Accounting
and
Society

Melville Series
on
Management, Accounting, and Information Systems

Consulting Editor   *John W. Buckley*

Mock and Vasarhelyi   APL for Management

Hill   Information Processing and Computer Programming:
An Introduction

Estes   Accounting and Society

Accounting
and
Society

Ralph W. Estes

School of Business Administration
The University of Texas at Arlington

 Melville Publishing Company
Los Angeles, California

Copyright © 1973, by John Wiley & Sons, Inc.
Published by Melville Publishing Company, a Division of
John Wiley & Sons, Inc.

Library of Congress Cataloging in Publication Data

Estes, Ralph W.
    Accounting and society.

    (Melville series on management, accounting and
information systems)
      1. Accounting—Addresses, essays, lectures.
    2. Social problems—Addresses, essays, lectures.
    I. Title.
HF5657.E85   658.1'5   73-4040
ISBN 0-471-24590-9
ISBN 0-471-24591-7 (pbk)

Preface

We are all concerned with the problems of our society. The professional accountant, however, is not widely viewed as one involved in working toward solutions to these problems. This view is incorrect! Especially in recent years, the professional accountant has been making a significant contribution to the solution of social problems, quite beyond his traditional role in financial and management accounting. Unfortunately, knowledge of this contribution is not widespread outside the profession; in fact many members of the profession itself are unaware of what their colleagues have been doing.

It is especially important that college programs in accounting give consideration to the broad contribution of accounting to society, not only to stimulate prospective accountants to become involved in such activity but also to present a more accurate picture of the profession. This concern is echoed by the Study Group on Introductory Accounting sponsored by The Price Waterhouse Foundation, which urges a shift from the traditional "preparer of accounting information" objective to a "function and social role of the accounting discipline" objective for introductory accounting (A New Introduction to Accounting, p. iii).

ACCOUNTING AND SOCIETY is intended to show how accounting skills and techniques can be (and have been) applied to the serious problems facing our society—problems such as urban blight, rampant crime, poverty, and pollution. Besides social problems, accounting contributions in such areas as the arts, economic development, education, and even divorce litigations are described. Although the greatest demand for accounting still comes from the traditional areas of financial reporting and management information for business firms, accounting's role goes well beyond the world of business. ACCOUNTING AND SOCIETY might be described as a sampler from the rest of the world of accounting—a world even larger and more diverse than many accountants realize.

The possible uses of this book include the following:

1. As a supplement to accounting courses at various levels.
2. As the primary source for courses and seminars dealing with the broad role of accounting in society, social accounting, socio-economic accounting, and the like.

3. As recommended reading for students concentrating in accounting, whether used in specific courses or not.
4. As a primary text or as a supplement in professional development and public administration courses.
5. As a source of ideas for professional accountants interested in becoming more involved with social problems.
6. For non-accountants, especially those concerned with governmental or social programs, who should know how accounting can help in their particular areas of interest.

Although some instructors will prefer to devote a few complete classes to this material, another productive approach is to assign selections from this book throughout the term in conjunction with assignments from a standard accounting text. Students would thus be learning "how to do" accounting while concurrently learning of the applications of accounting in their society.

As with many books, the title of this one was a problem. It could have been called SOCIO-ECONOMIC ACCOUNTING or SOCIAL ACCOUNTING, but these terms have been widely used to refer to national income accounting—only one of the areas discussed in these readings.

In using ACCOUNTING AND SOCIETY, it should be helpful to read the questions following each selection before reading the selection itself—the questions will thus serve as a guide to significant points to look for in the reading. Of course the questions and assignments should be actually undertaken only after the selection has been read.

The questions and suggested assignments included after each selection are somewhat unusual. Several call for the student to go out into his community to observe conditions and problems firsthand. Others require interviews or meetings with practicing accountants, community leaders, or representatives of community organizations. In addition, projects directed toward community needs and problems, and requiring limited application of accounting, are suggested.

It is of course impossible to prepare ideal assignments for a class without knowing something about the size, background, and composition of that class. Consequently some of the questions and assignments will require modification, but most should be adaptable to a range of situations, and should suggest ideas for other assignments.

Occasionally terms are used in these readings with which the reader may be unfamiliar, especially if he has no background in accounting. The range of possible readers' vocabularies makes it impractical to try to define all such terms. Readers may occasionally want to refer to an accounting or economics text or a suitable dictionary, such as Eric Kohler's A Dictionary for Accountants.

Thanks are due the copyright holders for permission to reprint their material; more specific acknowledgments are included with each selection.

In addition, numerous helpful comments and suggestions were offered by Professors John W. Buckley, University of California, Los Angeles; Lee Seidler, New York University; Charles Smith, University of Texas; and Alan Johnson, California State University at Hayward. These are all gratefully acknowledged.

Arlington, Texas   Ralph W. Estes

Contents

Accounting
and
Society

Section I
Introduction

The field of accounting is often divided into two parts: financial and managerial. Financial accounting is concerned with reporting the results of operations and financial position of a business firm to those outside the management of the firm, including stockholders. Managerial accounting deals with techniques, controls, systems and reports used internally by the managers of an organization.

This book is not directly concerned with either of these two areas. It explores what could be called "the other world of accounting," the broader and innovative application of accounting skills and techniques to the problems of society.

Of course, accounting has always contributed to a better society although many accountants and most non-accountants have not fully understood how. In a nonagrarian economy an adequate standard of living for most citizens is possible only when the economic system functions effectively. A capitalistic system thus requires that savings flow somewhat freely into investments. This will not occur unless savers/investors have confidence in the business firms which represent investment opportunities, a confidence which is greatly encouraged by reliable financial information. Financial information is a product of a firm's internal accounting system and is made more believable and reliable when the audit opinion of a CPA is attached. Thus by helping to provide reliable financial information accountants contribute to the functioning of our economic system and thereby to the economic well-being of the society.

This could be called the traditional role of accounting, and it is obviously an important and worthwhile role in our complex society—or in any society whose economic system has developed beyond the barter stage. But accounting and accountants can contribute to society in numerous other ways besides those traditionally recognized. As the selections in this book show, accounting is useful in attacking such problems as urban congestion and blight, crime control, environmental destruction, and economic development. Accounting is also helpful in measuring the national economic health, and may potentially contribute to the development of national measures of the quality of life. All these and other

1

contributions of accounting, past or potential, are discussed in later sections of this book.

Some might glance at the contents and say that all this is not accounting. But in most of the cases and engagements described the traditional tools of accounting were used: income and cost determination, information system design, tax advice, attestation, etc. The tools aren't novel, but the areas of application are.

The extent to which accountants "do" the things described in this book may be surprising. A survey of partners in the eight largest CPA firms in the U.S. produced the following responses to the question: "To the best of your knowledge, in which of the following areas has your firm been involved in social program engagements?"[1]

Area	No.	Percent
Education	28	88
Welfare programs (including programs to aid disadvantaged groups)	26	81
Health	24	75
Transportation	23	72
Urban, rural, and/or regional planning and economic development	21	66
Housing	21	66
Crime prevention and law enforcement	19	59
Recreation	16	50
Pollution abatement and control	10	31

These results do not reflect the number or significance of the actual engagements, but when the work of all CPAs and accountants is added to that of the "Big 8" firms, the role of accountants in social programs is surely impressive.

Involvement has not been restricted to accounting professionals; accounting students have also found ways to work on the problems of society. Student groups have provided assistance and advice to minority-owned businesses in cooperation with community action programs; established tax clinics in low-income neighborhoods; audited charitable and religious organizations; and participated in studies of pollution cost. The national professional and honorary accounting organization, Beta Alpha Psi, has strongly encouraged such activity among its chapters.

[1] American Accounting Association Committee on Measures of Effectiveness for Social Programs, "Report of the Committee on Measures of Effectiveness for Social Programs," The Accounting Review, Supplement to Vol. XLVII (1972), pp. 337-396.

The following selections by Linowes, Mobley, and Kulshrestha survey the range of services accounting can bring to bear on social problems; each article takes a different viewpoint and discusses somewhat different areas. The section is then concluded by the Griffin and Williams article which explores the meaning of the concept of the public interest and its relevance to accounting.

Together these selections provide a broad overview of the interface between accounting and society, as well as a foundation for the more specific readings to follow.

SUGGESTED CLASS ASSIGNMENT

Divide into several groups, with each group visiting the office of a different large accounting firm in the area. Discuss the sort of engagements the office visited has had in the social areas mentioned in this section's readings. Compare the experiences of the firms visited to those described throughout this book. (Note: if class size makes such visits impractical, partners from several firms might be invited to class for a panel discussion and a question and answer session.)

ADDITIONAL REFERENCES

1. Featherstone, Richard L., "Accounting Power—A New Tool?" The Federal Accountant, June 1970, pp. 68–76.
2. Grady, Paul, "The Increasing Emphasis on Accounting as a Social Force," The Accounting Review, July 1948, pp. 266–275.
3. Lawler, John, "Accounting: A Bridge Across the Generation Gap," The Journal of Accountancy, May 1971, pp. 44–48.
4. Ma, Ronald, "Accounting as a Social Force," The Pakistan Accountant, October–December 1965, pp. 13–23.
5. Most, Kenneth S., "The Accountant and Social Accounting," Accountancy (England), October 1967, pp. 661–662.
6. Nelson, Edward G., "Science and Accounting," The Accounting Review, October 1949, pp. 354–359.
7. Savoie, Leonard M., "Social Accounting—An Opportunity for Service," The CPA, November 1967, p. 3.
8. Scott, DR, The Cultural Significance of Accounts (New York: Henry Holt, 1931).
9. Trump, G. W., "Accounting—A Social Force," The Arizona CPA, May 1966, pp. 8ff.

Economists, sociologists and statisticians all perform accounting—often without an understanding of accounting principles and concepts. In collaborating with these groups, CPAs could increase efficiency in the private sector of the economy much as they have done in the public sector.

Socio-Economic Accounting

by David F. Linowes

The accounting profession has long been regarded as essentially an adjunct of business. In fact, accountancy is sometimes described as "the language of business." In the last several years, however, this definition has been giving way to "the measurement and communication of economic and financial data"—without specific reference to a business orientation.

There are good reasons for such an enlargement of concept. The fundamental job of accounting is to make events more intelligible and manageable by describing them in quantitative terms. The accounting discipline, in its dual functions of evaluation and verification, is therefore applicable in many areas. Inputs and outputs, whether expressed in dollars, tons or college graduates, are all quantitative elements.

Once the scope of accounting is enlarged beyond the business horizon, the profession finds itself confronting the information systems of education, private and public social programs, and government. There is challenge and opportunity in this development.

SOURCE: Reprinted by permission of the author and the publisher from The Journal of Accountancy (November 1968), pp. 37–42. Copyright 1968 by the American Institute of Certified Public Accountants, Inc.

4

The area of accounting beyond the field of business has sometimes been refered to as "social accounting." It includes the activities denoted by the terms "national income accounting," "government accounting" and "macro-accounting." I shall use the term "socio-economic accounting" to designate the accounting function discussed in this article.

Socio-economic accounting is intended here to mean the application of accounting in the field of the social sciences. These include sociology, political science and economics. Economics, of course, deals with the production, distribution and use of income and wealth; sociology with the development, organization, and functioning of human society; and political science with the conduct of government. These disciplines use measurements—whether they be indexes, ratios or trends. Thus, in the broad sense of the term, accounting is already common to all the social sciences. I submit that CPAs, by becoming more aware of this fact and by being alert to the concerns of the social sciences, can contribute importantly to the most effective use of accounting techniques in these disciplines.

ECONOMIC AREAS WHERE THE ACCOUNTING DISCIPLINE IS NEEDED

In recent decades, economists have moved from a methodology of reasoning from postulates based on subjective assumptions about human behavior to one of reasoning from statistical data. This development has brought the disciplines of economics and accounting closer together. Once the economists began to base their studies more and more on statistics, they recognized the service performed by accountants as men skilled in assembling and ordering data. The accountants in turn, observing that the economists were requesting hard, creditable data, began to become more attentive to their needs.

It is the discipline of accounting which collects, tabulates and evaluates the data which permit both an understanding of the results of past activity and a projection of future possibilities. With this information, both business and government are enabled to make decisions about which projects should be curtailed and which expanded to make the best possible use of available money, materials and manpower.

For too long our nation has acted as though our resources were unlimited. As the result of international crises and domestic disturbances, we have been forced to recognize our limitations. Questions are being asked as to whether our social and economic programs are designed to give us a sufficient margin of return on the limited national resources which have been applied to them.

Obviously the problems of poverty, civil disturbance and the apparent commitment to underwrite democratic government throughout the world have forced a sobering reappraisal of how our national resources are being used. Our leaders grope for answers, answers which can only come from a study of creditable economic and social data.

Since the end of World War II in particular, government, through the Department of Commerce, has been providing figures on the nation's economic activity. Gross national product figures have been computed each year from accounting data furnished largely by business entities. These GNP figures have become the bases of major programs of the legislative and executive branches. Private industry also often bases plans on trends reflected in the GNP.

The elements which are added together to arrive at the GNP in any one year are: total sales of goods to consumers, including goods sold to national and local government agencies; the value of new construction (including homes) and equipment built; the value of increases in inventories; and net exports. These are accounting data, material with which every CPA is comfortably familiar. Yet CPAs have been strangely missing from the hierarchy responsible for the development of these data.

The lack of participation by CPAs has resulted in some unnecessary weaknesses in national income accounting. One of these is the use by the compilers of the data of terms not commonly used by accountants and businessmen.

Professor Richard Ruggles, economist at Yale University, maintains that the present form of accounting used by government cannot readily encompass related social and demographic information. For example, it is not possible to study problems of poverty and discrimination in the context of the data provided in existing national accounts. Despite the technological revolution in processing and handling data caused by the computer, this factor is not reflected in the design or use of our economic accounting system.

One observer believes, "Accountants and management generally have taken little interest in computations of national income, largely because of the general feeling that the methods used and the results produced have not been closely enough tied in with commercial realities; and because, too, the relationship of the individual business unit to the whole economy has seemed remote and almost wholly incidental. However, participation by accountants and business management in further rationalizing the concept and in making the annual report more useful would doubtless be welcomed by the present compilers."[1]

It seems clearly important that those who tabulate these data recognize the generally accepted accounting practices in classifying business operating statistics.

FORECASTING

Forecasting has always been an important function of economists. In the past, most forecasts were based on personal observations, largely because of the unavailability of large reservoirs of data. More recently, however, national economic data have become available. From a coupling of these quantitative data with empirical economic information, and using statistical methods, there has developed a branch of economics known as "econometrics."

While the economist has been moving into econometrics, the CPA has been moving into operations research. The former applies scientific method to interactions taking place through markets, whereas operations research applies scientific method to the interactions within a particular organization. Both work with uncertain data and both use statistical methods for making projections. Although CPAs have involved themselves in operations research, they have shown no comparable interest in econometrics.

As econometrics grows and increasingly becomes a principal instrument for economic projections, so the credibility of the basic data becomes more critical. These data are essentially accounting material but are now being handled chiefly by non-accountants. Some concern has already been expressed by econometricians about this weakness.

George A. W. Boehm, former associate editor of *Fortune* and author of *New World of Math,* made this observation, "Some econometricians are bothered about inaccuracies in the data they do have. Oskar Morgenstern has gone so far as to write a book on the topic. . . . Even the official figures of the GNP are in doubt; they are usually revised several times in the course of a year or more, but their revisions do not converge to any particular value. Most other econometricians, while admitting that Morgenstern makes some compelling points, tend to remain calm about inaccuracies in general. . . ."[2]

CPAs are uniquely qualified for the collection, classification and validation of quantitative information. It would seem clear that they should be more involved in econometric projections.

The CPA is closely bound up with the income tax system through his assistance to corporate and individual taxpayers in the preparation of their returns. In addition to this service, the profession, through the AICPA's committee on federal taxation, has made significant contributions to tax administrative efficiency through consultation with and suggestions to the Internal Revenue Service.

Practically all this involvement, however, has concerned technical detail. In contrast, the more basic issues—effects of one type of tax as compared with another, economic consequences of special credits and allowances, rationale of the various facets of income tax laws—have largely been ignored by our profession. Yet, because of the familiarity with the tax system which CPAs acquire in the course of practice, and the numerous examples they see of the impact of the laws and regulations in actual cases, they are especially well qualified to consult on questions of tax policy.

BUDGETING

The government, like other entities, deals with income on the one hand and expenditures on the other. Each year the President and Congress spend much time and effort examining the new budget. The cost of each program is studied and weighed against the other items. Finally decisions are made to cut some and perhaps to augment others. But the fact is that the full cost of several programs cannot be determined from the budget, nor is it available in usable form elsewhere. There is no adequate accounting for such items as cost of natural resources programs, special programs for subsidizing large areas of agriculture and some businesses, and certain old-age assistance programs, to name a few. The true total expenditures for these items do not appear in the budget, and are not available because they are effected through allowances in the income tax administration.

As a matter of public policy, taxes are often used to encourage certain social or economic objectives. However, when the dollar-values of tax concessions, through such devices as depletion allowances and double exemptions for the aged, are not known to policy-makers, they cannot view real overall expenditures in perspective or evaluate one program as opposed to another.

Massive sums of money are today dedicated by government agencies and by foundations to research projects of many kinds. But budgeting standards for these projects are often inadequate and controls virtually nonexistent. To a large extent this is attributable to the fact that expenditure of research grants is usually in the hands of scientists who, while expert in their own disciplines and probably better able than anyone else to determine the relative importance of different elements of a project, have scant, if any, training in budgeting. When they make decisions involving, say, such a costly item as computer operations, their unfamiliarity with the allocation of computer time-sharing costs can lead to cost-assignments that are far from realistic.

The effectiveness of research programs themselves is an area requiring the keen attention of measurement specialties. What type of institution is most effective for the various kinds of research conducted? Many institutions—colleges, foundations, government, industry—undertake research programs largely paid for by the taxpayers' dollars. What kind of institution does what kind of research best? What standards should be used to evaluate the results?

Another budgeting accounting dimension in which the CPA is rather conspicuous by his absence (or, at best, limited presence) is PPBS—planning, programing, budgeting system. This form of budgeting is an accounting function and an easy extension of normal business budgeting practices.

Although the principles of the system are familiar to any trained accountant, the CPA has been largely on the periphery of its application to governmental accounting, and the job has been done by economists, political scientists, sociologists and statisticians.

PPBS rests on tabulation and evaluation of alternative courses of action. These tabulations are quite similar to the computations made by accountants to assist managements with make-or-buy decisions, expanding or contracting a production division, or investment in a new facility.

There is wide opportunity for applying PPBS techniques at state and local levels of government; however, only a handful of CPAs have begun to involve themselves.

Here is how one such application was described by a CPA who participated in it: "The Philadelphia school district in 1966-67 moved from a traditional organization line item budgeting and reporting system, which identifies cost with departmental responsibility and object of expenditure—wages, books, supplies—to a program budgeting system, which *also* relates expenditures to educational and other goals of the school district. In the system, financial budget elements are expressed primarily in terms of what the districts are getting out of the expenditures and, secondarily, in terms of what they are putting in. Thus, the system presents the educational program by function and activity, according to objectives or 'outputs.' For example, an 'output' of an elementary program would be boosting student skills in reading or arithmetic; and 'input,' thus, would be a specified number of teaching aids, requiring a specified number of dollars."[3]

Another example of the type of service which can be performed by CPAs occurred in Cleveland. Several years ago an accounting firm devised a plan to revitalize that city's downtown area. It created a balance sheet of Cleveland's assets and liabilities. Among the assets were listed a central retail core; existing office complex; finance and government services; and a good transportation complex. Among the liabilities were listed high land costs; automobile congestion; and absence of integrated community leadership. From these inputs the plan programed objectives and recommendations for carrying them out to achieve a renaissance of the city.[4]

SOCIAL AREAS REQUIRING MEASUREMENTS

Like corporations formed for profit, nonbusiness institutions involve people working in organizational patterns, tangible assets (such as roads and bridges, or buildings and equipment) and products (perhaps intangible, such as education and health).

The institutions need budgets, systems of managerial control, records. These things are presently provided to them, most often not by CPAs but by sociologists, economists and political scientists, some—probably most—of whom are not trained in accounting. As might be expected, the quality of the data used to guide extensive and costly social programs is often not as good as it should be.

The abilities of CPAs can be applied to improving the efficiency and controls of institutions, both private and governmental, that address themselves to social problems.

The efficiency of social programs may be regarded from the viewpoint of return on investment. One of the normal measurements used in business is the return (amount of profit or benefit) obtained relative to the capital employed.

To evaluate social programs, it is necessary to determine the resources put into a project and then measure the resulting benefit. When it is practical to state the investment and return in dollars, we are dealing with the same units of measurement employed in business. In social programs, however, it is usually impossible to measure results solely in monetary terms. For we are dealing here with human beings—with levels of education or of health, with intangible needs and satisfactions. To find methods of measurement, we must call upon sociologists, psychologists, educators, even ecologists. Creating meaningful standards may be difficult or, in some instances, impossible. Recognition of the difficulties, however, ought not to deter accounting and other disciplines from collaborating to evolve appropriate methodologies. Too much is at stake.

To pose a simple example from an accounting standpoint, consider the relationship of the cost-benefit concept to a social program in the area of high school education. Assuming that our benefit or "profit" objective is to have the maximum number of students graduate from high school, that is, not to be dropouts, the quantitative unit is "one" for each student successfully completing his high school program.

Let us further assume that we have a fixed number of dollars which is the quantitative input toward achieving this benefit. These dollars can be applied to hiring competent, imaginative high school teachers; to the construction of well-equipped school buildings; or to some combination of these expenditures. What pattern of input will produce the greatest output?

It would seem that this kind of determination clearly requires the application of accounting concepts.

In this example the problem is oversimplified, of course, by relating output in units of high school graduates to input only in dollars. Output should also be considered in relation to the students' out-of-school environment, and other influences.

An example of the kind of measurement needed in the social field—and the difficulty of finding it—was identified recently by the Department of Health, Education, and Welfare. HEW sought to determine the extent of children's correctible health problems, in what social groups these problems prevailed, and the relative cost of programs to correct them. Although, after considerable effort, some information was obtained concerning the extent and the areas of concentration of child health problems, practically no estimates could be established concerning medical care effects. As the then Assistant Secretary, William Gorham, of HEW testified before a Congressional subcommittee, "We simply do not know whether children who receive medical checkups and continuous medical attention are healthier than those who do not."

Senator Walter F. Mondale (D-Minn.) has been pointing up the weaknesses in the measurement of government programs for some time: ". . . we know how many people take advantage of Medicare, but there are no public reports on the quality of this care. The same is true of education, criminal rehabilitation, and much of the poverty effort. . . ." He further maintains, "Critics of the Job Corps attack the cost per corpsman, while the Corps' effect on the corpsman's life and potential is ignored."[5]

Possibly, just possibly, the social scientist will be able to furnish the accountant in due course with concepts in these areas, from which quantitative standards can be derived.

COST/BENEFIT RATIO OF OTHER GOVERNMENT PROGRAMS

In business accounting, as has been noted, capital investment, operating costs, and profit are all expressed in dollars. The standards are clear-cut even if not always exact. Since the objective is profit, and profit is dependent upon price and volume of sales (and the effect of price upon the consumer's willingness to buy), the market place becomes the determinant of success. A business succeeds in its mission when it earns profit; it fails in its mission when it does not. Ruthless actions of the market place decree which organizations shall live and which shall die, which organizations shall expand and which contract.

This is not the case with organizations undertaking services to improve "the quality of life." More and more programs with this purpose are performed by government. Indeed, long before the public's current concern with "social" projects, it looked to government for national defense, police protection, highways and bridges, courts of justice, education, and so on.

But although the inputs to produce such services and facilities have been measurable all along in dollar costs, we still do not have adequate means for evaluating output. In allocating resources, should priority be given to building up the civilian police department or the military? Where will the expenditures produce the most good for the most people? We have no quantitative measurement. We do not know how to evaluate even different levels of military preparedness. We can tally numbers of troops, or planes, or the fire power of weapons, but these numbers do not necessarily measure benefit. What we are interested in is being sufficiently prepared to deter or, at last resort, to repel aggression. Measurement here requires the co-operative effort of military experts, and perhaps civil engineers and political scientists, as well as experts in the discipline of measurement.

The fact that work of this kind would require judgments which are quite subjective and which would derive largely from other disciplines is not new to accountants. In setting up the expected life of equipment for depreciation purposes, for instance, the accountant must rely upon the engineer's opinion as to how long the equipment will last. In valuing work-in-process, the accountant must rely upon the production manager's estimate of the stage of completion. In other matters, the CPA consults the actuary, geologist, appraisers in special fields, and other experts.

The major difference between accounting for business and socio-economic accounting is that in attempting to measure the benefits of such items as national defense, police protection and highways for purposes of setting priorities, there is no market place in which consumers register their preferences.

This distinction should not lead CPAs into thinking that socio-economic accounting is outside the realm of our discipline. It does point up that this function is one in which the accountant's expertise must be co-ordinated with that of other disciplines.

MEASUREMENT BEYOND TRADITIONAL ACCOUNTING

Quantification in areas beyond that of business is being performed today, however, inadequately. Sociologists, economists and statisticians all perform accounting (some might call it social-bookkeeping) in areas with which their respective disciplines are involved. They do this without an understanding of accounting principles and concepts, without familiarity with budgetary procedures and managerial control.

It would seem clear, therefore, that collaboration among these disciplines and the accounting profession is becoming increasingly critical.

One task which needs doing is to identify areas where information is lacking. Some data are lacking only because we are not aware they are needed. In other cases, data exist but are not being used, or, if they are, are not being properly applied. In many areas all that is required is the competent application of established concepts. In other areas, measurement concepts may have to be invented.

Until quite recently the budget of the Department of HEW did not identify the total services performed or the groups of people affected by the Department's programs which in 1966 cost over $43 billion. In no one place, for example, could there be found the total cost of our country's health services because the programs are spread over the Public Health Service, the Social and Rehabilitation Service, the Social Security Administration, the Food and Drug Administration, the Administration on Aging and the Office of Education.

Under the pressures of a greatly accelerated pace of social evolution, our nation is undertaking unprecedented programs without adequate knowledge of the overall costs. If trained accountants were engaged in this problem, solutions might begin to evolve by perceptive dissection of proposals, for the purpose of quantitative treatment. This would assist decision-makers in their priority judgments. The need for such judgments is one of the most important unsolved problems of our day. The President and Congress realize that they need more help in this area.

Out of a federal budget approaching $186 billion, how much should be spent to deal with the causes of poverty? How much on space exploration? On highways? On the military establishment in general? How important is it that the federal government spends almost $4½ billion on space exploration, and less than $3½ billion on education? Programs for the needy take slightly over $7 billion, or about 10 percent of our military budget. Is this ratio appropriate? Supersonic transport development takes over $350 million. Could this development safely be postponed?

Not all questions can be answered and some answers must be based on political consideration. But many quantitative fragments are determinable and would inform and sharpen the action of legislators, administrators and the voting public. Furnishing Congress and the President with the facts and analyses which CPAs can supply would help them to do their jobs more effectively.

As it has done for the private sector of the economy, the accounting profession can help significantly to enhance efficiency in the public sector.

CPAs can do this in several ways: by accepting assignments or positions with government departments, social agencies or foundations; by accepting appointments to advisory commissions and committees involved in economic and social programs; and by arranging for accounting firms to undertake feasibility studies and investigations within these enlarged parameters. But it is not enough to await the opportunity to accept these assignments. For CPAs to participate in this aspect of our rapidly evolving social structure, we should aggressively seek out the challenges. By so doing, we will demonstrate our ability to make significant contributions to social measurement.

The profession has a tradition of responding to the needs of society. Today it has an obligation to respond creatively to new problems.

I believe the time has come to identify and classify these new areas of opportunity and challenge, in no less fashion than we have identified and classified new services in the management advisory area during recent years.

FOOTNOTES

1. Kohler, Eric, L., *Accounting for Management,* (New York: Prentice-Hall, 1965), p. 261.
2. Boehm, George A. W., "How They Predict the Economic Future," *Think,* July-August 1967, p. 11.
3. Rappaport, Donald, "New Approaches to Public Education," *The Journal of Accountancy,* July 1968, p. 31.

4. Smith, Robert, "Renaissance of Cleveland, Ohio," *Management Services,* March-April 1966, pp. 44-51.
5. Mondale, Walter F., "Reporting on the Social State of the Union," *Trans-Action,* Washington University of St. Louis, June 1968, p. 36.

QUESTIONS

1. What does Linowes mean by the term "socio-economic accounting"?

2. What does the author cite as the principal difference between socio-economic accounting and accounting for business? What other significant differences can you list?

3. (a) According to Linowes, "The fundamental job of accounting is to make events more intelligible and manageable by describing them in quantitative terms." Do you agree? Explain.
   (b) Find three definitions of accounting from sources other than a standard dictionary (check textbooks, articles, publications of accounting organizations, etc.). Compare and contrast them with the above statement.

4. The article frequently refers to CPAs. Do its suggestions apply to accountants who aren't CPAs? Should they too be involved in socio-economic accounting?

5. Explain PPBS (check other sources if you are not clear on the meaning). Give examples of areas in which PPBS could be used. Could it be used by a business firm?

6. How would you go about deciding how much should be spent on military defense by the United States—how much is enough? How can accountants assist in resolving this question which arises in every national political campaign?

7. "In social programs, however, it is usually impossible to measure results solely in monetary terms." How might results be measured in:

   (1) a university,
   (2) a hospital,
   (3) a police department,
   (4) a church,
   (5) the Salvation Army,
   (6) a library?

8. Which do you think is more important—for accountants to study economics or for economists to study accounting? Explain.

The world of accounting is expanding beyond the traditional financial and managerial areas. This broader world of accounting, which might be referred to as "socio-economic accounting," will present challenges to accountants in areas such as national income accounting, accounting for enterprise social product, assessment of social effects of business activities, measurement of cultural acceptance, and reporting on corporate social responsibility.

The Challenges of Socio-Economic Accounting

by Sybil C. Mobley

Socio-economic accounting is an idea so new that accountants are still unsettled on its definition; in fact, each writer seems to twist the concept a little to give it his personal flavor. The failure of accountants to adopt a common definition of socio-economic accounting is not mentioned as a criticism. With a new notion, exploration should be unrestricted and the great diversity of direction of investigators in socio-economic accounting attests to the great opportunity which exists. No attempt will be made in this paper to distinguish between the shades of meaning as they are used in the literature. However, it would be remiss not to refer to David Linowes, who may well become known as the father of socio-economic accounting. David Linowes has defined socio-economic accounting as "the application of accounting in the field of the social sciences. These include sociology, political science and economics."[1]

SOURCE: Reprinted by permission of the author and the publisher from The Accounting Review (October 1970), pp. 762-768.

The term socio-economic accounting will be used in this paper in its broadest sense. It refers to the ordering, measuring and analysis of the social and economic consequences of governmental and entrepreneurial behavior. So defined, socio-economic accounting is seen as encompassing and extending present accounting. Traditional accounting has limited its concern to selected economic consequences—whether in the financial, managerial or national income areas. Socio-economic accounting expands each of these areas to include social consequences as well as economic effects which are not presently considered.

Governmental and entrepreneurial activities generate *economic* consequences which are only partially reflected in the national income computations for the economy and the net income figures for the firms and *social* consequences for which we have no tabulation. Today society demands responsible behavior—behavior which is responsible in its consideration of all of the social and economic consequences which result as entities direct their efforts to maximizing their selected goals. Full consideration of these consequences is the charge of socio-economic accounting.

The purpose of this paper is to indicate some of the challenges of socio-economic accounting by establishing that there is a substantial and growing need for socio-economic accounting, and by suggesting approaches to and areas of research.

The thesis of this paper is that: *The technology of an economic system imposes a structure on its society which not only determines its economic activities but also influences its social relationships and well-being. Therefore, a measure limited to economic consequences is inadequate as an appraisal of the cause-effect relationships of the total system; it neglects the social effects.*

NATIONAL INCOME ACCOUNTING

Technological development has moved the nation toward economies of scale, natural monopolies and the resulting expediency that more and more goods and services fall under the classification of "government provided." This development suggests areas which concern the accountant such as the effectiveness of the highway and other transportation systems, of government-sponsored medical research, of city planning, and of housing development. Accounting for these activities as it relates to the stewardship function has long been provided. The present need is for an accounting which permits a meaningful ranking of priorities consistent with the goals of society in the planning stage and a measure of effectiveness in the evaluating stage. Today we also have government-sponsored slum-clearance projects, medical care, education and public welfare. In these projects, social and psychological goals rank equal with economic goals, and evaluation of either goal in isolation is meaningless.

ibilities. Some specific
of communities, exer-
segments of the com-

accept the pure com-
commercial self-gain
illing to settle for the
d pursuit of greater

ately providing for a

ly not take a social
*per*efficiency? Can't
way to give workers
couple of units per
paychecks. . . These
ble luxury when we
ogy complex.] But
tory if, like Charlie
c notions of relent-

iving has increased
e certain economic
ay be met. That is,
roblem for which
ed that accounting
well as individual
ing measurements
at the firm level.⁷
conomic concepts
at material goods

luces more than
-products should
o be maximized.
ce view.

ment and there-
Concept: New

iomic efficiency excludes
uit of economic efficiency
ede the realization of the
d economic measures, the
asured to assure that sub-
comes economically secure,
hich are not so adequately
chological, offer the greatest
re, to be effective, govern-
he social and psychological

its counterpart in economics,
ion of specific economic units,
or national income accounting
economics, which is concerned
employment, total output, total
ion, socio-economic accounting
a which will find its counterpart
sis. General equilibrium analysis
effects of given disturbances or
nell has said:

"the big splash" of an initial dis-
s the waves and ripples emanating
he waves and ripples are relatively
to be a tidal wave which changes
from the big splash viewed in

equilibrium analysis, will identify
e mutually decided; it will identify
nsideration of certain results as inde-

d both the firm's opportunities and
nodated business enterprises in their
must now accommodate society in its

efforts to assure that these enterprises assume their respons
areas of concern are environment pollution, disfigurement
cise of power positions to economically exploit significant
munity, the nation and the world, and resource depletion.

Leslie Dawson holds that society is no longer willing to
petition model which insists that the persistent search for
somehow leads to the ultimate good for all; society is unw
accidental by-products generated by business' self-centere
market opportunities and profit.[4]

Louis Banks discusses the feasibility of enterprises deliber
"social product":

> Since economic equilibrium is a social achievement, wl
> dividend? Do we any longer have to be servants of a *su*
> those students of Human Behavior in Organizations find a
> a sense of achievement in production, even at the cost of a
> hour? Can't we generate family pride in work as well as in
> are quality-of-life factors; they were, perhaps, an unthinka
> were building the apparatus [the business-science-technol
> the world's richest society will look very silly indeed to hi
> Chaplin in *Modern Times,* it continues with the spasmodi
> less efficiency when it no longer needs to do so.[5]

In the same vein, Bedford contends that as the standard of
it may be desirable for individual firms to allow and encourag
inefficiencies so that pressing social and psychological needs m
in the future, the economic problem may not be the only
society will hold business responsible.[6] Lloyd Amey has posit
measurements might well be based on community interests as
firm interests and he considers a means of developing account
of economic efficiency from the total community point of view

All of this may be viewed as entirely consistent with our e
dealing with those things in scarce supply. The notion here is th
and services do not represent the only significant scarcity.

The economy's business-science-technology complex prod
material products; it also generates social by-products. These by
be planned, controlled and evaluated if the benefit to society is
An accounting limited to economic effects provides only a surfa

MANAGERIAL ACCOUNTING

Today adjustments must take place in the orientation of manage
fore in managerial accounting. In his article, "The Human

Philosophy for Business," Leslie Dawson presents a provocative analysis of the new management era.

Dawson notes that Robert Keith has identified three distinct phases of management orientation in the 20th century: Production orientation (1900–1930)—an emphasis upon production volume and plant efficiency in response to newly developed technology for mass production and expanded markets; sales orientation (1900–1950)—an emphasis upon aggressive sales and distributive practices; market orientation (1950)—an emphasis upon consumer satisfaction.

Dawson suggests that we are no longer living in a marketing era and that we are witnessing the start of what may be called the human era and that the actions of many leading companies today, do, in fact, testify to the gradual replacement of the marketing concept with a more embracing philosophy which may be called the human concept.

Dawson points out that the marketing concept represented an outward extension of environmental awareness and sensitivity in contrast to the more inward-looking production and sales orientations. Yet, the perspective of the marketing concept has remained essentially confined to the *proximate* environment. The marketing concept stresses a consumer orientation; it directs the attention of the firm only to the fraction of society which supports it; its concern is only with the individual's role as a buyer or consumer and it is therefore limited in scope and one-dimensional in nature. Preoccupied as the marketing concept has been with customers and competitors, it has not been attentive to the healthfulness of a firm's relationship to the various dimensions of the *ultimate* environment. Wroe Alderson defines these two crucial environment levels which exist in the cultural ecology of business as first, the proximate environment, the external domain with which a system is in direct and continuous contact (for a marketing firm, the market in which it buys and sells and competes) and, second, the more embracing ultimate environment, which is composed of the technological, ideological, moral and social dimensions of the culture. In the long run, the business enterprise must maintain dynamic ecological equilibrium with both environments. If an enterprise fails to do so, it may not survive.

Dawson further points out that today, some of the most successful industries in terms of the consumer-oriented marketing concept are the most vulnerable. For instance, the tobacco industry, which has been most effective in terms of consumer satisfaction, finds its major threat to survival forces emanating from the non-smoking sectors of society. Another example of this vulnerability is the small firearms industry. This industry has also been very successful in satisfying its customers, but its future will not be determined by the segment of society which supports it. In other words, an industry may find its future influenced far more by cultural acceptance than by mere consumer acceptance and technical product improvement.[8]

Cultural equilibrium must constitute a significant management consideration in a world of rapidly changing values and priorities. Management accountants must devise a barometer capable of both registering current cultural acceptance and forecasting cultural obsolescence. The socio-economic accountant must provide management with indices sensitive to the ultimate environment if management is to assume social responsibility. These cultural considerations insist that managerial accounting be greatly expanded to provide creditable and meaningful data which will accommodate the expanded focus now required of management.

APPROACHES TO RESEARCH

The new dimensions of accounting should be developed in consideration of the same doctrines, assumptions, conventions and postulates which have required consideration in traditional accounting. Just as the going concern assumption is relaxed when there is evidence that the firm is in fact a quitting concern, other assumptions will be relaxed as we extend our concern to social effects. However, additional postulates, which will define new constraints, may be found to apply. Indeed, the study of the superstructure of accounting as it will apply to this extended concern will constitute an open area for challenging and, hopefully, fruitful research efforts. Examination of just a few concepts in terms of the questions posed by socio-economic accounting will indicate the magnitude of the research opportunity afforded.

The entity concept has been basic in accounting. For financial accounting, the entity has been the firm; for social or national income accounting, the entity has been the economy or the industry. Neither of these entities may be completely applicable for the broader concern of socio-economic accounting which may find it necessary to develop a variable entity concept. That is, inputs required for a particular activity may relate to one specific entity, while the collection of output data may require consideration of a different entity; or, to go one better, the waves and ripples may, in fact, extend to several entities.

What will be the point of realization? Should there be a single point or will the socio-economic accountant have to provide for meter readings at several stages? Will he measure the initial impact of an activity, then the impact of the multiplier and the accelerator?

How will the periodicity convention hold? The socio-economic accountant must select a time frame, but must he be restricted to just one? Is it not possible that the short-run effect will be reversed in the long-run? Which should be of greatest concern? Can the fact that the time period considered by participants in trade-off decisions is limited to their anticipated period of ownership or their interest in posterity be reconciled with the fact that future generations figure importantly in societal values—e.g., depletable natural resources?

For conventional accounting, which limits its concern to economic consequences, money is the unit of measure. This may or may not be so with socio-economic accounting which is concerned with both the social and economic consequences. The economic or dollar effect of a certain program may be cancelled by the non-economic, non-monetary effects of the program thus vitiating the value of money as a barometer or measure of total benefit. It may be appropriate to measure some benefits in man years of effort, increase in leisure, or the decrease in discomfort.

Whose interest would conservatism protect? What about the reverse? What will be the requirement of verifiability of these additional measures? Will it be as great or even greater than in conventional accounting?

These questions suggest that socio-economic accounting will require a very flexible framework. Accountants have borrowed the economist's technique of examining one variable while assuming that all others remain constant. Hence, the inflow and outflow of money or claims on money are measured while assuming that human capital, market position and consumer demand remain unchanged. In socio-economic accounting, as in general equilibrium analysis, several variables must be manipulated at the same time. This, of course, will require sophisticated models and highly skilled and knowledgeable accountants. The socio-economic accountant must develop accounting models which will yield data that will provide the needed basis for planning, decision making, control or corrective action and evaluation.

The accounting profession has already developed some tools, techniques and methods which will be helpful in accommodating some of the requirements of socio-economic accounting. In addition, others have been developed by related professionals.

The Planning, Programming, Budgeting System, known as PPBS, has much to offer. PPBS provides for a program-oriented budget. Rigorous analysis must be made of competing and/or conflicting goals. Priorities among national goals are not to be assessed by the accountant. They are established largely through the operation of the political processes. However, this fact does not preclude the opportunity and responsibility that belongs to accountants to provide the cost and benefit data needed to rank objectives.

With a government composed of many agencies—many of which have overlapping functions—with responsibilities for different segments of specific programs being spread over many agencies, a program-oriented, physical output-oriented budget has much to offer in terms of maximizing social and economic benefits or minimizing social and economic costs. At present, most applications of PPBS have been with governmental units. Other nonprofit institutions which invest social and economic capital to generate social and economic benefits will increasingly recognize the merits of PPBS. However, in the human era of today, it has been pointed out that profit-oriented enterprises are now being required to consider both the social and economic effects of their behavior. These entities will be striving to maximize an output that will not be traded in the market and therefore cannot be objectively translated into revenue dollars. In considering the profit-oriented activities of these firms, appropriate trade-offs can be easily determined because there is a common denominator, the dollar. However, trade-offs relating to their social functions involve measures which may not be expressed in common terms in some instances; in other instances, the common denominator may be votes, protests or restraint from protests, cooperation or the lack of it. PPBS provides a useful framework for such nonmonetary output measurements.

PPBS is conceptually related to input-output analysis. Input-output analysis, originally a macro-economic tool, will have wide applicability in socio-economic accounting. Input-output analysis gives insight into the interdependencies of the various entities. In some instances, we may need to consider a system of relationships as the relevant entity. Input-output tables can facilitate analysis of these inter-relationships.

As for techniques of data gathering, the socio-economic accountant will make use of sophisticated statistical concepts for sampling, extrapolations and interpretations.

So much for the positive side of the profession's present capability. The need for vigorous research is great. Because socio-economic accounting is concerned with activities which affect many people, the requirement of "creditability of data" is crucial. Disclosure must be explicit and evidence conclusive in order that judicious changes in the patterns of thinking and courses of action will be generated.

Studies are needed in terms of the value of the information generated. Not only must measures be reliable enough to justify the effort, but the information must also be useful enough.

SUMMARY

Changes in the economy have prompted changes in the information needs in all areas of accounting. New cause and effect relationships develop and new concepts emerge which must be given accounting expression. The accounting profession is therefore faced with a need for accounting data which must be accommodated. The magnitude of the challenge reveals the magnitude of the opportunity. There is every reason to believe that socio-economic accounting will provide the thrust necessary to tremendously expand the world of accounting. In this connection, there is an old Hindu saying which seems appropriate here, that "There is no door, but only a small window, that leads to a great new world." However, the saying requires a bit of paraphrasing for, actually, in this case, there is no window. Nevertheless, accountants do have access to, perhaps, a keyhole. The light provided by this small keyhole reveals that there are numerous answers to the challenges posed by socio-economic accounting and they all focus on research.

FOOTNOTES

1. David F. Linowes, "Socio-Economic Accounting," *The Journal of Accountancy* (November 1968), p. 37.
2. In a class lecture at the University of Illinois, 1962.
3. Campbell R. McConnell, *Economics: Principles, Problems and Policies* (McGraw-Hill Book Company Inc., 1963) pp. 576–577.
4. Leslie M. Dawson, "The Human Concept: New Philosophy for Business," *Business Horizons* (December 1969), p. 35.
5. Louis Banks, "The View through Youthful Eyes," *Fortune* (April 1970), pp. 118–121.
6. In a class lecture at the University of Illinois, 1962.
7. See Lloyd Amey, *The Efficiency of Business Enterprises* (George Allen and Unwin, Ltd.) 1969.
8. Leslie M. Dawson, *op. cit.*, pp. 29–38.

QUESTIONS

1. (a) As the terms are used by Mobley, what is the difference between social accounting and socio-economic accounting?
    (b) Compare and contrast Mobley's and Linowes' (see previous article) definitions of "socio-economic accounting."

2. Mobley suggests that today social and psychological concerns offer the greatest opportunity to increase total satisfaction. Does this mean we have resolved our economic problems? If not, what economic problems remain?

3. What does Mobley suggest are a business firm's responsibilities? How would you define a firm's responsibilities in today's society?

4. What does the author mean by "cultural obsolescence?" Of what concern is such obsolescence to accountants?

5. "Priorities among national goals are not to be assessed by the accountant." Why not?

6. "Profit-oriented enterprises are now being required to consider both the social and economic effects of their behavior." List several of the social effects of the activities of (1) General Motors, (2) the largest bank in your community, (3) a national grocery chain such as Safeway Stores.

7. By reference to accounting and economics texts, determine the meanings of any of the following terms with which you are not familiar:

    (1) the entity concept,
    (2) the going concern assumption,
    (3) realization,
    (4) the multiplier,
    (5) the accelerator,
    (6) the periodicity convention,
    (7) conservatism in accounting,
    (8) input-output analysis.

The interests of society require that account-
ants adopt more of a social attitude about
their work, and to recognize that dividend
policies, depreciation policies, cost account-
ing methods, and many other accounting
decisions have an impact on society.

Accounting as a
Social Science

by H. S. Kulshrestha

Accounting, when born, must not have been more dismal a subject than economics. At least, it has never been condemned as a "Gospel of Mammon." But later
on, as all know, when economics aimed at the welfare of man as a member of
society, it got popular and now occupies an important position among the social
sciences. Accounting, however, continued serving individuals. As a result, the
economist acted as thinker, author and orator on society; whereas the accountant worked at the desk shabbily dressed and "sincere" to his master. The secret
of this significant development in and popularity of economics lay in its social
approach to the well-being of man, which unfortunately accounting failed to
have.

The selection of the title for this paper, though not guided with a feeling of
envy or an attempt to suggest copying, has been made with a sort of conviction
that the progress and usefulness of accounting depends on the good it can do to

SOURCE: Reprinted by permission of the publisher from The Chartered
Accountant (India), October 1964, pp. 208–211.

society or the human race as a whole and not on the services rendered to individuals. In fact, a start has already been made and it is to be seen as to what extent accounting has followed and can follow the footprints of economics.

Accounting is the science of recording, classifying and summarising everyday business transactions (movements of value), generally in terms of money, and includes the checking, analysing, interpreting and reporting of the same to the parties interested in the affairs of the individual, firm, company, government or the nation to which the transactions relate. The controversy whether accounting is a science or an art is of secondary importance here and may be summarily solved by pointing out to the fact that correct accounting is always based on reason and, therefore, is a systematised knowledge based on cause and effect. Then, like every branch of knowledge accounting too has something of art, but not enough to prevent it from being a science.

IMPACT OF ACCOUNTING ON SOCIETY

Social science is the study of the group life of man.[1] It studies the actions of man in so far as they are influenced by his association with society and "attempts to develop understandings and inventions that should enable man to cope effectively with the kind of world in which he lives." Now the question is whether accounting, as a whole or a part of it, is in the nature of a social science or not. If not, is it possible and advisable to make it so, both for its own development as well as for the good of society? The answer to this basic question will depend on two considerations. Firstly, whether in practising accounting or in professing the principles thereof a social approach is possible and advisable or not. Secondly, whether the subject matter which the science of accounting records, classifies, summarises, checks, analyses, interprets and reports are related to man as a member of society or not. To some extent, these two questions are related to the one fundamental inquiry whether accounting studies or can study group life of man or not. However, it will facilitate our task if they are separately dealt with.

Taking up the second question first, as it is easier and less controversial, it may be observed that primarily accounting deals with the transactions relating to an individual business man, firm or joint-stock company or even a government. Ordinarily speaking, none of these accounting units study their transactions as if they are of a member of society. Their transactions in their respective individual capacity are recorded, classified, summarised, checked, analysed, interpreted and finally reported to the persons or groups of persons concerned. However, in case of public limited companies,* governments and nations, accounting deals with figures and problems pertaining to large groups of persons as members of society.

*EDITOR'S NOTE: Public limited companies are essentially the same as corporations.

Not only that, the accounting units in all these cases are large groups of people and in their case a social point of view is inevitable. The manner in which a particular transaction is dealt with in the accounts of a public limited company, government or the nation is bound to have some impact on man as a member of society. In the latter two cases, practically all transactions relate to the society as a whole. In fact the last field of accounting has been named as national accounting or social accounting.

DYNAMIC SIGNIFICANCE OF ACCOUNTING

The significance of this newly developed branch of accounting is beyond controversy. Accounting, in the life of a society or the nation, is as essential and useful as in the case of an individual. Recording classifying, summarising, checking, analysing, interpreting and reporting of the transactions taking place in a nation and between nations have become a necessity in this age of planned economy and in the face of the complicated financial problems a nation has to solve. It helps the nation to keep a record of the national wealth and to assess the national income, which in turn serves the whole society and enables the government to make successful plans for national development and defence. In day-to-day working, the government may be assisted by social accounting exactly in the same manner as the business man is helped by management accounting.

The due recognition of the role of accounting in the administration of the State even in ancient India is evident from the fact that accounting had been given its appropriate place by Kautilya in his "Arthshastra," which is a comprehensive treatise on the art of governing. The propriety of government accounting being included in or treated as social accounting is confirmed by the fact that it is the society in whose wealth governments deal. Governmental accounting is undertaken for and on behalf of the tax-payers who constitute the society.

Turning to company accounting, it is to be noted that the company form of organization does enjoy certain facilities and concessions at the hands of the government or the society. Irrespective of the public interest in the affairs of such companies on account of their corporate structure, large-scale operation and monopolistic or semi-monopolistic position make their accounting policies influence a vast group of society and sometimes the whole of society.

Their dividend policy, depreciation policy, method of cost accounting and many other decisions—which also form part of economics but are ultimately and physically dealt with by accounting—do have their impact on society. From this point of view, even the accounting of individuals and partnership firms may have some features of social accounting. As is pointed out in an editorial[2] under the caption "The Horizons of Accounting," "it can scarcely be denied that in our present world there are costs to society—services provided at the expenses of tax payers—involved in the operations of every kind of enterprise. Sooner or later some accountant (or some economist with an understanding of accounting) will develop the technique for figuring them out."

Besides the element of cost borne by the society indirectly and pointed out in the above editorial, there may be some cost which cannot be expressed in monetary terms and has to be considered by the modern accountant in view of the expanding horizons of accounting. This is exactly what Mr. Adolf A. Berle[3] as quoted in the above editorial expects when he writes that some day we shall have true "social cost accounting" which will show not merely what it cost a producer to produce—that is, what he paid out—but also what it cost *society to produce*. The technique of social cost accounting has yet to be invented. This all goes to show that not only the subject matter of government accounting or national accounting relates to society, but in case of individual business enterprises too a part of accounting has to be related to society to keep pace with the changing times and circumstances.

AUDITIVE ACCOUNTING

The auditive part of accounting has still more scope for being studied and looked upon as a social science. Besides serving as a check on the dishonesty of the persons concerned, which itself is a social problem in its wide sense, auditing tells the truth about accounting—not only that of business but also of societies, governments, nations and the tax-payers. To act as the public's watch-dog has become a recognised function of modern accounting. It is only on account of this social significance of auditing that the question of its being nationalised has become the subject matter of a controversy.

There is no doubt that society, for its welfare, will have to depend on the accountant so as to have "more and better information about the financial facts of life." The role of such information in the successful operation of democracy and free enterprise, both of which have been responsible for a marked development in the social condition of man, can very well be imagined. It is no exaggeration to say that "the heart of any democratic, free enterprise system is accountability. Together with a free press, the free flow of reliable financial information is the most effective safeguard against abuse or incompetence. Without reliable financial data there is no valid way to measure performance. An economy of free men, working voluntarily in a free market, would be helpless without sound financial information. The credit and investment machinery, domestic and international, would collapse. The tax system would disintegrate. Corporate managers could not control the vast industrial complexes. Labour disputes could find no rational solutions. Government fiscal policy will flounder in a vacuum. Government regulation of utilities and other enterprises highly charged with public interest would be impossible."[4]

SOCIAL APPROACH TO ACCOUNTING

Now, the propriety and possibility of a social approach to the preaching and practising of accounting principles can very well be examined. As indicated earlier, the future development of accounting depends upon the good it can do to society and not to individuals. In Australia (and maybe in many other countries), though it has been rightly called a hindrance in the progress of the accounting profession, there was a tendency "to regard the accountancy profession as consisting only of those who were in public practice and to treat the important branch of the profession which offered its service to a single employer as being outside the profession."[5]

This very tendency in the past and its being called a hindrance by modern accountants awakened to their social responsibility both go to show respectively, that even in the initial stage of its development, serving the public was the main criterion of the accountancy profession. Now there is. need for accountants serving single employers to adopt a social attitude towards their job—they are not to forget their obligation to society while helping their respective employers. All this partly proves the propriety of a social outlook in accounting.

The propriety of a social approach to accounting is further strengthened in the present age on account of the increased number and scope of public enterprises and public utilities, fast and marked expansion of the corporate form of enterprise having monopolistic or semi-monopolistic position, more and more of tax laws and many other similar factors. A social approach to accounting problems in state enterprises and other economic activities of the government is not only proper but essential for safeguarding the social and economic interests of the public. Similarly, determination of fair utility rates is not possible till the subject matter of accounting in public utility concerns is dealt with on a social level.

RELATIONSHIP OF ACCOUNTING TO SOCIETY

Company accounting is virtually public accounting in more than one sense. The wealth and income accounted for actually belong to people other than those who manage them. The manner in which company accounting is done and finally profit ascertained is to influence the society as a whole. Accounting plays an important role, though indirectly, in determining dividends and wages through ascertainment of profits and the price of the product or service through cost accounting.

Exactly the same functions are performed by economics but in an abstract and strictly social sense. An indirect determination of dividends by accounting is implied in its dealing with the problems of capital and revenue, stock valuation, depreciation, depletion and amortization, transference to various reserves, both specific and general, and finally in advising the management on the need of ploughing the profits back into the business or otherwise. In case of wages too, the ultimate source to know the maximum amount which can profitably be paid to the labourers is accounting. Although one should not be led to think that accounting has any superiority over economics in determining wages, no amount of abstract thinking as is done by economists can help the business enterprise in the matter.

A social approach by the accountant in dealing with all the above problems is but essential, if not legally, at least, ethically. After all, accounting alone can be instrumental in doing justice to the shareholders—present and prospective—workers, customers and the creditors and ultimately to the society and even to different accounting or trading periods.

Exactly the same arguments, though in a limited sense, can be applied to the accounting of individuals and partnership firms. Because of the comparatively small scale of operation of their activities, the manner in which their accounting problems are dealt with has, individually, little effect on society. But such accounting units as a whole and the accounting used by them have definitely some social significance. In more than one way, their accounting methodology may cause economic and social changes. Surely, the subject matter of the accounting of individuals and partnership firms does not relate to society; but while recording and studying their economic activities, accounting cannot and should not forget society and the fact that even these accounting units are parts of society. If this is not done, accounting will fail to serve the cause for which it is most capable.

Having established the propriety and urgency of accounting being treated as a social science, it may be examined whether it will be possible for accounting to be professed and practised as such by academicians and practising accountants respectively. For the academicians, the proposition may seem to be not only possible but easy and befitting to their social and national responsibility. They are the builders of the nation and are expected to raise the moral standard of those who come in direct or indirect contact with them. If they are really interested in the development of society and the subject, they must try to teach and profess principles which, when practised, will help not only the students, but the whole of society, to progress. The fact that individual selfishness does not make for general good, that unselfishness makes for personal good, is to be realised in its real sense by both academicians and their students.

The possibility of putting these ideas into practice shall not be doubted if the practising accountants too realise their own responsibility to society. The example of economics is enough to show that accounting will also develop on scientific lines when its approach in recording the economic activities of man becomes social. Some may criticise that preaching is easier than practising. Economics being just an abstract thinking in terms of inanimate objects, such approach is quite possible; but, in accounting, nothing can be professed or practised which does not help the accounting unit to make more profit—rather immediate profit. Here, one has to adopt an appropriate attitude not only towards accounting but towards life.

To keep this discussion limited to the field of business, it may be remarked that the success of American business is the result of translating Christ's teaching that "he who would save his life must lose it" in their business language as "he who would save his profit must lose it". Only the practice of this fundamental and immortal truth in its true sense has made the American business enterprises spend a sizeable portion of their earnings in advertisement, market and factory research, development research and many similar objects. This makes them progressive and their society prosperous. There is no reason why this sort of change in the nature and attitude of accounting cannot take place in whole of the accounting world.

INTERESTS OF SOCIETY

The only thing which accountants are to do is to think, while dealing with the accounting problems of their clients, about their economic impact on society so that injustice is done to none. The matters affecting the ascertainment of profit and cost are of maximum significance in this regard. Side by side with safeguarding the interests of different classes of society—shareholders, creditors, labourers, customers and so on—accounting has to protect the interest of society as a whole.

Its principles should not permit the erosion of social capital and should help in an accurate calculation of the social or national wealth and income. They should be harnessed not only to calculate the cost of the goods to the producers but also to the society; and even non-monetary costs should be taken into consideration. This will be done by scientific approach to the problems and it is possible that in doing so, long-practised and conservative golden rules of overstating one's losses and liabilities and understating his profits or assets may have to be given up.

Accountants are to think more than once in assuming all anticipated losses as real losses and in ignoring any anticipated profits without any regard to the degree of the probability of their becoming real profits. Liberalism or conservatism is to be followed a bit cautiously and as far as possible nothing should be made a matter of personal opinion and judgment; and this is actually the main characteristic of a science so essential and appropriate in the present age when almost every branch of knowledge is tending to become a science.

ACCOUNTING AND ECONOMICS

Before concluding, a common criticism, rather an item of confusion, must also receive our due attention. Some may think that, firstly, accounting is not a separate science as far as social aspects are concerned, and, even if it is so, it is merely a tool in the hands of economics. Truly speaking, the subject matter of study in both economics and accounting is the same—economic activities of man—the former studying them in abstract and the latter reducing them in writing and thereafter processing and reporting the same.

Both the sciences are of mutual help. Accounting makes use of the principles of economics in solving almost all its problems and in its turn helps economics to make its (economics') studies more realistic by making available accounting information. To say which of these two is the tool in the hands of the other is rather difficult these days, when social accounting has become a must for political, economic and social administration of a country. The various concepts of economics are used by accounting and accounting information is used by economists to improve the study of economic activities of man by making them more realistic.

Here, one is not to forget that modern accounting is not merely to record the activities but also to study, analyse, check and report their records. What is intended to be conveyed to those interested in a scientific development of accounting is the fact that although accounting records, studies and reports the economic activities of man, the concepts of economics are interpreted and understood by accountants as by laymen. Now is the time for accounting to become more useful to society by using various economic concepts in their technical sense. This will automatically give a social bias to accounting and will bring it nearer to economics, which is the most closely associated social science. Only such a change in the outlook of accountants, both academicians and those in practice, will enable these two social sciences to work jointly for achieving their ultimate aim, i.e., the well-being of man as a member of society.

FOOTNOTES

1. Elgin F. Hunt, *Social Science—An Introduction to the Study of Society.*
2. *Journal of Accountancy,* June 1963, page 28.
3. Adolf A. Berle, *The American Economic Republic.*
4. Maurice H. Stans, "Accounting and Human Progress," *The Australian Accountant,* March 1963.
5. "The Social Responsibility of Accountants," Summary of an address by Sir Alexander Fitzgerald, *The Australian Accountant,* August 1963.

QUESTIONS

1. A social science "studies the actions of man in so far as they are influenced by his association with society and 'attempts to develop understandings and inventions that should enable man to cope effectively with the kind of world in which he lives.' " According to this definition, is accounting a social science?

2. "To act as the public's watchdog has become a recognized function of modern accounting." How does accounting act as the public's watchdog?

3. "There is no doubt that society, for its welfare, will have to depend on the accountant so as to have 'more and better information about the financial facts of life.' " Is the accountants' role just to report the financial facts of life? Compare this statement to the arguments of Linowes and Mobley in the two preceding articles.

4. "The future development of accounting depends upon the good it can do to society and not to individuals." Do you agree? Explain.

5. What is "social cost accounting?" How is this related to "accounting for social costs" as discussed in the selection by Estes in Section VI?

6. What are non-monetary costs? When the author states that non-monetary costs must be taken into consideration, do you think he means they must be reported as data on the books and in financial statements? Explain.

7. What does the author mean when he suggests "a social approach by the accountant?"

8. The author notes that the question of auditing being nationalized has become the subject matter of a controversy in India. There have been rare but occasional suggestions in the United States that the practice of auditing and certifying financial statements should be nationalized? Why do you think such suggestions have been advanced? Discuss both the pros and cons of nationalizing auditing.

9. Summarize Kulshrestha's remarks concerning the role of business accountability in a democratic free enterprise system. Relate these ideas to the role of accounting in a country seeking rapid economic development.

10. Is accounting a tool of economics or is economics a tool of accounting? Discuss.

*Although accounting actions are often
defended on the basis that they serve the
public interest, relatively little attention
has been given to the basic characteristics
and manifold implications of the public
interest doctrine. This essentially explora-
tory study dramatizes the doctrine's elu-
sive character—primarily to generate
interest in more sharply defining an expression common to the vocabularies of all
accountants. "Public interest" is examined
here in terms of its essential properties, its
special relevance to business, the credentials
of those who are motivated to serve it, and
areas of accounting which exhibit special
sensitivity to its influence.*

"In the Public Interest"

by Charles H. Griffin & Thomas H. Williams

Economic thought prior to 1890 patently emphasized the importance of competition as the mechanism to harmonize private and social interests. This ideol-
ogy, commonly attributed to the "natural harmony" school of Rousseau, Locke
and Bentham, receded in importance after 1890. In the post-1890 period the
famed Alfred Marshall rejected the notion of the mystical merging of private and
public interests through competition, observing that the individual is typically

SOURCE: Reprinted by permission of the authors and the publisher from The
Federal Accountant (Spring 1965), pp. 86–97.

short-sighted and seldom reckons the consequences of his actions. Marshall believed that the public interest is not achieved by an aggregation of individual self-interests; rather, it is attained only by a carefully conceived and well directed public policy.[1] Unfortunately, however, there is no apparent consensus as to a precise delimitation of the public interest doctrine.

CONFLICTING CONCEPTS OF PUBLIC INTEREST

Recent interpretations of public interest either define it as an attribute of broad—even universal—scope, or seek to particularize the concept in terms of specific and discrete actions. F. J. Sorauf, in recounting some of the more common definitions of the phrase found in contemporary literature, noted that the public interest is variously conceived to be:[2]

- A commonly-held interest or value
- A wise or superior interest
- A moral imperative
- A balance of interests
- An undefinable object

Reviewing these properties, Sorauf argued that, at best, the public interest merely *"symbolizes the process of group accommodation."*[3]

Those who support Sorauf's *aggregationist* view assume, albeit cautiously, that the process of summation of a seemingly heterogeneous collection of individual and group interests is meaningful if it is based upon the judgment of enlightened people. However, in reply, the argument is made by *unity* proponents that "if the different reasons why a policy is or is not in the public interest, or the different respects in which it may be said to be in the public interest or not are not species of a common genus—if they have nothing strictly in common—then they cannot be summed or ranked according to any one scale. . . ."[4] Consequently, it appears that in any preliminary discourse upon the definition of public interest, attention should focus on the calculation or creation of a public or publics to accommodate the various interests of individuals or groups. If a unity concept is to be adopted, the common attributes of a single, transcendent public interest can be inferred therefrom; if, on the other hand, the aggregationist concept appears to be more workable, a value scale of some order is needed to accommodate subsequent summation or comparison.

In regard to social groups, John Dewey contends that the public is itself an ephemeral object which:

. . . cannot for any length of time identify and hold itself. It is not that there is no public, no large body of persons having a common interest in the consequences of social transactions. There is too much public, a public too diffused and scattered and too intricate in composition. And there are too many publics . . . and each of them crosses the others and generates its own group of persons especially affected with little to hold these different publics together in an integrated whole.[5]

The latitude usually ascribed to meanings of the word "interest" is likewise unrewarding as to casting any particular illumination upon the scope of the public interest. "Interest" is described by some as an attribute of need, desire or motivation, which can be established by empirical investigation; others regard it as an exercisable claim or legal right.

Repeated efforts to synthesize the views of the aggregationist and unity proponents have met with persistent failure. For the present, it would seem clearly more reasonable to grant the existence of several—perhaps many—public interests than to attempt to homogenize the separate, manifestly dissimilar, interests. The economic and social class pluralism which characterizes national institutions in the United States militates against current efforts to identify a common or unit interest. As a research goal, however, methodological refinements in the behavioral sciences may facilitate more precise measurements of the common interest pervading the socio-economic system.

RELEVANCE TO ACCOUNTING

In broad perspective accounting is essentially a system of communication by which information about the enterprise (or an affiliation of enterprises) is transmitted to various parties at interest. Because the information required by these parties is often used for different and important purposes, it is difficult to support the thesis that there is a single public interest served by an integrated system of accounts and reports. More than abundant evidence indicates the presence of many publics whose separate interests compel the accountant's attention. Four collections of such interests stand out:

Management Interests.   Authority for the orderly conduct of an enterprise rests in the hands of administrative and operating management. The achievement of the goals of the enterprise, including, among others, profit maximization and social betterment, is the special responsibility of this group. The accountant's role in the collection and timely reporting of relevant information is a vital prerequisite to the attainment of these objectives.

Equity Interests.   For a meaningful appraisal of financial condition and operations, equity interests—proprietary or creditor, present or prospective—require pertinent information regarding earnings history and projections, liquidity circumstance, legal and other constraints upon resource employment, and other important indexes.

Labor Interests.   The contributions of labor must be carefully measured if its reward is to be an equitable distributive share of the firm's resources. Clearly, the accountant has a unique responsibility in the calculation of this share.

Government Interests.   Tax agencies and regulatory commissions must rely upon information assembled and reported by the accountant as a basis for the assessment and collection of taxes and for the testing of compliance with relevant statutes and regulations.

Additional beneficiaries are:[6]

- Millions of people [who] provide for their future or their dependents, or protect themselves from loss or liability, by insurance, and must rely on examinations and reports in appraising the soundness of the provisions they have made.
- Contributors to charitable and social causes, and these are many more than a few wealthy philanthropists, [who] know only from reports that their contributions have been used as they intended.
- Taxpayers, and this includes everybody, [who] know that the funds assessed against them to meet costs of government are properly used and accounted for only by the fact of honest, competent, and adequate examination of municipal accounts.

Recent expressions concerning accounting theory also focus on the pluralism of accounting publics, for example:

Accounting supplies much of the comprehensive and dependable information that management needs to control and administer the resources in its charge efficiently and productively. It also supplies the data that management needs to fulfill its responsibility to report to owners, creditors, government, and others with *bona fide* interests. In turn, these owners, creditors, government, and others rely on accounting reports to assist them in determining and evaluating the performance of management and the business system.[7]

. . . the one basic accounting postulate underlying accounting principles may be stated as that of fairness—fairness to *all segments of the business community* (management, labor, stockholders, creditors, customers, and the public), determined and measured in the light of the economic and political environment and the modes of thought and customs of all such segments—to the end that the accounting principles based upon this postulate shall produce financial accounting for the lawfully established economic rights and interests that is fair to *all segments.*[8]

Important questions, as yet unresolved, are: "Can these separate interests be concurrently served? Can one system of accounts and reports so harmonize these interests as to be meaningful to each?"

The accountant who would serve these interests must be motivated to a service other than to self. Manifestly, he must be technically competent. More importantly, however, he must be endowed with a keen sense of equity and must demonstrate an attitude of professionalism and personal integrity. Only in this spirit can the accountant—public or private—begin to comprehend, and judiciously assign some type of measure to, the affected interests.

A QUESTION OF MEASUREMENT

As in the case of many qualitative attributes, it is difficult to evaluate the various interests served by the accountant. Clearly, the assignment of an absolute magnitude is not now possible; however, it is possible and useful to indicate ordinal preferences. A determination of relative magnitudes is particularly important where the interests of the various accounting publics appear to sharply diverge. In such an instance a value succession must necessarily control. Where there is no clearly established superiority of one interest, the accountant is importuned to elect that course of action which prudently compromises the several apparently equal interests.

The dilemma which confronts the accountant in respect to the problem of a conflict of interests is easily illustrated by the accountant's duty to make full and complete disclosure in published financial statements, such that the statements may be not misleading. Reports which are responsive to the needs of various external accounting publics must also satisfy a more immediate and more compelling need—that of corporate management. These interest segments are not always best served by the same types and amounts of information. Informative disclosures which satisfy an important need in respect to the management function may be singularly deficient in meeting the needs of non-management interests. Additionally, the accountant must remain especially alert in protecting important confidences reposed in management.

Public disclosure of the projected operating details and anticipations of management may easily compromise and prejudice its forward planning. Yet significantly, pronouncements of the Securities and Exchange Commission in respect to its registrants appear to support the view that the withholding of information (from the "investing" public) is justified only in those instances where the projected injury to the enterprise from unwarranted revelation is measurably greater than the corresponding benefit to other interests. The balancing of these interests, and a determination of the consequence of their inequality, must be based upon reliable evidence; it is not sufficient merely to anticipate a projected injury from unwarranted disclosure for which there is no present supporting evidence.

In dealing with this problem some years ago, the Securities and Exchange Commission reached the following conclusion:

It is patent, of course, that tangible proof of the injury is not required in this type of proceeding. At the same time, however, it is necessary that the registrant establish the factual basis from which an inference of future harm can reasonably be drawn. A statement of the assertions and fears of management in the absence of showing that a reasonable basis exists is not sufficient.[9]

It would appear this regulatory authority has compared implicitly the enterprise interest against an undefined, yet clearly existent, unit public interest. Thus, where the various public interests appear to have a common genus, the accountant should be motivated to compound these interests. In those instances where a plurality of publics exhibit widely divergent accounting need, however, the accountant is perforce compelled to establish an ordinal sequence and serve each interest as indicated in the line of succession.

PUBLIC ACCOUNTANTS

Audited financial statements of most large enterprises are distributed to virtually all segments of the business community and those who rely upon them for financial data are reassured by references to independent audit examination of the reporting enterprise. The audit opinion which evaluates the fairness of presentation of an enterprise's financial statements invariably refers to audit standards. These standards relate to the auditor's technical credentials, professional independence, competence in field work and quality of reporting performance. Widespread compliance with these standards by public accountants provides audited financial statements with needed reliability important to the protection of the public interests. Confidence in audited financial statements is further strengthened by the public accountant's willing acceptance of a code of professional ethics replete with references to the public interest. In the 1964 code of the American Institute of Certified Public Accountants there appear, for example, the following statements:

1. The reliance of the public and the business community on sound financial reporting and advice on business affairs imposes on the accounting profession on obligation to maintain high standards of technical competence, morality, and integrity.[10]

2. In further recognition of the public interest . . . a member [of the American Institute of Certified Public Accountants] agrees to comply with . . . the rules of ethical conduct. . . .[11]

3. Competitive bidding for public accounting services is not in the public interest. . . .[12]

4. There is nothing contrary to the public interest . . . in a firm of certified
   public accountants coordinating its work with that of an engineering, legal, or
   other professional firm on a specific project. . . .[13]

Unfortunately, these and other similar expressions offer little to remove the
ambiguities as to the meaning of the public interest and the concept remains
essentially undefined by the public accountant; yet, clearly many of the functions of attest and review are performed in the name of this doctrine.

In many States, additionally, the requirements of certification of public
accountants are defended with the argument that they are affected with the
public interest. "Professional organizations, such as the bar associations (which
some State governments give a special status, involving the right and duty of passing on qualifications of candidates for entry into the profession and for enforcing
standards of conduct) act, in limited ways, as trustees or agents of 'the public.'
Recognition of such responsibility is appropriate. . . ."[14] The fifty States and
three territories have enacted statutes which relate to the qualifications of those
individuals who practice public accountancy; this legislation is of both a "regulatory" and "permissive" character. Notwithstanding this widespread recognition
of social responsibility, the accounting profession, like other professions, has
failed to shed much light on its fundamental purpose. The nature of the doctrine
apparently must be inferred from specific legal or ethical controversies.

ACCOUNTANTS, CORPORATE EXECUTIVES AND THE PUBLIC INTEREST

Any organizational system contains a number of variables of indeterminate magnitude, the relative importance of which must be established if predetermined
goals are to be achieved. Such a plan of organization emphasizes the behavioral
relationships which connect the items or components of the system. The corporate executive presides over a complex organization function in which men,
property, products and service are equally important variable factors. Given such
a system for a modern corporate enterprise, the consequences (not all of which
are known) of alternative courses of managerial action may be predicted, and the
corporate executive, subject to certain cognitive limits on rationality, may then
order the consequences or sets of consequences. The selection of a specific
course of action by the corporate executive compels him to evaluate the operational objectives of the enterprise, surely one of which is social usefulness. In this
context, the public interest may be best served through workable compromises
resulting from conflict situations in which the executive encounters other management interests whose objectives assume different value bases. This notion of
the public interest—a description of what it is not in specific situations involving
conflict and compromise—appears reasonable for today's loosely defined, plural-
istic society.

Any description of the management function in a modern corporate enterprise focuses sharply on the importance of an effective and timely communication system. Accounting was described earlier as such a system. Given an effective system, the accountant, particularly the controller, is uniquely equipped to render important aid and offer valuable counsel to other corporate executives by making known to them relationships which certain decisions will alter or shape. For example, a decision may relate to management's election to use retained earnings to finance programs for expansion—that is, withholding cash or investing it in assets when it might otherwise have been distributed as dividends. Accountants are increasingly making use of new concepts, such as the cost of capital concept, to point out the implications of this type of election to corporate management.

To the extent decision choices of the executive have important environmental associations which affect various accounting publics, the analysis must be further broadened to recognize an increasing social responsibility. With the growth of a computer technology, it may be expected that business management will become even more dependent upon the accountant for systematizing the factors vital to the decision process in which are revealed public policy implications. With respect to the developing of a systematic approach to the decision function of management, the accountant is well qualified to contribute to the formulation of policy in a burgeoning socio-economic environment. The efficiency of the accounting-controlled communication system, in which are connected various decision centers, provides a basis for rational judgments. The resulting accuracy in interpreting data should appreciably refine the value of decision outputs which are relevant to the public interest.

FURTHER RESEARCH NEEDED

Accounting's affection with the public interest is confirmed by governmental action as well as professional self-regulation. Commissions which, in addition to other functions, regulate financial statement form and content are motivated to protect the interests of various accounting publics. Regulation which is self-imposed by the accounting profession primarily relates to the licensing function, the accountant's special sensitivity and increasing awareness of the numerous accounting publics, and the creation of codes of professional conduct and ethics. Additionally, the business community is increasingly responsive to its manifold obligations to consumers, employees, stockholders and other groups. Each of these contributes measurably to the accountant's acceptance of social responsibility; each endows him with a public trust.

The authors are impressed with the argument that many interests served by the accountant do, in fact, have a common genus. Theoretically, the common properties of these interests accommodate to the arithmetic process of summation. The texture of such an interest sum (or average), while consisting of many strands, is nonetheless composed in one fabric. Yet, there are other interests of a strikingly dissimilar nature which seem to defy any process of amalgamation. The communication system which is accounting must accordingly accommodate both interest categories, as each represents separate, but important, accounting publics. However, it is important to be mindful of the cautionary note sounded earlier by John Dewey that the public "cannot for any length of time identify and hold itself. . .it is too diffused and scattered and too intricate in composition."[15]

Further research in this important area of accounting responsibility should thus carefully consider the following five unresolved, yet fundamental, questions:

1. *Of what does the "public interest" consist?* Does it have a unique identity? Does it relate, for example, to economic classes, political subdivisions, ethnic groups, business or governmental units? Or, rather, is it an aggregate of all or a collection of special interest groups? What are its most salient features? What are the credentials of those who serve it (technical competence, an attitude of professionalism, motivation of public service, personal integrity. . .)?

2. *What criteria are available to measure the magnitude (or strength) of the "public interest"?* Is it possible that in serving the "public interest" other interests may be prejudiced or compromised? How may these conflicts be resolved.

3. *What motivates the accountancy profession in serving the "public interest"?* Does not the mere identification of data to be collected and recorded indicate a recognition of social responsibility? Is not the subsequent classification schema a further indication of this awareness? Are many of the currently controversial accounting topics merely manifestations of individual uncertainties in assessing the nature and implications of the public interest?

4. *What is the responsibility of the corporate executive (or more generally, business management) in serving the "public interest"?* How does the accounting executive aid in the discharge of this responsibility?

5. *Whom does the public accountant serve in its attest and review function?* If conflicts of interest are met here, how are they resolved? What is the relevence of the accountant's legal and social responsibilities? Are they of equal importance, or does not one occupy a superior relative position?

As answers to these fundamental questions are gradually assimilated within a professional framework for accountancy, an underlying set of basic principles—indeed, a philosophy of accountancy—may well emerge and guide the future accountant in his deliberations and actions.

FOOTNOTES

1. Homan, Paul. *Modern Economic Thought*, New York, New York: Harper and Brothers, 1928, p. 224.
2. Sorauf, F. J. "The Public Interest Reconsidered," *Journal of Politics*, 19 (November 1957), 616–39.
3. *Ibid.*
4. *See*, Leys, Wayne A. R. and Charner Marquis Perry. *Philosophy and the Public Interest*, Chicago, Illinois: The Committee to Advance Original Work in Philosophy, 1959. 72 pp. $1.00. Included in this document is a letter from Warner Wick presenting on page 21 the view quoted.
5. Dewey, John. *The Public and Its Problems*, New York, New York: Henry Holt, 1927, p. 137.
6. Wilcox, Edward B. "Accounting in the Public Interest," *The Journal of Accountancy*, 60 (September 1939), p. 152.
7. Sprouse, Robert T. and Maurice Moonitz, *A Tentative Set of Broad Accounting Principles for Business Enterprises*, New York, New York: American Institute of Certified Public Accountants, 1962, p. 1.
8. Arthur Andersen & Co., *The Postulate of Accounting*, Chicago, Illinois: Arthur Andersen & Co., 1960, p. 31 (emphases supplied).
9. American Sumatra Tobacco Corporation, 7 SEC 1052 (1940).
10. American Institute of Certified Public Accountants, *Code of Professional Ethics*, New York, New York: American Institute of Certified Public Accountants, 1964, p. 28.
11. *Ibid.*
12. *Ibid.*, p. 32.
13. *Ibid.*, p. 38.
14. Leys, Wayne A. R. and Charner M. Perry, *op. cit.*, p. 43.
15. Dewey, John. *The Public and Its Problems*, New York, New York: Henry Holt, 1927, p. 137.

QUESTIONS

1. What is "the public interest?"

2. Do accountants serve the public interest, or are they exclusively involved with private interests? Explain.

3. List the groups of "publics" served by accountants. Did Griffin and Williams omit any?

4. "Informative disclosures which satisfy an important need in respect to the management function may be singularly deficient in meeting the needs of non-management interests." Give several examples of information needed by management but which would not be particularly useful to outsiders. Is there any information needed by the various publics served by accounting which would not be particularly useful to internal management? What problems result from using the same accounting model and the same internal information system to generate information for both management and outsiders?

5. How can CPAs undertake to serve a public function through certification of financial statements, when their fees are paid by the very firms being audited?

6. Respond, as well as you can, to Griffin & William's five concluding questions.

Section II

Accounting's Social Responsibility

The purpose of life is a question of primary interest to philosophers; accountants sometimes appear to be more concerned with such fundamental issues as whether the debits equal the credits. But every person, including the accountant, must explicitly or implicitly make some judgement as to the purpose of his life. In other words, everyone must have implied or stated objectives to guide decisions and actions throughout life.

If philosophers have not been able to resolve the issue of life's purpose, it is doubtful that we can reach agreement here. Nevertheless, there seems to be a pretty fair consensus that every person should try to leave the world a little better than he finds it—in other words, in addition to providing for his own needs and pleasures each person should also try to improve society. (It is possible to reconcile this view with a philosophy of pure hedonism, but to do so would take us too far afield.)

This argument is especially applicable to professional persons. Professionals are generally expected to hold a commitment to public service above their commitment to personal economic gain. In addition, professional persons are accorded especial esteem by society and receive above-average economic rewards. Consequently, members of professions such as accounting have an extra obligation to work for the improvement of society.

Complementing their obligation to society, accountants have special abilities needed in the solution of the ever growing problems of society. The accountant's

45

analytical and evaluative skills, as well as his independence and ethical standards, permit him to make a significant and unique contribution to protecting the public interest, controlling and improving public programs, attacking environmental problems, working for economic growth, and improving the overall quality of life. Ways in which accountants are contributing and can contribute in these particular areas are presented in the sections to follow. We should first look, however, at accounting's social responsibility in its broadest context, and examine the general response of accountants to this responsibility.

The articles by Richard Austin, a black accountant, and by Letricia Gayle Rayburn, a woman, deal with the questions of discrimination and opportunities in accounting for minority group members and for women. Progress in these areas has been substantial, but much more is needed in a profession which was practically closed to all but white males prior to the decade of the 60's.

The following article by Estes explores the possible scope of the accountant's social responsibility, describes one CPA's involvement in the formation of a neighborhood war-on-poverty organization, and suggests similar areas in which accountants might become involved.

Neubauer next describes the formation and functions of the Accounting Aid Society in Des Moines, Iowa. This organization was formed by a group of accounting students and continues to use student help, with assistance from professional accountants, to provide accounting and financial counseling services to individuals, small businesses, and nonprofit organizations with limited funds in low-income communities.

The next two selections describe specific cases of young professional accountants' involvement in social/community problems. William Morris describes a volunteer tax counseling service in a low-income neighborhood, while Willard Archie and Alford Sweet tell about bookkeeping courses taught by professional accountants in the Bedford-Stuyvesant area of Brooklyn and the Harlem and the Lower East Side areas of Manhattan.

The last article in this section is a spoof on television series presenting young professional doctors and lawyers deeply involved in community problems. The author's apparent intention was to use a profession where involvement in community problems was so unlikely that to describe such involvement would be ridiculous and consequently funny. In view of the cases described in the other selections in this section, see if you share Shayne's image of the accounting profession.

ADDITIONAL REFERENCES

1. "A Gift of Service," The Price Waterhouse Review, Summer 1968, pp. 18–33.
2. Aiken, William, "The Black Experience in Large Public Accounting Firms," The Journal of Accountancy, August 1972, pp. 60–63.
3. Lang, Edwin R. and John Ashworth, "Integration in Fact—A Test of the Professional Accountant as a Citizen," The Journal of Accountancy, April 1971, pp. 41–46.
4. Lelievre, Clara C., "The Social Responsibility of the Accounting Profession," The Woman CPA, November 1969, pp. 5–9.
5. Linowes, David F., "Social Responsibility of the Profession," The Journal of Accountancy, January 1971, pp. 66–69.
6. Nolan, James, "A Philadelphia Story: CPA Chapter Helps Minority Businessmen," The Journal of Accountancy, March 1970, pp. 20ff.
7. Valentine, J. A., "The Responsibility of the Accountancy Profession in the Community," The Accountant's Journal (New Zealand), March 1967, pp. 301–303.
8. Wheaton, Perry, "Black Capitalism and the Social Role of the CPA," Lybrand Journal, vol. 52, 1971, pp. 47–50.

*In a speech given at Michigan State University
in 1971, the then Michigan Secretary of State
challenged accountants to increase black
involvement in the profession.*

The CPA's Social, Civic, and Political Responsibilities

by *Richard H. Austin*

The last ten years have produced the most drastic, rapid changes the world has ever experienced. Life is whizzing by so swiftly and progress—if we can call it that—is so rapid that we're forced to travel at jet speed just to stay in the same place. So we have to find ways to move even faster.

These speedy changes have affected different sectors of business and society in different ways. The phenomenal growth of business firms—incorporations, mergers, the formation of giant holding companies—all these escalations in size

---

SOURCE: Reprinted slightly abridged by permission of the author and the publisher from <u>The Journal of Accountancy</u> (December 1971), pp. 64–66. Copyright 1971 by the American Institute of Certified Public Accountants, Inc.

have brought an accompanying growth in the size of accounting firms. Our accounting giants now render their services worldwide. This trend toward ever larger accounting firms will continue, I am sure, as long as business itself continues to grow. At the same time our small practitioners manage to survive and some even to prosper. The gulf, however, between the megafirms and the mini-offices is ever widening.

But whatever the size and whatever the specialization, life in recent years has compelled all of us to reassess our attitudes, our prejudices and our basic relations with the chaotic world around us. Our kids especially have forced us to think less about our personal advantages and professional privileges and more of our social obligations and our civic and political responsibilities.

One has only to read the newspapers to recognize that none of us is above the battle. Involvement is no longer a matter of personal choice—it is a fact of life. You cannot be long apart from the contradictions, the pathos and the struggles of today's turbulent happenings. They are all-encompassing. The poverty, the under-education, the racism, the violence—each of these massive areas of discontent and injustice requires a response. To remain passive and silent is either to acquiesce or to surrender. And I don't know anyone who would choose either of those alternatives.

I am by no means recommending the abandonment of one's career or life-goals to become an activist. Each of us must respond to the pressures of today's America in his own way. But response is a *must*.

No one can do someone else's "soul-searching." And I do not suggest that my response is the best. But I'd like to talk about the reasons that led me to wander somewhat from my chosen life's work for another route. Let me take a moment to indulge in this self-history. Some of you have heard parts of this story before. (My story can be summed up in the often repeated suggestion: "When you book passage on the Titanic, you might as well go first class.")

Like yourselves, I was not born into our profession. I'm a self-made CPA and a self-generated professional drop-out, too. The pleasures and the rewards of accountancy are many, and I sincerely and enthusiastically recommend the pursuit of this career to every qualified and ambitious youth whose interests lie in this direction. Here, however, is precisely where I began to veer away from the confines of my chosen life work. Not too many years ago, I began to see more vividly and more angrily the facts about our profession—indeed, about all of America. This new vision widened my horizons and at the same time led me into other pursuits.

In a recent speech, Dr. Benjamin Mays, former president of Morehouse University in Atlanta, Georgia, explained why he felt compelled to write *Born to Rebel,* an autobiography which recounts the peculiar struggles of a black intellectual in the South. His reason can be summed in two words: Discrimination—Degradation.

I don't think that you who are born white, free and equal can truly share the feelings and experiences of black kids who struggle for identity and who try to claw their way out of obscurity and poverty. It was difficult for every CPA in this room to achieve "certification." But generally speaking, you had only the obstacles of scholastic requirements, tuition and discipline. If you were black, there would have been other, far more formidable obstacles.

There would have been a 400-year history of degradation, repression and violence concentrated against people of color. There would have been social ostracism, educational segregation and professional rejection. You would have been subjected, from the moment you could comprehend the language, to a hundred and one indignities and insults, challenging your boyhood, your manhood and your very life.

If you were black and you were so daring and unrealistic as to choose accountancy for your profession, you would have suffered the crowning rejection before you started, namely, the realization that the profession did not want you. This partly explains why it is so difficult to interest black youngsters, today, in accounting as a career.

I know that there are many individuals . . . doctors, lawyers, CPAs and whatever, who can rightfully deny their complicity with the system that segregates. I have such friends, and they are many. Some are here tonight. But these are not the ones who run the system. Indeed, they are as much victims of it as are my black brothers.

Look at the evidence, then tell me who is without shame.

In 1967, there were more than 110,000 CPAs in the United States. Of these, no more than 150 were black. There are perhaps over 200 today. That, my friends, is less than two-tenths of 1 per cent. That is perhaps the weakest participation by blacks in any profession in our country. There are proportionately 15 times more black doctors and dentists, despite the fact that less than 2½ per cent of the members of those professions are black.

In Michigan, the black population is about 15 per cent of the total. In Detroit, 45 per cent of the 1½ million people are black. To my knowledge, there remain six, perhaps seven, black CPAs in the state, all in Detroit; three of us are in one firm. I believe only eight or nine altogether have passed the CPA exams in Michigan. (Maybe more by now.) While I served as a member of the Board of Directors of the Michigan Association of CPAs, the appearance of the official family gave the illusion of an integrated profession, but the staffs were not integrated.

Only three states in the union in 1967 had more than ten black CPAs: Illinois, New York and California.

In 1954, the United States Supreme Court declared in its now famous school desegregation ruling that "equal but separate" educational facilities were not at all equal. We who fought for equality and believed in the democratic credo were overjoyed with the verdict. It was a landmark in the struggle for human rights and personal dignity.

Now, nearly 20 years later, we see the emptiness of the promises that had been made.

This country of ours is in great turmoil. Make no mistake. We are all in serious crisis. The tensions and frustrations have erupted into social upheaval. The problems of poverty, hunger and war are not being dealt with—they are being ignored. The festering cancer of racism is not being cured—it is being tolerated. It has reached our grade schools where disruptions are having a devastating effect on the education process.

Whether you are a factory worker or an accountant, whether you are rich or poor, whether you are trapped in a ghetto or cocooned in a suburb, you are at once a victim and a sacrifice to this oppressive and restrictive system.

Unless you strive for change, you are part of the problem, not a contributor to the solution.

We who have a professional commitment to objectivity and excellence in our craft cannot ignore the talent and the promise of so many deserving black youth.

We who have a moral commitment to honesty, decency and equality of opportunity know the strivings and the pleadings of so many black youths who have the capacity and who need to learn to share but who need direction and proper motivation.

We who are successful cannot escape our individual responsibilities to help others to be successful.

If you face tomorrow without making a personal commitment to positive action on this matter, you are, in effect, accepting the present rate of growth of black public accountants in the United States.

If you have had questions as to the roots of black frustration, the causes of black militancy, the reasons for black campus rebellion, look around you. Look into your own profession. If we accept the premise that our profession is a necessary part of the American system and economy, then we must recognize that it must have significant participation from all segments of our society—otherwise alienation and frustration will persist.

We can no longer live at peace with standards which deprive so many Americans of an equal right to professional equality. Whatever it takes, we should be prepared to furnish.

Whether scholarships, apprenticeships or special aid, it is incumbent upon you—each of you—to find the way and make your move. You have the talent, you have the skill, you have the organization and you have the money. Do you have the will to do it?

I commend the American Institute of Certified Public Accountants for its forthright stand on the issue of assistance to disadvantaged minorities and their promotion of the Accounting Education Fund for Disadvantaged Students. Establishment of the fund is a significant first step toward encouraging black recruits for the profession. I wish also to commend the Institute's Council for its grants to black colleges and for going on record urging a campaign to recruit and train young people from disadvantaged groups. These, however, are but empty gestures until the membership responds adequately and translates the pronouncements into action. (Let us not be like the company that spent $5,000 on pollution control and $212,000 bragging about it.) Those of you who have actively participated in black economic development projects deserve the profession's highest commendation. I see, at the same time, evidence of a lack of awareness by many members of my profession of what the decade of the seventies will be all about. I have, and I am sure many of you have, read the booklet, "Objectives of the American Institute of Certified Public Accountants." I see no mention of the responsibility of our profession to increase black involvement. I see no word in that document that would reflect a willingness to move out of the ingrown circle to embrace outsiders who have never been invited.

I hope this rather long exposition provides some insight to the circumstances which motivated me to move toward political involvement. I hope also it may serve to broaden the horizons of those who visualize their talents and their expertise as tools which can and should be assigned—in part at least—to the social good.

Each of us is propelled to participate along the lines of his own unique background and ambitions. I have tried to indicate the things that motivated me. I hope from all of this you can agree that politics is not necessarily a nasty word.

For me it is my way of helping in a small way to reach for the hopes and dreams I have for my people, my country. I am like all of you. I want all of us to attain freedom from want, freedom from conflict, freedom from hate. I want better housing, better schools, better medical care, cleaner streets, safer cities. I want an America liberated from prejudice, bigotry and racism. I want an America at peace with every other nation.

I want you to join me in working for these common goals. Let us begin by first examining the lives we ourselves live, the places we work and the people we work with. Can you do more to help yourself than by helping others? If you want to, you will find the way.

QUESTIONS

1. Why aren't there more black, Chicano, and Indian CPAs?

2. Assume the answer to the first question is prejudice and willful discrimination (many would disagree, of course, but assume it for the moment anyway). What action would you recommend to produce more professional accountants from minority groups?

3. Should the accounting profession provide special encouragement and assistance to minorities, or is elimination of barriers such as discrimination enough? Discuss thoroughly.

*An analysis of the experience, attitudes,
and characteristics of women in accounting
reveals that some prejudice still exists, but
that by and large ability and personality
have become the major factors in success.*

Recruitment
of Women
Accountants

by L. Gayle Rayburn

Despite what might be inferred from the activities of the women's liberation
movement, many doors are open to women accountants. Many prejudices have
been overcome with regard to hiring women accountants. However, more information concerning the success with which women CPAs have been acclimating
themselves to the "male" accounting profession is needed to further reduce
existing prejudices.

In the hope of obtaining this information, the writer mailed 902 question-
naires to the members of the American Woman's Society of Certified Public Accountants (AWSCPA) in June 1970. Second requests were mailed within about
six weeks. In total, 663 questionnaires containing sufficient information for classification were returned. This represents 73.5 per cent of the group surveyed.

The returned questionnaires present a comprehensive picture of a broad cross
section of American women CPAs. However, the sample is not fully representative, since it excludes women CPAs who do not belong to AWSCPA.

SOURCE: Reprinted by permission of the author and the publisher from The
Journal of Accountancy (November 1971), pp. 51–57. Copyright 1971 by the
American Institute of Certified Public Accountants, Inc.

Although 663 responses were received, not every respondent answered every question. Therefore, in some of the accompanying tables, the number of responses is a lesser sum. Also in several of the tables the part-time and nonaccounting-related respondents are excluded.

While the purpose of the survey was not to obtain women's complaints about discrimination, it was interesting to note that many respondents indicated that they thought the questions were slanted to anticipate discrimination. Some said that though they did not doubt that specific cases of discrimination existed, they were proud to say that they had never experienced any discrimination. Many felt that situations existed where the fact of being a woman was used as an excuse for poor performance or lack of knowledge on her part. Others suggested that most women who think they have been discriminated against because they are women are usually inferior in their work performance. Almost all agreed that there is a greater respect for talent than for sex in the accounting profession.

REASONS FOR CHOOSING ACCOUNTING

Prospective employers are often interested in knowing the reasons why women chose accounting as their profession. Some male recruiters believe that the majority of women are not deeply concerned with their future work or careers. However, this survey showed otherwise.

The AWSCPA members were asked to indicate their primary reasons for choosing accounting. Some respondents marked more than one of the reasons listed in Table 1.

TABLE 1.   Reasons for Choosing Accounting

	Number of Respondents
Interesting, challenging	506
Salary	70
Prestige	38
Felt had aptitude for working with numbers	26
Best opportunity for professional status	16
Enjoyed previous accounting-related job	11
Security—knew jobs always available	10
Influence of close family member who is an accountant	9
Encouragement of college or high school accounting teacher	8
Could obtain accounting instruction through other than college or university, i.e., business school and correspondence course	4
Occupation with potential full- or part-time home employment	3
Received accounting scholarship	3

Several respondents said that accounting was as close as they were advised to get to the engineering or legal professions, which were not open to women at that time. Others stated that they chose accounting because it was beginning to show a greater acceptance of women.

EMPLOYMENT CATEGORIES

Respondents were requested to indicate in what field of accounting they were presently employed. They were also asked to state whether their employment was full time or part time. Full time was defined as more than 35 hours per week for 40 or more weeks per year. Of the 663 replies, 570 were employed in full-time accounting work while 60 worked part time. Of the remaining respondents, 28 were not presently employed, 4 were engaged in full-time nonaccounting work and 1 was employed part time in a nonaccounting field. Table 2 shows the distribution among the accounting fields.

TABLE 2.   Number and Percentage of Respondents by Fields of Accounting

	Full Time		Part Time	
	Number	%	Number	%
Public accounting	369	65.0	48	80.0
Manufacturing	21	3.6	2	3.3
Education	55	9.6	4	6.7
Government	56	9.8	–	–
Service	25	4.3	4	6.7
Commercial	44	7.7	2	3.3
	570	100.0	60	100.0

The categories of annual professional earnings were indicated in the questionnaire. The lowest category was under $2,999 while the highest category was $30,000 and over. Annual professional earnings was defined in the questionnaire to exclude rent, interest, dividends, capital gains and inheritances. Table 3 illustrates the income pattern for those in full-time accounting employment, in full-time nonaccounting employment and in part-time employment. Six respondents did not state their salaries.

It was expected that the earnings of those employed part time in accounting-related fields would be low. However, 9 individuals, or 15 per cent, of those employed part time in accounting-related fields earned more than $9,999.

TABLE 3.   Income[1] by Main Categories

	Full Time		Accounting-Related Part Time
Earnings	Accounting-Related	Nonaccounting-Related	
Under $2,999			21.7%
$3,000–$4,999	.7%		21.7
$5,000–$6,999	2.6		16.6
$7,000–$9,999	14.3	25.0%	25.0
$10,000–$11,999	19.9		6.7
$12,000–$14,999	27.0	25.0	8.3
$15,000–$19,999	20.4		
$20,000–$24,999	7.3	25.0	
$25,000–$29,999	3.9		
$30,000 and over	3.9	25.0	
	100.0%	100.0%	100.0%
Total respondents	564	4	60

[1] Salaries and adjusted gross business income only, excluding rent, interest, dividends, capital gains, inheritances.

EFFECT OF MARRIAGE AND CHILDREN

Table 4 shows that 133 women CPA respondents under age 31 are employed full time while 16 are employed part time. Only 8 respondents under age 31 are not employed. This, insofar as the AWSCPA sample is valid, tends to refute the comment that women leave employment to marry and raise a family. Many employers have felt that the likelihood of retaining the woman CPA is less than that

TABLE 4.   Number and Percentage of Respondents by Age

	Full Time		Part Time		Not Employed	
Age	Number	%	Number	%	Number	%
Under 31	133	23.9	16	25.9	8	29.6
31–40	105	18.9	16	25.9	8	29.6
41–50	164	29.3	13	20.7	3	11.1
51–60	113	20.2	4	6.5	1	3.7
Over 60	43	7.7	13	21.0	7	26.0
	558	100.0	62	100.0	27	100.0

of retaining the male accountant. They have not been convinced that the woman CPA is serious enough about her career to continue working after marriage. However, it must be admitted that the data are based on a sample only of members of the AWSCPA, who by virtue of their membership are either employed, in practice or expecting to go back to work soon after temporary absence from work. Data from such a sample cannot conclusively answer the criticism that women leave employment to raise a family.

One question asked if the individual quit work at the time of marriage. Of those replying, 295 individuals, or 73.8 per cent, said that they did not, and 51 women, or 12.9 per cent, indicated that they did leave work when they married. The remaining 53 individuals, or 13.3 per cent, said that they were not working at the time they married. Thus, the majority of the women's labor force in accounting is not made up of young women who plan to work only a few years before marriage. Table 5 analyzes the present marital status of the respondents.

TABLE 5.   Present Marital Status by Employment Classification

Marital Status	Full Time	Part Time	Not Employed
Single	222	9	3
Married	255	43	21
Divorced/Separated	49	6	0
Widow	26	3	2

Only 33 of the respondents indicated that they worked for the same company as their husbands; 17 of these respondents were in partnership with or in the employ of their husbands. Of the remaining, 4 were employed in education with their husbands, 3 were employees along with their husbands in public accounting firms and the remainder were employed in government and industry.

One respondent said that she used her maiden name professionally to avoid competition with her husband who was employed by the same firm. The majority of the respondents listed only advantages for working in the same company as their husbands. The sharing of common interests and professional responsibility were often cited as advantages.

Motherhood seems to be no great deterrent to an accounting career. The AWSCPA members were asked to indicate how old their youngest child was when they began working or returned to work. A large percentage were working within a few months after the child's birth, as illustrated in Table 6.

Of the 198 replies, which included only respondents employed in accounting-related employment, 125 were employed full time when they first returned to work after their children were born and 73 were engaged in part-time employment. This is evidence that even though the female CPA plans to marry and raise a family, she also plans to continue her career. Firms do not lose their investment in female CPAs, as is often assumed.

TABLE 6.   Age of Youngest Child When Began or
Returned to Work

Age of Child	Number of Mothers	%
Under 2 months	52	26.3
2-4 months	23	11.6
5-6 months	12	6.1
6-12 months	12	6.1
12-18 months	8	4.0
2 years	15	7.6
3 years	14	7.1
4 years	8	4.0
5 years	7	3.5
6 years	8	4.0
7 years	3	1.5
8 years	4	2.0
over 8 years	32	16.2
	198	100.0

ABSENCES

A Public Health Service study[1] of worktime lost by persons 17 years of age and over because of illness or injury shows an average of 5.6 days lost by women and 5.3 days lost by men during the calendar year 1967. Slight differences were noted between men and women in the amount of time lost because of acute or chronic illness. Women lost an average of 3.7 workdays because of acute illness, whereas men averaged just 3.3 days away from work for this reason. On the other hand, men were more likely than women to be absent because of chronic conditions such as heart trouble, arthritis, rheumatism and orthopedic impairment.

Another analysis has also indicated that women's illnesses usually keep them away from work for approximately the same period of time that men's illnesses do. The Health Information Foundation of the University of Chicago[2] studied the total loss to the American economy from work absences that occurred because of illness or injury between July 1959 and June 1960. Since women lost more worktime because of acute conditions and men because of chronic conditions, the study found that the total financial loss caused by women's absences was about the same as that caused by men's.

The AWSCPA members were asked to give the number of days missed due to specific reasons. Table 7 analyzes the results from only those employed in full-time accounting work. Several members included their maternity leave in the "over 30 days of personal illness" classification. Absences due to deaths and funerals were included in the personal business classification.

TABLE 7.   Absences in 1969 of Respondents Employed Full Time in Accounting Fields

Personal Illness			Illness of Children		
Number of Days	Number of Respondents	%	Number of Days	Number of Respondents	%
0	216	39.8	0	143	81.2
1	51	9.4	1	13	7.3
2	69	12.7	2	15	8.5
3	49	9.0	3	3	1.8
4	30	5.5	5	1	.6
5	51	9.4	6	1	.6
6	14	2.6		176	100.0
7	6	1.1			
8–15	31	5.7			
16–30	18	3.3			
Over 30	8	1.5			
	543	100.0			

Illness of Other Family Members			Personal Business		
Number of Days	Number of Respondents	%	Number of Days	Number of Respondents	%
0	515	92.3	0	406	74.1
1	12	2.1	1	48	8.8
2	9	1.6	2	37	6.8
3	5	.8	3	11	2.0
4	2	.4	4	9	1.7
5	4	.7	5	21	3.8
6	2	.4	6	2	.3
7	1	.2	7	2	.3
8	1	.2	8–15	7	1.3
10	3	.5	Over 15	5	.9
12	2	.4		548	100.0
30	1	.2			
40	1	.2			
	558	100.0			

Even though their answers indicate a low absence percentage, supervisors of
women are not doing their female employees a favor by allowing them to miss
more days of employment than their male employees. This builds resentment on
the part of the male employees and it is reflected in the way they treat women
on other occasions. Women should also be held to the same standards as their
male co-workers with regard to the length of coffee and lunch breaks.

TRAVEL

The problem of out-of-town travel is often cited as a reason for not employing women accountants. Many firms have felt that their male staff would frown on any special concessions given to female staff members and also that the wives of the male staff members would be unhappy if their husbands travel with female staff members.

The AWSCPA members were asked to indicate their experience with regard to traveling in connection with their employment. Of those replying, 407 respondents, or 87 per cent, stated that their companies' policies allow them to travel out of town with their male associates, while 64 respondents, or 13 per cent, gave a negative reply. A different view can be obtained, however, from the replies to the question asking if their jobs require out-of-town travel. In answering this question, 315 respondents, or 55 per cent, gave a negative answer, while 260 respondents, or 45 per cent, indicated that their jobs did require out-of-town travel.

The members were also asked how many days in 1969 they spent out of town on voluntary professional business meetings and on trips in connection with their employment. Table 8 shows their answers in an unequal division of the number of days in order to give a more concise breakdown.

TABLE 8.   Days of Out-of-Town Travel

Number of Days	Number of Respondents	%
1–5 days	136	34.6
6–10 days	96	24.5
11–20 days	81	20.6
21–30 days	38	9.7
31–40 days	8	2.1
41–75 days	22	5.5
Over 75 days	12	3.0
Total	393	100.0

Of the respondents, 208, or 91 per cent, indicated full acceptance by the male associates with whom they traveled out of town; 15 respondents indicated partial acceptance; 3 respondents indicated limited acceptance; and 2 respondents indicated neither full, partial nor limited acceptance.

OFFICE FACILITIES

Employers of accountants are interested in knowing the problems of hiring women insofar as this would affect office facilities. The members were asked if any of their past or present employers ever had to make any changes in their office facilities primarily because they were hired. Only 11 respondents said that changes had to be made in the office facilities for them. Several of the 11 respondents indicated that before 1950 some changes were necessary because some of their clients did not have restroom facilities for women. Since such a high percentage, 98.3 per cent, stated that no changes in office facilities have been necessary in the hiring of women, this should not be a factor in recruitment.

JOB ASSIGNMENTS

Since there is a stronger resistance to female accountants in public accounting than in other accounting fields, the writer questioned the AWSCPA members concerning their public accounting experience. Of those who had worked in public accounting, 266, or 51 per cent, said that there was no difference in the way the jobs were assigned between men and women when they were first employed as staff accountants. Of the 250 respondents giving a positive reply, 60 per cent were first employed in public accounting before 1960, 28 per cent in the period 1961–1965 and 12 per cent in the period 1966–1970. However, only 4 respondents indicated a difference in job assignments between sexes for the year 1969. There was a sharp decline in the positive replies with each succeeding year, which naturally indicates a decreasing distinction in job assignments between sexes.

It is occasionally said that a woman cannot go into the "rough places" that are required of a new staff accountant in public accounting; however, the replies to the questionnaire do not confirm this. The members were asked if they received more jobs suited for women, such as retail and service establishments, rather than manufacturing or industrial assignments when they were first employed as staff accountants. Of those who had worked in public accounting, 76 respondents, or 15 per cent, indicated always; 127 respondents, or 26 per cent, indicated often; 172 respondents, or 35 per cent, indicated occasionally; and 120 respondents, or 24 per cent, indicated never. Since more than half of the respondents indicated occasionally or never, this objection is not valid.

Public accounting firms also occasionally state that their resistance to hiring female accountants involves their inability to perform inventory observations. The members were asked to give the frequency of their inventory observations in comparison with others of their experience and background. Of the total replying, 118 respondents, or 26 per cent, indicated equally as frequent; 78 respondents, or 17 per cent, indicated almost as frequent; and 253 respondents, or 57 per cent, indicated less frequent inventory observations. Even though the percentages reveal less frequent inventory observations for women CPAs, it should not be difficult to keep women busy on engagements in which no rough places are involved.

The AWSCPA members were asked about discrimination in their job assignments. Of those replying, 278 respondents, or 59 per cent, said that they felt completely accepted; 144 respondents, or 29 per cent, felt accepted most of the time; 13 respondents, or 3 per cent, did not know; 33 respondents, or 8 per cent, felt there was some discrimination in the job assignments. Four respondents, or 1 per cent, felt there was a large degree of discrimination in their job assignments.

CLIENT OPPOSITION

Many public accounting firms in the past have hesitated to hire female accountants because they expected their clients to resist. However, the answers received to questions concerning this topic strongly suggest that this objection is without merit. Most of the opposition appears to come from the profession itself, not from its clients.

While 230 respondents indicated that they knew of clients who had objected to a particular accountant, only 26 respondents said that their clients had a definite prejudice toward women accountants. Of these 26 respondents, 8 stated that they knew of clients who did not feel women were as competent as men at first but later accepted them freely. Many respondents described situations where they had been asked to assume supervision of an audit because clients felt women accountants performed better.

Of the remaining 18 respondents who knew of client opposition to women, most said the opposition came from clients with older management. Some of these clients did not feel free to discuss their financial problems with women or to take women to business meetings as their financial advisers.

Incompatibility of the accountant's personality with the client was the reason given by 111 of the 230 respondents who indicated knowledge of client opposition to a particular accountant. Twenty-six respondents knew of situations where the client's lack of confidence in the competency of the individual accounted for the opposition. Other grounds for opposition from clients included poor work habits, accusing rather than helpful attitude, failure to treat client's personnel with proper respect and specific religious affiliations.

A more specific question regarding the present attitudes and prejudices of clients was then asked. Of the 421 respondents working in public accounting in the last five years, 350 said that none of their firms' clients had shown any restrictions as to age, sex, color or national origin of accountants during that time. Of the 71 respondents indicating client restrictions, 23 were for sex, 19 for color, 8 for religious affiliation, 6 for age and 2 for national origin. Some of the respondents did not explain the reason for client restriction.

CONCLUDING OBSERVATION

Even though some prejudice against women still appears to exist, the opportunities today are much greater than ever before. Sex is no longer the main consideration; ability and the personality to inspire confidence and respect are most important. If a woman today has mastery of the profession, she may find opportunities not available to the men. For example, she may be able to offer sounder advice in family financial transactions with a better understanding of the problem. As more women accountants expect to be held as responsible for their work as their male co-workers, the need for women CPAs will be recognized more readily by business firms.

FOOTNOTES

1. U.S. Department of Health, Education, and Welfare, Public Health Service. *Vital and Health Statistics, Current Estimates From the Health Interview Survey,* United States, 1967, PHS Publication No. 1000—Series 10-No. 52, Tables 8 and 16, May 1969.
2. The University of Chicago, Graduate School of Business, Health Information Foundation. *The Economic Costs of Absenteeism,* In Progress in Health Services, March–April 1963.

QUESTIONS

1.   What is the ratio of women to men students in your class? Is this approximately the same as the ratio of women to men in society? If not, how would you account for the difference?

2.   The article refers to the professions of law and engineering. Call or visit three lawyers and three engineers, and obtain their views on women in their professions. Based on this information and Professor Rayburn's article, which profession—accounting, law, or engineering—do you think is most open to women?

3.   "Accountants didn't start hiring minorities and women until the need for qualified people became so great it couldn't be filled by white males."
     "The accounting profession was opened to minority group members and to women in response to purely moral considerations—it was right, so we did it."
     Evaluate these statements.

4.   Do women make better accountants than men?

*How the accountant can help solve such
social problems as unemployment, inadequate educational preparation, discrimination and inadequate inner city housing.*

The Accountant's
Social Responsibility

by Ralph W. Estes

"Give a damn!" reads the legend on a button currently popular with young people. And they do. Despite what may appear to those of us over 30 to be excessive
impatience and intolerance in seeking solutions to the manifold problems which
plague our society, no one can deny that the current younger generation does
care, and more and more its members are insisting that we demonstrate our concern too.

The accounting profession has been well-rewarded by our society and by our
economic system. That we have devoted many years to preparation and have
tried to earn these rewards is not denied. But we must also recognize our debt to
the society and economy which afforded us the opportunities to develop and
prosper, and both as accountants and as citizens we have an obligation to try to
repay this debt by working to insure that everyone has the same opportunities
we have had.

Do accountants "give a damn?" Most can honestly say they do. "Civic responsibility" is generally recognized as one of the several obligations of the professional accountant, and most accounting and industrial firms make a point of

SOURCE: Reprinted by permission of the author and the publisher from The
Journal of Accountancy (January 1970), pp. 40–43. Copyright 1970 by the
American Institute of Certified Public Accountants, Inc.

encouraging participation in civic activities by their employees. The purpose of this article is to argue that the traditional forms this participation has taken are not sufficient and are not directed toward the root causes of the more pressing problems of society, and to suggest ways in which we can become *more* involved.

The typical professional accountant can reel off an impressive list of civic activities in which he is and has been involved. As an indication of the nature of these activities, consider the following list which resulted from an informal sampling of several acquaintances:

Church work (service on boards and committees, fund-raising, audits)
United Fund
Junior Achievement (service as advisers and sponsors, on boards of directors, and fund-raising)
Service organizations, such as Lions, Rotary, Kiwanis, and Optimists
Art, opera and museum associations
City and county governing bodies
School boards and PTA
Red Cross
Big Brothers
YMCA, YWCA, and YMHA
Boy Scouts
Boys' Clubs of America
Jaycees
Chamber of Commerce

Any accountant could develop such a list of his own and his associates' activities, and it would probably be just as impressive. Further, as anyone who has participated in the work of these organizations can testify, the effort is not only rewarding but clearly productive.

ACTIVITIES COMBATTING SOCIAL ILLS

My argument is that, while productive, these activities are not directly aimed at the problems which have only recently been recognized as contributing heavily to the tremendous social unrest and even potential for revolution manifested by our youth and by minority groups. These problems have been generally identified as unemployment and underemployment, inadequate educational preparation, discrimination (yes, it still exists), inadequate inner city housing—all contributing to a depressing quality of life for far too many American citizens. The types of activities just cited, those in which accountants most often become involved, usually have as their goals the improvement of health, cultural opportunity, and life for citizens in the middle and upper economic strata of society.

In his inaugural address as president of the American Institute of Certified Public Accountants delivered in October 1968, Ralph E. Kent identified four problem areas, or needs, which "now compel our attention as professional CPAs."[1] He first cited our need to identify and meet our broad responsibilities as citizens, a need which, as I've indicated above, is perhaps being met by most accountants. But the second need mentioned by Mr. Kent was "our need to recognize and respond to our pressing responsibilities to the disadvantaged."[2] He went on to state that "It is not an exaggeration to say, echoing the words of Lincoln, that our response to this crisis of our times may well determine whether this nation—conceived in liberty and dedicated to the proposition that all men are created equal—can long endure."[3] Mr. Kent believes that there are at least three ways in which professional accountants can assist:

1. We can participate in the current efforts of the National Alliance of Businessmen and similar organizations to provide additional jobs for members of minority groups—particularly for the "hard-core" unemployed and individuals yet to be initiated into gainful lines of employment, called the "functionally illiterate."

2. We can also arrange to connect our expert accounting counsel to a growing number of businesses operated by residents in ghetto areas.

3. And we can increase our efforts to facilitate the entry of disadvantaged youth into the accounting profession itself.[4]

In the following paragraphs I would like to expand on these opportunities and indicate several other ways in which professional accountants can productively assist in working toward solutions to "the crisis of our times."

NEIGHBORHOOD ACTION, INC.

Let me begin by reciting a personal experience. In early 1967 a lawyer and I, along with our wives who had been socially active, perceived the need for community organization in Fort Worth poverty areas of the sort designed to get neighbors working together on mutual problems, such as cleaning up the neighborhood; pooling transportation and child care or baby-sitting resources so more could work; obtaining needed street improvements, traffic control, and bus service; improving neighborhood schools' facilities and quality of instruction; and learning to use what power could be mustered by participating fully in the political process. Prior to this time, leadership and co-operation in these neighborhoods had been virtually nonexistent, resulting in continuous deterioration in the neighborhoods. We discovered that a grant might be available if an organization was established with these purposes, and so we created and incorporated Neighborhood Action, Inc.[5] After several meetings designed to develop support in the poverty neighborhoods, we next applied for an Office of Economic Opportunity grant for a sum in excess of $200,000.

Office of Economic Opportunity regulations required that any such application include a statement by a CPA indicating that he had reviewed the proposed organization's accounting system and that, in his opinion, it included internal controls adequate to safeguard the assets of the organization, check the accuracy and reliability of accounting data, promote operational efficiency, and encourage adherence to prescribed management policies of the organization. This obviously required a commitment of the CPA that, for a new organization which had not yet commenced operations, he would continue to oversee the development and implementation of an adequate accounting and reporting system. Considering that the people who would probably be directing the organization had no accounting or, for that matter, business experience, this was no small commitment. Since no funds had as yet been awarded, it was not possible to engage a CPA for a fee. In this case, of course, a CPA was involved in the creation of the organization and was available to provide the assurance OEO required. I submitted the required statement to OEO and subsequently developed the organization's accounting system, supervising it until personnel were trained and the system was working routinely. The grant was then awarded.[6]

We later learned that OEO considered the presence of a CPA in the organizing group to be a major consideration in approving the grant and that, since community organization was (and still is) at best somewhat politically controversial, the proposal might well have been disapproved had *not* a CPA been actively involved.

For the first several months after operations began, I attended the board meetings of Neighborhood Action to offer advice on accounting and financial matters. Although this advice was evidently quite important to the organization, it usually involved matters that practically any professional accountant would be competent in, no matter what the level of his professional work. The important point to recognize here is that the people involved, as I mentioned above, had virtually no business or accounting training or experience, and so required advice in some of the most elemental areas.

THE RESULTS

I have since been able to limit my involvement with Neighborhood Action since the staff is now fully trained, a competent bookkeeper was employed, and, with funds now available, another certified public accountant has been engaged on a fee basis to perform the annual audit and routine accounting assistance.

What did this "assignment" pay me? No fee, of course, but the rewards were nevertheless more than worth the effort. Not only was the "client" fully appreciative of my professional opinions (and what accountant has not seen his well-researched advice go unheeded by clients and management), but tangible improvements have been made in the neighborhoods served by Neighborhood Action, Inc. It may be purely coincidental that there have been no riots in Fort Worth, but Neighborhood Action has been fairly active in calming residents of its neighborhoods down when tensions flared, and has also worked to eliminate some of the problems which have led to riots in other communities.

AREAS OPEN TO ACCOUNTANTS

Any accountant in an urban community can find similar opportunities for voluntary service. Although the War on Poverty is apparently being de-escalated, Community Action Programs are evidently going to be retained. Furthermore, a panorama of neighborhood organizations is appearing across the country. Each of these will be managed by someone and will receive and disburse monies, even if these don't come from OEO. Thus, each can use competent professional advice and assistance and, despite past mistrust, will most likely welcome such assistance if it is offered in the right spirit.

Mr. Kent mentioned providing expert accounting counsel to businesses operated by residents of ghetto areas. This is certainly a fruitful area in which accountants can meet their social responsibility, although it may be difficult at first to identify these opportunities because of the vast communication gap (and perhaps credibility gap) separating professional accountants and ghetto residents. In my own case, I am presently helping a black friend, whom I met through Neighborhood Action, establish a number of black franchises and small businesses. An effort to establish communication with Community Action Agencies and other War-on-Poverty organizations, black chambers of commerce, and community leaders in ghettos and poverty areas should be productive for any accountant in identifying ways to make his advice and assistance available to minority businesses on an individual basis.

Accounting and business firms and local accounting organizations have a unique opportunity to provide such assistance on a broader scale. Free accounting and business training can be offered on a regular basis, at night, in churches and other neighborhood meeting places. Any banker can testify to the need for such training on the part of minority businessmen, who rarely present adequate financial documents when applying.

Along this same line, accounting and business firms and accounting organizations can establish a local consortium to serve as a clearinghouse to match accountants willing to volunteer their services with local needs. This would help alleviate the problem of accountants perfectly willing to become socially involved but unaware of just where their services are needed in the community.

70 Accounting's Social Responsibility

POSSIBLE EDUCATIONAL PROGRAMS

Accountants can also do a lot more in the area of education for the disadvantaged. Mr. Kent's suggestions[7] in this regard are, of course, good and should be considered by all accountants. Accounting and business firms might undertake to establish scholarships in accounting for disadvantaged youth. It won't be enough, however, to simply provide colleges with so much money earmarked for such students. A more realistic approach would be to try to encourage high school sophomores to consider accounting as a career. Aptitude tests could be given to high school classes to identify potentially good accountants. Those so identified should continue to receive personal assistance (sometimes monetary) and advice through high school. Then, prior to their enrollment in college on scholarship, they should be counseled into those programs designed to compensate for mathematical and communication deficiencies. It might even be necessary to create such a program, using staff people for individual tutoring. Finally, an effort should be made to establish summer internships for these students to further reduce the financial burden of going to college.[8]

Some firms might find it worthwhile to carry this approach even further by "adopting" a high school in a poor neighborhood. Assistance could be provided not only in the form of counseling, but also by buying needed instruction and recreation equipment, conducting field trips, establishing Junior Achievement companies (in this case especially for disadvantaged youth), and sponsoring social and athletic activities. This approach is already being tried by the Chrysler Corporation, for one.[9]

To develop accounting competence in ghetto and poverty areas, those few minority group accountants that do exist could be brought into major accounting and business firms as interns for a temporary period to broaden their experience and help them pass the CPA examination. (It might be necessary to do this for only one or two days a week so these accountants could also carry on their regular work.) Not only would this serve to improve accounting in the ghettos and poverty areas, but it would also contribute to the general upgrading of the accounting profession, a goal professional accountants have always accepted.

Once this internship had been completed, a greater effort should be undertaken to provide referrals to these accountants from the minority groups.

Finally, a greater effort could be made to channel research grants into those projects which hold some promise of alleviating social ills. The Ford Foundation has already begun to concentrate its grants in such projects, but accounting and business firms many times make unrestricted grants to colleges and researchers without any real regard to the social impact of the research.

SUMMARY

In this article I've tried to offer some concrete suggestions as to ways in which professional accountants can become socially, as opposed to civically, involved—

ways in which we can work to solve some of the problems of the inner city, the poor, and the disadvantaged, and thus repay our debt to this society and preserve the economic system which has been so good to us. As David Rockefeller said:

> We must do this, in part because of what is sometimes termed "enlightened self-interest." We must realize that our efforts are essential if we are to maintain the healthy social and economic environment so vital to the very existence of our corporations. We must demonstrate our conviction that our democratic society and free market system depend on our assurance that all people enjoy the full opportunity to participate.[10]

FOOTNOTES

1. Ralph E. Kent, "The Needs of the Profession," *The Arthur Young Journal* (Autumn 1968), pp. 2–8. Similar points were made by Robert M. Trueblood in his address to the annual meeting of the AICPA in 1966. See the Touche, Ross, Bailey & Smart (now Touche Ross & Co.) *Quarterly* (December 1966), pp. 2–6.
2. *Ibid.*, p. 2.
3. *Ibid.*, p. 5.
4. *Ibid.*, p. 5.
5. It should be mentioned that a Community Action Program already existed in Fort Worth at the time, but it had never been particularly interested in community organization.
6. The grant was renewed for 1968–69 and for 1969–70, and the organization is generally recognized in the community as having made significant progress toward achieving its goals.
7. Kent, *op. cit.*, p 6.
8. This financial burden is often greater than we realize, for not only must such students face the cost of college, but they must give up the money they might be earning in a full-time job which could go toward supporting their parents, brothers and sisters.
9. David Rockefeller, "The Social Responsibilities of Business to Urban America," *Financial Executive* (January 1969), p. 16.
10. *Ibid.*, p. 19.

QUESTIONS

1. It has been said that: "Accounting's role is to serve business and thus make the economic system work, thereby improving the lot of everyone. This is its full social responsibility; anything else detracts from this role and should not be undertaken by the accountant who is really responsible." Evaluate this argument.

2. "It may be desirable for accountants to tackle social problems, but it certainly isn't their responsibility." Comment.

3. List the organizations in your community or area which might benefit from volunteer professional accounting assistance.

4. Contact local accounting organizations and try to determine and catalogue the extent and nature of involvement by professional accountants in social/community problems. (Local organizations might include chapters of your state's Society of CPAs, the National Association of Accountants, the Financial Executives Institute, the Internal Auditors Association, and Beta Alpha Psi.)

5. Several black leaders, such as Jim Brown and James Meredith, have argued that "green power" (economic power) is a more important objective to blacks than "black power." To what extent, and in what ways, should the accounting profession be concerned with improving the economic status of minorities? Of the poor in general? Of small businesses?

*A young man explains how the accounting
profession can involve itself in innovative
programs that are directed toward satisfying the basic needs of the poor.*

The Accounting
Aid Society

by John C. Neubauer

To retain its stability a society must provide its members with opportunities to
satisfy their basic needs. Such needs include income, housing, consumer goods
and services and education. The opportunities to meet these needs are not now
available to many of the nation's poor. The resultant dissatisfaction has been
reflected in increasing frustration and alienation, which has periodically exploded
into riots.

Helping the poor to satisfy their needs is not entirely the responsibility of
government, social workers and individuals. The professions, too, have an important role. Each must contribute its expertise to the fulfillment of society's needs.
The legal profession, for example, has established a legal services program, and
the teaching profession, a teacher corps program. The accounting profession, on
the other hand, has been subject to criticism and pressure because it lacks an
organized approach to helping the poor. Criticism has been heard from the
growing numbers of liberal-minded college graduates who are joining the profession's ranks, as well as from established members of the profession, who believe

SOURCE: Reprinted by permission of the author and the publisher from The
Journal of Accountancy (May 1971), pp. 55–59. Copyright 1971 by the American
Institute of Certified Public Accountants, Inc.

the accounting profession should take a more active social role. Pressure has been exerted both from within the profession and from private citizens and government agencies. The Department of Housing and Urban Development, for example, will soon be releasing a manual on minority entrepreneurship. One chapter in the book deals with the present nominal involvement of the accounting profession in government programs and suggests that accountants find new ways to participate in social action projects.

Individually, accountants have exhibited their social concern by participation in many civic, philanthropic and humanitarian activities. Unfortunately, as pointed out by Ralph W. Estes, "The traditional forms this participation has taken are not sufficient and are not directed toward the root causes of the more pressing problems of society."[1]

It is time for the accounting profession to involve itself in innovative programs directed toward satisfying the basic needs of the poor.

A MODEL PROGRAM

One such program is the Accounting Aid Society, which was organized recently and is already operating successfully in Des Moines, Iowa. The Accounting Aid Society offers professional accounting and financial counseling services to individuals, small businesses and nonprofit organizations with limited funds in low-income communities. It works toward educational and legislative solutions to the low-income community's consumer and financial problems. By combining the volunteer efforts of local CPAs, accountants, businessmen, college students and faculty, the Accounting Aid Society provides needed professional services to economically deprived individuals and groups who normally could not afford them.

While there have been isolated attempts in other parts of the nation to develop various accounting services for the poor, the Iowa program is considered by local citizens and recognized by federal officials to be the first of its kind that provides extensive volunteer accounting services to all elements of a community. The Accounting Aid Society has been acclaimed by and has drawn support from the Iowa Society of Certified Public Accountants, the regional chapter of the National Association of Accountants, the State Auditor's Office and Drake University in Des Moines.

It has also received official recognition from the Office of Economic Opportunity in Washington, D.C. Effective July 1, 1970, OEO granted to the Accounting Aid Society $76,566 to provide professional money-management and consumer affairs assistance to the low-income communities of Des Moines.

A close examination of the origin, activities and plans of the Accounting Aid Society will demonstrate how the accounting profession can make an important contribution to the solution of social problems. Hopefully, it will also encourage an organized effort to expand the program to other communities throughout the country.

ITS ORIGIN

One might expect a unique program like this to have been the idea of a specialist in urban problems in an industrialized, politically liberal state. However, this idea was conceived in April 1969 by a socially concerned accounting student at Drake University. During May 1969, the idea was discussed with the Drake accounting faculty, prominent Des Moines CPAs, the Legal Aid Society and the Iowa State Auditor's Office. At the annual convention of the Iowa Society of CPAs in May, W. J. Hunzelman, the society's new president, who practices in Storm Lake, Iowa, emphasized the need for the social involvement of CPAs and suggested that accounting students could be involved with them. When Mr. Hunzelman was made aware of the idea from Drake, he personally committed himself to assist in the development of the program.

Throughout the summer of 1969, support was sought and obtained by the author. The Des Moines residents and community action programs such as Model Cities and supportive service agencies pledged their moral support and cooperation. Drake University funded a planning grant to cover initial costs and provided manpower and materials during the implementation stages. The Iowa Society of CPAs provided the key contribution toward making the Accounting Aid Society a reality. In August, the Iowa Society formally endorsed the program by committing initial operating funds to meet expenses for six months and by encouraging Des Moines CPAs to volunteer their time.

The excitement which generated this support stemmed from the program's commitment to three goals: (1) to provide needed professional accounting and consumer services and education to low-income communities, (2) to provide an opportunity for college business students to apply their classroom skills and (3) to provide an opportunity for the accounting profession to work effectively toward the solution of social problems.

With this backing from all segments of the community, the Accounting Aid Society officially opened its doors on October 8, 1969, in the heart of the Des Moines Model Cities area. The office was a converted gas station with boarded windows, "automatic air conditioning" during the winter months and room for only two desks.

ORGANIZATION

The initial operation of the Accounting Aid Society was under the direction of a volunteer, John Henss, CPA, vice president and comptroller of a Des Moines insurance firm. Subsequently, the author, who had been serving as president of the board of directors and later as deputy director, was employed as full-time executive director on July 1, 1970, with responsibility for administering the day-to-day operations of the office under the general guidance of a 25-member board of directors.

The board of directors is composed of 14 representatives from the low-income community and 11 professionals (3 of whom are CPAs). Their powers consist of overseeing and managing the business and affairs of this nonprofit corporation. Such powers include staff compensation, personnel policies and funding. The executive director and his staff of 11 carry out the orders and directions of the board.

The services of the Accounting Aid Society are made known to those in the low-income community in various ways. Radio advertisements and distribution of flyers act as the best sources of communication. Also, referral systems have been developed with many community organizations.

When a potential client requests the services of the Accounting Aid Society, he is interviewed by a staff member to determine his needs and his qualifications. If the professional assistance of a CPA is required, a volunteer CPA and Drake students are assigned to the case by the director or deputy director (who presently is Julius Guy, former All-American football player from the University of Wichita). Fourteen CPA firms in Des Moines have made themselves available to participate on such cases. Follow-up is then done by the deputy director.

As mentioned earlier, the Accounting Aid Society assists three principal groups in the low-income area: individuals, small businesses and nonprofit organizations.

AIDS TO INDIVIDUALS

For persons having an annual income of less than $4,500 plus $600 for each dependent, the Accounting Aid Society provides tax services and individual financial counseling which includes prorating debts, developing budgets and intervening with creditors. The Accounting Aid Society counsels only in how each person can best handle his own problems. The income limitation was established by the board of directors.

Case Report.   A divorced mother with three children, an income of $400 monthly and $2,000 in unpaid bills came to the Accounting Aid Society because she wanted to pay her bills. When confronted with this kind of problem many low-income persons become frustrated and worried as unpaid bills accumulate. They become frightened when they can find no way to pay their bills without sacrificing the needs of their family.

In this case, instead of reapportioning the family budget to pay the bills first, the Accounting Aid Society set up a budget that would meet the family's needs first and the creditors' demands second. The Accounting Aid Society arranged a pro rata payment schedule with the remaining money, contacted the creditors and convinced them that it would be to their advantage to accept the payment schedule. By working with the Accounting Aid Society, this working mother was shown how to avoid an expensive consolidation process and disastrous bankruptcy procedure.

AID TO SMALL BUSINESS

For small businesses, the Accounting Aid Society has established accounting systems for a number of businesses owned by members of minority groups and has trained their bookkeepers to operate the systems. It has represented minority-owned businesses in negotiating for working capital with the Small Business Administration and other lending institutions. Financial statements and projections have accompanied these negotiations. In each of these cases, the SBA required as contingent to funding the establishment of an accounting system and instruction therein. For some businesses which were unaware of their tax responsibilities, the Accounting Aid Society has prepared and filed delinquent tax returns. Currently the Accounting Aid Society is conducting marketing surveys and feasibility studies to identify the community's consumer needs and to assist new and existing businesses.

Case Report.   One low-income individual was interested in developing a business that would promote live entertainment for young people, but he did not have the knowledge or capital to do it. He requested the services of the Accounting Aid Society, which contacted the Small Business Administration and acted as his representative in applying for the $25,000 loan. It also assisted him in the establishment and maintenance of an accounting system. Two CPAs—one a partner of a Des Moines accounting firm, the other a vice president of a Des Moines business—were assisted by a Drake student and worked 30 volunteer hours with the prospective businessman on his case. The volunteer time contributed to this case would be equivalent to about $600 in regular fees for an accounting firm's services.

Because such expenses often prevent many small businessmen from acquiring necessary accounting services, the contributed services of the Accounting Aid Society allow more needed small businesses to develop in the low-income area.

Case Report.   After two months of operating a cafe specializing in "soul food," a small businessman in the low-income community had no indication of whether or not he was making a profit. When the five paper bags which contained his limited accounting records were stolen, he contacted the Accounting Aid Society for advice. He requested a reconstruction of his financial situation for the past two months and asked that an accounting system be developed. One Drake student, who donated 30 hours of work, and one CPA, who contributed 5 hours of time in providing direction and supervision to the student, completed the case work that normally would have cost about $250. The records of the previous two months were reconstructed and the small businessman was shown how to manage his own accounting system. He was also counseled about the use of a checking account rather than a cash-in, cash-out basis. He was advised to get an employer's identification number and was informed of his tax responsibilities. Two months later, he could determine the financial status of his restaurant, and, as a result of the Accounting Aid Society's efforts, showed a $300 profit—a remarkable accomplishment for a beginning business.

Case Report.   A small businessman, trusted by the low-income community, had an idea that would provide a needed service to the community: an honest used-car business. Following through with this idea, he applied for a $16,000 loan from the local Small Business Administration, and the loan was approved. However, because he had not understood the complicated loan forms and their instructions, the federal office rejected the loan stating that he had presented fraudulent information regarding his past history. The rejection of his loan led him to consult the Accounting Aid Society. In solving the application problem, the Accounting Aid Society established communications between the small businessman and the federal SBA office. By working with Senator Jack Miller's office in Washington, the Accounting Aid Society was able to show the SBA office that the man's mistake was an honest one and was successful in persuading the SBA to approve the loan. Subsequently, the Accounting Aid Society helped him set up an accounting system and work out the withholding taxes and tax obligations for his new business.

No monetary value can be assigned to the value of community trust, the trust existing between buyer and seller. Through the efforts of the Accounting Aid Society this low-income community was given access to another reputable and trusted businessman.

AIDS TO NONPROFIT ORGANIZATIONS

For nonprofit organizations with limited funds, the Accounting Aid Society has developed accounting systems, trained low-income persons to operate the systems, prepared financial statements and audit reports and resolved tax problems. Child care centers, minority youth centers and street social workers are among nonprofit organizations served by the Accounting Aid Society.

Case Report.   A Des Moines Day Care Program was not required by its funders to be audited, but its conscientious board of directors wanted an examination to determine the operational merit of the organization over the past two years. To have a CPA firm conduct an audit would have cost about $500, an amount that was not available. After 20 hours of work, two Drake students and one accounting professor completed an examination, prepared supportive financial statements and made recommendations to the child care center concerning improvement of its accounting system and controls. As a result of the examination, the center could clearly define its progress and weakness and take corrective action to improve operations.

Case Report.   A black social action group was organized in a low-income community to deal with people on a door-to-door basis and to help them solve their problems. After one year, the group found itself in financial and legal difficulties because it had failed to withhold payroll taxes or to maintain an accounting system. When the group sought assistance from the Accounting Aid Society, a CPA and a Drake University student volunteered more than 30 hours of their time to resolve the problems. An accounting system was developed, an employer's identification number was obtained and past payroll tax returns were prepared and filed. The Accounting Aid Society was able to provide the needed accounting assistance at a nominal fee—$5 instead of $400 that would have otherwise been charged for such services.

AN EVALUATION

Has the Accounting Aid Society been successful in achieving its objectives? Has it provided needed accounting services and education to low-income communities, an opportunity for college business students to apply their classroom skills and an opportunity for the accounting profession to work effectively toward the solution of social problems?

The case reports should speak for themselves. There is no doubt that the Accounting Aid Society has provided needed accounting services and training for the low-income community it serves—and it has just begun. Student participation has been overwhelming. The enthusiasm, motivation and determination of the students have been responsible for much of the excitement and involvement of the accounting profession and the community. During its first eight months of operation, 40 Drake University business students worked on Accounting Aid Society cases. The desire of students to apply classroom skills to the solution of social problems has been channeled successfully and beneficially into the low-income community of Des Moines. Until February 1970, students at Drake worked on a volunteer basis only. Now they receive credit toward their undergraduate degree for participation in the work of the Accounting Aid Society.

The accounting profession has participated in the program in two ways. First, the state society's financial contributions sustained operations through the first six months of the program. But more importantly, Des Moines CPAs have personally devoted many hours of work to Accounting Aid Society cases and have provided low-income persons and small businesses with professional accounting services for the first time.

The program's influence on the social problem has indirectly shown positive results. In less than one year, the Accounting Aid Society has helped low-income businessmen draw almost $200,000 in loans into the community for use as working capital. Twenty-five small businesses and 15 nonprofit organizations in the low-income community have been helped with the installation of accounting systems which they could maintain themselves. Over 150 persons in the low-income community have been assisted with their money-management and tax problems.

Through this education, the low-income community is better prepared to satisfy its basic needs for consumer goods and services.

POTENTIAL NATIONWIDE IMPACT

The concept of the Accounting Aid Society as a solution to pressing social problems dealing with financial affairs seems to offer potential on a nationwide basis. The Office of Economic Opportunity in Washington has recognized this potential and has approved a three-year demonstration grant to the Accounting Aid Society. The Des Moines program provides an effective model from which similar operations can be developed in other cities and states, and the Accounting Aid Society stands ready to assist in any way it can.

The Accounting Aid Society can be an effective social force, perhaps of even greater impact than the legal services programs since its efforts are directed at preventive measures rather than assistance "after the fact." It can provide an opportunity for the accounting profession to contribute effectively to the solution of social problems, and it offers an opportunity for business students to learn firsthand some of the excitement and the rewards of a career in accounting.

State CPA societies and chapters, hopefully with the co-operation of the American Institute, can be given the inspiration, direction and assistance to make the Accounting Aid Society a unified, nationwide, social action program.

FOOTNOTE

1. Ralph W. Estes, "The Accountant's Social Responsibility," *Journal of Accountancy*, January 1970, p. 40.

QUESTIONS

1. (a) How do the participating students benefit from working with the Accounting Aid Society? How do the clients benefit? The CPAs? The communities?

   (b) Who benefits the most?

2. (a) What problems would you expect to encounter in establishing an Accounting Aid Society in your community?

   (b) How many students would you expect to participate?

   (c) Where specifically would you go to seek professional assistance?

   (d) How could clients be located? Describe these potential clients.

3. What sort of work can an Accounting Aid Society competently perform? Is there any work which such a group should not undertake?

*The hand-lettered sign in the window, trans-
lated into English, proclaims "Spanish spoken
here—on Tuesdays and Fridays."*

*During the other five days of the week,
the languages in the tiny vacant store are
limited to two—English and the obtuse
bureaucratese which is used on income
tax forms.*

*The sign above the 10-foot-wide store-
front still says "Hosiery," but the one hanging from the rafters inside says "Welcome—
Bienvenido." Another in the window offers
"Free Tax Aid," and each night a dozen or
more taxpayers from the neighboring West
Side community stop in to have their taxes
figured out.*

—Charles Delafuente
New York Post, Thursday, April 9, 1970

Story Behind
a Storefront

by *William H. Morris, Jr.*

It was a young Presbyterian minister called Dick Ittner who got us started.
During my year in New York I lived near the Brooklyn parish of Fort Greene
where Dick runs a community center. With his encouragement, Jack Potter and I
became interested in helping set up a free counseling service for low-income taxpayers who might have difficulty filling out the Government's new long-form tax

---

SOURCE: Reprinted by permission from The Arthur Young Journal (Summer
1970), pp. 43–45. Copyright © 1970 by Arthur Young & Company.

returns. With help from our fellow tax residents in Home Office, we began operating a tax "clinic" in late February, using the basement of Dick's parish house. Unfortunately few customers showed up. Perhaps they didn't like to venture out at night in that area, or maybe they didn't believe that we would really help them for nothing. No doubt they thought we were Government inspectors of some kind. In the end we decided to join forces with another group of young professionals who were involved in a similar project on the West Side of Manhattan.

This project, known as "Tax Aid," was being organized by Jeff Gold, a 27-year-old CPA with a real estate company. Jeff had gathered a small group of lawyers and accountants who were willing to help and had persuaded United Artists and Alexander's, the old and new owners of a vacant store on 96th Street and Broadway, to let him use the store rent-free. For a few weeks prior to April 15th, the storefront office was open Monday through Friday from 6 to 9 p.m. and on weekends from 10 a.m. to 4 p.m. This time there was no lack of interest. Altogether some 250 returns were prepared for a wide variety of low-income taxpayers.

For those of us who participated in the program, it was one of the most rewarding experiences of our lives. Needless to say, the tax problems involved were quite different from those we had become used to in Arthur Young & Company's practice, but they were often just as complex, and the personal element made them particularly interesting. But reducing these people's stories to a few figures on a form could be very misleading. For the IRS computer $50 is just another set of binary digits, but for these people having to pay even an extra $10 can be a disaster. The irony is that in many cases those who had delayed filing a return for fear of having to pay more tax were actually eligible for a refund.

Although we filled out the forms and gave what other help we could, it was agreed with the IRS and the American Institute of CPAs that we would not actually sign the returns. The IRS gave its full cooperation to the Tax Aid project, which supplemented the IRS-sponsored Volunteer Income Tax Assistors (VITA) program, run during normal office hours.

Most people were surprised by the fact that we made no charge for our advice, and a few insisted on giving us presents. One loyal taxpayer gave us a glass replica of the Capitol building in Washington which, when the dome was lifted off, played the "Star Spangled Banner." Another memorable gift was a bottle of

EDITOR'S NOTE: When William H. Morris, Jr. attended Arthur Young & Company's Home Office tax residents program in 1969, he did not anticipate that some of the more rewarding experiences would occur not in AY's carpeted air-conditioned offices but in a vacant store on Manhattan's upper West Side. In this article Morris describes how he came to spend many evening and weekend hours with poor New Yorkers, many of them Spanish-speaking, providing free tax advice and assistance. A member of AY's Tulsa Office at the time this was written, Mr. Morris is now Tulsa's Commissioner of Finance and Revenue.

champagne presented to us by a lovely little old lady on the evening of April 15th.

The program was a great success, and plans are being made for its expansion. It is my own conviction that there is a need for a permanent year-round service of this kind, perhaps provided through an organization similar to the Legal Aid Society. There is also a need for such programs in other cities.

In June, I accompanied Jeff Gold, Shelly Barasch, and Alan Blake to Washington, following an invitation from Mr. Gabriel Rudney of the Treasury Department. Our discussions with Treasury and IRS representatives made it clear that they are well aware of the problems of giving fair tax treatment to minority and low-income groups, and are receptive to fresh ideas on the subject. As professional people we have the knowledge and independence to be of particular service in areas such as this. Judging from our brief experience with the Tax Aid program, any help we can give is well worth the effort.

Black accountants with CPA firms in New York City offer bookkeeping instruction on a voluntary basis, to provide residents of poverty areas with entry-level skills.

Meeting Our Social Responsibilities

by *Willard Archie & Alford Sweet*

Recently, much has been written about the social responsibilities of the accountant to the communities in which he works and lives. Most of the articles proclaim how civic-minded accountants are. One article pointed out that the 100,000 CPAs throughout the country represented a potent force which could be tapped to assist community groups. This same article noted that if every CPA contributed 3 hours a week for 40 weeks a year, some 6,000 man years per year of professional accounting experience would be available. These numbers speak for themselves. An organized, directed force of this magnitude could have an appreciable impact on providing minority and underprivileged peoples with the knowledge they need to become part of the mainstream of America. However,

SOURCE: © The Arthur Andersen Chronicle; June, 1971, pp. 12–15. Reprinted by permission.

most of the efforts of the accounting profession have been spent talking about what can be done instead of doing what needs to be done.

We, a group of black staffmen in the New York office of Arthur Andersen & Co., decided immediate benefits could be obtained if we used our professional knowledge to train minority peoples to compete in the business world. With this goal in mind, we contacted other black staffmen employed by the "Big 8" accounting firms to determine if they were interested in participating in our project.

At the same time we were planning our project, one of our group was working on the audit of Opportunities Industrialization Center (O.I.C.). O.I.C. is a manpower training agency that offers prevocational and vocational training to people in the Bedford-Stuyvesant area of Brooklyn and the Harlem and Lower East Side areas of Manhattan. The organization, with more than 90 branches at the end of 1970, was founded in 1963 by the Rev. Dr. Leon Sullivan (recently named to the Board of Directors of General Motors). O.I.C. offers training in fields such as I.B.M. keypunch, secretarial skills, industrial electricity, drafting, office machine service and repair, etc., as well as tutoring for high school equivalency diplomas.

We decided to approach O.I.C. about offering a course in bookkeeping. Representatives of our group discussed the idea with the Rev. Calvin O. Pressley, Executive Director of the New York branches of O.I.C. He was elated about the idea and asked for immediate implementation. We explained that a few weeks were required to handle administrative matters, such as recruiting a teaching staff, selecting textbooks, and developing the course curriculum.

By this time, one of the "Big 8" firms which heard of our project offered to make available, on a full-time basis, any of its staff desiring to participate. Numerous meetings were held to finalize administrative matters and to complete the teaching staff. The final group of instructors consisted of men and women, both black and white, who were sincerely interested in helping other people.

It was decided that two bookkeeping classes would be taught, one during the day and another in the evening. By offering two classes, the course would be available to persons with work or family commitments during either the day or evening periods. Representatives of the other firm would teach the day classes, the Arthur Andersen group would teach the night classes.

The day program began on June 1, 1970, and the evening program on June 8. The goal of the bookkeeping course at O.I.C. is to teach the principles of bookkeeping to the students so that they are equipped to obtain employment.

The course is structured so that it is beneficial not only to the student who completes the course, but also to the student who is unable to finish the entire program. (This was done in recognition of a high potential attrition rate due to work or family responsibilities.) Naturally, maximum benefit accrues to the students who finish the course since they then have an understanding of the *entire* bookkeeping cycle of a business enterprise. Major bookkeeping topics—accounts receivable, accounts payable, payroll, etc.—are independently taught so that the student is capable of obtaining a bookkeeping position even before completing the course. This is important since most entry level bookkeeping positions are for accounts receivable, accounts payable, or payroll clerks.

Approximately one-third of each class session is devoted to lecturing, the remainder to problem solving activities. Three or four instructors are present at every class session in order to give the students as much personal attention as possible. Homework assignments are given daily and tests are administered weekly. Instructional aids such as illustrative charts and case problems, which were supplied by the Firm, were valuable teaching tools. The students are continuously appraised as to their progress, and written evaluations of the students are submitted to O.I.C.

O.I.C. is responsible for scheduling job interviews for graduates of the program. At the half-way point of the course, O.I.C. is notified of the better students in the class and advised to begin job placement activities for them. Any student placed during the program is advised to continue the program until completion. When the program is finished, each student receives a diploma stating that he has completed a course in bookkeeping at O.I.C.

Since the project has been in operation, approximately 66 people have taken the bookkeeping course. About half of our students have been placed in bookkeeping positions. This might seem to be a small number in terms of effort expended, but we consider it a step in the right direction.

The area of job placement is one in which we hope to obtain support from the "Big 8" and other agencies. Most of the graduates obtained jobs either through their own efforts or the efforts of the instructors who, among other things, contacted personnel managers at various companies. We are planning to establish a rapport with the various accounting firms to solicit their help in locating jobs for the bookkeeping graduates. We hope that the firms will advise clients of this source of well-trained people for bookkeeping positions.

We are just completing our fourth bookkeeping class at the Brooklyn branch and will soon begin plans for the next session. In addition, we are planning to extend the program to the Harlem and Lower East Side branches of O.I.C. A tentative starting date has been set for the day classes at the Lower East Side branch, and we are actively working towards this goal. The instructors for this program are currently being recruited from the staff of the New York office of Arthur Andersen & Co. Because of this increased commitment by both the firm and individuals, we expect the program to be even more successful than in the past.

We realize that the bookkeeping program is only a small step towards alleviating the frustrations in our concentrated communities that exist as a result of the lack of hope and job opportunities. However, we feel a measure of satisfaction because we are doing something to fulfill our obligation to the community in which we work and live.

QUESTIONS

1. What services besides tax return preparation and bookkeeping instruction might accountants provide free to those not able to afford such services?

2. Should such free, or feeless, work be considered a part of the accountant's professional responsibilities, or should it be strictly voluntary with the individual accountant?

3. Do you see any difference between the type of volunteer work a practicing CPA might do and that an accountant in industry or government might perform?

4. Could college students effectively provide the services described by Mr. Morris and by Mr. Archie and Mr. Sweet? If so, how could or should they be organized?

*A modest proposal for a new TV series in
this year of 'relevance'*

"The Young
Accountants"

by Bob Shayne

Somewhere, deep inside the teeming city ghetto, is a small, dilapidated store. It
has been boarded up for years, ever since the candy man moved uptown—gum
balls, penny licorice and all.

Today the store is alive with activity. One young man rolls paint onto the
cracking walls. Another removes weather-beaten boards and puts in glass window-
panes. A girl tosses her hair out of her eyes as she mops the floor.

For today The Young Accountants are moving in!

They are setting up the world's first free accounting office, where the poor,
the ignorant and the oppressed can turn for help with their books.

The Young Accountants are three dedicated advanced-accounting-school students. Their motto is: "Why should only the rich be able to afford a CPA?"

Our lead Young Accountant is Mark Merritt. He's a tall young man with long
(but neat) wavy blond hair and something inside him that says, "Do it, Mark, because it's right!" His father is a powerful banker, who wants his son to follow in
his footsteps. But Mark, a born rebel, knows that the sterile world of banking
isn't for him. Only through accountancy can he find fulfillment.

Against his father's wishes, Mark moved out of the sumptuous mansion in
which he was raised and rented a flea-bitten room near USC. He pays for the room
by washing dishes and grating oregano leaves in an organic-pizza parlor near the

SOURCE: Reprinted by permission from <u>TV Guide</u> (Jan. 9–16, 1971).

campus. Of course, tuition at USC is so high his parents have to pay that. But otherwise, Mark is making it on his own, doing his own thing in an uptight world of conformity.

The second Young Accountant is right at home in the tenement store they use for an office. Roosevelt (Rosey) Robinson has known poverty all his life. The son of a Negro washerwoman, he grew up in the slums and spent many miserable hours with his nose pressed up against the window of the candy store that now has, ironically, become his office. His father was killed in World War II while serving as General Patton's mess steward. Rosey doesn't remember his father, but he cherishes the Good Conduct Medal sent to his mother when his father was hit at Anzio while pouring an *Apéritif*. Rosey wears his hair in a close-cropped (and neat) Afro and talks hip.

Our third Young Accountant is Lorna Chung Horowitz, a Eurasian beauty. Lorna has a vulnerable quality about her, but underneath she's strong. Daughter of a Chinese princess and a Jewish merchant seaman, she spent her childhood going from port to port, searching for roots. She is thin, waiflike, with long straight hair that generally looks neat.

The threesome's nominal salaries and the rent on their ghetto office and adding machines are paid by the firm of Ogilvy and Penrose, Certified Public Accountants. More precisely, they are paid by Brian Ogilvy. His partner, Rodney Penrose, wants to have nothing to do with the three young people. "They're just a bunch of bleeding hearts," says Penrose, who lately has taken to wearing a hard hat to the office. (You can see the potential conflict here that heightens the series' tension and realism.)

The stories are just as gripping as the characters—and they have the impact of today's headlines.

One week Mark, Rosey and Lorna help a Welfare mother prepare her Quarterly Report of Anticipated Earnings, which is particularly tricky in respect to the amortization of food stamps. As a result, she receives a refund from the IRS of $420, enough to open her own Minnie Pearl Chicken franchise.

But not all episodes will deal with the grim but heartwarming struggles of ghetto denizens. Others will deal with crises in the lives of your average Middle American. In one segment, for example, a small businessman turns to The Young Accountants for help. His whale-blubber import business is failing because of the dwindling supply of whales. He thinks he must declare bankruptcy. But the threesome manage to rearrange his books so as to qualify him for an oil-depletion allowance. (As you can see, there's room in this story for an ecology message too.)

Of course, The Young Accountants have love interests too. One episode deals with a controversial intercultural romance which blossoms when Mark helps a young girl from the hills of Kentucky fill out a W-4 form. She teaches him to square-dance and he teaches her to play polo. He takes her to a fancy French restaurant and shows her how much to tip, and in return she cooks up a batch of sour-mash bourbon for him in her hotel room. But, sadly, she returns to the farm ("That's where I belong—I'm not one for your big-city ways") to put into practice what Mark has taught her about acreage allotments, price-support payments, set-aside payments, diversion payments, public-access payments, marketing certificates and other details of H.R. 18564, the new farm-subsidies bill.

Rosey is attracted to a night-club singer from Harlem who asks him to rescue her from the clutches of a counterfeiting ring. She has been passing phony trading stamps for them because they are holding her little brother (an excellent tap dancer) hostage. She is fatally shot during an exciting climax, and Rosey joins her brother in a moving tap-dance duet at the funeral, fulfilling her dying wish.

Lorna falls in love with a young doctor who has sought out The Young Accountants to learn whether he can go public. He turns out to be the son of a Hebrew princess and a Chinese merchant seaman, and he succumbs in Act IV to Eurasian influenza.

These, then, are The Young Accountants. They are Now people, involved and concerned with the burning social issues of Today. They get it all together. They rap. They find out where their heads are at. And they tell it like it is.

They are three young people not just talking, but *doing*. Not tearing down, but building a better tomorrow through free accountancy.

In a word, The Young Accountants are *relevant!*

QUESTIONS

1. Evaluate Shayne's article and describe your reaction to it.

2. Based on other readings in this book and your knowledge of the accounting profession, in what ways and how well are accountants meeting their social responsibilities? Where are they falling short?

Section III
Accounting and Public Programs

Federal spending "will inevitably increase as the population grows and as the population becomes more highly urbanized," according to the United States Comptroller General Elmer Staats in an interview with <u>Nation's Business</u>. Not only federal but also state and local spending appear destined to increase with the growth in our population and with increasing efforts to solve the problems of society.

Public programs are paid for, by and large, with taxpayers' dollars. Thus Government acts as an agent of citizens in carrying out their desires for collective action, as manifested through their elected representatives. Citizens clearly have a right to a complete and accurate accounting for the use of their resources. Our profession must be able to provide that accounting and must provide as well the information, reporting and control essential for effective and efficient execution of public programs. The following articles deal with the role of accounting in public programs.

With billions of dollars involved, it is essential that public programs of all sorts be reviewed by an <u>independent</u> agency to insure both efficiency of operation and adherence to legislated goals and budgets. As noted in the first article in this section, "The necessity for an independent agency to examine how the Government spends public funds in the discharge of its responsibilities was obvious from the very beginning of constitutional government in this country." The agency which performs this function at the federal level is the General Accounting Office (GAO), an agency of Congress created in 1921.

With sophisticated new military hardware, innovative but unproved social programs, and automatic increases in established programs, all leading to an ever-increasing federal budget, the role of the General Accounting Office becomes more and more important. As noted in "GAO—Success Is a Problem":

In an era of increasing demands for more funds to finance needed social programs and increasing resistance on the part of taxpayers to provide these
funds, the GAO's task to seek out and find ways the Government can economize is to say the least a valuable one.

How the GAO fulfills its watchdog role is described in this article and the next,
"Where Government Can Cut Spending."

One major function of the GAO is to audit federal grants. In addition to
spending billions of dollars directly each year, the federal government grants
additional billions to state and local agencies, governmental and private, to carry
on programs which Congress has determined to be in the public interest. Determining that such grants are properly spent for the purposes intended, and that
the programs themselves are productive, is not a simple task. As Ellsworth Morse
points out in his article on auditing federal grant programs, "The indicators of
progress in a social program . . . are not yet fully understood nor are they readily
measurable." Measurable or not, the progress of such programs must be evaluated—
and accountants at all levels are working to develop ways of performing such evaluations. (A further discussion of social measurement problems is contained in
Section VIII, "Accounting for Social Progress.")

A somewhat different view of the accountant's role in federal grant programs
is offered by the publisher of Science, a publication of the American Association
for the Advancement of Science, in "Control by Accountants." His concern
should not be taken lightly; accountants certainly have the capacity for imposing too many forms, too many controls, too much red tape. Unreasonable requirements can defeat the original purpose of a program, or discourage its initiation
altogether.

Although Morse notes the importance of auditing in the administration of the
anti-poverty program, this is only one of several ways in which accountants have
contributed to the war on poverty. Kleinman and Sandle˜ describe several
methods by which CPAs can assist poverty programs—assistance in budget preparation, establishment of systems of accounts and of internal control, periodic audits,
and management counseling. (A report on one CPA's work with an anti-poverty
agency is contained in the article, "The Accountant's Social Responsibility," in
Section I of this book.)

In undertaking such assistance, the accountant needs to know the criteria of
success for an anti-poverty program. Bruns and Snyder give these criteria and
describe information system requirements in "Management Information for Community Action Programs" based on experience with the Seattle Community
Action Program.

"The Modern Management Approach to a Program of Social Improvement"
by Robert Beyer deals with a Touche, Ross, Bailey & Smart (now Touche Ross
& Co.) engagement to assist in Detroit's war on poverty. In this engagement a
social accounting program was developed which includes a base line data system

containing comprehensive information about clients, a client profile technique, and the use of simulation to test the effects of available alternatives. While this system was developed for a poverty program, its relevance is much broader—for the system described could be adapted to a great many different social programs. With the apparently inevitable proliferation of social programs, accountants will be dealing with this or similar systems for many years to come. These programs might well be viewed by accountants as opportunities, for as Beyer says:

> Most men of conscience like to feel they are contributing to the betterment of society. One would be hard-pressed to find an undertaking more gratifying to the professional accountant than personal involvement in the social improvement effort described.

Medicare is another such social improvement effort. This program was introduced in 1966 to assist elderly citizens in securing adequate medical care. Although the medical professions are responsible for the ultimate provision of services under medicare, there is nevertheless a substantial role for the accounting profession. This role is described by Imke in "Medicare—So What?"

Only a few public and social programs have been discussed in this section, but these discussions should give the reader—especially the reader with a good imagination—ample insight into the ways in which accountants have been and can be of service to these programs. Whether working with the government in the General Accounting Office or some other agency, in public accounting, or in a private capacity, the accountant has numerous opportunities to contribute to the success of public programs.

ADDITIONAL REFERENCES

1.   Ahart, Gregory J., "GAO Review of the Economic Opportunity Programs," The GAO Review, Summer 1969, pp. 37–42.
2.   "Auditing in Vietnam," The Journal of Accountancy, March 1967, pp. 22–25.
3.   Bayer, Sylvan, "PPBS—A New Management Tool," The Federal Accountant, December 1968, pp. 82–90.
4.   "Defense Contractors Fear New Standards for Calculating Costs May be Catastrophic," The Wall Street Journal, November 20, 1970, p. 34.
5.   Devaney, C. William, "Examples of Program Budgeting for Nonprofit Administrative Decisions," The Price Waterhouse Review, Summer 1968, pp. 44–53.
6.   "Feasibility of Applying Uniform Cost Accounting Standards to Negotiated Defense Contracts," The Federal Accountant, March 1970, pp. 5–20.

7. Killenberg, Gustav A., "Accounting Aspects of Medicare," The New York Certified Public Accountant, November 1966, pp. 837–840.

8. Knighton, L. M., "Improving the Audit of Federal/State/Local Programs," The Federal Accountant, December 1968, pp. 31–43.

9. Limbert, G. Christian, Jr., "Evaluating Federal Poverty Programs," The Price Waterhouse Review, Summer/Autumn 1971, pp. 50–59.

10. Ruff, Jean-Paul A., "Poverty Programs . . . A Business Management Approach," The Quarterly (Touche, Ross & Company), June 1966, pp. 24–32.

*The United States General Accounting
Office, established as an agency of Congress,
is the watchdog over use of the taxpayer's
money. It also reviews and audits all sorts
of public programs. Its growing role is
described in this article.*

GAO –
Success is
a Problem

On the threshold of its 50th Anniversary, the General Accounting Office—sometimes referred to as "the department of 20/20 hindsight"—is viewed with almost unanimous approbation. Its performance as government watchdog has been lauded in the halls of Congress and its cost-cutting achievements regularly noted in the nation's press.

But success has brought in its train the specter of new and greater challenges for this agency. For, like it or not, the General Accounting Office is being urged to take on even greater tasks, particularly in the area where it shines the brightest —audit and review of federal programs. In an era of increasing demands for more funds to finance needed social programs and increasing resistance on the part of taxpayers to provide these funds, the GAO's task to seek out and find ways the Government can economize is to say the least a valuable one.

SOURCE: Reprinted by permission of the publisher from Management
Accounting (April 1970), pp. 53–55.

Much of the pressure for GAO to expand its activities arises from the frustration of Congress in trying to achieve control of the enormous expenditures of Government—especially those of the Defense Department. Senator Abraham Ribicoff expressed some of these feelings in his opening statement at hearings held by a subcommittee of the Committee on Government Operations. "The Defense Department will spend $147,000 every minute of every day in fiscal 1970. Congress has an obligation to assure that this huge sum is spent as effectively as possible and that the money that is not needed is put to other uses." He noted that the hearings would help determine whether GAO needs more systems analysts, auditors or legal authority "to search out waste and cost overruns in the Defense Department."

At the same hearings, Senator Charles Percy expressed some of the feelings of Congress concerning the value of the GAO when he said: "I have experience of 25 years in business where independent accounting and auditing, both internal as well as external, became an absolute 'must.' It was an arm of top management that could not be done without. It was not just to record a history of the past, it was to have these professional men who were highly skilled put a picture together in figures. Then that picture can be used to help guide management into the future. . . . There have been more men, increasingly in recent years, taking top-management position[s] in industry from the accounting end, because they—and they only sometimes—have been able to put together the whole picture on how to control these gigantic enterprises. The business that we manage down here is the biggest of all, of course, and it seems to me many times almost out of control. You cannot get your arms around it. . . ."

Sen. Percy went on to say that he hoped the hearings would draw public attention and the attention of the Congress "not only to the past accomplishments of GAO but also to your future potential, because I think we are just really beginning to tap the potential that can be contributed to this end of Government." He added, "We are simply, as I see our jobs, running hard to merely keep up with what our responsibilities are. We have no time to quietly reflect and sit and think and try to plan ahead for the future. I think we really need an expanding, continuing creative role for the GAO."

What Sen. Percy and Congress mean by a "creative role" has become clearer as the result of hearings held in recent months by various committees of the House of Representatives and the Senate. Action in two specific areas has been urged either in legislation passed by Congress or in statements by various members of the national legislature. Regarding Defense expenditures, Congress directed the GAO to study the feasibility of developing uniform cost accounting standards. At the same time, a number of legislators expressed the wish for cost effectiveness evaluations of federal programs *before* funds were actually spent.

GAO AND DEFENSE

Since the Pentagon's budget is the largest single item in the national budget, it is only logical that Congress would concentrate on this department to achieve cost savings. GAO estimates 1,100 out of a professional staff of 2,655 are assigned to audit and review Defense expenditures.

But waste in the Defense Department continues to rankle. In testimony before the House Banking and Finance Committee in 1968, Vice Admiral H. G. Rickover charged that defense contractors were earning exorbitant profits and that such profits are sometimes concealed by the fact that contractors are not required to use uniform methods of accounting with respect to their Defense business.

As one of the results of the testimony of the highly respected Director of the Naval Nuclear Propulsion and Reactor Programs for the Navy, Congress directed GAO, in cooperation with the Secretary of Defense and the Director of the Bureau of the Budget, to ". . . undertake a study to determine the feasibility of applying uniform cost accounting standards to be used in all negotiated price contracts and subcontract defense procurements of $100,000 or more."

The General Accounting Office undertook the study with the assistance of accounting groups, including the National Association of Accountants, and representatives of industry engaged in defense contracting. Last January the massive, 558-page study was released. The study concluded that "It is feasible to establish and apply cost-accounting standards to provide a greater degree of uniformity and consistency in cost accounting as a basis for negotiating and administering procurement contracts." The next round in the attempt to develop such standards will probably begin in hearings before the Senate Banking Committee.

Concern over Defense spending led to the directive to study the feasibility of uniform cost accounting standards; it also produced a re-examination of the overall role of GAO in government. Senators were not overly happy with after-the-fact-audits of government programs, despite the savings that often accrued as a result. Some legislators would prefer that GAO furnish them with program alternatives before funds are spent.

Such a policy would, in effect, thrust the traditionally, nonpartisan GAO into a policy-making role. Some senators pointed this out and Comptroller General Staats added a note of caution: "We do not believe that it is the desire of the Congress that GAO *initiate* new program proposals to deal with social, economic, national security, or other problems or needs. Nor do we have responsibility for *initiating* recommendations with respect to program funding levels or budget priorities. In other words, the GAO does not have the authority nor should it seek to become a congressional Bureau of the Budget with responsibility for the review of departmental appropriation requests; i.e., to assess the need for particular funding levels based upon program needs or the priorities among different programs."

WHAT IS THE GAO?

In light of the increased responsibilities Congress seems to want GAO to shoulder, it is instructive to review why the GAO was set up, what it does and how it carries out its responsibilities in Government.

If the General Accounting Office did not exist, it would have to be invented. The necessity for an independent agency to examine how the Government spends public funds in the discharge of its responsibilities was obvious from the very beginning of constitutional government in this country. GAO was created by Congressional act in 1921, but it was vested with all the powers and duties formerly prescribed for the Comptroller of the Treasury by statutes extending back to the creation of the Treasury Department in 1789.

To fulfill its watchdog duties over government spending, the GAO was placed in the legislative branch. This assignment was in keeping with its creation as an agency of Congress and its responsibility to provide the committees and members of Congress with independent reports on the financial and management operations of the executive branch of government. To ensure the independence of the Agency, the enacting legislation provided that the Comptroller General and Assistant Comptroller General be appointed by the President with the advice and consent of the Senate, but the President was not given the power to remove the two officials. Appointed for a term of 15 years, they are subject to removal only by Congress through joint resolution or by impeachment.

With headquarters in Washington, GAO operates from 16 regional offices and 30 suboffices throughout the United States. Overseas responsibilities are carried out through offices located in Frankfurt, West Germany; Honolulu, Hawaii; Manila, The Philippines; New Delhi, India; and Saigon, South Vietnam. There are more than 4,500 employees of GAO, with approximately 2,300 auditors and accountants making up this total. GAO also employs specialists in management, engineering, statistical and automatic data processing.

The major purpose of the General Accounting Office is to serve Congress by searching for means of achieving greater economy and efficiency throughout the Government. Its responsibilities can be broken down and summarized in five categories:

It audits and reviews the manner in which federal programs are carried out;

It provides direct assistance to Congress and its committees;

It prescribes principles and standards for accounting in the federal agencies;

It provides, through the Comptroller General, legal advice and renders legal opinions;

It settles claims for and against the United States.

GAO gets involved in programs ranging from the most obscure to those right out of today's newspaper. For example, a recent GAO report on water pollution concluded that attempts by federal, state and local governments to clean up polluted streams, rivers and lakes were failing. GAO made a series of far-reaching recommendations to make the program more effective. The agency estimates that it makes an average of more than 900 audit reports a year; prepares more than 4,000 decisions by the Comptroller General; and submits more than 700 legislative and legal reports.

In order to carry out the responsibilities delegated by Congress, GAO demands—and gets—top staff members. To qualify for staff accountant (GS-7), for example, a student must be in the upper one-third of his class or make a "B+" or better, or be elected to a qualified honor society or meet other equally rigorous standards.

In addition to increasing its staff of professional accountants and auditors, GAO is also concentrating on adding staff members educated and experienced in other disciplines—economics, business administration, mathematics, engineering, and systems analysis "to achieve the capability to more effectively review and evaluate Government programs."

Like most responsible public bodies, GAO wants to improve its work. Comptroller General Staats would be the last to deny GAO needs to expand its activities and its staff to carry out its responsibilities. Mr. Staats has indicated in speeches that the GAO plans to step up its efforts "on extensive, across-the-board types of audit review" of programs in the areas of health, education, welfare, and urban development. The octopus-like ramifications of Government programs, however, have changed the extent of GAO audits. "Because these programs involve so many agencies and organizations outside the Federal Government, General Accounting Office audits are being carried to an increasing extent beyond the activities of the responsible Federal agencies into state and local agencies using Federal funds."

If asked to justify the agency's existence from a cost effectiveness point of view, GAO could make a good case for itself. In recent testimony before a Senate subcommittee, Comptroller General Staats estimated that its recommendations had produced savings of more than $200 million a year for the last five years. Considering GAO's budget is only $63 million, it seems that taxpayers are getting their money's worth—at least from the General Accounting Office.

QUESTIONS

1. (a) What are the functions of the General Accounting Office?
    (b) Compare the work of the GAO with that of a public accounting firm.

2. Should states and local governments have something similar to the GAO? Could these services be obtained equally well by contracting with the federal GAO? Could public accounting firms be used?

3. Senator Percy is quoted as saying: "There have been more men, increasingly in recent years, taking top-management positions in industry from the accounting end, because they—and they only sometimes—have been able to put together the whole picture on how to control these gigantic enterprises."
    (a) Why would accountants make good top executives in private corporations? In what ways would they be weak?
    (b) Would the same be true for accountants in top government positions? Explain.
    (c) In what ways would you expect an accountant to make a good President of the United States? In what ways would you expect him to be bad? (Okay—why don't you run for President?)

*An interview with the Comptroller General
of the U.S. who audits the government's
books.*

Where Government
Can Cut Spending

Federal spending is drawing concern from all sides. For some this may be no more than a passing interest. For the U.S. General Accounting Office it's a constant job.

The GAO looks at a broad spectrum of federal activities in the interest of economy. Savings of more than $10 million a year, for example, are being achieved by the military services because GAO recommended that excess Army beds be used by the Navy and Air Force rather than disposed of.

The agency recently told Congress it believes millions of dollars a year can be saved by consolidating the separate recruiting organizations and facilities of the four military services, and that hundreds of thousands of dollars can be saved if the U.S. will use more of the foreign currencies it owns abroad.

Created in 1921 to watchdog government expenditures, the GAO audits agency accounts and transactions, passes on the legality of expenditures and settles claims by and against the government.

It will administer the new law that allows taxpayers to funnel $1 of their income tax liability into a Presidential election campaign fund.

Some lawmakers want to strengthen GAO's hand in budget evaluation and have lobbies register with it rather than with the House or Senate.

In fiscal year 1966, the GAO figures it saved more than $130 million, $40 million of which will recur in future years. But more important than the specific

---

SOURCE: Reprinted by permission of the publisher from <u>Nation's Business</u> (December 1966), pp. 43ff. © 1966, <u>Nation's Business</u>—the Chamber of Commerce of the United States.

dollar savings is the discipline and incentive the GAO provides for more prudent expenditure of public funds throughout government.

The GAO practices the economy it preaches. In the past decade of generally burgeoning federal payrolls, it has cut its own staff by 25 per cent.

Our audits "don't just make sure the figures add," says Elmer B. Staats, who, as comptroller general, heads the GAO. "They see that the job gets done the way Congress intended: effectively, efficiently and economically and within the laws enacted by the Congress."

Mr. Staats moved into the top job at the accounting office last spring after serving as deputy director of the Bureau of the Budget under four different Presidents. At the swearing in ceremonies, President Johnson said he had full confidence that Mr. Staats would serve all branches of the government without "fear, favor or fuss." Mr. Staats is having no problems with the first two, but he doubts that a comptroller general can do his job without some controversy.

Nation's Business interviewed Mr. Staats to get an insight into where savings can be achieved and what course he is charting.

Mr. Staats, what are the major causes of waste in government?

There are many causes—many of them common to both industry and government. In my experience, waste arises in most cases not from deliberate or willful desire to waste funds, but rather from failures—failure to introduce economical ways of performing a particular job, from poor supervision, from poor contracting policy, including failure to obtain competitive bidding when competitive bidding is feasible. It can also result from poor information as to costs being incurred. This is one of the reasons we stress the importance of cost-based budgeting and adequate financial management and reporting for all agencies.

Where is the greatest potential for savings?

That's a difficult question to answer categorically. Many people would say we should reduce or terminate lower priority programs. While we in the GAO do not rule this out completely, we are primarily concerned with seeking ways to carry out programs more efficiently and at lower costs. That is why we stress competitive procurement, particularly in the Defense Department where total procurement now runs about $38 billion a year, some 85 per cent of which is still in the form of negotiated contracts. Other major areas we are stressing are manpower utilization, introduction of labor-saving equipment, and careful reviews of overseas military and economic assistance, including Food for Peace.

You're directing more of the GAO's effort at bigger government programs, aren't you?

Yes. This has always been the aim. But I wasn't satisfied that enough had been done, particularly with respect to some of the newer programs enacted in the past two or three years.

Which ones, in particular?

On the domestic side, housing and urban development, health, education and poverty—the whole array of Great Society programs. In the poverty program, we are reviewing Community Action projects, the Neighborhood Youth Corps and the manpower training operations. Some reports on these will go to the new Congress after the first of the year.

We have worked closely with the Social Security Administration in developing medicare cost principles, and will expand our audit coverage to this new program.

In the military and international area, we have already added substantially to our staff efforts on defense procurement, stemming from the Southeast Asia build-up. Roughly half of our staff is devoted to defense supply, defense procurement and other defense expenditures.

Military construction in Southeast Asia is another important area, as is the commodity import program to assist the Vietnamese economy. To meet the Southeast Asia build-up, we are establishing a new branch office in Manila.

Mr. Staats, the federal government today seems more inclined to adopt the business practice of more forward planning in budgeting and managing its finances. What does your agency contribute to this?

One of the highly important aspects of the GAO's job, one which is not widely known, is its responsibility to assist the federal agencies in improving their financial management practice.

We are increasing our efforts sharply in this area. The work to be done is great. To date, only about one third of the civilian agencies have accounting systems which meet current GAO standards. And within the Defense Department, the Corps of Engineers is the only activity which has an approved accounting system. We have quadrupled our efforts in this area, assigning approximately 10 per cent of our professional staff to it.

What is the Pentagon doing to correct this deficiency?

Under the immediate direction of Assistant Secretary of Defense Robert Anthony it has recently undertaken a major program which it hopes to complete by July 1, 1967, to relate costs more closely to the program budgeting system. This new program promises to be one of the most revolutionary developments in defense accounting in 15 years. It represents a logical extension and refinement of the program budgeting system which has been in effect for the last five years and, I believe, could save substantial tax money in the future. We are giving active assistance to Mr. Anthony in this effort.

How else does the GAO protect our tax dollars?

In addition to our accounting and auditing work, by our legal activities, the GAO is the office designated by Congress to make final determinations on the legality of the expenditures of federal funds. Unlike the courts, our jurisdiction is not limited to legal questions arising after the fact. The heads of the departments and agencies and other officials may obtain advance legal decisions before initiating new programs, before awarding contracts, before making payments of almost any type.

Also, any bidder on a government contract who believes that a proposed or actual award hurts him may protest to the GAO. The preservation of an effective procurement system depends on maintaining the confidence of all parties interested in doing business with the government. This can only be accomplished by treating all bidders fairly, impartially.

What pressures work against your agency in achieving an accounting of how the taxpayers' dollars are spent?

Perhaps the principal problem is the need for additional qualified personnel.

But we are improving, partly because of an intensive recruiting program and our own highly developed training program and partly by taking advantage of training offered by universities and private industry. We increased our accounting personnel and auditing and investigating staff, from 1,850 in 1960 to 2,280 in 1966. At the same time, we reduced our over-all staff. This is indicative of our effort to increase our professional capability.

We particularly want to strengthen our staff in some of the newer management specialties, for example, electronic data processing, systems analysis, operations research. Without this kind of capability we can't be sure the agencies themselves are carrying out programs at the least cost.

In too many cases there has been a lack of interest topside in the agencies in developing good cost-based budgeting, and at times resistance to our efforts to obtain needed information. As we see it, cost consciousness and cost-based budgeting go together.

How do you go about making an investigative accounting; Can you give an example?

Yes. The answer lies, in part, in the fact that our staff is professionally trained to analyze whether governmental operations being conducted are necessary, are the most efficient way and are in accord with the intent and purpose authorized by Congress and directed by the agency head.

The techniques we use vary all the way from actual observation of operations to complex financial analyses and evaluations.

To cite a very simple case, one of our reviews disclosed that eliminating the requirement for a lock on office desks purchased by Federal agencies would save about $250,000 a year. Agencies had been buying an average of about 170,000 office desks a year, each equipped with a lock.

Generally employees aren't required to lock their desks, so we felt the lock was an unnecessary expense in most instances. The practice of purchasing desks with locks has been discontinued.

A considerably more complex example concerns our review and analysis of Coast Guard plans to replace high-endurance vessels. We initiated a review after observing that the Coast Guard had used theoretical planning factors rather than actual operating data to determine its vessel replacement requirements.

Our report to Congress showed that the replacement requirements for the eastern area of the U.S. could be substantially reduced, saving about $55 million in capital costs and about $3.8 million annually in vessel operating costs.

For the Western area, we advised that the requirements could also be substantially reduced, saving about $45 million in construction and $3.6 million a year in operating costs.

So, as a result of these studies, the General Accounting Office was able to point out an indicated saving in just one agency of $100 million in capital costs and $7.4 million in annual operating costs. The Coast Guard agreed to re-examine its requirements and is using the approach we recommended.

Another example comes from an analysis our staff made of the cost allocation practices of the Post Office Department, which resulted in their selling stamped envelopes at a substantial loss. The department is required by law to sell stamped envelopes as nearly as possible at cost, but not less than cost.

The General Accounting Office found that the department had improperly deducted costs of about $10.4 million. Also, it had made certain computation errors, resulting in an overstatement of about $4 million in the cost allocation. We estimated, after considering these amounts, that the cost of selling stamped envelopes exceeded revenues for the four years ending June 30, 1963, by $7.5 million, as compared with the department's reported loss of $1.3 million.

The department subsequently announced an increase in the price of stamped envelopes.

The GAO has been criticized by some as being too negative about government spending. What do you think?

We are not against spending as such. We are against waste.

Perhaps the good auditor is never going to win a popularity contest any more than a good budget officer is. Both the Budget Bureau and the General Accounting Office are critics of agency operations. Although most of our work will continue to be directed primarily at undesirable conditions which need correcting, we will give increased attention to suggesting ways to prevent recurrence of errors.

Do you envision any new systems or procedures that will make your agency's watchdogging more effective?

Yes, although there will never be a substitute for independent and critical analysis of agency operations. We feel we can further strengthen our work in the area of improving financial management practices. We can emphasize newer management techniques which have been successful in government and private industry.

Traditionally, there is a rush on spending at the end of the fiscal year. What can be done about this?

This is an old problem which we have made many efforts to deal with, both in the executive and legislative branch. It stems partly from inadequate financial information with respect to the status of expenditures, from inadequate controls and from inadequate supervision.

There may be isolated cases where a large or disproportionate expenditure in May and June can be justified because of delays in enacting appropriations, or delays in reaching decisions at the agencies. But there is no substitute for good supervision and adequate financial controls to be sure that money which may be over and above immediate requirements is not spent just to avoid asking for the money the next year, or used for things which are really not essential.

Drawing from your extensive experience at the Budget Bureau, do you see any end to expanding federal spending?

The question is not whether federal spending will increase, because it will inevitably increase as the population grows and as the population becomes more highly urbanized. The real question is what will be the particular areas that will require this increase and the rate and total burden on the taxpayer of it.

There are many ways to evaluate or make a judgment on the desirable level of government spending. One which I feel needs more emphasis is the relationship of total spending by government—federal, state and local—to the gross national product, and our national income. These are better measures not only of the tax burden but also of the effect of government spending on the economy.

QUESTIONS

1. From the description of the GAO's various functions, how do you think accounting courses contribute to the successful performance of a GAO accountant? Be thorough and specific.

2. "Roughly half of our staff is devoted to defense supply, defense procurement and other defense expenditures." How might the GAO save American taxpayers money in connection with defense expenditures?

3. What is "investigative accounting?"

4. What are the pros and cons of allowing accountants to review technical decisions and plans, such as those of the Coast Guard to replace high-endurance vessels?

An official of the General Accounting Office describes its approach to auditing the anti-poverty program and other federal grant-in-aid programs.

Auditing Federal Grant Programs

by Ellsworth H. Morse, Jr.

The management job of conducting and administering the vast network of Federal grant programs is a staggering and complex affair. The management of something like $20 billion a year is very big business in itself but in the case of grant programs it is complicated by the large number of different programs with a great variety of authorized purposes, terms, and conditions, and the involvement of numerous and different levels of governmental entities.

The audit function is only a part of the total management job to be done. It is not a large part in relation to actual program administration, but since it includes—or should include—evaluation of the effectiveness of such administration, it is a highly important one.

The purpose of this article is to describe how the audit job to be done is viewed from the standpoint of the General Accounting Office; to refer to some efforts underway to more effectively carry out this function; and to suggest some possibilities for improvement.

First, let me outline very briefly what GAO is and where it fits in the picture.

SOURCE: Reprinted slightly abridged by premission of the publisher from a longer article in The Federal Accountant (June 1969), pp. 4–12.

WHAT GAO IS

The GAO is the independent auditing agency of the Federal Government located in the legislative branch. It is headed by the Comptroller General of the United States who is responsible only to the Congress of the United States. He is appointed for a 15-year term and once confirmed by the Senate, he is not removable except for extreme causes and then only by action of the Congress.

The GAO thus is a nonpartisan and nonpolitical office. It has 4,300 employees of whom 2,400 are professional accountants and auditors. Its audit responsibilities extend to almost all of the agencies of the Federal Government which are spending over $180 billion a year on a vast variety of programs, operations, and activities.

GAO Audit Policy

In the light of the great size and diversity of Federal agency operations and as a matter of generally accepted as well as efficient audit practice, the policy of the GAO is to determine its specific direction of audit work and the extent of it in any given problem area with due regard to the known interests of the Congress and to the effectiveness of an agency's management system. Preliminary surveys and reviews of agency policies and practices are made as the basis for such assessments.

THE FEDERAL GRANT PROGRAMS OVERALL

The grant-in-aid programs of the various Federal agencies are but one category of many types of programs that involve the application of Federal funds and about which the GAO has to be concerned. But it is an important category and a complex one.

Our overview of the total Federal budget for grant-in-aid expenditures focuses first on the individual agencies responsible for administering those programs. Almost all of the Federal departments and agencies have grant expenditures of some kind. Currently the major ones are found in the following:

	In billions (fiscal year 1969 budget)
Health, Education, and Welfare	$ 9.4
Transportation	4.4
Housing and Urban Development	1.7
Economic Opportunity Programs	1.4
Agriculture	1.3
All others	2.0
	$20.2

These totals in turn proliferate into specific programs of which there are
hundreds.

BASIC AUDIT APPROACH

With the application of such substantial amounts of public funds under these
programs, the GAO approach starts with the nature of financial controls exercised
by the administering Federal agency over each program and the quality of the
overall control from the standpoint of these six objectives which we define as
generally applicable to all Federal aid programs.

1. Whether the administering Federal agencies' policies and procedures are consistent with authorizing legislation, the objectives sought, and any constraints
   imposed.
2. Whether the aid provided is limited to authorized recipients and is within
   established monetary limits.
3. Whether the control procedures actually in use are adequate to assure that the
   aid is used for the purposes intended.
4. Whether the recipients have the capability of using the aid provided in an
   effective and productive manner and can provide the resources expected of
   them as their contribution to the project or activity.
5. Whether the timing of aid payments is geared properly to the time of need.
6. Whether funds provided are properly accounted for and any reversionary
   interests are exercised.

In working toward these broad audit objectives, we advise our auditors to
specifically inquire into the nature and quality of existing management review
activities such as—

- Regular managerial checks of the performance of recipients.
- Audits of the recipient by the donor Federal agency or by others such as
  under cross-servicing arrangements.
- Audits of the recipient by its own internal auditors.
- Audits by independent public accountants.

Inquiry into these functions is a prerequisite to our own determinations as to
the specific operations or problem areas that we may select for detailed and
penetrating audit work.

Our view is that the essence of management control is the action that adjusts
operations to conform with prescribed or desired standards or requirements.
Management at all levels needs timely and adequate information on performance
as a basis for action.

In the case of the massive grant programs, really effective control is hard to
come by and responsible managers need all the help they can obtain. Although

not the only source, one very important source of information for managers of government programs for use in improving their control is the internal audit function.

IMPORTANCE OF INTERNAL AUDITING

The General Accounting Office has for many years actively promoted the development of strong internal audit systems in all Federal agencies as an important part of the management machinery for bringing about effective, efficient, and economical operations. We examine into this function on all of our audit assignments in order to find out whether it is serving the management effectively with respect to the particular area we are auditing. This is a basic audit policy. It is not necessarily peculiar to our work—it is basic to all modern auditing practice.

In 1957, we prepared a brief statement of basic principles and concepts that we viewed as important in the development of improved internal audit systems in the Federal agencies. A revision of this statement was recently issued to reflect the benefit of over 10 years experience with this important and expanding function in government agency management.

While there is no time here to adequately summarize the new statement, I do wish to point out that we believe that all Federal agencies should have strong internal audit systems. They should be highly placed in the organization reporting either to the head of the agency or to a principal official who does report to the agency head.

We also urge a centralized audit organization rather than fragmented groups of auditors within a department or agency in order to provide an environment more conducive to the attraction and retention of good audit managers and staff and generally be in position to do a better audit job.

Our interest in internal auditing in the Federal agencies is essentially the same as the interest of state auditors in internal auditing within state agencies. Lennis Knighton points out in his excellent study of performance post auditing in State governments that an auditor's scope of work must be beyond financial areas if he is to really function as a broad review element in a control system. He adds that:

"before the performance post-audit review as conducted by the Auditor General can become fully effective, it must be accompanied by a similar extension of the scope of internal auditing at both agency and top-executive levels."[1]

GAO AUDITS OF GRANT PROGRAMS

Over the years GAO has done a great deal of audit work on Federal programs in which grants-in-aid to state and local government bodies are made. We have issued many reports to the Congress on our work in such Federal aid programs as those for highways; housing; and health, education and welfare.

We have extended the scope of our auditing in all Federal programs beyond a concern with propriety of financial transactions, fiscal accountability, and adequacy of accounting. We want our audit work directed also toward delving into whether public funds are being economically applied to accomplish the purposes for which they are made available.

Some state audit organizations are making good progress toward a comparable expansion of the scope of their audits and we hope that all of the states will in time be able to do so.

Here are some examples of GAO audit findings pertaining to "greater economy." These examples are drawn from reports sent to the Congress or agency officials on our work on Federal grant-in-aid programs.

Reducibility of expenditures for drugs in public assistance programs through the use of less expensive nonproprietary name drugs instead of comparable brand name drugs or more expensive nonproprietary name drugs. (B-114836, February 3, 1966; Welfare Administration DHEW (Pennsylvania).)

Overpayments for financial assistance because of ineligibility of claimants under terms under which such assistance was available. (B-114836, December 9, 1964; Welfare Administration, DHEW (Florida).)

Overallocation of State administrative costs to Federal grant programs because of use of improper or unrealistic allocation methods. (B-114836, December 29, 1964; Welfare Administration, DHEW (New York).) (Also B-114836, January 22, 1965 (Massachusetts).)

Failure to adequately implement procedures to assure that payments for drugs for welfare recipients were made only for correctly priced drugs prescribed under proper authority and actually delivered to eligible recipients. (B-114836, August 8, 1966; Welfare Administration; DHEW (California).)

Acceptance of appraisal reports for value of land for public projects to be financed in part by Federal funds which did not adequately support the reasonableness of such value. (Federal Aviation Administration, April and June 1967.)

There is no need to compound examples of fruitful areas of inquiry by auditors who feel that an important part of their job is to search for economy without impairing the accomplishment of the primary purposes for which public programs are conducted.

Audit of the Anti-Poverty Program

Nor does our concern stop with matters of economy.

We have one assignment involving Federal grants-in-aid that we are currently performing that is probably as technically difficult and challenging as auditors can encounter anywhere. This is our examination of the Federal programs and activities for reducing poverty which utilize funds authorized under the Economic Opportunity Act of 1964 ($1.4 billion for this year).

Last year when it enacted the Economic Opportunity Amendments of 1967, the Congress displayed a degree of discontent with this program, and directed the General Accounting Office to make a comprehensive examination of the program from two standpoints:

1. The *efficiency* with which the programs and activities are administered.
2. The extent to which the objectives of the original act—the Economic Opportunity Act of 1964—were being met (in other words, an evaluation of the *effectiveness* of the program.)

We are making this examination right now and we expect to issue our final overall report in a few months. We have had over 300 auditors working on this program, plus three contractors who have been engaged to assist in certain aspects and a half a dozen individual consultants who are expert in various social fields.

As in all professional audit work, we are working on a selective basis and are examining in some depth such component programs as:

Job Corps,
Community Action,
Neighborhood Youth Corps,
Work Experience,
Special Impact,
Volunteers in Service to America (VISTA).

We are examining into the conduct of these programs in different parts of the country. Many problems have been encountered in this type of audit and many more will crop up before we can complete it if such an assignment can ever be really completed.

Probably the most important problem is deciding on the standards for making judgments. The indicators of progress in a social program such as this one are not yet fully understood nor are they readily measurable. Nor is there really much agreement on what the best indicators are or whether they can be reduced to significant numbers or any other measure. We will be dealing with some of these problems in our report.

I cite our work on the poverty program not only because it involves Federal grants-in-aid but because it is also a good illustration of the really important work that will confront the auditor of the future. That auditor's concern, which will be derived from the concerns of top management including the Congress or other legislative bodies, will be largely with effectiveness of operations or, simply, just how good a job is being done? This is an easy question to ask but a hard one to answer even when verifiable and agreed upon indicators of success or progress exist.

We think that the answers, at least in part, can be supplied by accountants and auditors and that they have the capacity to expand their scope of operation to be of great assistance to management on this kind of a question.

CONCERN WITH ALL AUDIT COVERAGE

In our audits of grant programs, where Federal funds are passed to other governmental organizations for use or allocation to yet additional levels, our concern does not stop with the Federal agency's audit surveillance, including its audits of third parties. We also wish to be informed on the quality of the management by the recipient organization and on the quality of its internal auditing. Primarily, we will undertake to gain this information through the eyes and ears of the Federal agency managers and auditors.

The overall audit objective is to find out whether the granted funds are used for the purposes intended, are serving those purposes effectively, and are not being wasted. GAO testing will search out how effectively the sum total of the audit machinery is being operated to arrive at conclusions on these objectives and to communicate appropriate recommendations to the Congress and to management officials for consideration in bettering future operations.

FOOTNOTE

1. Knighton, Lennis M., *The Performance Post Audit in State Government*, Bureau of Business and Economic Research, Graduate School of Business Administration, Michigan State University, 1967, p. 55.

QUESTIONS

1. What is an audit? What is an internal audit?

2. To whom is the GAO responsible?

3. How do federal grants-in-aid differ from direct federal expenditures?

4. What differences in objectives and approach would you expect to find between audits of grant recipients by (1) the GAO, (2) the donor federal agency, (3) the recipient's internal auditors and (4) independent public accountants?

5. When a grant recipient has an effective internal audit system, is there any need for a GAO audit? Explain.

6. Find out about federal grant programs operating within your university and your community. (Consider anti-poverty programs, transportation grants, criminal justice program grants, model cities programs, city and regional planning, training programs, education grants, welfare programs and research, etc.) As assigned by your instructor, visit (individually or as a member of a team) the office administering a selected grant and ascertain the types of audits utilized. Has the GAO ever audited the office? If so, ask to see the GAO's report, and summarize it for the rest of your class.

7. Does your school have an internal audit department? If so, determine the nature and scope of its activities. If not, find out why.

8. Determine the type of auditing system used by your state. Prepare a brief report on this system for presentation to your class.

A view from the sciences on the danger of
accountants influencing grant programs.

Control by
Accountants

by Dael Wolfle

Science is coming more and more under the influence of accountants. Here are some examples:

1) The *Administration of Government Supported Research at Universities,* a compilation of much information on federal grant programs and many recommendations on the management of grants, was written by the Bureau of the Budget. One of the principal spokesmen for universities was the National Association of College and University Business Officers.

2) The Department of Health, Education, and Welfare has recently appointed a Grant Administration Advisory Committee, a majority of whose members occupy positions of financial and administrative, rather than research or educational, responsibility.

3) The Department of Health, Education and Welfare has announced the availability of a pamphlet of instructions, *Time or Effort Reporting,* to aid universities and other grant recipients in complying with the requirements of Bureau of the Budget *Circular A-21,* the controlling document on financial records of government grants to universities.

4) National Science Foundation auditors are in some cases extending the principle of time or effort reporting, which now applies widely to staff members

SOURCE: Reprinted by permission of the author and the publisher from Science (19 May 1967), vol. 156, p. 895. Copyright 1967 by the American Association for the Advancement of Science.

working directly on project activities, to others who are only indirectly involved. In other cases, NSF requires separation of those expenses of a project the NSF auditors classify as "off-site" from those expenses of the same project they classify as "on-site," so that indirect charges can be paid at different rates on the two categories.

5) Additional accounting records will have to be kept by universities and scientific associations if the Internal Revenue Service succeeds in imposing a proposed regulation (*Science,* 21 April 1967) whereby nonprofit organizations would be taxed on the advertising income of scientific (and other) journals they publish.

Records must be kept; government funds must be accounted for; carelessness in grant administration and the use of public funds cannot be condoned. It is therefore necessary to have close understanding between the auditors and accountants in government agencies and the administrative and business staffs of their grantees. Nevertheless, the original purposes of the federal grant programs are endangered by having too many of the rules written by accountants. Although scientists and accountants, in and out of government, are aware of the other's point of view, they consider scientific activities and the grants that support them from fundamentally different vantage points. The scientific interest is primarily in the purposes for which funds are granted and in the accomplishments made possible by grants. The accounting interest is primarily in seeing that the accounts balance accurately and that there is a proper piece of paper on file to justify each expense item. The danger of having too many of the rules written by accountants is the obvious one that the form will be given more weight than the substance. Accountants, however, are not solely responsible for this situation; they have been filling a gap the scientists have allowed to develop.

Twenty or more universities in the United States are now developing programs of research and study on "science and government" or "science and society." Most seem to be concentrating on political theory, political science, congressional responsibility, social philosophy, or kindred matters. It may seem cynical, but it is realistic to suggest that it would be timely for at least one of these universities to study the effects of science on current accounting practices.

QUESTIONS

1. "The original purposes of the federal grant programs are endangered by having too many of the rules written by accountants." Why?

2. "The scientific interest is primarily in the purposes for which funds are granted and in the accomplishments made possible by grants." Are

accountants interested in the original purposes and the accomplishments? According to Ellsworth Morse in the article preceding this one, does the GAO concern itself with purposes and accomplishments in auditing federal grants?

3.   Should scientists be encouraged to study accounting? Why or why not?

Accountants have a unique opportunity to enlarge the scope of their services, by involvement in the system, budget and auditing services of federal poverty program grants. In addition, the accountants may help assure the proper fiscal management of the funds by close attention to their handling by the usually fiscally-inexperienced program managers.

The CPA's Role in the Accounting for Anti-Poverty Program Grants

by Bernard D. Kleinman & Stanley L. Sandler

The 1964 Economic Opportunity Act authorized substantial allotments of funds to localities for approved anti-poverty programs. These funds are transmitted by the U. S. Treasury to municipalities (grantees); they, in turn, may allot them to approved local organizations (delegate agencies). In New York City, for example, the Community Development Agency (CDA) is the City department responsible for distributing funds, as well as regulating and controlling their expenditure.

This article will discuss the procedures for an agency to receive a grant, the accounting and other requirements and the role of the accountant and his service.

SOURCE: From The New York CPA, September 1967, pp. 673–678. Reprinted by permission of the publisher, The New York State Society of Certified Public Accountants.

THE ROLE OF THE CPA

Certified Public Accountants play an important role in this effort. They can help avert the problems that plague some of these well-intentioned agencies.

The CPA can serve in these important ways:

- To assist in preparing the budget and proposal that must be submitted to the local administrative agency to secure a grant.
- To insure compliance with the grant.
- To set up a system of accounts and internal control consistent with regulations.
- To make periodic audits.
- To prepare or review the financial reports that must be submitted to the administrative agency.
- To counsel with the directors of the agency.

THE APPLICATION FOR A GRANT

Local organizations submit a proposal to the grantee. In it, they state the problems of their neighborhood and outline their program for eliminating them. The proposal should include a detailed budget of the expenses the organization expects to incur. The grantee reviews the proposal and, if it is acceptable to it and subsequently to the federal government agency, a contract is agreed upon and signed. Each contract is based on a budget year, usually ending on the same date as the federal fiscal year, June 30th. (Special projects, such as summer programs, may run for shorter periods.)

CONTENT OF THE BUDGET

Most organizations are staffed by local residents with little or no background in accounting or budgeting. Therefore, professional assistance is usually needed in preparing the budget. The stipulated budget form consists of seven major categories, to wit:

Personnel costs: Salaries, wages and fringe benefits. Fringe benefits include: payroll taxes, workmen's compensation insurance, hospitalization and medical plans, etc.

Consultants' and contract services: Legal and accounting fees and other professional services (doctors, psychologists, etc.).

Travel: Local transportation, mileage payments for authorized use of personal auto, rental of autos, buses, etc.

Space costs and rentals: Rent paid for space, utilities and renovation costs, if necessary.

Consumable supplies: Stationery, postage, other office supplies and small office accessories with a unit cost of $50 or less.

Rental, lease or purchase of equipment: Furniture, office machinery, special program equipment, maintenance equipment, etc. with a unit cost of more than $50.

Other costs: Insurance (other than that included in personnel costs), telephone, printing and publications, over-time meals, food used in the program and other sundry expenses.

In addition to totals for each category, the organization must show the basis for the cost estimate. For example, personnel costs must list the job title for each anticipated employee, his monthly salary, the number of months employed during the budget period, and the total cost.

As to consultants and contract service, the organization must show the type of consultants needed, an estimate of the days they will be required and the daily rate expected to be charged. Regulations prohibit the use of consultants on a retainer basis. They must be paid per diem and at rates not to exceed federal guidelines.

Rental of space is generally limited to a cost not to exceed $3 per square foot.

In preparing the budget for equipment, it may be necessary to list each item and its unit cost. Generally, no unit cost should exceed the cost listed in the General Services Administration (GSA) catalog, even though the purchases need not be made through GSA.

A Flexible Budget is Desirable

A flexible budget will enable the delegate agency to allow for such things as increased activity resulting from expanded services. For example, in a new program it usually is best not to begin operating at full personnel strength. People must be trained and worked into the program. If personnel costs are estimated at full capacity from the beginning, much money will not be used during these early months of the grant period. Regulations do not permit these unexpended funds to be used up as excess expenditures towards the end of the grant period. Any monies unexpended at the end of the period must be returned to the grantee and ultimately to the federal government. If funds have to be returned because of a faulty budget, the community is the loser since this money could have been used for other worthwhile programs.

Some Common Budget Deficiencies

Budgets prepared without professional assistance have been found to contain errors which the well informed accountant would have avoided. For example, in preparing the personnel cost budget, proper provision may not have been made for payroll taxes, workmen's compensation insurance, disability insurance, etc., due to a lack of knowledge of governmental regulations. In other instances, budgets were prepared which did not provide for enough desks for budgeted employees. Some budgets were prepared without sufficient research into prevailing wage scales. In one instance, the proposed salaries for social workers were far below those normally paid in the New York City area. The result? The organization could not hire qualified people after receiving approval to launch their program. Here are some other expenses miscalculated or omitted from budgets: insurance, utilities, postage and protection expenses.

Departures From the Budget.   Once a contract is signed, the organization must adhere to the budget. It may not, under any circumstances, spend money in excess of it. However, specific categories may be increased if others are correspondingly decreased. Changes in personnel costs of up to 10% of the total cost, or $2,000 (whichever is greater) and changes in other categories of 20% of the category, or $1,000 (whichever is greater) may be made without the permission of the federal government. However, in New York City, CDA must approve all budget modifications. Proper budgeting techniques would avoid such revisions and speed the progress of community projects.

PRELIMINARIES TO THE RECEIPT OF FUNDS

(The following procedures are followed in New York City. They may not apply in other communities.)

After the budget is approved and the contract signed, the organization must take out an insurance policy, payable to the City of New York, bonding employees who sign checks and/or handle large amounts of cash. The policy may be either a blanket position or name-scheduled bond. It must be delivered to CDA before any money is released to the organization.

After it receives the bond, CDA will release a percentage of the total budget as a revolving fund. Additional money is released only after the organization submits a request for reimbursement of expenditures.

REIMBURSEMENT REPORTS

To recover expenditures from CDA, the organization must submit a request for reimbursement on forms prescribed by the City. These data must be supplied: date of expenditure, check number, payee, amount paid, budget category to be charged, and total paid in each category for the period in question. The original copy of each paid invoice should be attached to the reimbursement request. It should carry the date paid, check number, and signature of the Executive

Director of the agency under the word "approved." If items are paid by petty cash, the original voucher, approved by the Executive Director, with substantiating instruments attached, must also be submitted.

A request for reimbursement of personnel costs must include a copy of the payroll register containing the employees' names, job categories (as detailed in the budget), rate of pay, gross salaries, payroll deductions, net salary and number of the check used to pay each employee.

These reporting requirements must be met in full to insure prompt reimbursement by CDA. Unauthorized expenditures will not be reimbursed, and the Executive Director of the organization may be held personally responsible for them. If the organization inadvertently pays sales tax to vendors, CDA will not reimburse it. As a delegate agency of the City of New York, the organization is not required to pay sales tax on items purchased; a sales tax exemption certificate is given to it by CDA when the contract is signed.

The completed reimbursement reports are submitted to the Fiscal Department of CDA for audit. Upon approval, payment is made to the organization.

CASH BASIS FOR REPORTS

Though the organization submits its reimbursement reports to CDA on the basis of cash expenditures, it is important that its accounts be kept on an accrual basis. For this reason, it is better to use a voucher register combined with cash disbursements journal than merely a cash disbursements journal. Knowing what expenses are "as incurred" rather than "as paid" is essential if the organization is not to exceed its budget. For example, if the budget for consumable supplies is $50,000, and $40,000 was spent by a certain date, the person responsible for purchasing may assume he can still purchase $10,000 worth of supplies. In reality, there may be an additional $5,000 in supplies that has been received but not yet paid for. Such a miscalculation can create serious difficulties with CDA on future funding; it can also lead to personal liability by the Executive Director.

By using a voucher register, the organization can tell at any time how much money is still available in any category. This is done simply by comparing the amounts budgeted with the expenses incurred per the general ledger and the current month's voucher register.

RECORDKEEPING

Generally accepted accounting principles for non-profit organizations apply. The governmental requirements for accounting records are flexible but the following books and records are minimum requirements for proper reporting and for insuring proper budget control.

Books of account: General ledger, cash receipts journal, voucher register combined with cash disbursements journal, payroll register, general journal.

Reimbursement reports: It is extremely important that the organization retain a complete file of all submitted reimbursement reports along with duplicate copies of all attachments.

Time Sheets for all employees: The regulations require that signed time sheets be kept for all employees, and that payrolls be prepared accordingly. The employee's immediate supervisor should approve all time sheets in writing.

Individual employee earnings cards: These should be maintained for preparation of quarterly payroll tax returns.

Copies of Leases: These should be maintained in the event they must be submitted as proof of rent expense.

Contracts with consultants and other professionals: These may be necessary to prove that the services performed were authorized by the directors of the organization.

Property record: This record should indicate the nature of the property, the date acquired, its cost and location. At the end of the grant period, the organization must submit to CDA an inventory of furniture and equipment on hand. Title to all property acquired with anti-poverty funds remains with the government. If the organization does not receive a new grant, the property can be given to other agencies by CDA direction.

AUDIT OF INTERNAL CONTROL AND ACCOUNTING SYSTEM MANDATORY

The Community Action Program Guide, Volume II, Financial Instructions, states that "each grantee shall arrange for periodic financial audits to insure that the accounting system and related internal controls are operating effectively and that adequate records are being maintained." The City of New York also requires a financial examination of all delegate agencies by independent public accountants at the end of each grant period.

An accounting system based on sound internal control principles is as necessary for an anti-poverty organization as it is for a commercial one. Even if the organization is doing an excellent job of combating poverty in the neighborhood, it may be hindered in receiving additional future grants by poor financial control.

In addition to usual internal control procedures, there are certain procedures required under governmental regulations pertaining to anti-poverty programs. Some of these are:

- All checks must be signed by at least two persons who are bonded.
- The organization cannot pay its employees for overtime work. An employee may only be given compensatory time off.
- A separate bank account must be maintained for each program. Cash received under a grant cannot be combined with cash received under other grants, even if received from the same governmental agency.

REQUIRED AUDIT PROCEDURES

Selection and Approval of Independent Auditor.   The federal government, through its official agency, the Office of Economic Opportunity (OEO), has recognized the importance of maintaining adequate fiscal controls by establishing regional audit offices. However, it has also indicated that primary responsibility for control lies with the grantee. Each delegate agency must employ the services of independent certified public accountants or licensed public accountants to examine and render opinions on the internal control procedures and financial statements of the projects.

A recent OEO publication states that a grantee agency (other than governmental agencies or their subdivisions) shall promptly select an independent public accountant. Within one month of receipt of the notice of grant approval, the grantee shall inform the regional OEO auditor of the name of the auditor or auditing organization selected. OEO will indicate if the auditor nominated is not acceptable. A preliminary audit survey must be started not more than three months from the effective date of the grant.

Preliminary Audit Survey.   This is to determine if the agency has an accounting system which "includes internal controls adequate to safeguard the assets of the agency, check the accuracy and reliability of accounting data, promote operational efficiency and encourage adherence to prescribed management policies of the agency."

A preliminary audit survey is required in the following cases:

- An agency receives its first grant.
- A delegate agency receives its first contract.
- An agency receiving a renewal grant contemplates a major change in operation, or there is a significant increase in the funding level. OEO will inform the grantee if the change requires a preliminary audit survey.
- An agency receives a renewal grant but has not been audited in the twelve months prior to its effective date.

- A short-term program agency which was not audited in the previous year receives a grant or contract.

In addition to periodic financial examinations, OEO requires an annual examination. OEO has published an Audit and Examination Guide detailing the scope of audits and reports required.

THE COMMUNITY SERVICE ROLE OF THE CPA

The anti-poverty programs offer the certified public accountant an area of service beyond the usual accountant-client relationship. In addition to the audit and attest role, the CPA has an unusual opportunity in the area of public service through the furnishing of management and financial advice.

Most organizers of the various programs are people with social work backgrounds who are weak in the areas of budgetary planning and fiscal policy. Until they gain this skill through time and experience, it must be provided by the accountant. The success of a program may very well be measured by the extent of his professional assistance.

BIBLIOGRAPHY

1. *Community Action Program Guide, Vol. I and II.* (Office of Economic Opportunity, Washington, D. C., 20506, June 1965.) (Presently being revised.)
2. *Guide for Grantee Accounting.* (Office of Economic Opportunity, March 1966.)
3. *Accounting System Survey and Audit Guide for Community Action Program Grants.* (Office of Economic Opportunity, 1967.)

QUESTIONS

1. What is a budget? A flexible budget?
2. "Even if the organization is doing an excellent job of combating poverty in the neighborhood, it may be hindered in receiving additional future grants by poor financial control."
   (a) If an organization is doing an excellent job of combating poverty, why shouldn't it continue to receive grants regardless?

(b) Compare the above quotation to the argument advanced in the article, "Control by Accountants."

3. What requirements does the OEO place on grantee agencies with respect to engaging independent public accountants? Why are these requirements imposed? Do you think they are reasonable?

4. A disgruntled delegate agency executive director recently observed: "The real beneficiaries of the war on poverty have been the public accountants." Do you agree?

The financial and control aspects of a community social welfare program have much in common with business, yet accountants are just beginning to take a key role in such programs. Here are some guides.

Management Information for Community Action Programs

by William J. Bruns, Jr. & Robert J. Snyder

Problems of planning and control in publicly sponsored social programs are receiving increasing attention from program managers, government officers, and taxpayers. Social problems such as those stemming from urban and rural poverty weigh heavily on the public conscience. However, the resources available for pursuing solutions to national problems and fulfilling international commitments are limited and must be allocated carefully. Better management techniques are needed at every level of the public resource allocation process.

SOURCE: Reprinted by permission of the authors and the publisher from Management Services (July-August 1969), pp. 15–22. Copyright 1969 by the American Institute of CPAs.

Accountants can and should play a major role in the development of these techniques. One pioneering effort in this field, the development of a computerized information system for planning and evaluation of results in Detroit's war on poverty, was conducted by a CPA firm.*

This article deals with techniques that have been found to be appropriate for one endeavor of the Office of Economic Opportunity, the Community Action Program, based on experience with Seattle's Community Action Programs. Our focus is at the agency level.

The broad, overriding goals of a Community Action Program are established by the legislation that created it—to alleviate the conditions and causes of poverty. However, the determination of specific operational goals requires specific information about the geographic location, population variables (age, sex, etc.), educational levels, regional economic status, cultural background, and so forth of the people to be helped. Only with this kind of information can the policy-making management of a CAP set the scope and direction of agency operations. CAPs were meant to be innovative and aggressive; to be successfully so, their managements need a realistic understanding of the poverty environment in which they work.

POVERTY "MARKET" NEEDS

The poverty in a CAP's geographic area defines the "market" the CAP will serve; the services to be offered depend upon the market needs. The similarity to a business's market for goods and services is clear. The profit success of a business is decided by market acceptance of products at a price in excess of cost. A prime input to business success, then, is market information. Exactly the same is true for CAPs. Success in achieving goals demands thorough understanding of the "market."

Good information about conditions may make it possible to predict both client and nonclient response to programs, side effects, and ramifications, including congressional reaction. The success of a project or program may depend upon ability to predict outcomes, and prediction for a CAP, just as for a business, depends on proper understanding of the market to be served.

One source of "market" information is, of course, the CAP policy and advisory boards. Congress has required that the poor participate in CAP decision making "to the extent practicable"—at least partly, one speculates, to ensure that their feelings, observations, and poverty "expertise" will be a source of information.

*EDITOR'S NOTE: See the next article in this section, "The Modern Management Approach to a Program of Social Improvement."

A second source is the collected statistics of poverty. Data such as crime rates, school dropout rates, incidence of disease, housing conditions and occupancy levels, unemployment and underemployment, birth rates, racial relations, etc., are indicators of the problems and pinpointers of the location of poverty. To know something about these conditions is to know something about the affluence and/or poverty of a community, and it is, of course, just such information that CAP management planners must have.

Such "statistics of poverty" are usually collected by other public agencies. Medical, employment, and educational data are often available in a form that suits the needs of CAP planners, or they can be modified to satisfy those needs. The Bureau of Economic Research of Rutgers University prepared a document entitled *The Dimensions and Location of Poverty in Burlington County, New Jersey*[1] by working primarily from existing census information. In Detroit a well developed system was designed to transform data from many agencies into information useful for planning and managing antipoverty activities.

The individual techniques of information gathering and processing that can be used depend very much on the size of the agency, the nature of the poverty area, and the sources of data available (such as police records, school statistics, etc.). But in all cases a formal document setting forth the known "market" information to be considered (similar to the New Jersey document prepared by Rutgers) should be prepared for the policy and advisory boards and other interested parties. This document becomes the basis for planning programs.

CAP CAPACITY FOR SERVICE

In addition to an appraisal of the "poverty market," CAP planners must have an understanding of the internal capabilities and limitations of the operating agency. Appraising the capability of the CAP organization is a two-part job. First, the objectives of the organization as expressed in tentative projects or programs must be translated into organizational demands. That is, quite simply, the CAP planners must decide what type of organization is needed to carry out a project. The second step is to measure the existing organization against these requirements. If the organization is inadequate, either it must be strengthened or the program must be re-evaluated. If the organization is more than adequate, then perhaps additional opportunities for service should be sought, subject, of course, to other constraints.

The elements of organizational strength that must be catalogued are several; they include personnel members and qualifications, physical facilities, professional expertise, leadership availability, morale, ability to attract additional talent, political climate, etc. It is clear that each of these factors presents problems of quantification and objectivity; however, planners for CAPs must in some fashion evaluate the characteristics of their organizations if they are to direct activities realistically and successfully.

Each tentative project should be considered in light of factors in addition to organizational demands, of course. The physical and financial resources required for the project need to be considered in several ways. The resources needed must be compared to those available; it is useless to begin a project for which funds will never be allocated. Often, more than financial resources must be considered; for example, the necessary physical space to carry out some project may be essential information if space is limited. All resource requirements, availabilities, and shortages are important information for planning.

It is hard to be specific about the sources of and procedures for collecting information. *The Community Action Program Guide,*[2] published by the Office of Economic Opportunity, explains some of the expectations of and limitations on an agency. Experience of managers and discussions with other CAP managements, regional OEO administrators, etc. can add to this information. Information regarding the community's willingness and ability to participate can be collected from people experienced in the community with a knowledge of the political tenor of the area. The organization's capabilities may be the most difficult information to obtain; since people very close to the organization will be doing the appraisal, they may be excessively optimistic (or pessimistic) about the organization's potential or may overlook the real problems because they are focusing on desired ends.

The early stages of planning should lead to an understanding of the restrictions and limitations that are present in the situation of the CAP. A document should then be prepared that states specifically the goals of the agency and the best judgments on each factor critical for success so that they are clear to all persons involved and can be referred to again when reviews of progress are undertaken. However, planning is not complete when goals are selected; it becomes more detailed and specific as it seeks to establish means for achieving them. We call this process operational planning and scheduling.

PLANNING AND SCHEDULING

Operational planning and scheduling are concerned with the major requirements and expectations for each step of a project; they deal with flows of funds, material, and personnel; with dependence on other projects; and with the dependence of other projects on the planned project. Information needed for operational planning and scheduling relates to the transformation of resource inputs into results. Therefore, the kinds of information needed include transformation functions, the factors which affect them (for example, regional economic conditions affect the transformation of unemployed people through a job training program), the inputs required, and the results demanded by policy management and the funding entities. The significant variables that appear to be least predictable and the effect of that unpredictability on desired results are of particular interest; information about them provides the basis for judgments about project risks.

Typically, there are many sources of useful information. The policy board of the CAP supplies the objectives—the expected results—and very probably some broad outline of the desired timetable of results. The experience of the CAP in past projects and the related experience of other agencies are often helpful. Some other kinds of information commonly relevant to the operational planning and scheduling process in CAPs include:

1. *Personnel requirements:* numbers, skills, experience, whether organization employees or community volunteers are needed
2. *The exact "market" to be served:* a certain segment of the juvenile population, school children, etc., or a certain neighborhood, for example
3. *Time constraints and goals:* a project that must be completed before another can be undertaken, for instance
4. *Other programs:* programs that must be integrated and meshed
5. *Physical requirements:* school space, hospital space, etc.
6. *Other resources required:* supplies, materials, training equipment, etc.
7. *Budget requirements:* how much money must be spent to procure the resources needed and the timing
8. *Community receptiveness:* Will the client population participate? Will the project conflict with any religious or cultural values? How difficult will it be to attract (communicate with) participants?
9. *Participation:* What is the "maximum feasible participation" of the poor? How will their participation affect the outcome? How will it affect planned progress? What extra resources/efforts will it require? How can the project derive maximum benefit from the "expertise" of the participants and give them maximum benefit in return?
10. *Results:* What is the frequency distribution of probable outcomes? That is, what is the range of possible outcomes and side problems? What is the "risk"?
11. *Scheduling:* How much time must be allowed as "slack" to absorb the results of one stage of the program before the next stage can begin?
12. *Public reaction:* What cooperation/objections will the members of the nonparticipant population offer? What is the best way to communicate with them to exchange views of the project?

Usually a formal plan is only as good as the assumptions and intelligence that went into making it; therefore, a statement of those assumptions and that intelligence on relevant variables will be important to many readers of the plan. This entire flow of information from external source to ultimate statement of the plan is a vital part of each CAP management information system.

The planning process—ideally well informed with such information as mentioned—culminates, informed or not, in some statement of actions to be taken, resources to be committed, and results expected. This statement, especially its financial aspect, is often referred to as a budget. A discussion such as this can hardly end without taking up the place of budgeting in the information system of a CAP.

BUDGETING

A budget is the middle ground between a plan and a review of performance. It is both the tool by which the plan is communicated to operating personnel and the standard against which performance is evaluated. Therefore, the essence of budgets and budgeting might be summed up as follows: (1) A budget serves both as control and plan, according to the user, and (2) a budget is largely financial in nature.

The isolation of variables in a budget can be extremely useful; in a profit-motivated organization those variables that affect revenue and cost are of vital importance to the manager and should be included in the budget. One problem in budgeting for a Community Action Program is that the goals of any Community Action Program are financial only in the long run. In the short run, measures of CAP performance are mostly nonfinancial and only partly quantitative. In considering the performance of a CAP for immunization, for example, a manager is interested in how many people can be immunized, how many will be missed, what the costs per immunization are, what kindred effects there may be (such as stimulating parent concern with child health problems), and how the project fits into the overall program. In considering these criteria it seems evident that financial and nonfinancial, quantifiable and nonquantifiable information are all important. It is not clear which is most important; and such is the problem of budgeting for CAPs: *Although the financial cost can be fairly well planned and stated the nonfinancial results often cannot be.*

Control of a Community Action Program—like control of any organization—is a process of measurement. Drucker says, "The basic question is not 'How do we control?' but 'What do we measure in our control system?' "[3] And this is precisely the question that every agency manager must ask himself as he exercises control over the activities of a CAP. What variables must be considered in order to evaluate the progress of the whole organization, individual project, or subpart?

The importance of considering all types of relevant information—demographic, socio-economic, political—without neglecting the importance of the financial budgeting process was stressed earlier. In this discussion of control it should again be emphasized that measurements of all types are indicators of CAP performance but not to the exclusion of, or with sole reliance on, financial cost data. Cost data most often are used as a measure of *efforts*; other information must supply the measure of *effects*.

"EFFORT" MEASUREMENT

The Office of Economic Opportunity has published a *Community Action Program Guide, Financial Instructions* that defines in general terms the type of accounting system expected of a CAP. Such an accounting system is but part of the record system, which includes detailed records such as client contacts, personnel records, correspondence, purchase contracts, etc. The OEO *Instructions* state: "OEO recognizes that the accounting system utilized in grantee organizations will vary from a pure cash receipt and expenditure system to a very extensive accrual system. OEO will not dictate the type and format of the system to be used, since the interest of the Federal Government is satisfied if a system is established which is adequate to account for program funds, which provides accurate and current information relating to program progress, and which may be audited without undue difficulty."[4]

COST ACCOUNTING

In designing, operating, or renewing a CAP cost collection system, the same considerations involved in any managerial accounting system should be taken into account. Such considerations include the materiality of an expense, whether it is variable or fixed, whether it can be assigned to a responsibility center or not, precisely what kind of an expense it is, whether a valid allocation can be made, what goes into any transfer prices, and so forth. Because an accounting system is part of the information system, it should yield relevant and useful information. In this regard, it is well to remember that much information of an accounting nature is meant for users outside the organization—the OEO, the public, Congress, etc.—and as such might not be in useful form for managerial use. Thus, in the design of a cost collection system for a CAP, both the need to report externally and the needs of management must be considered.

The exhibit on the next page shows two account systems; one is designed only to furnish the reporting minimum, and the other is designed to provide management with significant data in excess of the minimum.

The depth and detail of the cost accounts depend on the need for management information. Obviously, if $250 a year is spent on rent and the total grant runs to six figures, there is little justification for collecting any more than minimal data. However, in a situation where labor is the principal expenditure, a relatively complete classification and analysis might be warranted.

A Minimum Cost Account System and a More Inclusive One

Minimum: For a Period

Cost	Program	Components	(Grants)	Total
Personnel				
Consultants				
Travel				
. . .				
Total				

More Inclusive: For a Period

Cost	Responsibility Centers and Components (Grants)					
	Component I					
Overhead	Center A			Center B		
G & A	Budget	Actual	Variance	Budget	Actual	Variance
Personnel						
Consultants						
Travel						
. . .						
O/H Allocation						
Total						
Total	Total–Component I					

	Component II								
Overhead	Center A			Center B			Total		
G & A	Budget	Actual	Variance	Budget	Actual	Variance	Budget	Actual	Variance
Personnel									
Consultants									
Travel									
. . .									
O/H Allocation									
Total									
Total	Total–Component II								

In general, the criteria for judging the appropriateness of a CAP cost system are these:

1. The requirements of external reporting;
2. The requirements of management for planning, controlling, and operating;
3. The essentials for safeguarding assets and ensuring efficient allocations of resources;
4. The cost of collection, summarizing, and reporting.

Incorporated in the budgeting system, at least in complex CAPs, there should be potential for review by exception. The system illustrated in the exhibit has such a potential. In addition to the cost information already discussed, data on receipts, contributions, progress toward fulfilling the community's responsibility to contribute X per cent, etc. must be collected, processed, and reported. Such information is an important part of the system, but it is probably not as voluminous as the cost information in most cases. The accounting system to handle this task should reflect the same considerations as the cost collection system, namely, external reporting requirements, internal management requirements, basic efficiency and protection requirements, and the cost of the system itself. The reporting for this portion of the financial information, like cost reporting, should be on an exception basis.

MEASUREMENT OF "EFFECT"

The following passage illustrates the problem of measuring the effects of Community Action Programs: "How does the data required differ from that necessary to measure the performance of an industrial concern or a commercial enterprise? Of course, the War on Poverty does not have a profit motive in the business sense; but in all other respects the similarity is striking! Businesses as well as any of the programs of the Office of Economic Opportunity have goals they attempt to reach through a plan. . . . . They can compare the results obtained after a given period of time to the results which were expected from the plan and then take the necessary corrective action. By reporting against the plan they can measure both performance and can also update the plan, review the allocation of resources procedure, identify the areas which deserve more attention to meet objectives on schedule, and, finally, provide the information necessary for internal management as well as the data which will satisfy public demand."[5]

The ultimate success of every poverty program would be elimination of the causes and effects of those social conditions defined as poverty. In movement toward this ultimate goal, many subgoals will be set that should build toward final accomplishment, and one subgoal certainly will be basic CAP management efficiency, including a system for recording, retrieving, and using financial data.

But a CAP that does not ultimately contribute to elimination of poverty is not successful, regardless of how sophisticated its cost accounting system may be. Similarly, any CAP that alleviates poverty in its assigned geographic area is successful; the lack of an adequate accounting system might decrease its efficiency but does not take away from its ultimate success. The essential task in CAP performance measurement, then, is to evaluate its success in affecting the indicators of poverty considered representative of community ills.

There is no definitive list of indicators for measuring this success, nor are there definitive methods of collecting data. Because the problems are unique and diverse, the statistics and procedures must also be diverse. But some indicators may be common to many CAPs. The Detroit system has designed into it a selection of indicators, covering a broad range of variables and sources of data, that might be generally applicable to many other CAPs.[6] They include the following:

Police Department offense complaints;
Police Department arrests;
Police Department Youth Bureau contacts;
Police Women's Division law enforcement;
City Welfare relief openings;
City Welfare food stamp openings;
City Welfare food stamp closings;
Registration Bureau service inquiries;
Visiting Nurses service requests;
Social Hygiene Clinic VD cases;
Tuberculosis Clinic TB cases;
Sanitary Engineering complaints and violations;
Health Department births;
Health Department deaths;
Health Department stillbirths;
State Welfare Aid to Dependent Children openings;
State Welfare Aid to Dependent Children closings;
State Unemployment openings;
State Unemployment closings;
State Welfare Old Age Assistance Aid to the Disabled or Blind openings;
State Welfare Old Age Assistance Aid to the Disabled or Blind closings;
Legal Aid Bureau requests for aid;
Board of Education truancy;
Board of Education dropouts.

This list suggests the type of analysis that is required to evaluate the success of a CAP. In very large programs a sophisticated computerized system might be necessary. In smaller programs a manual system with many fewer indicators might be adequate. For example, actual canvasses of the poverty population and area or use of a sampling technique might be possible, depending on the size and diversity of the problem area.

The CAP's primary tasks are to identify the problem of poverty, its causes, and its effects and to plan to alleviate those factors. The variables that indicate the existence of poverty to the planner ought to be, of course, among the variables used to measure program success. For example, it's obvious that for any program meant to improve school dropout rates the change in dropout rate should be an indicator of success.

The essence of CAP control is to seek out those measurements and measurement techniques that indicate progress toward meeting established goals. Necessary for such measurement are a stated set of goals and a plan of action against which to compare the results of efforts.

The list of social indicators offered earlier could be extended, of course. Some indicators may very well be inexact, perhaps even misleading, but this should not detract from the search for variables to test progress. If CAP managers are to allocate efforts effectively, they must have indicators of success; if the taxpaying public—through its legislators—is to continue to support programs, measures of overall performance must be made available.

Our examination leads us to the following conclusions about management information for community action programs.

1. The task of managing a CAP is quite complex and is different in important respects from the task of managing a profit-oriented business. A management information system provides a means of linking objectives to management processes, processes to efforts, and efforts to achievement. The nature of the CAP requires careful attention to the design of the management information system to provide information for goal formulation, project selection, operational planning and budgeting, and control and appraisal of progress and performance.

2. In most cases the management information for a CAP will have to be created by program managers for each program. Differences between programs prohibit creation of a standard system for all CAPs. A system to provide needed information should be installed at the inception of a program, nurtured to develop needed information if it is not originally available, and evaluated periodically to eliminate useless data or unnecessary detail.

3. Planning processes in a CAP depend upon management information just as they do in a business. Planning forms a basis for operational statements such as budgets which direct activity and provide a basis for performance review and control. The management information system is the communication link among each of these processes.

4. Control of a CAP depends upon the measurement of *effect* as well as *effort*. Control of efforts is required by the public nature of support for the CAP; evaluation of effects is required for sound allocation of resources and for evaluation of the alternative courses of action open to a program.

5. When the management information system is operating, planning and control processes operate simultaneously, each providing data and information for the other. Haphazard phasing of these processes is eliminated, and the likelihood of effective use of resources is increased. Data on efforts and effects provided for control lead to information for goal formulation, organization analysis, and project selection. Goals and plans lead to statements of expected results to which actual performance can be compared. Management information becomes the basis for systematic management.

FOOTNOTES

1. *The Dimensions and Location of Poverty in Burlington County, New Jersey,* a report prepared at the request of the Rural Community Action Program, New Jersey State Office of Economic Opportunity (Rutgers University, New Brunswick, N. J., 1965).

2. United States Office of Economic Opportunity, *Community Action Program Guide,* 2 vols. (Government Printing Office, Washington, 1965).

3. Peter F. Drucker, "Controls, Control and Management," *Management Controls; New Directions in Basic Research,* Charles P. Bonini, editor (McGraw-Hill Book Company, New York, 1964), p. 289.

4. United States Office of Economic Opportunity, *op cit.,* Vol. II: *Financial Instructions,* p. 15.

5. Jean-Paul A. Ruff, "Poverty Programs—A Business Management Approach," *Touche, Ross, Bailey and Smart Quarterly* (June, 1966), pp. 24–25.

QUESTIONS

1. What is the ultimate goal of the poverty program?

2. "CAPs were meant to be innovative and aggressive; to be successfully so, their managements need a realistic understanding of the poverty environment in which they work." Would this also be true of CPAs who work with CAPs? If so, how can CPAs obtain this understanding?

3. How does this article show that the CPA must be concerned with more than just reporting financial facts?

4. What are the OEO requirements for a Community Action Program's accounting system?

5. "Cost data most often are used as a measure of efforts; other information must supply the measure of effects." How does an income statement reflect this idea?

6. Carefully study the exhibit in this article. In your own words, describe the sort of useful information you would expect to obtain from the middle report ("Component I").

7. How are the information requirements of a Community Action Program similar to those of a business firm? How are they different?

8. ". . . the lack of an adequate accounting system might decrease (a CAP's) efficiency but does not take away from its ultimate success." Do you agree? Explain.

9. "If the taxpaying public—through its legislators—is to continue to support programs, measures of overall performance must be made available." As a taxpayer, list several of the measures of performance you would like to see for a Community Action Program. (Note: it might be helpful to scan Section VIII of this book, "Accounting for Social Progress," before answering.)

10. Invite the executive director or some other official of a local Community Action Program to class to discuss (1) the information needed to effectively operate the program; (2) how accountants—both internal and external—have helped (and maybe how they have hindered) the program.

How an accounting firm helped set up an effective management information system by quantifying the unmeasurable aspects of human needs for Detroit's war on poverty.

The Modern Management Approach to a Program of Social Improvement

by Robert Beyer

America the beautiful has an ugly scar across her face.

Her cities are torn by violence and crime. Prejudice and racial hatred flare harshly. Her rivers and streams are polluted. Her hospitals are overcrowded and poorly staffed.

Despite much-publicized affluence, pockets of poverty throughout the nation swell with bitter and hopeless men and women in search of dignity, opportunity and self-respect.

Something has gone wrong in our society and something must be done to correct it. Not next year. Not tomorrow. But now.

SOURCE: Reprinted by permission of the author and the publisher from The Journal of Accountancy (March 1969), pp. 37–46. Copyright 1969 by the American Institute of Certified Public Accountants, Inc.

This is not to say that nothing has been done, or is being done. Billions of dollars are being poured into action programs designed to alleviate society's ills. The question is: How effectively is this money being used?

Are the programs reaching the right people? Are we properly defining the needs of the disadvantaged? Are we attending to the needs in their proper order of priority? Are we paying sufficient attention to alternative ways of helping the poor? Are we reversing the tides of deterioration in our nation?

It would be difficult for even the most talented administrator, program director, or sociologist to come up with precise answers to such questions if left to his own devices. But aided by the accountant's knowledge of handling data, he should be able to set up a system to measure these so-called unmeasurable aspects of human needs.[1]

Touche, Ross, Bailey & Smart pioneered such a project in 1965 for Detroit's war on poverty. The firm was asked to work with the Mayor's Committee for Human Resource Development to structure a modern information and management system that would help the city with its vast and complex problems.

We thought the project challenging and agreed to try to design and develop such a system.

The preliminary survey took about a month. During this time the management services consultants, supervised by Jean-Paul Ruff, who had been working since 1960 on measuring nonmeasurables in terms of human needs, examined what information was currently being generated and how, and what further information would be needed to manage the program most effectively. The information requirement boiled down into two main categories: (1) data needed to justify the appropriations of the funding agencies involved, most notably the number of clients to be served (the hard practicality of the matter is that without proper justification, funding is not possible); (2) internal information needed to upgrade the effectiveness of management judgments and action.

Mr. Ruff and his management team studied objectives of the organizations participating in the program. They attended several meetings organized by program administrators and held in modern business offices. Other meetings called by loosely organized groups representing the city's poor were held in empty flats. Present at the meetings was a cross section of program administrators, educators and sociologists; also counselor-aides and members of the hard-core poor and unemployed along with their leaders and representatives.

Based on the preliminary analysis, a set of basic conclusions was drawn up:
1. It is vital to the success of the program that maximum participation of the poor be achieved in defining client needs, determining corrective actions to be taken, and setting goals.
2. A definition of client needs must be clearly spelled out and agreed upon by all parties involved in the program, recipients as well as planners and administrators.
3. Prompt and decisive action must be taken to streamline paperwork and simplify business type problems.

Two principal objectives were spelled out following the preliminary investigation. The first was short-range. Its purpose was to design a system for keeping track of individual clients and services rendered. This would establish a foundation for analysis and it would generate the data required for funding and action. It would also establish a base for the overall system. As experience testifies, a system is no more effective than the input it receives.

Objective number two, the long-range goal, was to outline the total management system. This was designed to measure what had been done in the past in order to improve on a continuing basis the effectiveness of future planning and action. Subgoals of the total management system were:

1. Measure the relative urgency of various client needs.
2. Measure the resources—manpower, money, equipment, supplies, etc.—available to meet these needs.
3. Develop techniques to assess the alternative plans proposed for the allocation of available resources.
4. Provide the methodology for responding to changes in concept or procedure with regard to any aspect of the program when the measurement program indicates the desirability of such change.
5. Set up an information feedback network that would serve management in its continuing effort to optimize its planning and action.

After the preliminary analysis was completed, we were asked to continue working with the mayor's committee to design and develop the total management program.

THE MODERN MANAGEMENT APPROACH

The social accounting program which Mr. Ruff's team used is unique. For one thing, it quantifies and measures human needs and characteristics—long deemed incommensurable. For another, it utilizes concepts familiar to business systems and technology of modern management.

The basic differences between social and corporate management are well recognized. In social endeavors the chief "product" involved is the fulfillment of human needs. Thus no traditional market results are available to gauge the effectiveness of "product development"—in this case, the effectiveness of action programs that are instituted.

On the other hand, experience shows that important similarities exist between administering a large-scale social improvement program and running a corporation. In each case substantial resources of manpower, money and equipment must be allocated. Complex problems arise in both enterprises, and fact-based management decisions are required to solve them.

By using the strategies and technology of modern management, the social accounting program provides what is needed by the sociological community: a built-in system of evaluation and feedback which continuously assesses not only results, but the measurement system itself, thereby upgrading the organization, planning and implementation of resource allocation.

The concept of the social accounting program is easy to understand and can be implemented by accounting firms of various sizes for projects that differ in size and complexity. But one thing should always be remembered: It is the accountant's job to handle the data; not to decide what data to handle. That task is turned over to the sociologists, psychologists and other staff of the program. A social accounting program is by its nature an interdisciplinary effort.

Objective number one is to point out and measure the individual's needs. This provides the input that is required to extend the measurement to groups of people. Once individual and group needs are determined, the program will work out the distribution of the means best suited to take care of the needs. After this, the results are measured.

The social accounting program then answers the questions that administrators, sociologists, program directors and funding agencies need to have answered to get maximum value out of dollars invested: What has to be done? What resources do we have to do it with? What plans do we need to do it? How are we doing it? What do we do next?

How can this total picture be obtained readily? The system is highly computerized. It takes full advantage of sophisticated scientific management strategies such as operations research, simulation and linear programing. It applies advanced managerial concepts and eliminates guesswork with proven professional controls.

Thus, with optimum flexibility assured, traditional limitations cannot scotch objectives.

But what about the measurement? Is it foolproof? Far from it. At the outset it will be full of flaws. But the important point—and one that planners increasingly are coming to recognize—is that even a relatively uncertain system of measurement is more desirable than no measurement at all. The trick is to structure the system so that it continuously evaluates and upgrades all aspects of the program so that it will be refined to a high degree of reliability.

THE BASE LINE DATA SYSTEM

Information about individual clients—the term used by most social service agencies to designate recipients of aid—is recorded in the base line data file. The BLD file consists of three main categories of information:

Client Information.   This includes name and address, age, sex, etc., along with the identification number assigned to every client. The information is recorded only once and is normally located at the site of the first interview. An on-line identification center for the entire system is maintained at a point accessible by telephone from every service agency. The pooling of client identification data is handled by phone rather than computer for a number of reasons. For one thing, it is the easiest way for nontechnical people to operate.

Also, the effect of this arrangement is to eliminate client harassment. Traditionally, in a multiservice organization, the recipient is shunted from office to office and required to recite for interviewers the same information again and again.

Under the base line data system, when a client appears at a service point a second time, a call is placed to determine whether he is a former client. If he is, his file is located, and repetitious questioning dispensed with.

The base line data system also assures the confidentiality of the client file. The identification center is authorized to communicate only two kinds of information: the client's routine identification data, and the location of his BLD file. The file is available only at the source location and at the discretion of the agency or program director. It is not available to clerical personnel, and cannot be given to the unauthorized caller.

Objective Client Data.   This portion of the BLD file records information required by the funding organization relating to the housing of clients, their employment, schooling, health, etc. It is not so much the purpose of the system to keep on hand all information about the individual as it is to locate the source of such information when it is needed. Thus the client's medical file, as an example, might be in his base line data file.

The objective data is not a diagnostic tool. It is sometimes used by the social service agent to help with decisions regarding client eligibility to participate in certain programs. It is also used to prepare required statistical reports.

The amount of objective information used varies. This would depend on the needs and reporting requirements of the agency through which the client is processed. Often no more than 15 or 20 per cent of the Objective Client Data is utilized. But if it is required, it is available.

Client's Service History.   This section of the file records what happens to the client as he takes advantage of the services offered. It is used for reporting purposes, and as a follow-up on the client's activity and progress. Each quarter the program generates a report showing the current status of each client. This encompasses all clients and all agencies. Thus an up-to-date record of client activity is available on a year-round basis.

Also, as will be seen later, the client's service history is used in combination with the identification portion of the base line data file to generate samples needed for the measurement of client needs.

HOW THE BASE LINE DATA SYSTEM WORKS

Identification, historical and service information is fed into the system at client entrance points and service agencies. Standard checks and controls of the type used in modern corporate accounting systems insure maximum accuracy. The problem of reliability was tackled early. Pitfalls and hazards were taken into account as carefully as they would be in setting up a corporate payroll or accounts receivable system. One such consideration was the large number of clerical personnel that would be needed to operate the system. Another was a predictably high rate of turnover. A third was the average person's lack of familiarity with accounting and numbering systems.

Thus one target agreed upon was maximum centralization and control. As a result, the program requires that base line data be centrally edited by a small group of personnel trained by the agency with the help of the consultants. They are to be guided by a set of clear, simple and carefully spelled-out rules. Control functions are designed to be further mechanized through a small third generation computer programed in COBOL to generate exception reports which indicate clerical errors, incomplete information, missing documents, questionable logic and the like.

Provisions are also made for the responsibility for accuracy to be channeled to a single control person whose job it will be to correct errors and see to it that data flows properly to and from the various input and output points of the computerized system.

Finally, the computer will be utilized on a monthly basis for the updating of all files and the production of reports. As is the case with any computerized system, reporting becomes an automatic by-product of the data fed into the system.

If the practitioner has no direct access to a computer installation, he can expect to use the system of the municipality or organization engaging his services, since most programs of this type are linked to a large organization.

Generally speaking the base line data system has been designed to produce two kinds of reports. The first includes all of the documentation that is required for funding and statistical purposes.

The second are those necessary for better management of the service centers. Here typical examples would include: current status and completion results by service; number of clients referred to, and placed with, each major service according to referring service; services requested and services referred to for new clients by location of client intake; source of intake by intake location.

What's most important is that base line data reports can be produced in time to allow prompt action on the conditions revealed. They can be produced in time to anticipate trouble before it erupts and to make changes and adjustments as required. Many other reports which formerly were not feasible because of time or cost factors involved can now be routinely generated at minimum cost because the required data is already available on punched cards or magnetic tape ready to be fed into the computer.

HOW THE INDIVIDUAL IS MEASURED

How does one determine and definitively state the needs of socially disadvantaged persons in a particular area? The idea is to start from the base of a single individual. If the needs of one person can be determined and quantitatively expressed, samples can be taken and aggregate population figures extrapolated in accordance with accepted statistical procedures.

In setting up a measurement system, the logical place to start is with the client population. The needs selected by the clients and social scientists in the program are those which, improved by the social action endeavors, will work to achieve the objectives of the program. Suppose, for example, we are dealing with a system designed to upgrade the level of public health. The needs would be defined to include such significant factors as speed of health care, accessibility of emergency services, availability of nursing care, pollution controls, etc.

Or take a poverty program. Here health, as a prime factor determining the employability of people, would be a characteristic in itself.

For each characteristic relating to the program's objective—in this case, the elimination of poverty—a numerical scale will be structured through consultation with the needy. What follows is an illustration of how a typical health scale might look:

Health Scale Model

Rating	Condition of Health
7	Excellent health
6	Generally good health with minor problems
5	Some health problems requiring doctor's care between two and four weeks
4	Continual poor health or periodical health lapses
3	Severe health problems requiring continuous doctor's care
2	Very severe health problems requiring periodic hospitalization
1	Failing health or continuous hospitalization

The poor should have a major role as well in the setting of needs priorities because the more accurately the needs set up by the program mirror the true feelings of the disadvantaged, the more successful the program will be.

It is also important in setting up a measurement system not to lose sight of what it is we are trying to measure. In a poverty program, for example, the goal is to identify all characteristics that contribute to poverty. In our health example, regardless of why the client's health is poor, measurement must be geared to reflect the amount of financial impairment imposed on the individual. Thus a client whose cancer is under control might rate higher on the scale than a person suffering from an ingrown toenail, since the former could function economically and the latter could not.

Finally, for each characteristic a target level is defined at which the client is in a position to stand on his own feet and, therefore, be terminated as a client. Thus the individual need is measured by the difference between a person's current rating and the level defined as acceptable.

What constitutes an acceptable level for a given characteristic? Experience has taught us that the actual level labeled as "acceptable" is not an all-important factor. As we shall see, the impact of this decision will be practically tempered by the varying weights assigned to the different population types.

RELATIVE IMPORTANCE OF CHARACTERISTICS

It's obvious that the work experience of a four-year-old child is unimportant regardless of how the work experience scale may read. There are thus two choices: to change the scale when considering a four-year-old child; or set up a series of weights to reflect the relative importance of work experience where a four-year-old child is concerned. Taking this latter and more practical course of action, the question now arises: In establishing weights, into how many different segments should the population be divided? And should other criteria besides age—i.e., sex, race, nationality—figure in the picture?

Working on this aspect of the program, the social scientists and administrators, the clients and the accountants decided that age, sex and race might all be valid criteria. The population was then broken down into 72 categories to reflect all significant combinations involved. When the results of this breakdown were analyzed, it was found that race was a totally indifferent criterion and that it had no effect on the weights. Though blacks may have more needs than whites, the conclusion was reached that in this situation the relative importance of needs is the same for people of all races.

As a result of these findings, the table of types was revised, reducing the original 72 categories to 11 basic types.

A set of weights was produced to reflect the importance of each need for each population type. The scale for each need will be tempered by the individual weights applied, and the acceptable level will be modified to meet the requirements of each population type.

THE INDIVIDUAL

The ultimate objective, in developing input data that properly reflects the client population, is to establish a profile for each individual with his current needs and his target levels spelled out. Source material can be obtained in either of two ways. It can be developed through depth analysis involving long question-naires and the services of professional social scientists. This method has proved to be time consuming, expensive, and not well received by the people being served. In addition, there is no proof that depth analysis produces more accurate results. The more practical method is for the sponsoring agency to train nonprofessional interviewers, and equip them with decision tables, procedure manuals and other aids.

In any case, after the necessary data is obtained, a profile for each client is drawn (see chart). This ties in with the base line data system. It enables statistical samples to be taken and extrapolations to be made to determine aggregate needs for the total population and for each segment of the population by client type and location category.

John Doe's total needs are 327, of which 80 derive from insufficient family income, 51 from inadequate education and training, etc. For the program to succeed, it must eliminate the needs specified and terminate him as a client.

This can also be used to measure any nonclient (a disadvantaged person not yet absorbed into the system)—at any time and at the completion of services. The measurement of nonclients as well as clients is significant, since it is the program's objective to serve all members of the community.

DEFINITION OF PROGRAMS

However well the program director is fortified with the ammunition of modern management, his work is still cut out for him. His main task is to use the resources available to him to fulfill the greatest number of needs in the shortest time. The system and the planning model he utilizes to distribute resources to the program will make all the difference.

Before resource distribution can be optimized, each program must be defined in terms of: (1) the number of needs it is capable of fulfilling for each type included in the client population, (2) the number of people of each type that might be helped under each of a variety of alternative programs, and (3) the number of resources required for operation under each of the alternatives specified.

Program alternatives are important. Most programs can be designed to operate with differing numbers of participants and a variety of client types. As long as the anticipated benefits per participant are the same, each level considered is a program alternative.

Client Profile—John Doe

Characteristic	Condition	Rating	Acceptable Level	Nonweighted Need	Weight	Weighted Need
Health	Some health problems	5	6	1	20	20
Employment status	Part time, irregular	10	15	5	12	60
Work experience	Mechanic 2 years	4	7	3	13	39
Education and training	10th grade, no vocat'l	4	7	3	17	51
Housing	Sound, 1.6 pers.pr.rm.	9	14	5	7	35
Family income	$2,650	8	16	8	10	80
Public assistance income	None	0	0	0	4	0
Family stability	Nonsupportive, adequate	3	7	4	9	36
Social problems	No relevant problems	7	7	0	6	0
Urban adjustment	Moderate	4	7	3	2	6
					Total Needs	327

Evaluation of alternatives—before selection, while in progress, and after completion—is of key importance. To insure that dollar investment is sound, an answer to this question should be available at any time: To what degree is this program succeeding in the fulfillment of client needs?

This question has often been asked by social scientists, program administrators, funding agencies and representatives of the poor. In most cases, straight and simple answers have been hard to come by.

In designing the social accounting program, our management services group made a special effort to provide these answers. A key objective was the simplification of the communications and intelligence gathering effort. The voluminous documentation traditionally used to evaluate programs and decide on alternatives has been distilled to a single sheet of paper that the program director and other interested parties can easily absorb. Titled the program report, it provides a clear, simple, and total picture with regard to needs, resources, participants and benefits, both anticipated and achieved.

The program report serves as both a guide and a control. Unlike prior planning aids, it requires the program director to include alternatives for each program proposed and to specify the number and type of clients involved. Equipped with a total information picture one may easily find the most promising program alternatives and reveal planning weaknesses.

Perhaps the single phrase that plagues a program director most consistently is "What if . . . ?"

Suppose that a particular need is not being adequately improved. What action should the program director take? Here again scientific planning generates valuable leads to conclusions. Perhaps the need is unfulfilled because no program exists to fulfill it. Perhaps it is unfulfilled because a program is not being implemented. Whatever the reason, planning, made simpler and more systematic by such tools as the program report, enables the program director to base his critical judgment on the evidence of proven results rather than on guesswork.

Another factor contributing to the replacement of instinct by scientific judgments is the program's use of the mathematical model and sophisticated simulation techniques to assist the decision-making process. The computer's ability to formulate program by program comparisons, to analyze different alternatives, combinations of programs, and varieties of client mixes is virtually unlimited. Never before has management been better equipped to test the workability of a proposed effort before committing its resources to use. Guided by simulation we are able to superimpose any number of factors and probabilities on the model.

RESULTS EVALUATION

Evaluation after the fact is another consideration of importance to the program director and to all agencies involved in the social improvement effort. Program

X, for example, has been in operation two years. How well is it doing in comparison with other programs? Is it living up to expectations? These questions involve difficult and complex aspects of social program management where multiservice operations are in force.

Many clients participate in more than one program. Assume, for example, that during the past 12 months client Jane Doe took advantage of a health program, an educational program, a social adjustment program. Today, gainfully employed, she is no longer a client. Where should credit for the fulfillment of her needs be applied? Obviously, an accurate evaluation of the existing plan is essential if we are to determine the best course of action to take for future Jane Does.

The social accounting program is geared to provide such assessment for single programs and for any combination of multiple programs through which a client might be processed. Consider, for example, the case of three clients. Client 1 goes through Program A, eliminating 10 of his needs, Client 2 goes through Program B, eliminating 90 of his needs. Client 3, taking advantage of both programs, A and B, has 130 of his needs eliminated. It is necessary in a system of results evaluation—the equivalent of profitability accounting in corporate management—to assign credit for achievements gained in order to evaluate the effectiveness of dollars invested. In our illustration, therefore, 10 per cent of the credit where Client 3 was concerned might be applied to Program A and 90 per cent to Program B on the basis of individual gains recorded. Though not necessarily accurate, it is one way of dealing with intangible elements and allocating credit in a practical and consistent manner.

ALLOCATION OF RESOURCES

Let us return briefly to the commercial enterprise analogy. Marketing research, we will assume, has told us what is needed and wanted. What next? At this point in a manufacturing operation, production would be consulted to determine what tools, materials, facilities and manpower we would need to function at various levels of productivity. By matching the resources to the needs of the program, a production schedule would be developed. Next, the schedule would be reviewed, alternative strategies considered, and a final plan evolved. Later, when the plan went into effect, results would be reported and compared with expected production.

Resource allocation under the social accounting program follows this same general concept. However, under a production setup dealing with human needs instead of widgets, unique problems and uncertainties arise. Program constraints relating to manpower availability, budget, equipment shortages and other resource limitations complicate the planner's life to a greater degree than they do in industry.

For example, if earmarked funds enter the program as a constraint, to what degree will needs be fulfilled? On the other hand, if the constraint is removed, in what measure would the need fulfillment be altered? The difference between need fulfillment with and without the earmarking constraint is a measure of the constraint's cost.

The social accounting program's mathematical model has been geared to answer such questions. It helps to identify the best theoretical allocation of resources to programs in order to reduce the inventory of needs to a minimum compatible with given constraints.

STRUCTURING OF POLICY CONSTRAINTS

This does not imply that allocation alternatives generated by the computer are always satisfactory. To illustrate, in one case analysis might indicate that not enough was done to reduce certain education needs. Perhaps 5 million needs exist, but the program calls for elimination of only 3 million. And analysis produces the conclusion that taking care of at least one million, or 50 per cent of the remaining unfulfilled needs, is of prime importance to the program. The program director might therefore introduce a policy constraint which states that the additional one million needs must be eliminated within a given period. The question is how many other needs must be sacrificed to satisfy the constraint.

Needless to say, the structuring of such policy constraints will have an important bearing on the distribution of resources and the fulfillment of needs. Under the social accounting program, the policy constraints would be first introduced as input to the mathematical model. Each constraint will be tested by simulation and an analysis of its effect made, independently and in combination with other constraints. Aided by the analysis, the program director will be able to determine which constraints are feasible, where adjustments are needed, where new possible constraints are required.

When the simulation process is completed and all policies sharpened, refined and agreed upon, the net result will be a listing of policy decisions designed to put available resources to use to fulfill the most needs in the least time. This listing would be available to the press, to funding agencies, to representatives of the poor, and to other interested parties. Most important, the program director would have at his fingertips the documentation required to explain why particular policies were selected, and to relate policies to needs and accomplishments to policies.

The mathematical model, apart from its usefulness in supporting and justifying key decisions, functions primarily as a decision-making tool. It computes costs, explores innumerable alternatives, makes endless tests and comparisons at microsecond speeds. Quantification of the model's input is consistent with methods previously described.

The overriding objective, of course, is to whittle down to negotiable size the infinitely expandable number of "ifs" that crop up during the course of any social improvement program.

A key aim of the model is to produce a detailed operational plan for every program in force. This plan will include the number of participants expected by type and location, the needs expected to be fulfilled, and the resources that will be required for fulfillment. As a by-product of the plan, the budget will be prepared.

In another sense the planning model serves as special consultant to the program director. He might ask the computer: "What will be the effect on employment needs reduction if child day care services are increased by 30 per cent?"

Good, bad, or indifferent, the computer would take about ten seconds to come up with an answer.

SYSTEM REPORTING AND FLEXIBILITY

Although the measurement process begins with initial determination of the individual needs, the client profile is a starting point and no more. However scrupulously drawn, it is subject to the imperfections of human judgment, as are the programs designed to eliminate human needs. Thus, to work effectively, a measurement system must be designed with the goal of continuing improvement in mind.

Needs rarely remain static. They improve, or intensify. They are influenced by many factors, some of them outside the program. The degree to which they are reduced, and the time it takes for reduction to occur, is the acid test of a program's success. Continuing measurement, reliably controlled in the best accounting tradition, provides a valuable instrument of continuing evaluation. The absence of this ingredient is responsible for the failure of more social improvement programs in the past than any other single factor.

The feedback reporting system of our social accounting program has been tailored to measure progress. It is achieved by selecting random samples from the base line data file at given points of time. The sample data determines the total contribution of each program by need characteristic and client type. It also allocates specific contributions to specific programs where clients participate in two programs or more.

The beauty of a well-organized computer-based system is its great flexibility. Once data is gathered, checked for accuracy and validity and fed into the program, it may be recalled at will, and at electronic speeds to provide feedback reporting in any form desired.

The social accounting program's feedback system has been geared to measure program results at different stages of development. Reports compare planned and actual results. They record contributions by program and location for specified periods of time. Changes in client need characteristics are reflected, not months later, but as the changes are taking place, so that corrective action can be taken as required. This is essential because social measurement and resource allocation are in a constant state of flux. It would be significant for a program director to know, for example, that, after 10 weeks of a 52-week program, 90 per cent of all benefits expected were already obtained.

Feedback reporting helps police the entire endeavor. Where programs do not perform in line with expectations, variance reports are produced that point out problem areas in need of attention and revision.

Most men of conscience like to feel they are contributing to the betterment of society. One would be hard-pressed to find an undertaking more gratifying to the professional accountant then personal involvement in the social improvement effort described. We believe the main benefits of this modern management approach to social action accounting to be the following:

1. The program upgrades the efficiency of administration and processing at all levels.
2. It centralizes and consolidates client information, permitting better analysis while providing the utmost in the confidentiality of privileged client information.
3. It satisfies the management information system reporting requirements of the funding agency, whether government or private.
4. Client needs and program resources are consistently quantified on an individual and aggregate basis. The system's input and output are scientifically controlled and reliably measured in the best traditions of management science and professional accounting.
5. Resources are allocated on a pre-planned and pre-tested basis.
6. Advanced and sophisticated techniques of operations research, simulation and linear programing are applied to refine the analysis of individual programs and program alternatives.
7. The social accounting program takes into account the constantly changing needs of a dynamic client population—influenced by factors both internal and external to the program. Measurement and evaluation are continuous.

The social accounting program, though initially designed for Detroit's war on poverty, is equally applicable to other areas of social improvement such as health, education, air and water pollution, housing, etc. Though programs vary substantially from area to area and problem to problem, the general concepts of scientific management, measurement and control are broadly superimposable.

Does any of this imply that the system described is infallible? Far from it. Flaws most certainly exist. Certain aspects of the program are debatable.

But in attempting to improve the quality and effectiveness of social action programs, no guide serves so well as hard-won experience. "After the event," as Homer said, "even a fool is wise." But experience in the area of social improvement, however well conceived and formulated the research, diminishes in value as time passes. Conditions in the disadvantaged community change drastically from month to month and year to year. For research to be constructive, conclusions must be predicated on today's situation and tomorrow's needs as well as on yesterday's historical data.

With this in mind, we are of the "action now" school. The objective, we believe, is to get the best possible program under way as rapidly as possible. Gradually, as results are examined and expectations continuously compared against performance, improvements will be made, and imperfections worked out of the system in a scientifically controlled debugging operation.

In the meantime progress, long overdue, will be made.

FOOTNOTE

1. David F. Linowes, "Socio-Economic Accounting," *The Journal of Accountancy,* November 1968, p. 37.

QUESTIONS

1. (a) What is a "social accounting program"?

   (b) Two criticisms of the social accounting program described might be that (1) it's too sophisticated, too difficult for the user (who's not an expert) to understand, and (2) it's too expensive, requiring the use of a computer and costly mathematical techniques. Evaluate these possible criticisms.

2. Summarize in two or three paragraphs the work done by Touche Ross for Detroit's war on poverty.

3. What has been the most important single factor in the failure of social improvement programs in the past, according to Beyer?

4. "The basic differences between social and corporate management are well recognized." What are these basic differences? What are the similarities?

5. What types of information does the base line data file contain?

6. Describe the reports the base line data system is designed to produce.

7. "It is the accountant's job to handle the data; not to decide what data to handle."

   (a) Does this mean that accountants are to collect and report all data?

   (b) Does the accountant choose what data to report?

(c) Do you agree with this quotation? Why?

8. Frequently poverty agencies must obtain and store information about clients of a confidential nature. How does the Detroit program protect the clients' right to privacy?

9. In the exemplary client profile given in the article, John Doe's total needs are 327. Explain, in simple terms, the meaning of this figure.

10. Summarize the expected benefits of the "modern management approach to social action accounting."

The author points out the impact of the Federal Medicare Program on the accounting profession and the accountant's place in the program.

Medicare – So What?

by Frank J. Imke

Probably all CPAs are aware that a multibillion dollar medicare program became effective July 1, 1966. Apparently many of them are not aware of the obligations, challenges, and opportunities the program presents for the public accounting profession. One hospital official recently said, "not only do the CPAs not know about the accounting implications of medicare, they don't seem to care." And, a CPA who has been closely associated with the accounting problems presented by medicare stated that he was embarrassed for his profession that CPAs were so uninformed and unconcerned about the accounting problems of medical services organizations. Such observations may excessively accentuate the negative. Apparently, however, CPAs are not adequately providing a needed service that is within their area of responsibility.

Traditionally, components of the medical and health care services have tended to avoid constraints, both real and imaginary, generally associated with efficient business operations. To place emphasis on business efficiency would, it was feared, result in less desirable and perhaps less effective medical care. Many hospitals and other health care units have sought to maintain a personal, family-type operation. Undoubtedly it is necessary to preserve an element of the

SOURCE: Reprinted by permission of the author and the publisher from The Texas CPA (April 1967), pp. 29–32.

159

"personal touch" in health care services. However, since medical services now constitutes one of the largest economic sectors, it must be recognized as big business, and the individual operating units must seek certain economies and efficiencies associated with well-managed business operations.

A trend toward increased business efficiency had been well established before the advent of the medicare program. For example, many hospitals had hired controllers, engaged independent auditors, and utilized CPAs in various types of management services engagements. Also, the American Hospital Association had prepared guides to accounting systems and cost-finding techniques for hospitals. Requirements associated with administration of the medicare program are causing a significant acceleration in the trend. The introduction of medicare has compounded the accounting problems of the providers of medical services to a degree that is yet to be fully understood.

Medicare has gone into effect in a tentative atmosphere—many questions remain unanswered, many problems are unsolved. Decisions and solutions that evolve during this initial period will be instrumental in shaping the future of the medicare program. Whether or not CPAs as individuals are in sympathy with the program, as professional accountants they should be interested in helping to assure that wide decisions and efficient solutions are forthcoming in its administration. Therein lies an opportunity for an important service to society.

THE MEDICARE PROGRAM

In general, the medicare program provides that persons 65 and over may have in-patient hospital services, post-hospital extended care services, post-hospital home health services, out-patient hospital diagnostic services, and medical and other health services paid for by the Federal government. The program is administered by the Social Security Administration in accordance with provisions of Public Law 89-97. Responsibility for supervising the program and monitoring the costs incurred under the program has been delegated to "fiscal intermediaries." In most of the states, the fiscal intermediary function will be performed by Blue Cross-Blue Shield associations. In other states, and in those states where more than one intermediary has been selected, some insurance companies have been selected as fiscal intermediaries.

Specifically, the fiscal intermediaries will apply principles of reimbursement established by the Social Security Administration and make payments to providers of services. The principles were published in the Federal Register, June 2, 1966, under the title "Principles for Reimbursable Costs." The principles offer certain alternatives and options designed to fit unique circumstances of a provider. Further, the principles include alternatives that may be selected until such time as adequate systems can be established for the collection of statistical and financial data necessary for accurate cost determinations. The fiscal intermediary also has the responsibility for furnishing consultative services to providers for the purpose of developing accounting and cost-finding systems.

CPAs HELP NEEDED

Obviously the fiscal intermediaries and the providers of medicare services need accounting know-how in establishing and administering the program—systems, cost finding techniques, reimbursement procedures, and auditing. The principles for reimbursement, for example, are based on the following objectives:

1. To assure prompt (current) payment.
2. Retroactive adjustment of costs, where appropriate.
3. Positive separation of costs between beneficiaries of medicare and other patients in order to reflect actual costs of services for medicare patients as opposed to average costs of serving all patients.
4. To provide, especially in the beginning, for the great differences among providers in the state of recordkeeping.
5. To assure equitable treatment of both non-profit and profit-making institutions (thus, for example, the value of donated services to a non-profit organization are reimbursable costs).
6. To provide for growth and improved quality of services.

Some providers now have adequate systems to obtain the information needed, but most of them do not. There is (and will continue to be for some time) a need for a significant amount of systems work. Fiscal intermediaries do not have the staffs to provide the required systems, cost finding, and other consultative services. Nor do they have the staffs to perform all the required audit work. The intermediaries and providers will look to CPAs for help. A significant amount of that help can be provided by local CPA firms. Some of the specialized services will require resources generally available only to the regional or national firms.

CPAs also should help resolve some accounting problems created by provisions of the principles for reimbursable costs. Depreciation is to be allowed and is to be based on cost. But suppose cost records do not exist? The principles provide an optional allowance based on a percentage of operating costs. Computation of the allowance obviously requires utilization of accounting knowledge. Also, an allowance to "secure, preserve and improve service-rendering capability" is provided. It represents in part a direct return on net capital investment and in part a recognition of "various uncertainties" inherent in the application of any cost formula. The allowance applies to both non-profit and profit-making institutions alike. Again, proper application of the provision will require more than a little accounting know-how. There are, of course, several other similar problems. The purpose here is not to enumerate the accounting problems, but to illustrate that significant accounting help is needed in the administration of the medicare program.

THE ATTEST FUNCTION

The validity and accuracy of claims for reimbursement will have to be determined and several aspects of the attest function of CPAs may be involved. For example, the provider's claims for reimbursement must be certified either by an official of the claimant (for example, a hospital administrator) or by an independent accountant. Conceivably, many providers will seek help from local CPAs in the preparation and certification of requests for reimbursement of services rendered to medicare patients.

Fiscal intermediaries will be required to audit the claims of providers either before or after disbursement. The Social Security Administration will reimburse the intermediary for its appropriate share of the cost of such audit services whether furnished by employees of the intermediary or by an independent audit firm. For the most part, intermediaries will rely on the services of CPAs rather than establishing their own audit staffs.

A third level of attest involves audits of the fiscal intermediary. The audits may be performed by employees of the Social Security Administration or by independent public accountants. Since most of the fiscal intermediaries now engage independent auditors, it seems likely that the same auditors can meet the needs of the Social Security Administration for audits related to administration of the medicare program.

Application of the attest function at the different levels will likely result in greater reliance on local firms of CPAs. Current arrangements for audits of financial statements prepared by hospitals and other providers should not be disturbed. Indeed, as a result of a new awareness of the importance of accounting systems, internal control, budgeting, and financial reporting, many more organizations will seek the services of independent auditors. In some instances, fiscal intermediaries may contract with one audit firm to perform all the required audits of providers' claims for reimbursement, but in other cases, local firms will be used on an individual contract basis.

Initially, there was some question whether a CPA firm that was engaged as independent auditor by the provider could also audit claims for reimbursement. Some observers believed the dual role of auditing the provider's financial statements and auditing reimbursable costs on behalf of the fiscal intermediary would result in a possible conflict of interest. The AICPA's Committee on Professional Ethics and the Social Security Administration have both indicated that there is no conflict of interest in such circumstances. Conceivably, a CPA firm may have occasion to audit the financial statements of a provider, "certify" costs in claims for reimbursement filed by the provider, and audit reimbursable costs on behalf of the fiscal intermediary. Utilization of the same firm to perform the three types of attest would obviously result in reduced cost in administration of the medicare program. CPAs who combine the three functions must be especially alert to assure that they will be properly regarded as independent in the particular circumstances.

CONCLUSIONS

The relative social benefit to be derived per tax dollar spent in providing medicare services will depend in large measure on the accounting function. Although the program is now in operation, many problems remain unsolved. CPAs are best qualified to develop solutions to many of those problems, and they will render an important service to society by providing help in the administration and operation of the medicare program.

QUESTIONS

1. Describe the medicare program.

2. Contact a medical doctor (your family doctor if possible). Discuss medicare with him and report his reactions to your class.

3. "CPAs are not adequately providing a needed service that is within their area of responsibility." Define, in broad terms, the area of the CPA's responsibility as you see it. Is the responsibility of an accountant who is not a CPA and is not in public accounting any different? Explain.

4. What is the attest function of CPAs?

5. How has the introduction of medicare "compounded the accounting problems of the providers of medical services?"

6. Imke says that professional accountants should be interested in helping to assure that wise decisions and efficient solutions are forthcoming in the administration of medicare. Yet it is often asserted that accountants should provide information but should stop short of actually participating in decision-making; in fact, Beyer in the preceding article says that "it is the accountant's job to handle the data; not to decide what data to handle." Should accountants, whether dealing with social programs or with business

firms, stay out of decision-making, or should they actively participate in the decision-making process? Discuss fully.

7. (a) How can accountants be of service in connection with the medicare program?

(b) Should such services be donated, should they be at a reduced fee, or should a normal fee be charged?

8. What problems would you expect to develop in the medicare program if accountants were not involved with it at all?

Section IV

Accounting and Urban Problems

Urban problems have multiplied within recent years to the extent that a new term, "urban blight," has entered our vocabulary. Urban blight respects no economic or social boundaries, although of course the inner-city poor suffer the most. Even the most affluent citizens are unable to escape the problems of congestion, crime, pollution, deteriorating streets and facilities, inadequate transportation, and dilapidated housing.

Solutions to all these problems may never be found, but at least conditions can be improved. No one profession or trade has a monopoly on the skills needed; the problems are so broad that practically every discipline can make a valuable contribution. This includes accounting!

The accounting techniques which can contribute to an improvement in urban life are essentially the same tools the accountant brings to business problems: measurement, data collection, analysis, and communication. Efforts to improve urban conditions require condition measurements to determine where to allocate resources, analysis to decide how to attack the problems, results measurement for evaluation, and frequent communication/reporting to permit redeployment of resources into more promising projects, elimination of unproductive programs, etc.

The accounting firm of Ernst & Ernst has undertaken community development, urban revitalization, and economic projects for a number of cities, public agencies, and industries. Their approach is to try to serve as "coordinators who help develop and guide community leaders to work together for the benefit of all sectors of the community." Robert Smith describes an Ernst & Ernst engagement resulting in recommendations for significant changes in downtown

165

Cleveland. This is a story of a broad-based attack on the entire collection of problems constituting "urban blight" in Cleveland and a good illustration of the variety of talents a large accounting firm can marshall on a consulting engagement.

The article by Brounstein and Meikrantz describes a Peat, Marwick, Mitchell & Co. engagement to adapt and install a prototype information system in several Model Cities programs. Communication and information are key elements in Model Cities programs. Adequate progress reports must be received from delegate agencies and forwarded to the Department of Housing and Urban Development; information is needed for self-evaluation and improvement of programs; and control of funding and expenditures requires an effective financial information system.

In undertaking this assignment, the PMM&Co. consultants encountered several unique problems. Distrust, secrecy, lack of cooperation, restrictions on access to other agencies, and political motives had to be dealt with. These and similar problems will continue to confront accountants on engagements dealing with urban problems. Whether they can be effectively resolved, given the different educational and cultural experiences of professional accountants and the urban poor, will to a large extent determine the success of such engagements.

In the story of the Bay Area Rapid Transit system Albert Newgarden discusses Arthur Young & Co. engagements which, though well within the limits of what is considered to be traditional accounting work, illustrate the breadth of involvement by accountants in major public projects. Information and control are essential in practically every organized human activity, and these are areas in which accountants are particularly qualified.

City management is not all exciting renovations, model cities programs, and innovative transportation systems. Routine operations also present problems which can become opportunities for service by accountants. Such services may not always be welcomed, however—at least by some city officials. In Newark the newly elected Mayor attempted to bring in a national accounting firm to conduct a special audit and review of the city's books, financial procedures, and controls on money. As described in The New York Times article by David Shipler, this effort was blocked by the City Council. The Council preferred instead to continue to engage the accounting firm which had been handling the audit for the last 24 years, even though one of this firm's clients was the reputed head of organized crime in Newark. It is especially interesting to contemplate, while reading this article, how the morally neutral field of accounting could provide either a service or a disservice to the City of Newark and to the public interest, depending on how it was practiced.

As these articles show, accountants have numerous opportunities to work on solutions to urban problems. The problems are too great and the accountants' skills are too necessary for us to refuse these opportunities.

ADDITIONAL REFERENCES

1. Croner, Melvyn D., "Organization Planning for a New City, " The Arthur Young Journal, Summer 1971, pp. 42–48.

2. Gibson, Charles, "Cities in Financial Crisis: CPA Firms Can Offer Services," The Journal of Accountancy, August 1972, pp. 83–85.

3. Joplin, Bruce, "Local Government Accounting: It's Your Responsibility, Too," The Journal of Accountancy, August 1967, pp. 38–43.

4. Schriever, Barnard A., "Urban Crisis and the Emerging National Response," World (Peat, Marwick, Mitchell & Co.), Spring 1969, pp. 2–9.

5. Tannian, Philip G., "How Public Accountants and Consultants Can Serve Our Cities," The Journal of Accountancy, June 1972, pp. 65–67.

Most of the problems to be found in any large urban area will be found in Cleveland. In the face of such problems some people throw up their hands; Ernst & Ernst accountants rolled up their sleeves. Cleveland still has massive problems, but they would be worse if these accountants had "stuck to their books."

Renaissance of Cleveland, Ohio

by Robert Smith

Like most large cities, Cleveland, the eighth largest city in the United States, has its problems. Its population dropped by nearly 50,000 between the 1950 and 1960 censuses while its suburbs grew by more than that amount.

It is the largest metropolitan area centered in the East-West axis between New York and Chicago, and its overall growth pattern is typical of that of other mature Northern industrial cities such as Detroit and Pittsburgh.

Retail sales in its major downtown shopping area declined by 14.6 per cent—$68 million—in the nine-year period between 1954 and 1963. In the outlying areas, on the other hand, retail sales more than doubled during the same period.

Cleveland's downtown area, which should be the healthy retailing, transient, and entertainment center for a prosperous city, is instead a grim, rather unprepossessing business and manufacturing center, thronged by day, deserted by night, surrounded by a ring of prosperous suburbs.

SOURCE: Reprinted by permission of <u>Management Services</u>, March-April 1966. Copyright 1966 by the American Institute of CPAs.

168

But Cleveland, after many false starts and some mistakes, is doing something about its problems. Predominant in the planning is an ambitious program developed by the CPA firm of Ernst & Ernst to revitalize downtown Cleveland.

A bit out of character for an accounting firm? For many it would be, but for Ernst & Ernst it is a familiar role. During the last ten years, Ernst & Ernst has undertaken economic, community development, and urban revitalization projects for a broad cross section of cities, public agencies, and industries alike. Ernst & Ernst, like many accounting and consulting firms, were old hands at industrial development and site location. Many urban redevelopment programs employed the same process in reverse.

What can a community do to make itself more attractive to business or a better place in which to work and live?

The basic approach involves the application of a set of simple criteria:

1. Create a balance sheet of applicable community assets and liabilities.
2. Develop a plan to eliminate or minimize the liabilities and simultaneously capitalize on community assets.
3. Involve all sectors of the community—newspapers, politicians, and business and labor leaders alike—to help create the "vehicle" or task force necessary to carry out the plan.

ECONOMIC APPROACH

Thus, Ernst & Ernst approaches community redevelopment primarily from an economic viewpoint rather than in terms of the area's physical needs. They believe that lack of sound economic and financial planning and "selling" of concepts through the active involvement of many different interests has been the principal reason underlying the failure of many urban plans.

The Ernst & Ernst economic development specialists are not city planners. Rather they view themselves as coordinators who help develop and guide the community leaders to work together for the benefit of all sectors of the community.

Cleveland has run the gamut from the traditional planning approach to the more fundamental but more effective development approach espoused by Ernst & Ernst. And now, after years of stagnation, radical changes are under way in its downtown area—changes for the better.

Let's briefly review the Cleveland situation. In 1959, the Cleveland City Plan Commission, with the financial assistance of several local foundations, prepared a new and ambitious plan for future downtown development entitled "Downtown Cleveland—1975."

And that was what it remained—a plan. The plan was primarily oriented to downtown physical needs with little consideration of the economic "facts of life."

Moreover, community cooperation had not been enlisted. Local property owners, real estate interests, and banks, always conservative, were slow to cooperate. Buildings built in the early twenties were left as they had been. The general attitude was: If a building's making money, why spend anything on it?

But the Cleveland Development Foundation, headed by Cleveland's industrial, financial, and business leadership, including Republic Steel's Thomas F. Patton, Eaton, Yale & Towne's John Virden, and others, proved too resourceful to accept this defeat.

The Foundation had been organized to promote closer cooperation between business interests and the city administration—primarily in the areas of public housing and urban redevelopment. Now the city and progressive elements in the Cleveland Development group teamed up for a swift coup that prodded the more conservative business group into doing something about the entire downtown area.

ERIEVIEW

With the full support of the Development Foundation, the city administration, then under the leadership of Anthony J. Celebrezze, who later became Secretary of Health, Education, and Welfare, carved out one of the largest-scale downtown urban renewal programs in the nation—Erieview.

A 163-acre site in the northeast section of the downtown area was designated an urban renewal area. Under urban renewal status, the development authority has the power of eminent domain. Slum and blighted structures can be condemned and razed; all new structures must conform to a rigid code and be designed for specific uses.

Venture capital was found and Phase 1 of the Erieview project got under way—the construction of a major new office building, one of the first built in the downtown area since the early twenties. Phase II of the project visualized high-rise and low-rise apartment houses—the first residential construction in downtown Cleveland in decades.

The effect on the somnolent downtown interests was immediate. Erieview Tower, the skyscraper office building, was new, sleek, and glamorous; it not only attracted new headquarters offices to the downtown area, but it began to siphon tenants away from its forty-year-old competitors. Real estate groups that had experienced high occupancy rates in their old buildings suddenly found that they were losing tenants. And various downtown interests that had been at odds with each other for years suddenly found themselves faced with a common peril.

NEW PLAN SUGGESTED

With the stimulus of the Cleveland Development Foundation, the principal interests, conservative and progressive alike, in the community began to recognize the need for collective action to rehabilitate the entire downtown area. And Ernst & Ernst, as the best known Cleveland consulting organization with experience in urban redevelopment, was brought in to help coordinate efforts.

An Ernst & Ernst team, headed by K. S. Caldwell, a firm principal, and G. McCay, a top economic development specialist, studied the plans made for Cleveland for 1975, what had already been done in the Erieview project, and Cleveland's economic prospects.

Many elements of the 1975 plan had been incorporated into the Erieview project; thus the 1975 plan was no longer valid. A tremendous need was foreseen to have more people working in the downtown area. More people would occupy more office space, help retail trade, and serve as an important economic "generator." But it would be difficult to get more people—which means more major employers—to move to Cleveland unless downtown Cleveland could be made competitive with other major office centers.

So Ernst & Ernst suggested in its overall report, "Guidelines for Action," two complementary plans, one a short-range program that could be implemented within a year to two years to make the entire downtown area more attractive and livable, the other a strong concrete effort by the entire downtown community to attract more businesses to Cleveland.

The short-range program was directed toward these objectives:

1. Improving the physical appearance and housekeeping of the downtown.
2. Improving circulation, transportation, and parking in the downtown and access to and from it.
3. Providing a better mix of goods and services in the downtown section.
4. Coordinating and unifying the efforts of the area's merchants, property owners, and realty and development organizations to promote the downtown, its office facilities, stores, and services.
5. Creating a physical plan for the total downtown and specific development plans for projects to enhance downtown investment, economy, and service.

CENTRAL GROUP STIPULATED

And finally, Ernst & Ernst warned, to be successful, an effective and unified downtown organization must be developed to carry out needed plans—an organization which must represent all major downtown interests. They pointed out that Cleveland's downtown had much going for it. Its assets included:

• A central retail core (currently with few vacancies) that was oriented toward the most modern regional shopping center design with a mall (Euclid Avenue), anchored at either end by major department stores, that provided a wide variety of goods and services.

- A strong existing office complex and an emerging new one that had brought Cleveland national recognition and was stimulating added confidence and investor interest in downtown.
- A wide range of finance and government services along with one of the nation's largest and most modern exhibit convention centers.
- A concentration of the above functions that made them easily accessible to one another.
- Good access from a central transportation complex of air, water, rail, highway, and suburban rapid transit not found in any other downtown in the country.

Liabilities were listed as these:

- Increasing urban sprawl.
- High downtown land costs.
- Increased auto congestion brought about by limited highways, streets, and parking.
- High downtown property operating costs—taxes, labor, rents.
- Lack of the downtown or community leadership needed to help overcome core area problems.

However, many of the assets are potential assets rather than existing ones. The central retail core—stretching almost a mile along Euclid Avenue between two major department stores—would be an asset if it were properly developed with the proper mix of shops and services.

By the same token, Cleveland's overall transportation system is good. However, its Rapid Transit System was designed for the commuter, not for the downtown shopper. This is unfortunate in that the shopper coming from an outlying area to the downtown has to go to the railroad station and then make his way by bus to his eventual destination. This might be a mile or so away. But still, Euclid Avenue and the Transit System are strong assets; the facilities do exist; they are not planners' dreams.

The shop buildings exist along Euclid; it is a question of improving their appearance and upgrading merchandise and selling methods. The Rapid Transit System is there. It would have to be extended to serve the downtown.

By the same token, there is adequate office space in downtown Cleveland in total. Many buildings must be modernized; in some cases they will need new facades. But they are not so dilapidated that they must be razed.

Each is an asset—if it is improved. And improvements in any one will benefit the others. If the stores improve the quality of their goods and their promotion methods they will draw more people away from suburban shopping centers. If the transit system is developed so as to get people closer to their ultimate destination, the number of downtown shoppers will increase. If the offices are improved and more tenants are found for them, the number of people circulating in the area and shopping in downtown stores will increase.

Obviously, achieving these multiple, interrelated goals will take cooperation and participation by all segments of the downtown community and integration of the many different downtown interests into one coordinated organization.

Ernst & Ernst stimulated creation of such a group and spelled out as its main objectives:

"To undertake and/or assist in developing action programs and worthwhile projects conducive to the continued progress of the downtown community.

"To assist in formulating policies, enacting legislation, and encouraging private codes or public ordinances necessary for renewal of the downtown.

"To develop a close and effective liaison with the City of Cleveland and other public and private agencies concerned with the downtown.

"To develop specific recommendations regarding all the following:

- Traffic transportation and parking
- Assessment practices and land use
- Public and private facilities and services
- Merchandising and promotion
- Property maintenance and development."

It was recommended that the needed Downtown Organization be organized as an independent, special-purpose arm of the Cleveland Growth Board—the regional industrial development agency—to work closely with the Chamber of Commerce, the Growth Board, the Cleveland Development Foundation, and the Convention and Visitors Bureau.

Also recommended was creation of an Advisory Council of Architects, Engineers, and Planners to assist the Downtown Organization to evaluate existing structures in the downtown to see which could be rehabilitated or redeveloped and which areas should be entirely replanned and redeveloped; to develop standards for downtown revitalization; and to perform the physical planning itself.

PLANS GEARED TO 1980

The end product of these efforts was to be an updated general plan for the Downtown Cleveland of 1980, including a definition of its functional character, its transport pattern, its land use, and its development schedule.

A similar Real Estate Advisory Board was also suggested in "Guidelines for Action" to provide advice, counsel, and assistance in such areas as:

- Assessment and taxation
- Appraisals
- Market and re-use studies
- Building management costs and problems
- Leasing and financing criteria for developments
- Attraction of tenants.

Plans were also outlined to coordinate the work of the new Downtown Organization with that of existing promotional and development organizations.

The key element of the development program was one effective organization representing all downtown interests, receiving advice from and channeling its plans through two paid technical groups—the Advisory Council of Architects, Engineers, and Planners and the Real Estate Advisory Board.

Downtown industry was also given careful consideration in the proposed development plan. Downtown Cleveland is primarily a white collar and merchandising area. What industry there is is that often associated with office concentrations. Ernst & Ernst and State of Ohio projections indicated that manufacturing activities in the downtown area would continue to decline but that office employment would probably rise. So the desirable industry was not a plant, or several plants, but large clerical enterprises—perhaps an insurance company.

The city must be ready for such a windfall if and when it comes through. And it is working toward that goal, not by wholesale destruction and reconstruction in given areas, but by trying to plan development activities so that each area of the downtown can concentrate on the activities in which it is strongest today or which offer the greatest development potential. Another Ernst & Ernst suggestion, in line with their whole approach to the problem, is to build on economic realities first, to improve the strong points and gradually eliminate the weak ones.

PLANNING AREAS

Thus, the firm divided the entire downtown area into seven project planning areas, centered around:

1. **The Core Area.**   This included the most built-up section of Euclid Avenue, the town's major artery, and the Public Square, a four-block open area where Euclid Avenue starts. This was designated as the primary retail, office, and government center and included the pioneer new office complex already constructed at Erieview I.

2. **Lakefront-Port Area.**   This region, traditionally a transportation and distribution area, was reserved for these uses with a further suggestion that recreational facilities might be expanded. It already houses a stadium and Burke

Lakefront Airport. Runways at the latter could be extended to 6,200 feet, which would make the Downtown Airport practicable for both short- and medium-range jet planes. If this were done, Cleveland would have an airport capable of receiving trunk and local air carriers far closer to the center of town than most other major cities. Moreover, airports traditionally breed nearby hotels or motels, and this is another of Cleveland's needs if it is to attain its full potential as a convention city. Conventions, of course, would bring people— to the benefit of the adjacent core area.

This would further strengthen the need to develop recreational facilities clustered in the center of the Lakefront Area near the stadium, with Burke Airport to the east and the shipping port facilities to the west. Eventually, plans call for a special bus service connecting this area directly to the retail center at the core, with service possibly subsidized by downtown department stores.

3. Erieview II Area.   Immediately to the East of the Erieview I office complex, now part of the core area in Ernst & Ernst plans, Erieview II has already been planned primarily for residential facilities. It thus fits neatly into the overall plan since it can serve as a second "anchor" for the Euclid Avenue retail complex, which formerly had the Public Square transportation center as its focal point. It also, of course, if successful, will bring more shoppers into the downtown.

4. Northeast Area.   On the extreme northeastern fringe of the downtown section, it was planned that this area should continue to function in its traditional role—as a manufacturing, wholesaling, and distribution center. It can also serve to house businesses and people displaced by changes in the other areas. This area, badly run down now, is close to the railways, the highways, and Cleveland's port so it is naturally suited to both manufacturing and distribution. Perhaps even more important, it borders on the two areas in downtown Cleveland slated for heavy residential development, Erieview II and the University Area.

5. The University Area.   The development of Cleveland State University in the downtown is a key element of the redevelopment program. The Ohio State University, at Columbus, the state's third largest city, has a student population of more than 34,000. But Columbus, in the center of the state, is far from the greatest center of population—the Cleveland-Akron area. A major extension of the State University system has long been planned for the Cleveland area, but it was generally thought it would be located somewhere in Cleveland's pleasant suburbs rather than in the downtown. However, the Cleveland Development Foundation and city officials, realizing what a boost a major university could give the entire downtown region, campaigned hard, and when the final decision was made, the downtown had been selected for the major campus.

Lake Erie

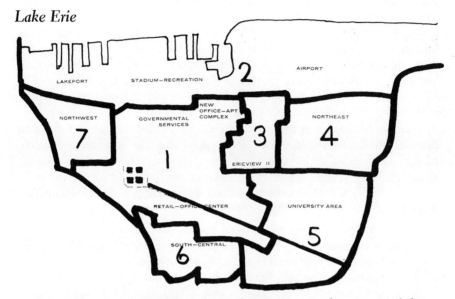

Map shows seven distinct areas in downtown complex suggested by Ernst & Ernst. Square and line running from Area 1 through Area 5 are, respectively, the Public Square and Euclid Avenue.

Cleveland State University, which plans to enroll 12,000 full-time-equivalent students by 1970 and 20,000 by 1980, will spawn a multitude of supporting businesses. It will also offer the prospects of a heavy residential concentration in a formerly underdeveloped area of downtown. Finally it will provide another "anchor" in the downtown.

6. South Central Area.   Immediately south of the retail heart of Euclid Avenue, this area is planned for development as a future major office complex when the core area has reached saturation point. Interim plans call for broadening the retail mix in the area to include such items as imports, gifts, handicrafts, and specialty household items. Automotive repair and garage facilities will also be concentrated in the area.

7. The Northwest Area.   Like its corresponding number, the Northeast Area, this is reserved for manufacturing and wholesaling activities. Like the Northeast, it is on the railroad, close to the port, and has good highway connections. Again like the Northeast, its buildings are largely obsolescent. Its recommended development closely parallels that of the Northeast Area.

The development plan, "Guidelines for Action," also set forth a number of recommendations applicable to the entire core area. Of prime importance was a proposal that the city designate the Downtown Organization a Redevelopment Agency to undertake selective rehabilitation and redevelopment projects and to coordinate and direct downtown redevelopment activities. Programs sponsored by the Downtown Organization should be privately financed wherever possible and should, said Ernst & Ernst, include:

- "Identification of the specific areas and/or structures where condition, appearance, or use detract from or limit the development of the downtown.
- "The architectural, engineering, and planning studies necessary to evaluate present use, condition, and potentials for the areas and/or structure concerned.
- "Development of local or state ordinances necessary to properly utilize the city's powers of eminent domain in designating redevelopment areas.
- "Assembly of sufficient land parcels to make possible desired developments.
- "Coordination and direction of the redevelopment program, including the elimination of blighted or nonconforming structures and the upgrading or improving of substandard areas or structures.
- "Preparation of recommended changes in the ordinances, building, and safety codes necessary to prevent future blight or deterioration.
- "Development of suggested criteria to be used in the acquisition and demolition of properties, the relocation of present tenants elsewhere in the downtown, and the manner in which new tenants can be attracted.
- "Coordination of survey and planning activities with potential developers, investors, and land and building owners.
- "Preparation of a general physical plan for each of the designated renewal areas concerning land use, transportation, parking, and services."

EMINENT DOMAIN NEEDED

The city's power of eminent domain was a key element in the proposed development program. "Guidelines for Action" spells out the reason:

> While most cities have problems in their downtown land ownership patterns, our analysis has revealed some major Cleveland roadblocks which must be overcome. A number of downtown properties are owned by nonresidents who are primarily interested in return on their present investments. A large number of key properties are owned by individuals in the community who have placed high values on their properties or who are not interested in disposing of or developing them for other purposes.

Ernst & Ernst, drawing on previous reports by other groups, made other specific recommendations for immediate improvement. These included setting limits on the type, size, and appearance of signs and displays throughout the downtown area, street plantings along the two main shopping streets, installation of street furniture, uniform arcades over the sidewalks, and installation of false fronts on some of the older buildings. Also urged were an improved street lighting and building illumination plan to make the area attractive by night as well as by day and construction of multilevel garages instead of the open street-level parking lots that are so ubiquitous in Cleveland today.

RETAIL CORE

But perhaps the most ambitious immediate program is one aimed at revitalizing the retail center of the city along Euclid and Prospect Avenues. The CPA firm has proposed to the Downtown Organization that these two streets should be considered as a retail entity—like a suburban shopping center—with an overall plan to provide a mix of merchandise and services that will ensure maximum customer demand. Together with this, Ernst & Ernst has made certain recommendations (based on a concurrent study of downtown Cleveland's traffic, transportation, and parking problems by Wilbur Smith and Associates, New Haven engineers) for rerouting of traffic on some downtown arteries, construction of one additional rapid transit station immediately to serve the Cleveland State University area, and the extension and expansion of some downtown streets to improve traffic flow.

One of the most difficult problems throughout the study has been to weigh the time factors so that office and residential construction will be ready for new people when it is needed but will not lie idle for long periods of time before it is needed.

A small amount of residential construction is not too great a gamble; in a city the size of Cleveland a market exists for quality apartments in town. Erieview II can meet this need. By the same token immediate residential needs in the Cleveland State University area can be predicted with some reliability. Office construction or remodeling, though, involves some risks. The development program calls for at least 15,000 new office employees by 1975; leading interests are campaigning hard to lure more large concerns to Cleveland. But in the interval, it is possible that some fairly expensive renovation of existing buildings may be necessary in order to retain existing tenants.

While Ernst & Ernst have projected space needs on a year-by-year basis, they have also emphasized that some developers or property owners may have to be prepared to accept an occupancy rate of 80 per cent or lower at one time or another during the next ten years, depending on the timing of developments. In effect, they are employing another standard business technique—planning ahead for several years and then modifying the plan for the period immediately ahead. Thus, if one new building siphons tenants from a remodeled building and they are not immediately replaced by new workers, plans for construction of more new buildings would be re-evaluated.

FINANCING REDEVELOPMENT

How is all this to be financed? Estimates are that 50 million dollars a year will be required for the next twenty years—a billion dollars all told. This is a great deal of money, of course, but no higher than the present level of capital investment in the downtown area. The main difference is that now there is the beginning of an overall, integrated plan to be followed in which each dollar spent will reinforce the effect of every other dollar spent. Moreover, under the new program a substantial part of the required investment will come from Federal and state sources through urban renewal grants and funds for Cleveland State University. The City of Cleveland too will have to contribute heavily. Both Erieview II and the Cleveland State University complex will require new schools; money will have to be spent on tighter building inspection and code enforcement procedures, on street extension, and on improving housekeeping services.

All told, approximately twenty million dollars a year is expected to be supplied from Federal, state, and municipal sources. The balance—thirty million dollars a year—should come from private sources.

No one in Cleveland seriously doubts that the money will be forthcoming now that there is a clear forward direction in which the city can move. The plan so far is not really that; it is only a guide to a plan. But it appears feasible, it makes sense, it can be done. And best of all, it has helped to bring the combined attention of the community as a whole to bear on the problems.

PROGRESS TO DATE

Substantial progress has already been made. In the several months following submission of "Guidelines," the Downtown Organization has been established as an arm of the Greater Cleveland Growth Board, and an aggressive fund raising program is under way.

William Slayton, U.S. Urban Renewal Commissioner, said recently:

Cities have to command a voice in deciding their own fate, not just leave it to the private developers. The cities in the ascendency in the next ten years are going to be the ones who have analyzed their potential, attracted the new, and encouraged change—in short, entrepreneurs, instruments of activity. They must take advantage of all the tools and not just urban renewal—which has become a term of fear, conjuring up mass demolition and displacements.

Renewal has to be used along with code enforcement, park acquisition, schools, highways, beautification—in the best ways and combinations that a clever entrepreneur can find.

He might have been describing the exact process Cleveland is currently going through.

QUESTIONS

1. Ernst & Ernst is an accounting firm, a partnership of CPAs. How was <u>accounting</u> involved in this engagement?

2. (a) According to this article, the first step in improving a community is to "create a balance sheet of applicable community assets and liabilities." List <u>your</u> community's assets and liabilities, considering such things as transportation facilities, geographical features, climate, parks, recreational facilities, congestion, pollution, leadership, educational institutions, crime and police protection, property tax base and other (present or potential) revenue sources, etc.

    (b) Try to assign a weight or value to each of these factors. What problems do you encounter? Can the assets and liabilities be meaningfully balanced with a net surplus or deficit result?

3. With several classmates, arrange an appointment with a top official in your community (e.g., mayor, city manager, director of planning, council member or alderman). Discuss the Cleveland effort with him and explore the feasibility of a similar program for your community. Write a brief (3–4 pages) report on your meeting. (Note: Large classes may prefer to invite one or more city officials to campus, or the class may be divided into several groups, each group to meet with a different official.)

4. (a) What happens to the occupants when dilapidated houses are condemned and razed by the city? Where do they go? Is this properly a concern of the consultants, or should it be left strictly to city policy-makers?

    (b) In a broader sense, should professionals such as accountants and lawyers serve their clients without regard for the broader societal effects? Or should such professionals either attempt to change their clients' policies to avoid apparent negative societal effects or else refuse to participate?

(c) Is the comparison of accountants and lawyers in the preceding question appropriate? Explain.

5. "A number of downtown properties are owned by nonresidents who are primarily interested in return on their present investments. A large number of key properties are owned by individuals in the community who have placed high values on their properties or who are not interested in disposing of or developing them for other purposes."

(a) As assigned by your instructor, present the arguments either for or against the use of eminent domain by the city to acquire such properties.

(b) Assuming eminent domain is to be used, how would you go about arriving at a fair value for each piece of property?

*Peat, Marwick, Mitchell & Company's assign-
ment to help the Department of Housing and
Urban Development (HUD) administer its
controversial Model Cities program turned
out to be an engagement with built-in human
hurdles rarely faced by a team of management consultants—hurdles involving suspicion, political gamesmanship, and racial
tension. In this article two consultants tell
it like it was.*

Model Cities

by Sidney H. Brounstein &
John F. Meikrantz

The assignment from HUD's Model Cities Administration, in September 1969,
sounded routine: prepare a proposal for technical assistance in adapting and
installing a prototype information system for City Demonstration Agencies
(CDAs) and provide staff training for CDAs in 13 of the participating cities.

The Washington Office quickly formed a group of ten consultants from
seven offices for the engagement which began two months later. Their first
task was to attend a two-week HUD-sponsored training session in Fredericksburg, Va.

The session was designed to acquaint consultants from four firms with the
Model Cities program in general, and with the development of information systems, and CDA staff training, in particular.

Like the Model Cities program itself, the Fredericksburg seminar raised
more questions than answers. Participants wondered how they could ever
fulfill the terms of the contract. Part of the problem was an almost total lack
of unanimity among the speakers on how best to cope with the obstacles they
faced in trying to make the Model Cities program work.

SOURCE: Reprinted by permission of the authors and the publisher from
World (Winter 1971), pp. 48–51.

Speakers dwelled on the need for "sensitivity," a word used again and again—how to be sensitive to the ghetto environment, how to be sensitive in dealing with politicians, how to be sensitive about the inexperience of CDA directors and their staffs, how to be sensitive about the participation of citizen's committees in a technical operation.

By the time the two-week session ended, the word "sensitivity" had become an obsession to most of us. PMM's consultants were brought together again for another week of special study at the Firm's Sterling Institute training facility in Washington's Watergate.

The men arrived with serious doubts about the engagement that lay ahead. There was much give-and-take but no unanimity about how best to tackle the assignment in such dis-similar cities as Newark, N.J., and Gainesville, Ga. Four weeks into the contract our team spirit still consisted of ten individual egos.

Then, a newly-hired group of local consultants arrived. These six black professionals, hired by PMM&Co. to complement the project team, were to work part-time assisting the Firm's consultants in relating to the community and to the agencies. They, too, had individual doubts about their roles in the Model Cities assignment.

Some were afraid of being caught in the middle between ghetto residents and the CDAs; others feared they might be charged with "tokenism," or being the "house black" for an "establishment" firm; still others wondered just why PMM wanted them as part of the project.

The ten PMM consultants, reacting to the doubts of their new teammates, put to use what they had learned during the three preceding weeks. They began to try to resolve the reservations of the six local consultants and by doing that, most of their own reservations disappeared. Finally, they began to function as a team.

Just what is this project that has prompted so many doubts and fueled so much controversy in its brief life?

When President Lyndon B. Johnson signed the Demonstration Cities and Metropolitan Development Act of 1966 he saw it as the capstone of his Great Society.

He asked Congress at the time that $2.3 billion be spent over five years to elevate the nation's urban areas from "sewers of despair and neglect" to become "masterpieces of our civilization."

He saw his Model Cities program as a way to eradicate neighborhood blight by alleviating social distress as well as tending to brick-and-mortar needs. It was to be different from the old "war on poverty" administered by the Office of Economic Opportunity (OEO). OEO's controversial Community Action Programs (CAPS) organized citizens to operate outside the existing political structures, thus alienating local government in many instances. Mayors rebelled on two key issues: their authority was being undermined, and frequent duplication of municipal services. Model Cities is a "mayor's" program within the existing political structure that involves the persons being helped and offers them a voice in the decisions affecting their lives.

President Nixon recently endorsed Model Cities (with certain changes in direction) following a long debate within the Administration about its future. As a way of helping to achieve the "new federalism," more money and more authority over the program will be allotted by this Administration to state and local governments that demonstrate creative and effective use of Model Cities resources. The aim is to further reduce direct control from Washington over urban affairs while increasing state and local government responsiveness to the total community. Cities that do not show reasonable progress run the risk of being phased out of the program. In fact, three were recently dropped.

The 1966 Model Cities legislation empowered HUD to grant aid to cities that imaginatively mobilize physical and social rehabilitation services in a "total attack" on neighborhood blight. Unlike CAPS, which attempted to serve all poor people in a city, Model Cities concentrated scarce resources in "model *neighborhoods*" within cities to be able to adequately fund comprehensive programs.

The first round of the program included 75 cities, ranging from Alma, Ga. (pop. 4,000) to Chicago and New York.

A year later 75 "second-round" cities joined to make the current total 147. The neighborhoods now covered by the program contain 5,934,000 men, women and children.

Of the second-round cities, 11 were contracted to PMM, making its total 24. By now, the contract has involved over 20 consultants from 10 PMM offices. In addition, a subcontractor, Opportunity Systems, Inc. joined the PMM consulting team.

HUD's first move on launching the Model Cities program was to make small grants to each city for the purpose of analyzing its most critical problems and preparing an attack plan.

For the cities this meant getting together with many municipal, state, and federal agencies; it meant a study of the most common ghetto problems, such as high crime rates, poor housing, and lack of education.

Based on this study and the statistical data that grew out of it, each city was asked to prepare a comprehensive development plan which, in effect, was to serve as its application for aid—80% of all its cost of staffing and managing the program and 100% of the cost of the project itself. The cities were given one year for the initial planning. But most found the going slow. The mayors' first job was to appoint a City Demonstration Agency director and form a citizens commission from the model neighborhood itself. The CDA directors and the citizens groups were to collaborate with municipal agencies and private and university consultants to devise a comprehensive development plan.

For most of the cities in the program this took all of two years instead of the one year targeted by Washington. And not all of the initial plans had met with HUD's approval.

The first Detroit Model Cities program, for example, included a legalized red light district in a draft of its comprehensive plan, a fact that quickly received nationwide attention and criticism.

But some of the other proposals from early applicants served as better barometers of the directions the Model Cities program might take.

Examples:

Crime Reduction.   Detroit, of course, had other plans, too. It selected a crime-ridden area in the city's heart as its target neighborhood and proposed a model correction center there as a major feature of its uplift program. The center was to stress crime prevention and rehabilitation of criminals. Judges of a model court, created especially to serve the neighborhood, would forego punishment as much as possible, in favor of directing offenders to various job training and counseling programs. The idea was to enable offenders to maintain contacts with the community during rehabilitation, rather than being locked away in jail.

Job Training.   Philadelphia sought to turn a shabby, largely black slum on its lower north side into a vibrant community that would include a thriving business district. The city envisioned as many as 10 new businesses in the area to produce a variety of items, such as electric parts. These "pilot production plants" would offer on-the-job training to neighborhood residents and would train managers at a special academy to be established in the area.

Open Housing.   St. Louis chose a crescent-shaped area with an evenly divided white and black population as its target neighborhood. The city wanted to break the area's segregated housing pattern, in part, by strategically relocating displaced black families.

Social Services.   Norfolk decided to locate the first of several planned Comprehensive Neighborhood Service Centers in a large, stable, though physically isolated section of its Model Neighborhood to help determine the viability of decentralized social service delivery. One conveniently located facility provides: a general health, pre-natal, and new baby clinic; mental health clinic; employment office; legal aid office; welfare services; adult education; homemaker services and handicraft and recreation. The individual or family enrolls at the center which coordinates referrals and follow-up services as needed. Special "out reach" services are provided, where center employees go out to the neighborhood to identify and advise eligible families who, because of lack of awareness or other problems, do not use available services. Norfolk was one of the first cities to inaugurate this type of service.

Education. The early plans of many cities aimed at concentrating school facilities so as to improve the education available to the poor and to encourage eventual racial integration. St. Louis envisioned a centralized "educational park" complex to operate 24 hours a day, offering adult courses at night. Philadelphia wanted to transform a street that runs through its target slum into an "education highway" of various kinds of schools to eventually serve the entire city. Waco saw in a shut-down Air Force base a potential educational compound to serve entire families—job training for fathers, homemaking instruction for mothers, and special small-class schools for the youngsters.

But having a draft plan is only the first step of a very long journey.

Once a program is started, the CDA director begins to function much like a broker. He contracts with "delegate agencies," such as schools, housing authorities, hospitals, and police departments, and pays each for its role in the Model Cities program out of the funds he gets from Washington. In addition, to get maximum mileage out of his funds, the CDA director will help sponsor other state and federally funded projects by using Model Cities funds to pay the "local" matching share; hence multiplying the overall effect of Model Cities funds.

The schools may be asked to provide adult education classes for people in the model neighborhood, or to conduct vocational training, remedial reading both for adults and youngsters. While most city school systems provide such services, the blighted neighborhoods need something different because the normal school system just doesn't seem to work for the ghetto.

The hospitals and health departments may be contracted to provide wholesale and controlled immunization, to establish clinics and to perform more frequent examinations to find and treat the diseases common among the underprivileged.

Police participation aimed at improving community relations may involve the assigning of policemen to meet and counsel with residents in the Model Cities area and to offer and supervise recreational programs for the young.

The job of the city housing authorities could be to build new housing units, to rehabilitate old ones, to enforce codes more vigorously, to relocate displaced residents, and to advise people on how to take better care of their homes.

Under the Model Cities program's five-year plan it also is the task of the CDA and the citizens committee to develop a "self-evaluation capability" and to serve as their own overseers.

They must evaluate the program as a whole along with the performance of the various agencies that get paid for being part of it.

Typical of the questions they must ask are:

Has unemployment and infant mortality been reduced? Has sub-standard housing and education been improved? Did the contracting agencies perform efficiently so far? Did they meet their schedules and budgets? Did they reach all the people they were supposed to reach?

Based on these evaluations, which are reviewed by HUD and its Model Cities Administration, comprehensive plans must be revised and submitted each year to obtain new funds to be granted for the continuation of a city's program.

To prove that it is doing its job properly and that it is monitoring its project effectively, a CDA must furnish satisfactory answers to a multitude of questions asked by HUD.

Even though HUD had imposed fewer reporting requirements than other Federal agencies, this makes for a mountain of paperwork. Despite recent HUD attempts to reduce unnecessary Federal forms, the paper pile continues to grow. HUD's full set of guidelines totals 400 pages, 25% more than a year ago.

PMM's basic assignment was to go into 13 first-round and later 11 second-round cities and adapt and install a CDA project performance information system and to train the staff of each CDA in the development and use of the information system.

In most cases the PMM team began by giving formal presentations to the CDA and agency staffs of what the prototype system was.

As it turned out, that was a wrong-foot start.

It soon became apparent that many of the cities were either not ready for training, or were very resistant to HUD and to the concept of a contractor paid by HUD coming in with a "canned" system. Even though HUD wanted the consultants to "tailor" a system for each CDA, it was difficult to convince the CDA it would be their own.

Here are some of the things that made this engagement challenging:

- To begin with, a lot of people wanted to know what a huge establishment accounting-consulting firm was doing in the ghetto.
- About half the CDAs were not yet funded when PMM arrived to give technical assistance. The pressure to get funding, as well as the problem of having small and poorly-trained staffs, diverted the CDA's attention. They just weren't ready to work with consultants.
- In some cities CDA staffs refused even to talk about information needs. They were too busy, they said, writing contracts so funds could be allocated quickly, and projects would become visible to the citizens.
- Most CDAs wouldn't allow the consultants, or members of their own staffs, for that matter, to contact citizens' groups. And in some cities, PMM&Co. was barred from contacting other city agencies involved in the project.
- Some CDA staffs had previously worked with another consulting firm and strongly resisted the new contractor sent in by HUD.
- In at least one city, the CDA was suspicious of everything: HUD, its information system, and any consultant who was to help implement it.
- In many cities CDA directors were basically local politicians whose sole goal at first appeared to be getting the Federal money into their city and spending

it as fast as possible. To some of these directors, delegating authority to manage and to develop information systems seemed designed to detract from the directors' total control of the local program.

These early roadblocks were difficult to clear. Delays were frequent due in part to poor communications from program personnel unaccustomed to a frank business dialogue with "outsiders." This was something that had to be found out the hard way.

PMM's consultants had other things to learn, too.

At the beginning, the consultants, having had no similar experiences to fall back on, approached the assignment as if it were a typical commercial engagement.

They tried to follow the HUD contract to the letter and attempted to implement the prototype information system with strict technical adherence to specifications, while trying to maintain formal client relationships. They were product oriented on the one hand and on the other they kept insisting the client meet certain conditions before he could be helped. This just wouldn't work.

So the methods of giving technical assistance changed. Consultants became less technical, more personal, and flexible.

They now sought to find out first what each city wanted to do and in what area it needed help the most. Technical assistance was tailored to each city's unique needs.

In most cases, it was found best to modify the formal approach in explaining the information system. This approach came across as too technical and sophisticated and tended to alienate people, making rapport impossible. Part of the problem was that consultants were introducing technical matters before they felt comfortable in the new working environment. They had difficulty relating technical matters by way of example to clients whose own business experience varied substantially from that of the consultants.

A Federal prototype, it was soon learned, could easily become a "home" system with very minor technical adjustments if adapted in a way a city could call its own.

The key to Model Cities became flexibility.

And as doors began to open, the consultants discovered that the cities needed their help on numerous activities—outside the scope of the contract—to put them in a position to use an information system.

They needed help in staffing and organization so that responsibility could be assigned to individuals for project monitoring and other management functions for which they would need information. They needed help in planning, contracting with delegate agencies, and evaluation.

By providing this type of help and getting the staff's cooperation, the consultants found that when the staff was ready for training in the development of an information system, progress was faster. They began to appreciate the value of a process called "project analysis," which helped the CDA and delegate agencies define and agree on the project's objectives, work program and reporting requirements. They could still get an information system installed, which, though it was a less sophisticated product, was one that could be understood and used. From HUD's point of view, it preferred a system that would be used by the CDA rather than one that was sophisticated and not used.

To HUD's credit, it recognized that greater flexibility was needed to give the CDA assistance in general management and evaluation. It modified PMM's, and other firms' contracts for second-round cities to include such flexibility. From the beginning, HUD adopted the refreshing approach that by building a better information system capacity at the local level, the total program would benefit more than by HUD imposing its own standardized requirements on all cities.

In analyzing the outcome there is now increasing evidence that the wheels are turning on the local level. Most of PMM's 24 cities have organized to get their programs going and to manage them as they get under way.

The communications process, a vital ingredient of a successful Model Cities program, is beginning to work as CDAs are receiving progress reports from their delegate agencies and are filing the results of their monitoring to HUD—a prerequisite for continued funding. Some cities are beginning to use these reports for self-evaluation and improving their own operations, which is what HUD is really looking for.

For PMM, an organization that is trying to broaden its involvement in community affairs, this, perhaps, indicated that it can effectively meet the challenge of the public sector.

To succeed, its consultants had to change themselves. They had to re-think their values and approach on what it takes to be a good consultant. In the process many learned that the greatest challenge in developing an information system is in working with people that must use it.

Conversely, the technical skills needed in this engagement were similar to those needed in commercial and even government engagements.

This engagement has not only shown that there is room for firms like PMM assisting urban affairs administrators, but that the firms' skills are needed. Skills in management, systems, training, finance, planning, measurement, and evaluation are especially needed by urban affairs staffs to complement their substantive skills (as in health, social planning, housing). Monetary rewards notwithstanding, the nation's expanding social consciousness demands that firms like PMM actively seek a role in urban affairs to fulfill a moral obligation to society.

QUESTIONS

1. What were the objectives of the engagement described in this article?

2. In your opinion, how critical was the work of the accountants/consultants to the success of these Model Cities programs?

3. How did this engagement differ from a normal engagement of a CPA firm with a business client? What unique problems were encountered? For each problem listed, how would you suggest overcoming it?

4. Suppose you were on an engagement such as that described. A local political activist, not involved in the Model Cities program, approaches you in the City Demonstration Agency office and says: "Hey, listen man, you cats are rippin' off a big chunk of this program's money for a lot of mumbo-jumbo that ain't gonna do any of us any good. Man, you can't even explain it—you don't talk no sense! That money you're getting ought to go right into the pockets of poor folk instead of with you back uptown. That way we'd at least get some beans on the table—instead of buying steak for you." Unfortunately, a reporter for the city's daily newspaper, which has editorialized vigorously against the Model Cities program, overhears and has his pencil poised to record your response. How would you justify your work and your fee?

Ground-breaking occurred in 1964 for what was scheduled to become a 75-mile network of high-speed, computer-controlled subways, aerial lines, and surface lines serving the San Francisco Bay area. The San Francisco Bay Area Rapid Transit system, or BART, was described by its designers and builders as "the world's fastest, safest, and most modern urban transportation system." Albert Newgarden of Arthur Young & Co. describes his visit to BART and the Bay Area Rapid Transit District, a client of his firm.

A Visit
to BART

by Albert Newgarden

The first person we met at the BART District offices on San Francisco's Mission Street was John M. Peirce, BART's director of finance. As Mr. Peirce told us about the early history of BART, and particularly about its financing, his eyes sparkled with what, for want of a better word, we can only call parental pride.

The story of BART, we learned, goes back at least as far as 1947, when a joint Army-Navy board recommended the construction of an underwater transit tube beneath San Francisco Bay. At that time, a number of Bay Area civic leaders were championing the cause of a modern rapid transit system for the region, and in 1951 the California legislature created a special commission to study the problem. Although considerable public interest in, and support for, a regional rapid transit system developed in the next few years, it was not until 1957 that the state legislature created the Bay Area Rapid Transit District to plan and, if approved, to build and operate a rapid-transit system.

For the next four years, BART District officials, with the help of engineering and financial consultants, were engaged in planning the system and mobilizing public support in the Bay Area.

Without any question, the most important date of all in the history of BART is November 6, 1962, when the citizens of three Bay Area counties—San Francisco and, across the Bay to the east, Alameda and Contra Costa—voted in a referendum to authorize a $792 million general-obligation bond issue to finance construction of the proposed BART system.

In July 1963, full-scale design engineering was begun by BART's engineering consultants, the joint-venture firm of Parsons Brinckerhoff-Tudor-Bechtel. Actual construction of the system was begun a year later, in June 1964, and in April 1965 the Diablo Test Track, a 4½-mile stretch of surface and aerial lines, was put into operation. At the Test Track, BART engineers and consultants from more than twenty U.S. corporations—including General Electric, Westinghouse, General Steel, and Budd Co.—are testing and refining virtually every element of the proposed BART system: ties, wheels, motors, undercarriages, suspension systems, sound-deadening devices, and the computer systems that will control BART's operations.

None of this, of course, just happened. Throughout these years, under the leadership of BART's president, Adrien J. Falk, former chairman of the board of S&W Fine Foods, BART officials spent an enormous amount of time and energy in "promoting" BART—mobilizing public support for the bond issue, enlisting the backing of leading members of the Bay Area's business and financial communities, and convincing Bay Area commuters that BART would be "faster, safer, more comfortable and more convenient than driving a private automobile on Bay Area streets and highways."

These last words are from a speech that BART's general manager, B. R. Stokes, made in 1962. The speeches that BART officials have made in the past eight years must number well up in the thousands. As Bill Stokes confesses, "We didn't turn down a single request. I gave as many as four speeches a day—breakfast, lunch, midafternoon, and dinner."

Although the pace of this promotional activity may have slackened a bit in the last few years, it still receives an important share of the attention of Bill Stokes and other BART officials. Through a superbly organized community relations program which involves, among other things, taking a 70-foot, $250,000 model of BART's prototype car to various strategic points around the Bay Area where citizens of all ages and temperaments can look, touch, sit, smell the upholstery, and even suggest improvements, BART officials are still working full-time at "enticing car-crazy Californians out of the driver's seat." General manager Stokes is more than slightly optimistic about the results of all this community relations activity. Commuters, he has said, "aren't going to *have* any real choice when they see how much more pleasant, comfortable, and certainly safer our trains are going to be."

THE MONEY PART

Of the total $1 billion estimated cost of the BART system, the major part is, as we have already noted, being raised by the sale of $792 million of BART District general-obligation bonds. These bonds will be supported out of a tax on real property levied throughout the three counties which the District comprises. The maximum tax rate required has been estimated at 71 cents per $100 assessed valuation, resulting in a cost of about $30 per year to the typical Bay Area homeowner.

In a heartening demonstration of forward-looking cooperation on the part of highway officials and automobile interests generally, $180 million for the building of the trans-Bay tube will come from auto tolls collected on the San Francisco-Oakland Bay Bridge and two other Bay Area bridges.

Another $71 million for rolling stock will be financed from BART fare-box revenues.

Because of the substantial interest of other U.S. cities and the nation as a whole in the testing program that is being carried on at the Diablo Test Track, the Federal Government has agreed to contribute at least $7.4 million of the estimated total cost of $11.5 million for the testing activity.

DETAILS OF THE SYSTEM

To permit high-speed transportation of large numbers of people with a maximum of safety and comfort, the BART system will be of the supported duorail type. The specially designed lightweight electric trains, constructed of either aluminum or steel and equipped with automatic operating controls, will have a maximum speed of more than 70 mph and will travel at an average speed of 50 mph, including station stops, over some 16 miles of subway and tunnel track, 31 miles of aerial track, 24 miles of surface track, and 4 miles of underwater track (through the trans-Bay tube).

There will be four main transit lines, all branching out from the trans-Bay tube. On the western side of the Bay, one line will extend southwestward from downtown San Francisco to Daly City. On the eastern side, three lines will branch outward from Oakland—one north to Richmond, another east to Concord, the third south to Fremont. All routes will occupy exclusive grade-separated rights-of-way, utilizing freeway median strips and existing rights-of-way wherever possible.

Multi-level subways with underground stations and pedestrian mezzanines will operate in downtown San Francisco, Oakland, and Berkeley. Of a total of 37 passenger stations throughout the system, 14 will be subway stations, 17 will be aerial stations, and 6 will be surface stations. Twenty-three of these stations will be equipped with commuter parking lots to provide a total initial parking capacity for some 30,000 automobiles.

Trains of from two to ten cars each will run at maximum daytime intervals of 15 minutes, with minimum intervals of 90 seconds during peak commuting hours. Each transit line will have a peak carrying capacity of 30,000 passengers per hour in each direction.

Train controls will be operated automatically through a centrally located computer, with an attendant assigned to each train. Fares also will be tabulated by computer—possibly through the use of a special "credit card" system.

Fares have been set low enough (25 cents minimum, 50 cents average) to assure the greatest possible patronage by Bay Area commuters—yet high enough to provide revenues adequate to pay all operating and maintenance costs. Trip fares will average 2½ to 3 cents per mile, with a possible discount for commuter fares.

AY AND BART

We asked San Francisco partner Joe Sullivan, who is in charge of Arthur Young's work for BART, to describe what our role has been. Here's what he told us . . .

"Our relationship with BART began back in 1958, when the Bay Area Rapid Transit District became a client of San Francisco Office. At that time BART was still in its infancy, and our involvement was limited to the annual audit. As BART's level of activity increased, from initial planning of the system in the late 1950s and early 1960s, through the voters' authorization to issue bonds in 1962, and the subsequent undertaking of detailed design and construction, our role increased.

"Within the past year, the scope of our work for BART has grown substantially. In addition to the annual audit, we have undertaken four special assignments:

"1. Design and implementation of a system for exercising cost control over the engineering and construction project.

"2. Development of accounting policies and procedures to meet the substantial increase in project activity.

"3. Design and implementation of a property accounting system to enable proper classification of invested funds and to provide meaningful information for purposes of accounting for assets and controlling operating performance.

"4. Assisting the BART internal audit staff in developing a program for auditing the many construction contracts that will be awarded during the next three to five years.

"Our association with the BART organization and its people has been a very gratifying experience for all of us. It has been exciting to see the Bay Area Rapid Transit system grow from an idea on a drawing board to its present stage of construction. But we're even more enthusiastic about what the eventual operating system will be like. The pride we take in BART as residents of the Bay Area will be that much greater because of the opportunity we've had to play a small part in its making."

QUESTIONS

1. Describe the work Arthur Young & Co. did in connection with BART.

2. (a) This work was described as "traditional accounting" work. What is "traditional accounting?"
    (b) To what extent were the Ernst & Ernst engagements in Cleveland and the Peat, Marwick, Mitchell & Co. work with the Model Cities programs (described in the two previous articles) "traditional accounting?"
    (c) Are there any boundaries at all to accounting? If so, how would you define them?

3. "The world should be populated with one-third philosophers and two-thirds accountants." Granting that the author of this comment was over-simplifying, why do you think he juxtaposed philosophers and accountants? Why do you think he chose these proportions?

*When Kenneth Gibson took over as mayor
of Newark, he succeeded a mayor who was
subsequently convicted on 64 counts of
extortion and conspiracy and inherited an
administration riddled with greed, ambition, and fiscal mismanagement. He sought
to call in Touche Ross & Co. to do a fresh
audit and review of the books. How this
effort was blocked by the City Council,
and the explanations given by the city's
long-standing outside auditor who also did
work for the reputed head of organized
crime in Newark, are recounted in the following* New York Times *news story of
September 20, 1970.*

Gibson Finds Graft Worse Than Expected

by David K. Shipler

The country's newest black Mayor and his aides are discovering that they have
inherited a city government even more corrupt, more debilitated by years of
fiscal mismanagement and more thoroughly riddled with resilient forces of greed
and ambition than they had expected.

Kenneth A. Gibson, after just over 10 weeks in office as the only black Mayor
in the Northeast and chief executive of New Jersey's largest city, has encountered the following among his problems:

- The political heirs and supporters of former Mayor Hugh A. Addonizio, who was convicted last July on 64 counts of extortion and conspiracy, have already become an obstacle to Mayor Gibson. In the City Council they blocked Mr. Gibson's attempt to hire an accountant who had worked on a grand jury investigation of organized crime to conduct a special audit and examination of the city's finances.

- Local business executives who are serving temporarily as aides to the new Mayor have uncovered $21-million in school operating expenses for this year that were kept secret by the previous administration to avoid the necessity of a tax rise in an election year.

- This imbalance between expenditures and revenue, compounded by other growing costs, will leave the city with $60-million less than it will need to pay its bills by the end of 1971, the Mayor's aides have calculated. Schools may have to close next spring because the Board of Education may run out of money.

- The conviction last July of Addonizio and other city officials has turned out to represent only the tip of a vast iceberg of corruption. Gibson aides have discovered that virtually every contract signed by the city in recent years was inflated by 10 per cent to allow for kickbacks to city officials.

- Corruption was made easier by a lack of personnel in city agencies. There are few at the middle-management levels who would dilute the power of top officials. And the city's Department of Public Works, which controls millions of dollars for sewers, roads and other projects, employs not a single licensed engineer—although it once had 20 to 25—to guard against fraud and error by private contractors.

- In its last few months, the Addonizio administration let certain private contracts lapse, stalling work on construction projects and depriving the city of certain privately rendered services. Federal funds were also cut off from several programs, leaving the city with no money to pay some employees when Mayor Gibson took office.

MAYOR'S MORALE HIGH

And yet Mr. Gibson seems to smile more than anyone else in City Hall these days.

To a recent question about the problems he faces, the 38-year old structural engineer grinned and replied evenly, "Well, they appear a little desperate, but they can be solved."

Calm, relaxed, deliberate, Mayor Gibson's cautious and undramatic approach to his job appears to have begun to steady the nerves of a city that has endured so many convulsions in recent years—rioting in the Negro slums in 1967 that left 26 dead, racial hatred, poverty and finally the exposure of the corruption that gripped the previous administration.

Mr. Gibson's calm has also won him the respect of the predominantly white business community, to the point where five major companies have lent him half a dozen top executives to help keep the machinery of city government operating until he finds permanent appointees.

The Mayor's friends see his caution and his slow pace more as a product of his own temperament than as a carefully constructed political style. But its effect is pragmatic, at least at the outset of his administration, for he is becoming known as a man who caters to no narrow group, whose broad appeal extends from militant blacks to middle-of-the-road whites.

There is a cross current to this respect for Mr. Gibson, however. While most of those who worked for him during the campaign appear to be reserving judgment for the moment on his performance in office, others within the Gibson camp are showing signs of being displeased with the new Mayor.

His avoidance of grand promises when he came into office, generally regarded as a wise move, annoyed some. His slowness in making key appointments has been met with thinly veiled impatience. The Mayor has become, in some eyes, an enigma, reluctant to trust anyone enough to take him into his confidence, to allow him to become a close adviser.

Mr. Gibson's caution, friends say, has become mixed with an apprehension about what law-enforcement officials tell him is a thoroughly entrenched structure of organized crime in the city. It is expected to attempt inroads into the new administration. In the first six weeks in office, the Mayor said he had "indications" that he could have received $31,000 "under the table" if he had responded to offers.

The Mayor said he had been told that the Police Director's job would be worth $15,000 to him, presumably if he appointed someone's chosen man.

And rumors have reached him of dissident policemen forming cadres to embarrass or thwart him. There is fear also of disloyalty among some civil servants in various agencies.

Gustav Heningburg, president of the Greater Newark Urban Coalition, and a campaign coordinator for Mr. Gibson, put it this way:

"By temperament and by training he's an engineer accustomed to careful analysis. Here's a 16-page report by somebody he doesn't know down in the bowels of City Hall. That lack of full knowledge tends to slow down his decision-making process. He reviews something six times instead of four."

'OWN ADVISER'

Furthermore, Mr. Heningburg continued, "He's his own adviser. He listens and he absorbs and then he goes off somewhere and makes decisions. There were people who worked in the campaign who knew more about campaigning than he did, and they had visible impact on his decisions. Now there is a normal kind of frustration."

The result has been that "some of his friends are peeling off," in the words of another close associate. Tired and somewhat hurt at not being listened to, they are withdrawing.

The major open dispute has been between the Mayor and Imamu Baraka, the black poet and playwright formerly known as LeRoi Jones. Mr. Baraka, who set out at least two years ago to get a black elected Mayor, took strong issue with Mr. Gibson's appointment of a white man, John L. Redden, to the sensitive post of Police Director.

"I was opposed to it," Mr. Baraka said recently. "This nation is a racist nation—I don't think that's any news. A lot of white people have a social attitude that will permit racist practices simply because they are not as sensitive to racism as black people."

BLACKS REFUSED

Mr. Baraka, acting for the Mayor, reportedly approached several blacks outside Newark to ask them if they would take the job, including Assistant Chief Inspector Eldridge Waith of the New York City Police Department. All refused.

"I talked to blacks," Mayor Gibson said. "They weren't really ahead of Redden. Whether you were black or white was really not the factor. The question was whether the guy could do the job."

Mr. Redden, a member of the police force since 1947 and formerly deputy police chief, has earned a reputation as "a tough, honest cop," as one businessman put it.

"The Redden appointment was excellent," said Frederick B. Lacey, the United States Attorney who prosecuted Addonizio. "He knows the Police Department of the City of Newark. This was the clearest demonstration of Gibson's intention to clean up the city."

Shortly after Mr. Redden took over, he promoted, demoted and transferred more than 200 policemen within the department. Scores of detectives were reduced to uniformed patrolmen pounding beats, and scores of patrolmen elevated to plain-clothes detective work.

RESISTANCE FEARED

Despite the Mayor's effort to establish firm control over the department, there is fear within the Gibson camp that dissident policemen may try to organize resistance to him.

Dominick A. Spina, former Police Director under Mayor Addonizio, and indicted, but acquitted, on charges of failure to enforce antigambling laws, retains a job in the department because of his Civil Service status.

He has tried to rally anti-Gibson sentiment among the uniformed forces, the Mayor's supporters say. And a recent three-hour meeting behind closed doors between Mr. Spina and former Councilman Anthony Imperiale, the white militant, has reinforced the apprehension that the two are working together against the Mayor.

At the end of August, an obscene hate letter was sent to policemen with Italian-sounding names. Gibson aides believe it was an attempt by whites who had access to the police roster to stir up black-white friction within the department.

The new Mayor ran into trouble from the outset on his appointment of Chief Redden, not only with blacks who wanted a black man in the job, but also with the nine-member City Council, which reportedly balked at first on approving the appointment.

According to sources at City Hall, Mr. Gibson had to use some muscle to get his man through. He reportedly threatened to get the three Councilmen who had run with him to oppose the election of Louis M. Turco, a 33-year-old lawyer as the Council President. At this, Mr. Turco and his supporters reluctantly voted their approval of the Redden appointment, and Mr. Turco was elected.

But the Council has remained an obstacle to Mayor Gibson, rebuffing his attempt to hire the accounting concern of Touche Ross & Co. to do a fresh audit and review of the city's books, financial procedures and controls on money. Touche Ross had been hired by an Essex County grand jury to work on a corruption investigation.

For the last 24 years, Samuel Klein & Co., a Newark accounting concern, has audited the city's books. The Mayor has observed that Mr. Klein's audits never revealed an irregularity.

"The way money was handled," Mr. Gibson said in an interview, "the way contracts were let, the way the city did business, how come the auditor who has been auditing the city's books for all these years has never raised a question?

"These are things that people have been indicted for—a Mayor and two former Public Works Directors—and yet nobody has found anything wrong with the bookkeeping."

AUDITOR REPLIES

In response, Mr. Klein, who has been in business for nearly 50 years, maintained "an auditing firm are not detectives, they are not an investigative body." "All I do is comply with the law," he said.

Contending that although he never found any irregularities, his work had a preventive effect, Mr. Klein remarked, "You didn't see any big defaultation or embezzlements."

In August, two days after the Council tabled the Mayor's request for a special audit by Touche Ross, Mr. Klein was subpoenaed to appear before a Federal grand jury investigating organized crime in New Jersey.

Mr. Klein recalled in a recent interview that he had delivered 16 cartons of his company's records and for 90 minutes, answered questions about the accounting he did for the family of Anthony (Tony Boy) Boiardo, the reputed head of organized crime in Newark, who was indicted along with Addonizio on extortion and income tax evasion. He is awaiting trial.

CLIENT FOR 30 YEARS

"I have represented the Boiardos for over 30 years," Mr. Klein said recently. "All I do is make out their tax returns." He said he also had among his 500 clients the Valentine Electric Company, in which Mr. Boiardo was once a part owner. "I see no conflict of interest."

But Mayor Gibson does. Asked if Mr. Klein's association with the Boiardos worried him, the Mayor replied, "It sure does—you better believe it. But you can't charge this guy with being a crook."

The Council had a different reaction. Mr. Klein appeared before them, discussed his relationship with the Boiardos and his past performance as an auditor and the Council voted unanimously to renew the $80,000-a-year Klein contract for another three years. It also tabled, and in effect killed, the Mayor's attempt to hire Touche Ross & Co.

"Klein dismissed the Boiardo thing," explained Council President Turco. "As an attorney I don't believe you can stigmatize a lawyer for defending people accused of committing a crime—it's the same for accountants. And the state of New Jersey has continued to issue contracts to firms that are low bidders and are involved in grand jury proceedings."

Mr. Turco, who supported Addonizio for re-election against Mr. Gibson, also rejected the need for a special audit, contending that it would be redundant, and that the city could not afford the $40,000 it would cost.

The Mayor's request for the audit grew out of a suggestion by Robert W. Smith, a vice president of Prudential Insurance Company who is on loan to fill in as the city's acting business administrator, a job similar to the city manager in other municipalities. Touche Ross, the concern that Mr. Smith recommended, is also the accountant for Prudential.

There were political overtones to the Mayor's request. Many of his advisers urged him to hire the accountant to make public the corruption and mismanagement that preceded his administration. Otherwise, they said, he would become responsible for it in a few months.

The same night the Council voted down the special audit, it appropriated $6,000 to buy Mr. Turco a new air-conditioned car. Mr. Turco defended the action by contending that bids would be taken on the car, so that it might cost less than $6,000. And, he said, "The last car was a 1964 Buick Electra which was run into the ground."

The city's financial difficulties are extremely severe, according to Mr. Smith of Prudential. The city's single source of revenue is its real estate tax. The rate is already nearly $8.50 per $100 of assessed valuation, one of the highest in the country and a level Mayor Gibson has called "confiscatory."

$162-MILLION BUDGET

The city's current budget is $162-million, Mr. Smith said, but expenses hidden by the previous administration will drive it to $60-million above what the city can expect to collect in taxes during 1971. If the property levy alone has to provide the revenue, it would have to rise to $13.53 per $100, he said, a rate that would surely drive out the remaining industry and middle-class property owners.

"We've reached the point in our society where the resources of the city are no longer adequate to meet the needs of the city," said Mr. Smith. "Newark has reached this point ahead of others, but there are a great many cities that aren't far behind us."

The Mayor, with the help of businesses in Newark, plans to present the State Legislature this fall with a package of proposed taxes to help the city out of its difficulty. Mr. Gibson has no details yet on the recommendations. But some observers are pessimistic about the prospects, noting that the Republican-controlled Legislature would like to stay Republican after the elections a year from November. In other words, a state income tax or city income tax—which would hit suburbanites who commute to Newark—is unlikely.

OTHER PROBLEMS FOUND

Mr. Smith found other problems when he arrived from Prudential, which is paying his salary for the 90 days he is to work for the city.

The lack of engineers in the Public Works Department was convenient, he said, since the city then had to rely on consultants to do the work. The consultant was often a contractor also, and the specifications it drew up could be met by only one concern—itself.

The result, according to Mr. Smith, was a recurrence of the same names of companies in the city's list of contractors.

Other sources at City Hall, who wished to remain anonymous, said that one sewer line was built that went nowhere. It simply ended underground and the sewage seeped into the earth.

On another sewer contract signed by the city for $78,000, new bids were taken after Mayor Gibson came into office and the city got it for $62,000.

The lack of middle management in city agencies appears to be a double-edged sword for the Gibson administration. On the one hand, as Mr. Smith observed, "the best guy in the world can't manage if he's got to get involved in every operating detail."

On the other, the structure gives the prospective Gibson appointees unusual power. And it means that organized crime must reach the top men if it is to corrupt the administration, giving the Mayor somewhat more control over the task of cleaning up the city government.

But many of the difficulties that confronted Mr. Smith the day he walked in had nothing to do with corruption. Construction contracts on which additional expenses had been encountered, for example, had lain dormant so that work was stalled on streets and sewers awaiting new appropriations.

The city's Federal housing code enforcement program had been denied Federal funds because the city had failed to meet the program's requirements to improve services and facilities in certain neighborhoods.

The contract with the private concern hired to remove abandoned cars had run out. Last week Mayor Gibson got the National Guard in to help with the job.

The city's computer operation, he explained, which makes up payroll checks, processes taxes and does part of the city's bookkeeping, is badly underutilized and understaffed. Only one man is employed who can program the computer, Mr. Smith said, and he keeps no records of his programs, so if he gets sick or quits, the system is threatened.

"In my judgment, the thing is hanging on a thread," he said. "If that thread breaks, we'll have trouble getting out the payroll."

Nevertheless, Mr. Smith and some of his colleagues insist that "this city is manageable—this thing can be made to run." The problem is finding someone to run it.

Some of the businesses that have donated executives for 90 days—Prudential, the National Newark and Essex Bank, the Fidelity Union Trust Company, New Jersey Bell Telephone Company and Public Service Electric and Gas Company—have also been conducting a nationwide search for a business administrator in the same way they would search for a corporation executive.

QUESTIONS

1. Why couldn't Mayor Gibson have called on the City's own staff of account-
    ants to conduct the special investigation he wanted? (Note that these ac-
    countants were employed by the city, and were associated with neither
    Touche Ross & Co. nor Samuel Klein & Co.)

2. The accounting firm Mayor Gibson wanted to hire had worked on a grand
    jury investigation of organized crime. Why would accountants be useful in
    such an investigation?

3. What are the scope and objectives of an audit? Should the firm which had
    been auditing the City of Newark for 24 years have discovered the irregu-
    larities? Discuss thoroughly.

4. Council President Turco is quoted as saying: "As an attorney I don't
    believe you can stigmatize a lawyer for defending people accused of com-
    miting a crime—it's the same for accountants." Do you agree? Explain
    fully.

5. What is your reaction to a CPA working, in a strictly accounting capacity,
    for organized crime?

Section V

Accounting and Crime Control

Crime is a problem throughout our country—in the cities, the suburbs, and even in rural areas and small towns. It occurs in the streets and corporate executive offices, in private homes and governmental agencies. There is evidence of regional, national, and even international networks and organizations involved in crime.

As our society becomes more crowded and more complex, the incidence and variety of crimes appears to increase. Clearly the well-being of a nation and its citizens requires that crime be held reasonably in check, and under present circumstances it is just as clear that this will require the mobilization of a variety of efforts and skills. The modern "war on crime" involves the sociologist, the chemist, the engineer, the psychologist, the physicist, and yes, the accountant.

As in other areas of society, law enforcement and crime control involve a great deal of organization and require the control of many resources. Information is at the heart of such efforts; and development of information processing and control systems is a principal part of the accountant's job.

Processing of defendants through the courts is an area replete with problems. Long delays, scheduling conflicts, and misplaced or misfiled case records resulting in dismissals do not serve justice not deter criminals. Sidney Brounstein describes how the accounting firm of Peat, Marwick, Mitchell and Co. assisted in the development of a defendant classification system for the District of Columbia by establishing a records system to show every event occuring on a criminal case—from the time it is brought into the prosecutor's office by the arresting policeman

205

to its final disposition by the courts. The system promises to contribute significantly to the smoother functioning of the Washington judicial system.

Thomas Sheehan notes that "one byproduct of the independent operation of multi-level criminal justice agencies and the overlapping of jurisdictions is the generation of prodigious masses of criminal data. The output of one agency becomes the input of another. And so the mountain of paperwork increases." To combat this situation the New York State Identification and Intelligence System (NYSIIS) was established with the help of the accounting firm of Touche, Ross, Bailey & Smart (now Touche Ross & Co.). (Most accounting firms provide a variety of services to clients beyond auditing and tax work. These activities include devising and installing cost control systems and information systems as well as a variety of special studies; at Touche Ross such work is called Management Services, and it is such a management services engagement which Sheehan describes in his article.)

On a more local level, the firm of Ernst & Ernst was engaged to try to improve the operations of the Louisville Police Court. The report of this engagement is summarized in "Assignment: Municipal Court." The conditions found by Ernst & Ernst appear to be the norm rather than the exception in communities throughout the United States.

Not every accountant has the opportunity to work with the courts and law enforcement agencies directly—but every accountant can be on the alert for signs of crime in business clients. Frederick Lacey, a United States attorney, suggests ways in which accountants can spot evidence of organized crime infiltration into business firms and what to do when such evidence is found.

Accountants are not policemen, despite the reputations some auditors have. But as the readings in this section suggest, accountants can contribute significantly in the war on crime.

ADDITIONAL REFERENCES

1. "Detecting and Preventing Organized Crime," The Journal of Accountancy, May 1970, pp. 45–46.
2. Downey, J. Russell and Ronald N. Nadler, "Federal Prison Industries," World (Peat, Marwick, Mitchell & Co.), Spring 1970, pp. 22–27.
3. Felkenes, George T., "Can the Computer Save Our Courts?" Datamation, June 15, 1971, pp. 36–39.
4. Hoover, J. E., "Accounting Investigations of the FBI," Management Accounting, August 1968, pp. 11–14.
5. Wormeli, Paul K., "The Search for . . . Automated Justice," Datamation, June 15, 1971, pp. 32–36.

*Law enforcement officers agree that to be
a deterrent, justice must be swift. By this
standard little deterrent exists in the United
States criminal justice system. This article
describes the contribution of Peat Marwick
Mitchell & Co. to the development of a
prosecutor's management information system designed to help speed up the whole
process.*

Programming the Criminal Courts for Justice and Efficiency

by Sidney H. Brounstein

*More money and more judges alone is not the real problem. Some of what is
wrong is due to failure to apply the techniques of modern business to the administration of the purely mechanical operations of the courts—of modern record
keeping, systems planning for handling the movement of cases.*

—Chief Justice Warren Burger

America's criminal justice system suffers as much from its own administrative
disorganization as it does from the pressures of rising crime. Criminals can't be

SOURCE: Reprinted by permission of the author and the publisher from
World (Autumn 1971), pp. 36–39.

blamed for scheduling conflicts that on the same day scatter policemen, witnesses, defense attorneys to several courts on different cases causing wholesale postponements; or for failure to notify in time, witnesses and attorneys that they are due in court, or that they aren't because of a last-minute shift in the calendar; or for the misplacement of essential records or files; or for the inability of the system to coordinate and bring together at the same time and at the same place chemists, physicians, handwriting analysts, and out-of-town witnesses vital to a case. And they certainly didn't invent the popular courthouse game in which one delay after another is sought in an effort to wear down the system.

The United States Attorney's Office in Washington, D.C., faced each year with the near-impossible task of trying to process more than 30,000 felonies and serious misdemeanors through the assembly lines of an overloaded, over-calendared court system, decided last year to do something about its organizational problems.

It set out jointly with the Washington, D.C. Office of Crime Analysis to develop a classification system designed to keep track of a defendant from the time of his arrest, through his prosecution and court processing, to freedom or prison.

The Office of Crime Analysis had been established by the District of Columbia to improve its court procedures and to coordinate the courts' work with law enforcement agencies.

Funds for the classification system were provided by the Federal Law Enforcement Assistance Administration, a part of the Department of Justice.

The heart and guts of this defendant tracking system is a computer-based information and processing technology that helps the prosecutor's office improve the key areas of its operation and to coordinate its work with that of the police and the courts.

Peat, Marwick was called upon to establish a records system to show every event occurring on a criminal case from the time it is brought into the prosecutor's office by the arresting policeman to its final disposition by the courts.

To accomplish this, a unique, never-before-tried computerized case accounting and information system had to be devised. The balance sheet in the system contained such hard-to-measure intangibles as criminal traits, human weaknesses, descriptions of crimes, and defense attorneys' ploys. It also meant keeping score on multiple cases, with some cases carrying multiple charges and multiple defendants. It meant accounting for changes in charges, changes in witnesses and, at times, changes in the cases themselves.

And the new system was to contain a set of values built into its operational process—values based on statistical data and criminological research and designed to provide priorities and a strategy for decision-making.

The process of designing the system and developing a method of programming it called for PMM&Co. to work closely with Charles Work and Frederick Watts of the U.S. Attorney's Office and with a team from the Office of Crime Analysis that included director Joan Jacoby, criminologist Dr. Stanley Turner, and systems analyst James Etheridge. In addition to the author, the PMM&Co. consultants responsible for this phase were William Hamilton, Robert Whitaker, and Dean Merrill.

Neither PMM's people nor the client knew exactly what ingredients were required in building such a system. This was a new and strange ballgame with no examples to follow. All the rules that were to govern the play were mainly informal and mostly in people's minds.

It might well have been called Project Innovation. As it turned out, it was named PROMIS—Prosecutor's Management Information System.

It took nearly a year for PROMIS to be born. It began to earn its keep on January 1, 1971.

PROMIS goes to work the moment an arresting policeman walks into the prosecutor's office with his offense report and "statement of facts"—data about the defendant and the complaint.

At this point, based on the "statement of facts," the prosecutor can refuse to prosecute the case (if he finds it too weak); can reduce the policeman's charge (if he figures it is unsupportable); can prosecute the charges the policeman instigated; or can add charges of his own.

Once the prosecutor makes up his mind on how to charge the case, he prepares an "input backup sheet." This contains personal information about the defendant, details about the evidence, the witness, and the victim.

All this will serve as an ultimate checklist to measure the urgency for prosecution and provide operational control.

Every bit of information gathered so far is punched out by a Magnetic Tape Selectric Typewriter (MTST) which sends its cartridge to a master tape housed in a System 360 computer.

This master tape already holds 10,000 case histories and the volume of its other criminal data is growing by the hour.

The next step in a criminal proceeding is the arraignment. And the circumstances surrounding it are now fed into the master tape. The date and place of the arraignment, the identification of all participants, the type of defense counsel being used, location of the defendant (on bail or in jail), initial plea, demand for jury trial and the date set for trial.

The trials in PROMIS' "jurisdiction" are held in two parts of the city court system. Misdemeanors go to the Superior Court of the District of Columbia and felonies to the District Court.

Each time a case comes to court—and the numbers can get pretty high these days—the master tape is told not only the action which occurred, but also the reason for each action. Every time a continuance is granted the tape is told whether it was ordered by the court (rare), requested by the government (rarer), or sought by the defense (frequent). Also listed is the specific reason for the order or request.

The last major computer input deals with the final disposition of a case and records the reasons for it. If a case is dismissed for want of prosecution, the tape will show why. A not-guilty verdict is evaluated to see if the prosecutor had presented a weak or strong case. A conviction will indicate if it was obtained by plea, verdict, or no contest.

Now this, in essence, is what goes into the computer. Here is what comes out:

The computer provides the prosecutor with two court calendars: The first, two weeks before a trial; the second, one day before. The calendars offer a most important service: each case is ranked for the prosecutor by its urgency for action.

A prosecutor's priorities are based on four factors: seriousness of the crime, defendant's criminal record, age of the case, and probability of winning a conviction.

The measure of what makes a "bad crime" is based on the seriousness of injury, the size of property loss, or the type of narcotic involved.

Another scale measures the man. The urgency of the case is rated on the extent of his criminal record, the number of his prior arrests and convictions, the length of time between his arrests, and his employment status.

The age of the case is a crucial element. PROMIS warns the prosecutor that the case is aging and that the probability of gaining a conviction is fading at a fast clip. One of the early lessons taught to the computer was: "The longer the time, the more distorted human memory will be."

Not unlike a bookmaker, the computer offers odds on the probability of winning. PROMIS takes guesswork and intuition pretty much out of this age-old practice of predicting. While it bases its odds partly on an experienced prosecutor's judgment, it depends on scaled factors such as extent of physical injury or property loss, relationship between the defendant and the complainant, availability of witnesses, involvement of narcotics, and whether the defendant is in jail or out on bail.

When the computer ranks a case urgent for any one or more of these four reasons, the U.S. Attorney's Office gets a chance to pick the case off the court assembly line and concentrate its scarce resources on it. It can, for instance, assign a more experienced assistant prosecutor to it. He, in turn, can take time out to study the defendant's history, the circumstances of the crime, the availability of witnesses, the need for special investigation. Now he can push for a speedy trial.

PROMIS also provides management control for the prosecutor's office:

- It reports to him cases that are languishing in the system because hearing or trial dates had passed without final action, or the setting of a new date;
- It tells him 14 days ahead of trial whether required chemical analyses had been completed and it updates this report the day before trial;
- It informs him of the number of continuances or postponements in each case and the reasons for them;
- It warns him to hurry because the arresting policeman is scheduled to retire soon and his unavailability would mean certain mistrial.

But PROMIS does much more than merely make the prosecutor's life easier:
It helps the entire system by keeping track of apparent conflicts in upcoming cases in the scheduling of policemen, defense lawyers, and expert witnesses and trying to reconcile them in advance of trial.

It helps police and courts by automatically generating subpoenas or notices for arresting policemen. It assists policemen, witnesses, defense attorneys, and defendants before each trial date, preliminary hearing and motion hearing date by automatically renotifying them when a hearing is postponed or canceled. And if there is not enough time left to mail subpoenas or notices, the computer turns to the telephone.

While PROMIS tries to prevent needless continuances by meshing court schedules and tracking down the people involved in a trial, it can't cope with human weakness.

A growing number of defense lawyers are known to play on the patience of witnesses as if on a fine stringed instrument. They use every ruse imaginable to win continuances until they finally succeed in wearing down witnesses.

As Charles Work, deputy chief in the U.S. Attorney's Office, tells it: "I know of one witness who dutifully showed up 12 consecutive times at a trial. Each time a continuance was gained. The 13th time the witness was unable to attend. Bingo! The case was dismissed."

PROMIS surely will prove to be a big help in making Washington's judicial system function smoother, Work says, but people, too, must do their share:

"We must improve police training so that reports will be more complete and the proper evidence is gathered; prosecutors must also be better trained in order to improve case preparation and courtroom presentation; more bench time by judges is needed (which could come from a combination of more judges and freeing them of burdensome administrative tasks), and lawyers must avoid the temptation of taking on too many cases per day and thus over-committing themselves for court appearances."

Meanwhile, PROMIS also tries to boost the effectiveness of the system by generating reports on cases scheduled for special hearings the next day.

It lists the cases for which hearings will be held to determine the mental competency of defendants; cases for which court-ordered police line-ups are scheduled and the cases scheduled for sentencing, including any sentencing recommendation based on bargained pleas.

PROMIS also provides police with hard copy and computer-readable magnetic tape outputs to update arrest records with final dispositions of the charges. And, as an important educational tool, it tells the police just exactly what happened to the charges they originally preferred.

It produces reports of defendants in new cases who are wanted by the courts as fugitives from other cases.

It provides a computer-readable magnetic tape containing pertinent data about defendants who have just been sentenced, enabling the Corrections Department to establish computer-based files on new inmates.

Bail agencies receive hard-copy outputs containing data on defendants released under the jurisdiction of the agency.

While it is too early to measure PROMIS' overall contribution to Washington's judicial process, the system already can be credited with one specific accomplishment.

The city has established a "special violations" unit to take advantage of PROMIS' brain, which holds a great deal of information from a multitude of crime-fighting sources throughout the nation.

Today, when PROMIS is fed the cartridge of a new case, it asks itself: "Is this person on my most wanted list?" If the answer is "yes," PROMIS prints out a special alert telling the police, the prosecutor and the courts that they have a "live one" on their hands.

New York and Philadelphia law enforcement agencies already are showing interest in bringing PROMIS to their cities. And PROMIS' proud parent, the Department of Justice, is studying the possibility of installing the system in several cities.

PROMIS has its hands full taking care of the present. But it already is looking to the future.

The day is not far when PROMIS will be asked to do more than just make the going great for the day-to-day administration of justice. It also will be asked to help prevent crime: by identifying patterns of success and failure in prison rehabilitation; by documenting the incidence of crime on bail; by analyzing and dissecting the ecology of crime, pinpointing the places where certain crimes are likely to occur, zeroing in on the likely time for that crime, and drawing a profile of the likely criminal.

And, perhaps most importantly, PROMIS will pinpoint the delay-causing problem spots in the criminal court system and recommend remedies to bolster the courts' role as a deterrent of crime.

QUESTIONS

1. "Peat, Marwick was called upon to establish a records system to show every event occurring on a criminal case . . ."

    (a) What are the main differences between this law enforcement records system and the records system of a business?

    (b) Very little economic information would appear in a law enforcement records system. Is this "accounting?"

    (c) Why do you suppose a public accounting firm was engaged for this work, rather than some other type of consultant?

2. What are the specific outputs of PROMIS?

3. Do you think the Prosecutor's Management Information System will help to reduce crime in the District of Columbia? Why? What other benefits does PROMIS promise? What costs and sacrifices are involved?

4. How might the system described in this article benefit an innocent defendant?

What positive, efficient, result-getting steps can be taken to upgrade the search, collection, retrieval, assembly and dissemination of criminal justice information? One answer is the New York State Identification and Intelligence System, developed with the assistance of Touche Ross & Co. and described in this article.

An Application of Management Services to Criminal Justice

by Thomas H. Sheehan

Napoleon Bonaparte once said, "The contagion of crime is worse than the plague."

In the U.S., crime is a plague indeed and a problem of the greatest national urgency. Yet public, and even official, understanding of the subject is woefully lacking.

Many Americans, of course, prefer not to think about the problem. "What business is it of mine?" they reason. "It is the job of the police to understand

SOURCE: Reprinted by permission of the author and the publisher from Touche Ross Tempo (June 1968), pp. 13–19. Mr. Sheehan is now with the management consulting firm of Spencer Stuart & Associates.

and cope with the criminal. Don't bother me with the issue. I have my own business to look after."

Others, increasingly alarmed by reports of the rocketing crime rate, feel that it most certainly is their business. They articulate their concern in the form of searching and disquieting questions: "Why does crime exist? What kind of individual commits criminal acts? How much does crime cost society? Are we capable of reducing crime? If so, how can this be done? What methods are practical? What methods are more effective than others? How much should we invest in the crime reduction effort?"

These are the questions in need of answers. But in all too many instances, neither are police able to provide the information nor are judges, penologists, probation and parole officials.

From the President on down, there is a sharp awareness of the need to ask the right questions regarding crime, and to come up with the right answers. As a result, numerous committees have been formed and investigations initiated to study the problem. The efforts continue. Some studies are relatively helpful, others worthless. The more effective probes tend to study the situation in much the same way a systems analyst would use to investigate a manufacturing process or an accounting system.

What works against getting meaningful answers that might help in combating crime is that the present network of American criminal justice was not conceived as an integrated whole. The system divides into a myriad of agencies—prosecution, criminal court, probation, prison, parole—each functioning independently in a way that does not necessarily relate to the whole. Under this setup, each agency is responsible to a different political structure. Villages, towns, counties, cities, states and the Federal Government each maintain separate criminal justice systems.

In many cases, the systems are archaic in concept. Origins of magistrate courts, for example, trial by jury, bail and appellate courts date back centuries, usually to English and European precedents. Provincial courts often stem from Colonial times. State courts were spawned in the post-Revolutionary period. Other components of the criminal justice system such as juvenile courts, probation, and psychiatric rehabilitation are more recent. But what the situation boils down to is a maze of functions, frequently unclear, sometimes overlapping, which makes the overall structure of American criminal justice difficult to define and even more difficult to upgrade.

Still, efforts are being made. And more than one agency has attempted to clarify the progress of criminal cases through the system. One such effort is outlined in Exhibit I. (From "The Challenge of Crime in a Free Society," a report by the President's Commission in Law Enforcement and Administration of Justice.)

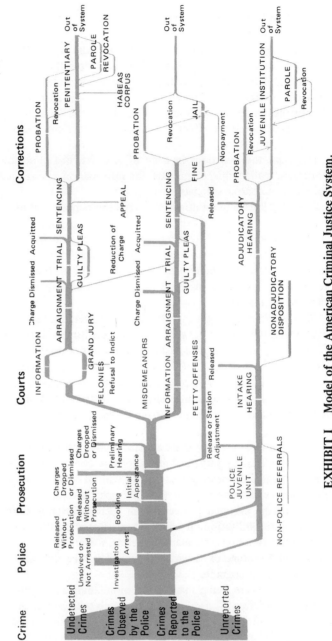

EXHIBIT I   Model of the American Criminal Justice System.

The varying line weights in Exhibit I suggest relative volumes. However, no nationally authoritative data exists to confirm or deny the suggested volumes associated with each part of the criminal justice model. Thus no one knows how to represent quantitatively the American criminal justice system. Neither does anyone know all the components of the system. Nor does anyone understand the significance should one or more of the components be missing. As a result, it becomes difficult if not impossible to accurately assess the merits of one proposal to reduce crime over an alternative proposal.

What, for example, would be the percentage of reduction in juvenile crime if all teenagers were required by law to attend daily classes on social responsibility? How effective would this measure be compared to an alternative proposal of assigning teenage law breakers in specified categories to a non-criminal "buddy" with a predetermined set of personality attributes?

Proponents for the classroom approach may well argue that this strategy would be the most effective way to tackle the problem. By the same token, "buddy" system advocates could present a very strong case in their own behalf. But which group is right? To which alternative could public funds be more efficiently applied? To get the answer, the benefits of each alternative would have to be scientifically documented. Then costs would have to be calculated and weighed against the gains. This is no simple procedure.

For one thing, both alternatives include a host of assumptions. The first alternative assumes that social responsibility could be defined and taught; that sufficient teachers could be made available; that adequate physical facilities exist or could be constructed. The second alternative assumes that "experts" would be able to predict the effect of personality attributes; that agreement could be reached regarding what it takes to qualify as an expert; that sufficient quantities of "buddies" would be available to make the program meaningful.

It takes far more than conjecture to satisfy these assumptions. One technique for coping with the problem is the decision table. Here is how a decision table geared to deal with the first two "buddy" system assumptions might be designed. (See Exhibit II.)

J = Judgment factor to be used at time of "buddy" assignment.

Although the decision table concept may be applicable to the consideration of alternatives, as yet there exists no precise and consistent sociological data with which to construct such a table. Obviously, the two alternatives proposed are naive in approach and do not represent operational alternatives. But they do illustrate the complexities of the American criminal justice system, and give some small insight into what is involved in the development and consideration of alternative crime reduction strategies.

One byproduct of the independent operation of multi-level criminal justice agencies and the overlapping of jurisdictions is the generation of prodigious

EXHIBIT II   Buddy Assignment Decision Table

IF: the teenage lawbreaker exhibits characteristics A, B, and C
in the combinations in the right of the table,

CHARACTERISTICS						
A	•	•			•	
B		•	•	•	•	
C				•	•	•

THEN: select a non-criminal buddy with the following
set of tested personality attributes.

ATTRIBUTES

physical strength	same	same		stronger	same	weaker
ethnic background	different	same	J	Table 2	same	
health	handicapped	same	same	J		
age range	-2, 0	3,5	3,5	4,7	3,5	0,3
race	different		different	same	same	
educational attainment	Table 3			2 yrs	Table 2	J
economic level				same		
sex	opposite	J		J		J

masses of criminal data. The output of one agency becomes the input of another.
And so the mountain of paperwork increases. Often, during the shuffling of data,
key facts are omitted, others are misinterpreted or erroneously transmitted. All
of which results in needless duplication and a correspondingly high cost of
operation.

Thus, as citizens, we pose the searching question: Where is the way out of the
labyrinth? What positive, efficient, result-getting steps can be taken to upgrade
the search, collection, retrieval, assembly and dissemination of criminal justice
information?

The need to present decisive answers to these questions was never more urgent. This urgency was stressed in the Report of the President's Commission on
Crime in the District of Columbia:

Nearly every agency involved in law enforcement and the administration of
justice is impaired by lack of facts pertinent to daily operations and long-
range planning. Information is either non-existent, incomplete, unassembled,

or incompatible at every stage of the criminal process—from offense to arrest, trial, conviction, sentencing, incarceration, release, and aftercare.

If data is not available at the local level, who is collecting, or planning to collect the data? And when it is collected, what will be done with it?

Several States are searching for answers. California, Colorado, Georgia, Kansas, Massachusetts, Michigan, New Jersey, New York, Pennsylvania and Washington are among them. Alameda County in California, the city of St. Louis, the Washington, D.C. Planning Commission, and the New England State Police Administrators' Conference have already taken positive steps to improve their data handling and dissemination.

New York State in particular has taken significant strides forward. Its experience is well worth reviewing.

NYSIIS

In 1965, the New York State Identification and Intelligence System (NYSIIS) was established to provide improved data for the more than 3600 criminal justice agencies in the State. The four principal goals of NYSIIS are:

1. to set up a state-wide criminal justice data bank,
2. to improve the accuracy and completeness of the data on file,
3. to respond rapidly and efficiently to inquiries from all criminal justice agencies regarding persons with a criminal history on file in New York State,
4. to aid in the speedier and more thorough processing of accused and convicted persons.

NYSIIS provides positive identification of an individual based on fingerprints; probable identification based on name, personal description and other identifying data; and responds to inquiries with a summary case history (SCH), photographs and other information.

The need for NYSIIS was underscored by the November, 1957 Apalachin, New York meeting of more than 100 crime overlords. The frustrations of sorting, assembling and retrieving data on these arch criminals triggered Governor Nelson A. Rockefeller's authorization in May, 1963 of the initial study project. In 1965, a statute established NYSIIS as an agency within the Executive Department of New York State. Its purpose: "To assist in the improvement of the administration of criminal justice by developing and establishing a computer-based information sharing system."

TRBS AT NYSIIS

NYSIIS started with a study group of five State employees. In less than a year it swelled to agency status. Demands on the small State group were considerable.

In August, 1965, Touche, Ross, Bailey & Smart was asked to supplement the efforts of the State staff. The initial task of the TRBS Management Services group was to aid NYSIIS in making a study of alternative methods of converting historical data from manually processed to machine processable form. The value of the systems approach became apparent early in the endeavor. The key elements of this approach are worth repeating.

Key No. 1—The importance of defining objectives and clarifying terms at the outset of the study.

Key No. 2—The need to establish project control procedures right from the start.

Key No. 3—The need to conceptualize, develop costs, explore and evaluate alternatives.

Key No. 4—The importance of hard work and depth probing. This includes attention to detail and a need for project leaders and analysts alike to understand the system under study as a whole as well as being able to spell out computer specifications at the data element level.

Key No. 5—The need to measure results against explicity stated objectives.

Key No. 6—The importance of pinpointing potential uses for such quantitative techniques as sampling, queuing theory and network analysis—coupled with the importance of remaining objective about their applicability.

Of prime importance, experience proves, is the need to remain flexible, particularly during the analysis process. Opinions and conclusions reached too early encourage rigidity and discourage the imaginative approach. In the end it leads to costly system modifications, frustration and disappointment. All of these keys played a vital role in achieving the objectives of the NYSIIS data conversion study on schedule, within budget, and with maximum efficiency.

A prime purpose of the data conversion study was to analyze the type of data required to satisfy the information needs of NYSIIS, its user agencies, and the New York State criminal justice system. The output of the study was a report supporting NYSIIS' fiscal 1966 budget request with cost estimates for converting data.

One goal of NYSIIS was to provide rapid access capability to historical data already on hand in the State's Division of Identification (DCI).[1] This readily available source included information on approximately 3.5 million persons, of whom one-and-three-quarter-million were known to be criminals. A primary task in planning the data conversion effort was to define the file to be converted. This meant identifying the various types of data, exploring, reviewing and deciding upon feasible conversion alternatives.

Here is where the systems approach became important. To determine the optimum conversion alternative, certain fundamental questions were posed by TRBS analysts:

- What are the operational definitions of a criminal and a recidivist? (A recidivist is a "repeater" who meets the following criteria: he must be under 55 years old, and if arrested only once that arrest must have occurred within ten years; if arrested two or more times, at least one of these arrests must have occurred within twenty years.) These definitions need not, and at NYSIIS did not, conform to the legal or dictionary definitions.
- Would the cost of converting all criminal records in the files be commensurate with benefits to be derived?
- If not, which records should be converted and how could they best be identified?
- What data elements[2] should be converted?
- Which document types provide consistent and accurate data?
- How much of the required information is missing or unavailable in existing records? What steps will be needed to obtain this information?
- What practical error level can be tolerated? How will this error level be measured?
- What are the conversion requirements in terms of manpower, money and time?

While operational definitions of a criminal and recidivist were being obtained, identification of the data elements to be converted was begun. The identification process was based on a statistical sample of the manually processed summary case history folder file, name index file, and fingerprint file.[3] The sample provided the quantitative measures needed to compute estimates of:

- The number of recidivist case history folders on file,
- The composition of recidivist case history folders by document types and volumes of documents they contained,
- The amount of missing information,
- The attributes of recidivists.

The sample revealed other interesting problems as well. For example, the average number of documents per recidivist case history folder was ten. But some folders contained as many as 192 documents; others contained none. The average number of fingerprint arrest cards per recidivist case folder was three. But some histories reported as many as 75 arrests. One person, arrested 8 times, showed seven different cities as his place of birth and an age discrepancy of 21 years. Another person with 12 arrests was recorded ten times as a male, twice as a female.

This will provide some insight into the degree of frustration involved in the findings. Despite this, the sample was extremely useful in developing routine conversion procedures. At the same time, it suggested different methods of handling exceptions in situations such as those outlined above. Finally, the statistical sample provided a laboratory for making time and motion studies and in estimating the amount of work involved to locate each data element, for coding or transcribing the data element, and for applying edit rules.

Another major task was that of describing the total work content in the conversion process. This was a highly detailed operation. It consisted of breaking down conversion activities into logically grouped categories. Specific recidivist case history folders had to be removed from the files, documents selected and microfilmed, data keystroked, and original material returned to the files. The time and motion estimates were used in conjunction with standard hourly rates to estimate costs for each activity as well as total costs for each conversion alternative.

In analyzing the proposed conversion alternatives, TRBS came to the conclusion that a substantial number of the one-and-a-quarter-million summary case history folders on file were not likely to be of much value. This bulk represented non-recidivists as spelled out in the operational definition (persons who had not committed a second offense in a great many years, or people beyond the 55-year age limit). The assumption was thus made, based on statistical findings, that the non-recidivist was unlikely to commit other crimes in the future. Selection procedures were consequently geared to segregate non-recidivists prior to conversion, reducing costs considerably.

Suppose, however, that the future actions of non-recidivists contradicted the general assumption. Provisions were made to convert and reactivate such files should the summary case history folders be required to satisfy the rapid response goal of NYSIIS to meet the criminal justice information needs of user agencies.

The final task of the data conversion study was to evaluate the proposed alternative conversion plans and to recommend the one that was best. Evaluation of alternatives was based on the following criteria: the ability to satisfy data base requirements, the cost of conversion, the implications of scheduling the required clerical staffs, and the projected effectiveness of practical control measures.

The data conversion system ultimately recommended estimated that approximately 500,000 summary case histories out of a population of one-and-a-quarter million would optimize the ratio of cost to benefits derived.

In November, 1965, NYSIIS invited TRBS back to implement the data conversion study recommendations. A joint NYSIIS-TRBS data conversion implementation team was designated. The team's new major tasks included:

● Planning the data conversion design, development and implementation effort using network analysis and a CPM computer program.*

*EDITOR'S NOTE: Network analysis and CPM (Critical Path Method) are techniques for scheduling complex projects.

- Preparing the EDP programming specifications.
- Performing a non-criminal data conversion study similar in scope to the initial data conversion study which considered only criminal data.
- Writing clerical data conversion procedures.
- Preparing a data conversion master schedule.
- Designing and monitoring a pilot study operation of the clerical procedures.
- Verifying the results of the statistical sample performed in the data conversion study.
- Establishing a statistical acceptance sampling procedure on vendor performed keystrokes.
- Training of the clerical staff and monitoring of the overall data conversion operation during the initial start-up effort.

In October, 1966, the application of Management Services Techniques was expanded. At that time TRBS joined the NYSIIS staff in designing an On-going system. This On-going system serves as the basis for accomplishing the four previously stated goals of NYSIIS.

In addition to the major tasks already discussed, the expanded scope of work included:

- Definition of the On-going system capabilities. This definition included a series of milestones against which progress can be measured.
- Identification of present departmental workload.
- Definition of the existing manual system and the proposed EDP system including present and anticipated costs.
- Analysis of future data communication needs for fast response information sharing.
- Preparation of flow charts, clerical procedures, EDP functional specifications, control procedures, and work station layouts.
- Documentation of the system design effort including: System Design Manual(s), System Design Change Notices, and System Description.
- Analysis of fingerprint classification procedures and performance of a controlled statistical experiment to estimate filing and searching error rates.
- Analysis of the feasibility of using microfilm to record storage, transaction control and system backup.
- Preparation of a training program.
- Development of project reporting and management techniques.
- Assistance in the preparation of budgets and schedules and their subsequent re-planning as required.
- Analysis of machine readable data files to determine missing, incomplete or unusable data elements.

- Estimation of costs to collect missing or unusable data elements.
- Development of decision rules to format-converted data into the On-going system.
- Specification of error correction EDP programs, clerical control procedures.

Although the list of completed NYSIIS tasks grows longer each day, considerable work remains to be done. Impressive strides are being made, not solely through application of the systems approach, but equally through the dedicated efforts of highly qualified people from several organizations who are pooling their knowledge and enthusiasm in the achievement of a common goal.

As yet New York State is a long way from solving its harrowing and complex crime problems. But a basic building block in the solutions, the ingredients of an improved data bank, are gradually being fitted into place.

IN CONCLUSION

Like NYSIIS, the national criminal justice system in America can be analyzed using the systems approach. Thus the same advantages inherent in the NYSIIS effort would apply to the national picture as well. One objective in designing an information system, for example, is to balance the value of information generated against the cost of supplying it.

Determining the value of data is essentially a management decision. In a criminal justice system, this comes under the province of police, court, prison, parole and probation administrators. By the same token, the cost of information is governed by technical considerations of systems design dictated by volume of data handled, response time, selectivity of response, accuracy and reliability.

The systems approach stresses the development of alternatives in order to achieve the best balance between value and cost. Yet the concept alone is no panacea. The systems approach requires competent personnel to apply its discipline effectively. At the same time the discipline of the systems approach permits competent personnel to ask the questions that need asking, to evaluate the answers and, if necessary, to rephrase the questions without losing sight of the objectives.

In criminal justice this is a must if we, as Americans, are to make significant progress in the reduction of crime.

FOOTNOTES

1. DCI was an organizational unit within the Department of Correction. When absorbed by NYSIIS it subsequently became known as the Bureau of Identification (BI) via a statutory enactment in April, 1966.

2. A data element is the most basic grouping of characters, or unit of data that one wishes to reference. It is sometimes called a "field" in computer terminology. Care must be used in defining data elements. NAME, for example (person's full name), is not a data element if one wishes to address those characters within NAME that refer to first name only.

3. The summary case history folder file represents one-and-a-quarter million persons who have two or more documents on file at NYSIIS. The name index file contains five-and-one-half-million names and name variants such as: nickname, alias. The fingerprint file contains three-and-one-half million master fingerprint cards, one for each person on file.

QUESTIONS

1. At the beginning of his article Sheehan raises the following questions:

   Why does crime exist?
   What kind of individual commits criminal acts?
   How much does crime cost society?
   Are we capable of reducing crime?
   If so, how can this be done?
   What methods are practical?
   What methods are more effective than others?
   How much should we invest in the crime reduction effort?

   How can accounting help in answering these questions? Which ones appear to be completely beyond the scope of accountants?

2. Does your concept of a "typical CPA" include the performance of management services?

3. Describe fully Touche Ross' role in establishing the New York State Identification and Intelligence System. Could non-accountants have performed this work equally well? Explain.

4. "...no one knows how to represent quantitatively the American criminal justice system....it becomes difficult, if not impossible, to accurately assess the merits of one proposal to reduce crime over an alternative proposal." Is it necessary to quantify components of the system in order to evaluate alternatives? Discuss.

5. "Determining the value of data is essentially a management decision." Do you think accountants determine the value of data? If so, how?

6. "The data conversion system ultimately recommended estimated that approximately 500,000 summary case histories out of a population of one-and-a-quarter million would optimize the ratio of cost to benefits derived." List the major costs and benefits you think were involved.

7. (a) The State Division of Identification maintained information "on approximately 3.5 million persons, of whom one-and-three-quarter-million were known to be criminals." Why would the Division maintain information on citizens not known to be criminals?

   (b) An attorney recently observed: "Bureaucrats, technicians, and number shufflers are so enthusiastic about using their high-powered techniques and massive computers to maintain data on every man, woman, and child that they ignore civil liberties problems such as invasion of privacy, inhibition of freedom of association, and the chilling effect dossiers have on the exercise of free speech." Do you agree? Do accountants fit this description? What are the responsibilities of the accountant to society, over and above his responsibilities to the client who pays his fees? (Note: you might want to scan the section on Accounting's Social Responsibility before answering.)

8. (a) You are a partner in the accounting firm of Luca Pacioli and Co. You have been approached by the governing body of your city to estimate the cost of crime to the community. Suggest ways in which the "cost" to your community of the following crimes might be measured:

   Murder
   Assault
   Robbery, burglary, and shoplifting
   Driving while intoxicated
   Heroin possession and use
   Bribery of public officials

   (Note: it might be useful to read at least the Appendix to "Accounting for Social Costs" in Section VI before answering.)

   (b) Choose one crime, not necessarily from the above list. Outline in some detail the steps you would take to estimate the cost of this crime to your community. When finished, consider whether what you have just done is "accounting."

   (c) Now assume you are the mayor of your city. How could you use the crime cost estimates provided by Luca Pacioli and Co. for policy and decision-making?

*How to get the most for their tax dollars is
an increasing concern for millions of taxpayers. The people of Louisville and their
city administration are no exception. Recently Louisville newscaster Clarence Jones
of WHAS-TV read an Ernst & Ernst report
he felt his viewers ought to know about.
He took the unusual step of airing it in
three installments. Portions of his script
are reproduced here in italics. The connecting passages are the thoughts of one of his
viewers—an E & E man who worked on the
assignment.*

Assignment:
Municipal Court

Suddenly you remember what it was like. It's eleven o'clock at night, you're relaxing in your living room, the news has just started, and the announcer is saying:

*An accounting firm, Ernst & Ernst, has just completed a major study of Louis-
ville Police Court. The survey was aimed at finding out how police court works,
and how it can be made to work better. For the story, here's WHAS newsman
Clarence Jones.*

And you remember that morning, soon after the assignment began, watching the people arrested the previous night being shepherded from city jail to the hold-over cells at the police court. And all at once realizing how different this assignment is. You've worked for a lot of clients who turned out a great variety of

---

SOURCE: Reprinted by permission of the publisher from E & E (Summer
1972), pp. 23–27.

products and services, but this client is unique; it's in the business of processing people. The people for the most part are an unshaven, shambling, unprepossessing lot. But it occurs to you that you wouldn't look your best either if you'd been bustled into a squad car the night before and herded into a jail cell to await the 9:00 a.m. reactivation of the judicial process. You'd be worrying less about how you looked than about your chances of getting a prompt and fair hearing. You remember reminding yourself that your report, when you come to write it, has to be not only totally factual and objective, but easily understandable by an intelligent layman. Well, it sounds as though newscaster Clarence Jones had little trouble understanding it . . .

The study stays away from statistics and complicated technicalities. It says in plain, everyday language that police court is badly bogged down in red tape and unnecessary paper shuffling. The report blames nobody. It says the system is the culprit, not any one judge or bailiff or clerk. Once the system begins to do something as part of standard procedure, whether good or bad, it is continued, passed on from employee to employee, until nobody remembers or understands why it is done. There is a rule, for instance, that says all city jail prisoners arrested during the night up until 6:00 a.m. will be brought before the 9:00 a.m. session of police court. So every morning, prisoners arrested in the pre-dawn hours are taken from city jail to the holdover cells at police court. On busy days, the paper work can't be completed for their cases to be heard at 9:00 a.m., so they must be taken back to city jail after court recesses, then hauled back again for a later court session. "This causes a great deal of confusion for both the police department and the court clerks," the report says. It could be eliminated if someone would simply review the time it takes to process paper work after an arrest, then make sure there has been enough time before prisoners are brought over from city jail.

You remember one clerk, in particular, who was industriously banging away at a typewriter. You asked her what she was doing. She looked up briefly from her keyboard to explain that she was typing case dispositions. What happens to them when they're typed? you asked. Why, she answered, they go into the judge's order book. What's the book used for? you asked. She didn't know. So you went to her superior. Why is this done? you asked. You learned why, and so did newsman Jones . . .

It's done because a city ordinance says it must be done. But nobody ever uses the book, the report says. The same information is available in other records that are easier to use.

You remember, during the first day or two, you spent a frustrating amount of time just finding your way from one place to another. This, of course, was no problem for the people who work there every day. But a city police court usually has quite a few strangers milling around. How do they get to where they're supposed to go? Here's Clarence Jones again, paraphrasing your report . . .

Clerks who work the cashier windows in the court clerk's office spend half their time, the report says, just giving directions to confused people who are trying to figure out which courtroom they're supposed to be in. Every day half the cases on the police court docket are continued to future dates. Cases are frequently continued because witnesses are not present. The report says that sometimes the witnesses are there, but sitting in the wrong courtroom. The report suggests that a simple sign system could correct some of these problems. If you've tried to telephone police court during the day and found the line busy for hours, the report tells you why. Lawyers, bondsmen, policemen and other non-court personnel constantly use the court clerk's phone for their private business, and the public can't call in.

Now newscaster Jones is holding before the TV camera a bill submitted to the police court by an outside detective agency for four days of summons serving. You've never been served a summons personally, and you hope you never will be, but you won't soon forget your first encounter with summonses. Jones covers the subject . . .

Late last summer one of the accountants conducting the court study discovered that nobody checked the detective agency's bills. One day, when the agency brought in a batch of summonses, the accountant counted them. The count showed a significant discrepancy between the bill and the returned summonses. From that day forward, clerks have counted the summons returns. . . . If the new, lower bills paid to the detective agency continue, the city will pay the agency about $20,000 per year less. The accountants' report shows that there are other problems in the summons serving process. In early October, WHAS reported that 44 percent of all Louisville parking tickets are filed away in police court. Twenty-five percent of all traffic tickets for moving violations are filed away . . . . The court survey shows that the process of issuing summonses is so antiquated that clerks simply can't write summonses fast enough to keep up with the case load. As a result, many cases are filed away. Each summons is now handwritten. The report says that with minor computer programming, the city-county data processing center could print summonses and eliminate the need for clerks to write between 50,000 and 60,000 summonses per year. Other cities have found, the report says, that mailing summonses is often more effective and much cheaper than trying to do it with personal service. The report recommends that Louisville study summons serving in other cities and consider changing the local system.

Now the newscaster is touching a particularly vivid memory . . .

Throughout the accountants' report there is a recurring theme: that various agencies in city government do not communicate with each other, and that this is the cause of many foul-ups.

You remember that your assignment involved you with three distinct entities: the police department, which tried its best to enforce the law; the court, which tried its best to administer the law on an impartial and just basis; and the data processing department, which tried its best to maintain an accurate and up-to-date record of what the police and the court were doing. Everybody, in short, was trying his best, but the result was far below what it should be, and the reason was that they weren't communicating.

Last February some of the court clerk's chores were assigned to the city-county data processing department. The task of preparing the daily court docket is now done by computer. But the report says there has been very little communication between the court, the data processing department, and the police department . . . Much of the report deals with the need for court processes to be further computerized. The report says the crush of today's caseload simply cannot be handled by clerks filling out forms in longhand.

You remember the court clerk, Mrs. Margueritte Younger, who knew exactly what her job demanded, and met those demands with professional competence, Now here she is being interviewed on TV by Clarence Jones.

Jones: Mrs. Younger, the court clerk, said one of the report's suggestions to help solve [the communications] problem has already been adopted.
Mrs. Younger: We have a clerk as a coordinator with data processing, as the report suggested. This keeps him busy full time, five days a week.
Jones: This is to let you really talk to data processing for the first time?
Mrs. Younger: Yes, and data processing has a person designated to work along with the clerk that I have and iron out all these problems that arise from starting something new of this sort. It's already beginning to show improvement, and I'm well satisfied with it.

You remember tripping over an open file drawer. You'd been aware, since the beginning of the assignment, that working conditions for the court's staff were anything but ideal, and this fact was certainly going to be emphasized in your report. But perhaps your sore shin lent eloquence to your prose when you wrote: "The overall physical arrangement is crowded and gives both workers and persons served by the clerk's office a feeling of untidiness. Illumination and ventilation are inadequate for good working conditions. The traffic patterns are poor and cause a great deal of disruption."

Clarence Jones of WHAS doesn't know you tripped over the file drawer, but he's read your report, and he knows that the wheels of justice in Louisville inadvertently leave civic bruises. Now he's signing off . . .

The report . . . is a good one. In plain, everyday language, it shows some of the ridiculous make work that present law requires clerks to perform. It is embarrassingly candid in spelling out quirks that common sense could have cured. It praises city officials for being willing to let the public take a peek at some of the court's dirty laundry. It says that for a court to process as many cases as we expect of this court, there must be far broader use of computers instead of clerks scribbling endlessly in longhand. It says, in the final analysis, that the system no longer works. That many cases get lost in the shuffle. Unless massive changes are made in the operation and organization of the court, then the cries . . . calling for a more effective war against crime are no more than hollow . . . words masking generations of neglect.

You turn off the TV, but the memories persist. Stair banisters with years of patina and nicks. Clattering typewriters; hurrying pens. The mustiness of basement rooms where aging records are piled in bins. The respectful rustle of a roomful of people rising when a judge enters the courtroom. The late-night cup of coffee offered to you by a friendly desk sergeant. All facets of a hoary but indispensable ritual that's feeling its age these days. If you've helped breathe new life into it, your time couldn't have been better spent.

QUESTIONS

1. Visit the Police Court (or its equivalent) in your community. Do the conditions you observe appear to be better, about the same, or worse than those encountered by the Ernst & Ernst staff in Louisville?

2. In terms of the work involved for the accounting firm, how did the Louisville police court engagement differ from one which might be undertaken to improve office operations in a business firm?

3. Do you think the engagement described is likely to have any direct effect on the lives of defendants charged in the Louisville Police Court? If so, how?

4. (a) In several readings in this book the accountant is involved with computers. How did computers figure in this engagement?
   (b) To what extent should accountants be competent in working with computers?

According to the author, who was U.S. Attorney in the State of New Jersey at the time this was written, organized crime is far broader than the two dozen families of the Mafia. And the evil it perpetrates goes beyond vice, gambling, extortion, narcotics and loan sharking—its ever-spreading tentacles threaten to poison the free enterprise system itself. In this article, he suggests that no one is in a better position to turn back the criminal infiltrators of legitimate business than members of the accounting profession, and indicates the actions the CPA might take to help legitimate business protect itself against criminal penetration.

How Accountants Can Fight Organized Crime

by Frederick B. Lacey

Ten per cent of all special agents in the Federal Bureau of Investigation are trained accountants. That figure underlines the FBI's recognition of the important role that the accounting profession can play in the war against crime. Nevertheless, CPAs in mufti don't ever seem to think of themselves as potential crime fighters. I think they should become more aware of the contribution that

---

SOURCE: Reprinted by permission of the publisher from <u>World</u>, published by Peat Marwick Mitchell & Co., Summer 1970, pp. 2–5.

public accountancy can make toward stopping one of the pernicious evils of the day—the infiltration of legitimate business by Organized Crime.

Even more than the lawyer, the accountant is singularly equipped to note the incipient stage at which organized crime begins its penetration of a legitimate business. Apathy, indifference, disbelief can only help the criminal spread his filthy and dangerous tentacles into our free enterprise economy.

Have no doubt about it: the underworld is moving in on the business community. And the infiltration—too often with the help of businessmen themselves—has been going on for a long time.

As far back as the Kefauver hearings it was reported that "in some instances legitimate businessmen have aided the interests of the underworld by awarding lucrative contracts to gangsters and mobsters in return for help in handling employees, defeating attempts at unionization, and in breaking strikes."

A few years ago the Illinois Crime Commission, after investigating a service industry in Chicago, stated: "There is a disturbing lack of interest on the part of some legitimate business concerns regarding the identity of the persons with whom they deal. This lackadaisical attitude is conducive to the perpetration of frauds and the infiltration and subversion of legitimate businesses by the organized criminal element."

In one city, Organized Crime gained a monopoly in garbage collection by preserving the business's nonunion status and by using its cash to offset temporary losses incurred when the mob company lowered prices to drive competitors out of the field.

One must not make the mistake of thinking that Organized Crime limits its takeovers to such businesses as garbage collection, jukebox distribution, and restaurant services. The President's Commission on Law Enforcement and Administration of Justice reported that control of "certain brokerage houses was obtained by foreclosing on usurious loans, with the businesses thereafter being used to sell fraudulent stock, causing a loss of $2 million to the public."

The Commission also reported that "The kinds of production and service industries and businesses that organized crime controls, or has invested in, range from accounting firms to yeast manufacturing. One criminal syndicate alone has real estate interests with an estimated value of $300 million. In a few instances, racketeers control nationwide manufacturing and service industries with known and respected brand names."

It can truly be said that every legitimate commercial enterprise in this country is a potential victim of organized crime. Of course, with the larger companies sophisticated means are substituted for the muscular extortionists often used by the mob to acquire control of local enterprises.

There is, for example, the use of foreign banking operations. The mob arranges for the transmission of its illegal gains to a foreign bank where, under the laws of secrecy that prevail, the identity of the criminals is concealed. The foreign bank is then used to acquire the stock of an American company and acts as a nominee, still concealing the name of the criminal investors. Thereby, as pointed out by Will Wilson, the Assistant Attorney General who heads the Criminal Division of the Department of Justice: ". . . substantial equity positions in key industries are being acquired with the proceeds of vice, gambling, extortion, narcotics and loan sharking, as well as from the illegal operations of legal businesses."

A variation of the foregoing procedure is to have a foreign trust owned and funded by American underworld interests lend money to a cooperative American businessman who, in turn, through a holding company, uses the proceeds of the loan to acquire major positions in public companies.

Attorney General John Mitchell has told of the dreadful incursions into the air freight business by organized crime. And we all have become aware in recent years that security of banking institutions and brokerage houses has been compromised in many instances. Trafficking in stolen securities is now an extensive mob activity.

The racketeer goes into legitimate business for three reasons: to make more money; to achieve an aura of respectability for himself and his family; and to establish a source of funds which, after taxes, is available for expenditures in an amount to explain his mode of living. The latter reason ameliorates the racketeer's gravest concern, income tax prosecution.

As indicated above, the criminal may follow any of a variety of roads in his penetration of legitimate business. He keeps tabs on the business proprietor who is a big-stakes gambler. Should the businessman run up a substantial gambling debt, he may be told that the only payment he can make is a transfer of a portion, or all, of his interest in the business to a member of the mob.

The businessman who is at the end of his line of credit with the banks might give in to the temptation to borrow from a shylock at an extortionate rate of interest. Ultimately the interest, which can be as high as 2% a day, becomes impossible to pay. At this point, the businessman is given a choice: live under the threat of severe physical injury from the shylock's musclemen or pay off his debt by transferring his interest in the business to the mob.

Sometimes business is penetrated through dishonest labor channels. The businessman, the crooked union representative and the mob he represents team up to keep labor peace.

And of course, the member of the mob with vast sums of cash on hand can simply buy his way into a business.

No matter how the criminal gets into the business, one thing is certain to happen when the mob takes control: cash will begin to flow out of the company. This is the hallmark of a company that has been taken over by criminals. At this point the mob, even though it controls the proprietor, is vulnerable to the alert CPA.

If the corporate financial records show that cash is being funneled out of the company into unusual sources, the accountant should immediately request that the client furnish him with the raw data supporting the outlays. The auditor should bear in mind that we have found from time to time in our own investigations that these cash outlays have been supported by invoices and bills that are not legitimate. Suspicions shouldn't be put aside too easily. Not only does the accountant have a duty to his profession but he should try to save the client from himself if he seems to be following the path of least resistance to the demands of the mob. There can be only one result: the businessman is going to lose his business and no one is in a better position to spell this out for him than his auditor.

Among the danger signs that the accountant should be alert to is the sudden appearance on the payroll of the names of men who are said to be performing services that in the past required no employees. Just possibly these new employees have been placed by the mob to serve as watchdogs over the newly penetrated business.

The accountant should act quickly when he senses the infiltration of Organized Crime. If he waits for things to develop, the company may be lost. The mob has been known to use arsonists to burn buildings and their contents in order to collect fire insurance. The syndicate is more likely, however, to put into play one of its favorite ploys: the planned bankruptcy. The working of a planned bankruptcy was recently illustrated by the plundering of a New York meatpacking firm that had passed into the hands of the mob as payment for gambling debts. While the original owners remained in nominal management positions, the mob used its control to place extensive orders for products, using established lines of credit, then selling off the finished product almost immediately at low prices before the suppliers were paid. A quick profit of $750,000 was made from the sale of the products. When the suppliers tried to collect, the company went into bankruptcy.

Unusual things begin to happen to a company when a criminal bankruptcy is being prepared. Credit is used heavily for unexplained increases in inventory. A customer makes large, but equally unexplained, increases in his orders. Remittances lag. The auditor should be aware that these are warning signals.

Without suggesting in any way that the CPA abridge his professional or ethical responsibilities, he should be prepared to aid law enforcement authorities. For one thing he should discuss his suspicions with his client and do everything he can to persuade him to meet with the proper authorities. Perhaps, before he goes to the client, it would be best to obtain assistance from the company's legal counsel. The two professions acting together might be more persuasive.

What should the accountant do if the businessman denies that there is a criminal element in his company or if he refuses to cooperate with the law? I don't want to get into the question of professional ethics, but I believe that the auditor is responsible ultimately if an annual report is published that does not truly reflect the real financial condition of the company. If he is fairly sure that organized crime has penetrated his client company, the accountant must take a strong stand. Either the client discloses to the accountant the true state of his affairs or the accountant abandons the client.

I have felt for some time that businessmen are not telling us, the law enforcement agencies, each and every instance when they have been victimized by organized crime in recent years. I ascribe it in part at least to a general apathy on the part of the public. Those guilty of this general apathy include businessmen.

It will be only when we get complete cooperation from the public in general, and business and the professions in particular, that we are going to eliminate or reduce Organized Crime to something that is not very meaningful in our society. Trade associations and chambers of commerce can be of help in conveying to the businessman, particularly those in small and moderate-sized businesses, the dangers they face if they fail to come forward at the first sign that someone is casting an illegal eye on their businesses. But no one is in a better position to point an accusing finger at the criminal infiltrator of legitimate business than the accountant. This is a challenge that I expect him to accept as a professional and as a citizen.

QUESTIONS

1. ". . . no one is in a better position to point an accusing finger at the criminal infiltrator of legitimate business than the accountant." Why?

2. What are some of the accounting clues that organized crime may be infiltrating a business concern?

3. You are a CPA auditing the Jones Company, a sole proprietorship. You discover that the company is obtaining all its raw materials at somewhat excessive prices from the Extortio Company, which you know to be a front for organized crime. When you bring this to the attention of Mr. Jones, he replies: "You think I don't know it! These guys are eating me alive. I can't blow my nose without checking with them first—but I'm not about to go to the D.A. The last guy that complained left a widow and seven kids behind!"

(a) Should you continue with the engagement: Why or why not?
(b) Assuming you continue, should you make any reference to this situation in your audit opinion on the Jones Company's financial statements?
(c) Should you go to the District Attorney in your professional capacity? In your capacity as a citizen? Explain.

Section VI

Accounting and the Environment

For thousands of years man has been able to use the earth and its resources without regard to conservation or destructive effects. The impact of early man was negligible and easily absorbed through natural processes.

Now humans literally swarm over the earth's surface. This population explosion alone would have produced an increase in resource utilization and organic waste sufficient to disturb the ecological balance—but rather than occurring in isolation the population explosion has been accompanied by technological "advances" which have multiplied our ability to destroy the environment.

We are now faced with a crisis, with most grave consequences. But we have at last begun to recognize the problem and to search for solutions. As with most crises, every citizen has a responsibility to contribute to the solution and citizens who happen also to be accountants are no exception. Accountants, though—like engineers, economists, lawyers, doctors, and other professionals—have additional capabilities and thus additional responsibilities.

In relation to environmental problems these capabilities and responsibilities fall primarily into three categories:

Cost determination (with particular regard to "social" costs)
Management services
Information services

These categories as well as the accountant's role as citizen are cited by the American Institute of Certified Public Accountants in its articulation of the

239

role of the CPA in environmental management. The problems of social costs and their estimation are discussed by Estes in "Accounting for Social Costs." Beams and Fertig suggest that present accounting methods actually contribute to environmental damage, and propose changes in the financial reporting model to reflect the effects of pollution and pollution control efforts.

Sawin next describes a Price Waterhouse & Co. engagement to assist in the development of an information system for a state water control program—an engagement which combined the management services and information services functions of accounting. Finally, in a twist on recalling defective automobiles, a group's efforts to get General Motors to recall its annual report to "correct some misleading claims concerning anti-pollution" is reported in the Wall Street Journal story, "Annual Report Recall Urged."

These articles do not exhaust the roles of accountants in dealing with environmental problems, but they do give an indication of the variety of such roles and the potential of accounting to serve society in this area.

ADDITIONAL REFERENCES

1   "Accountants Urged to Grapple With Pollution Problems," The Journal of Accountancy, January 1970, pp. 7–8.

2.   Bearse, Alvah W., "Air Pollution: A Case Study," Management Accounting, September 1971, pp. 16–18.

3.   Burton, Ellison S. and William Sanjour, "Multiple Source Analysis of Air Pollution Abatement Strategies," The Federal Accountant, March 1969, pp. 48–69.

4.   "Environmental Disclosures," The Journal of Accountancy, March 1972, pp. 76–77.

5.   Estes, Ralph W., "Socio-Economic Accounting and External Diseconomies, The Accounting Review, April 1972, pp. 284–290.

6.   Foy, F. C., "Let's Call a Cost a Cost; Social Costs," Forbes, July 1, 1971, pp. 66–67.

7.   Mason, Alister K., "Social Costs—A New Challenge for Accountants," Canadian Chartered Accountant, June 1971, pp. 390–395.

8.   Needles, Belverd Jr., James C. Caldwell and Doyle Z. Williams, "Pollution Control: A Framework for Decision Making and Cost Control," Management Adviser, May–June 1972, pp. 24–31.

9. Parker, James E., "Accounting and Ecology: A Perspective," The Journal of Accountancy, October 1971, pp. 41–46.

10. Wood, Thomas D., "A New Reporting Problem for Auditors—the Impact of Pollution Control on Financial Statements," The Journal of Accountancy, March 1972, pp. 75–76.

*Concern over environmental problems
prompted the American Institute of Certified Public Accountants to create a committee on ecology. Its objectives are
presented in the following article, along
with suggestions for other contributions
by accountants.*

Environmental Management: The Role of the CPA

Among the constituent committees of the AICPA's newly organized division of management advisory services is a committee on ecology. At the request of Louis M. Kessler, who recently completed his productive term as president of the Institute, this committee was formed for two purposes: compiling information on the work that has been done by CPAs in the area of environmental management and recommending methods by which the capabilities of the accounting profession can be used effectively in the effort to resolve the ecological crisis.

In a speech last December entitled "Intangible Values: A New Business Objective," Mr. Kessler noted two significant reasons for having confidence that we can make progress in the next few years toward restoring ecological balance. One reason is the extraordinary strength of our country's industrial capacity, with the continuing advances of science and technology. A second reason is

SOURCE: Reprinted by permission of the publisher from The Journal of Accountancy (November 1970), pp. 81–83. Copyright 1970 by the American Institute of Certified Public Accountants, Inc.

the refinement of techniques encompassed within the concept of "systems management."

The development of systems management techniques was rapidly accelerated during the 1950's to meet the military needs of this country. More recently, these techniques were used with dramatically successful results in the program to land men on the moon.

In the same ways that systems management methods have been used on limited-scope problems throughout the domains of business and government, it should be feasible to treat the ecology of a geographical area as a system, albeit a uniquely complex one.

Increasingly, accountants are extending their purview beyond account*ing* to other areas of account*ability*. Norton Bedford, former president of the American Accounting Association, has suggested that in view of the expanded role of the accounting profession there should be additional research into measurement methods and communication of results. The profession will have to address itself to the broad subject of socio-economic accounting—methods of measuring and reporting on "the adequacy of our efforts to develop a meaningful civilization."

The role of the accounting profession may be primarily in the area of cost-benefit analysis and evaluation. Additionally, the CPA's knowledge of scheduling techniques such as PERT and CPM should be useful in structuring the problem-solving projects.

Cost-benefit studies have been used in anti-poverty programs and the redesign of evolving traffic patterns, as well as in efforts to mitigate the problems of air and water pollution. A number of large accounting firms have worked with civic organizations, using operations research techniques to find the most effective solutions to problems of pollution control and abatement. The 83rd annual meeting of the AICPA, held in September 1970, included a case study in environmental management presented by a representative of a national accounting firm.

There are undeniable complexities in quantifying the effectiveness of government programs dealing with environmental control. The impossibility of assigning a numerical measure to ecological or aesthetic values will sometimes result in an "apples and oranges" comparison in the cost-benefit equation for a project that affects the natural environment. But as long as the monetary value on one side of the equation is quantified, and the other side is represented by expert predictions on the ecological effects, there is an improved basis for rational decision-making.

CO-ORDINATION OF THE EFFORT

Secretary of Commerce Maurice Stans has urged businessmen to direct their skills and resources to the social needs of our time, including the problems of air and water pollution. Since individual businessmen cannot continually increase their costs voluntarily while competitors use methods that cost less and pollute more, some central co-ordination is required.

A co-ordinated voluntary effort by business could limit the extent of government's intervention. Pending the development of long-range conservation programs on a national scale, business organizations can initiate and sponsor industry-wide studies of pollution control and abatement, and they can contribute financial support to academic studies of conservation and environmental conditions.

It may be inevitable that the major responsibility for co-ordinating solutions to the problem will be vested in the federal government. Even to the most ardent champion of individual initiative, this should not be a particularly alarming prospect, for our mixed economy has accommodated arrangements more paradoxical than this. Some of the staunchest advocates of free enterprise have sought monopolistic protection for their own operations; when they are unable even from this sanctuary to conduct a viable and respectable business, it is to the federal government that they turn for additional subsidization. The wasteful irony is that an incompetently managed institution continues to crumble no matter how much governmental underwriting is procured.

A worthier function of government is to protect the individual and collective security of its citizens. We have now become acutely aware of what conservationists have been telling us for years—that our survival and security are directly dependent upon the preservation of ecological balances.

One possibility that is being explored, in which the systems management approach would be applied to the environment, is the feasibility of a National Institute of Ecology which would utilize the resources of an electronic data processing bank for centralized analysis of field research data. This would be a co-ordinating agency for research and for programs executed by government agencies, industry, universities and civic groups. Whatever institutional forms eventually evolve, we should bear in mind that contributing to their success is not only the province of "scientists" and "politicians" but of "accountants" and all citizens as well.

CONTRIBUTIONS BY ACCOUNTANTS

The AICPA's committee on ecology has as one of its objectives compiling information on the work being done by CPA firms in pollution abatement and other environmental studies. This should result in a current body of knowledge on the subject of ecological programs within the profession. Particularly interesting case studies may be published as articles in *The Journal of Accountancy*. Conceivably, a professional development course could result.

In several ways, accountants could use their expertise in the area of taxation to promote effective policies on environmental management. Tax incentive programs for industry can be appraised; the impact of tax laws on the viability of conservation groups and foundations can be studied; the question of who should be assessed for local abatement measures can be examined.

To optimize the flow of information and to convey the immediacy of the problem, state societies and other accounting groups can make an effort to secure speakers on ecology for their meetings.

As members of various civic organizations, accountants are in a position to initiate programs that will influence governments and businesses on a local level to contribute to the effort of preserving environmental quality. All professional people should encourage the direct participation of specialists with expertise in ecology in the decision-making centers of government.

It is imperative that the recommendations of ecologists and other experts in the biological sciences be heeded in the planning and designing of industrial facilities. Any CPA, whether an individual practitioner or a member of a large firm, can use his advisory role in business to promote an awareness among clients of the pressing need for voluntary antipollution efforts.

Another way that individual CPAs could voluntarily make a contribution is by examining governmental budgets from the viewpoint of what is planned for the protection and proper utilization of natural resources. Numerous municipal budgets could undoubtedly benefit from the critical review of a CPA. The techniques of long-range planning and of programing and budgeting systems should be applied in public administration to the problems of planning the skillful allocation of natural resources.

CONFRONTATION WITH THE ISSUE

As we confront the problems of the eroding quality of our environment, some formidable economic and political choices will have to be made. The cost of pollution abatement and control will have to be paid through higher taxes and higher prices, and part of the cost may be a sacrifice of technological progress in some areas.

The *Harvard Business Review* has estimated that this country must spend $275 billion by the year 2000 to ensure the availability of clean air and water. More recently, the Center for Political Research has estimated that the private and public sectors will spend about $85 billion during the next five years to fight pollution—and that amount is less than one-half of what the Center estimates would actually be needed to keep pollution under control during the next five years.

Whatever estimate is correct, whatever costs may accrue, no cost-benefit study need be made regarding the desirability of the overall effort. Because the benefit is survival.

The *New Yorker* magazine has expressed it this way: "In the past, when we threw something 'away,' we pretty much considered that it had disappeared. But now, because of the ecological crisis, we know that there is no such thing as throwing something 'away.' There is only throwing it into the sea or into the soil or into the air. . . . Today, when we consider making something, we must expand our knowledge and concern beyond the moment of its service to us and take responsibility for its entire career on the earth. We must consider the effect it will have on all living things as it travels down our sewers or rises up our chimneys and makes its slow but inevitable circular progress through the chain of life back to our dinner tables or into our lungs."

Should this be someone else's responsibility but not ours because ecology is too tangential to accounting? Responsibility, it has been observed, is a unique quality—a property that is assigned in various portions to every individual. It is, in a very real sense, something that is impossible to evade. You can share it with others, but your own portion is not diminished. You can delegate it, yet it remains yours. And you can rationalize a refusal to honor it, but if it is rightfully yours, you thereby only increase its burdensomeness.

Eric Sevareid, who was a guest speaker at the AICPA's 1970 annual meeting, referred to the environmental crisis. What distressed him most on this issue was that the worst pessimism he encounters is from those people who have the greatest expertise. There is, he said, "an air of finality" about some of their observations. Nevertheless, Mr. Sevareid found a cause for hope in the presence of this problem, because perhaps no other issue is potentially as capable of unifying the efforts of disparate groups both within this country and internationally.

Our technological ingenuity has been impressive in making space capsules efficient life-sustaining systems for astronauts. But perhaps the most valuable lesson derived from the entire space program resides in the pictures of our own planet that have been transmitted back to us, because of their indelible reminder that we are all astronauts in the closed system of spaceship Earth.

QUESTIONS

1. Do accountants, as accountants, have any responsibility for ecological problems?

2. According to this article, how can accountants contribute to environmental management?

3. (a) What is cost-benefit analysis?

   (b) How does cost-benefit analysis differ from income determination, which involves matching of revenues and expenses?

4. "Increasingly, accountants are extending their purview beyond accounting to other areas of accountability."

   (a) Name several such areas.

   (b) In your opinion, is this trend good or bad? Explain.

*Firms which pollute air and water with im-
punity are being subsidized by society. The
author argues that such firms should be assessed for the amount of damage done, and
that in fact a system of such assessments
may soon be adopted. The implications of
such a system for accountants, particularly
with regard to social cost measurement,
are outlined.*

Accounting for Social Costs

by *Ralph W. Estes*

In this paper it will be argued that companies should be assessed for their "social costs." A social cost is a measure of the damage done to all outsiders (society) by the activities of a company. Thus, air, water, and aesthetic pollution; litter; and noise are forms of social costs. Such costs are generally not borne by the offending company at present.

Evidence of the acceptance of such assessments in the United States is presented, and the paper concludes with a discussion of the implications of social cost accounting for the accounting profession. An appendix describes several actual cases of social cost measurement.

ECONOMIC THEORY AND ASSESSMENT FOR SOCIAL COSTS

In our supposedly free market economy, exchange prices are assumed to reflect the values, or relative utility, of goods and services. Disregarding the relatively unimportant cases of upward sloping demand curves and of perfect elasticity or

SOURCE: A portion of this paper appeared in The Accounting Review (April 1972), pp. 284–290, under the title "Socio-Economic Accounting and External Diseconomies," and is used here by permission of the publisher.

perfect inelasticity, any increase in price means that fewer units of a good will be taken and vice versa.

A statement often made about our economic system is that "it works." There is not universal agreement as to what this statement means, but generally it is used to indicate that the flexible price mechanism causes the market to be cleared and results in goods which are desired being produced and ending up in the hands of those who desire them. Again, certain aberations and structural defects can be ignored for the present discussion.

This is all economic gospel, although we purposely interfere with the functioning of the "invisible hand" in many ways. For example, excise taxes discriminatorily increase the costs of certain goods and thus decrease the quantity taken in relation to other, untaxed goods. The oil depletion allowance subsidizes oil as a fuel and artificially encourages the use of gasoline and thus of automobiles. Maintenance of rivers and canals subsidizes barge lines and industries near the shores relative to other forms of transportation and to "inland" industries. Other subsidies include the investment credit, certain kinds of defense contracts designed to maintain a variety of suppliers rather than to obtain defense hardware at the lowest price, education for college students (the cost greatly exceeds tuition and fee revenue), and electric power in the Tennessee Valley. Of course, there is nothing inherently wrong with subsidies, but each should be justified on rational grounds. Such justification should generally be in terms of showing that the benefits to society outweigh the costs or sacrifices in the subsidy. We would expect an inappropriate allocation of resources if such subsidies could not be so justified.

Companies whose processes and products damage the environment are receiving such subsidies—subsidies not previously justified in terms of the expected benefits to society. For example, companies which dispose of their waste products in flowing waterways and are not fined or taxed therefor have, in the absence of restrictive legislation and penalties, lower costs of waste disposition than other companies, and also avoid the burden of paying for the damage done to downstream fisheries and recreational opportunities. Companies whose furnaces pollute the air have lower equipment costs than other companies and do not bear the cost of damage done to surrounding homes and to the public health, primarily in the form of respiratory diseases. Companies whose products are packaged in disposable containers burden society with the cost of ultimately collecting and disposing of such containers, a cost not borne directly by the users of the products nor passed on to them through higher costs or levies assessed against the manufacturer. Such subsidization results in a mal-allocation of resources and the production and provision of the wrong goods and services in the wrong quantities. Our well-being is thus diminished. We are worse off than we might be if products bore prices more consonant with their total costs, including the social costs.

How might social costs be brought into the cost structure of industry? The most feasible approach appears to be assessments on each polluting firm equal to the amount of the damage done.

Of course, many or most industries would find it cheaper to avoid doing the damage than to pay the assessment. Studies of the Ford Foundation-supported Resources for the Future, Inc. have indicated that the tangible costs of the damage done to the environment tend to outweigh abatement outlays by a factor of 16 to 1.[1] Furthermore, in most cases the additional costs should not be unbearable. Even in electric power generation, where the problems of air and water pollution join, economists figure that meeting maximum standards will add only 5% to production costs.[2]

THE TREND TOWARD SOCIAL COST ASSESSMENTS

The United States appears to be almost ready to institute a system of assessments for social costs. Anglo-Saxon legal principles have long included the concepts of equity and of damages awarded in compensation to the suffering party. This background has undoubtedly contributed to a more ready acceptance of developments such as the following.

1. Gasoline and automobile license taxes or fees are assessed against the users of highways in many jurisdictions, with the proceeds often committed to the maintenance of such highways and possibly the building of additional roads. The rationale for such taxes may be to assess the beneficiaries of highway construction—as with street and sidewalk assessments—but the effect is hardly different from charging users for damage done.

2. Similarly, park fees are usually used for maintenance of the parks, including trash removal and repairing damage done by visitors. This application of fees unfortunately fails to distinguish between those who do substantial damage and those who do little or no damage to the park facilities. Consequently such fees provide no incentive for park users to avoid littering and damaging the facilities.

3. A direct incentive is provided in recent strip-mining legislation requiring the mining companies to pay for or bear the land restoration costs.

4. The Genossenschaften of the Ruhr area of Germany are water resources cooperative associations with compulsory membership; members are principally the municipal and rural administrative districts, coal mines and industrial enterprises. The earliest were established by statute in 1904. The Genossenschaften plan and construct facilities for water resources management and assess their members with the cost of constructing and operating such facilities. The statutes creating the Genossenschaften specify that "the

costs of constructing and operating the system are to be paid for by those members whose activities make it necessary and by those who benefit from it."[3]

5. Acceptance of a system of assessments is manifest in the 1966 Report of the Council of Economic Advisers, which reports that one desirable method of abating waste discharges is a system of economic incentives, possibly including "fees or charges levied against a pollutor in accordance with the damages caused by his pollutants."[4] This report also notes that:

> . . . localities should collect revenues from the polluters, adequate to sustain the (waste treatment) system and to expand it in line with normal growth. Charges based on use of treatment facilities provide long-run incentives for the abatement of pollution.[5]

6. Legislation providing for "effluent charges," or assessments on the polluter based on the costs related to his pollution, is being proposed. For example, Senator William Proxmire plans to seek a national system of effluent charges to curb water pollution, and is also considering a bill "to impose a one-cent-per-pound fee on any manufactured product that must be discarded." [6]

   Similarly, a bill by Senator Gaylord Nelson would put a tax on packaging roughly equivalent to the cost of disposing of it.[7]

7. Even the President of the United States has taken up the call. In his 1970 State of the Union message, President Nixon urged that "the price of goods should be made to include the cost of producing and disposing of them without damage to the environment."[8]

8. In furtherance of President Nixon's apparent policy, Joel E. Segall, Deputy Assistant Treasury Secretary for Tax Policy, was recently reported to be considering a high tax to curb sulfur emissions, equal to the cost of sulfur damage to the environment.[9]

9. Similarly, President Nixon's Council on Environmental Quality noted in its 1971 annual report that "pollution charges would provide a strong abatement incentive and would tie environmental costs to the processes that generate the pollution."[10]

10. Complementing these developments is the relatively young environmentalist movement, and increased concern about the social responsibility of business. Together, these movements are creating a climate of public opinion more favorably disposed to taxation of business firms for their external diseconomies or social costs.

IMPLICATIONS FOR ACCOUNTING

These developments point clearly to a trend of assessments on business firms based on some monetary measure of social costs, with the objective of internalizing these external diseconomies. Such assessments will involve accountants at several levels, from the estimation of social costs through the ultimate inclusion of such costs in financial reports.

The most complex, and controversial, link in the assessment process is the determination of the social costs—monetizing the external diseconomies. Accountants are likely to resist involvement in such efforts because of the uncertainty involved, but such resistance is not justified. Cost determination is more the forté of accountants than of engineers and economists, yet these two professions have shown much greater interest and have undertaken considerably more research into social cost measurement than have accountants. Several examples of actual social costs estimates, along with descriptions of some techniques used, are presented in the Appendix; none of these estimates were made by accountants.

Assuming that actual social cost estimation will be done by public agencies at some level of government, it then seems not unlikely that the accounting profession will be called upon to attest to such estimates. Again, the accounting profession is uniquely qualified to perform the attest function, but its lack of involvement to date is liable to leave this function to some other less qualified group or profession by default.[11]

From a management accounting standpoint, decisions will be required between payment of assessments and abatement of emissions (or reduction of whatever social cost is involved). Such decisions should of course be based on estimates of marginal costs and marginal benefits. Some accountants have already (unavoidably) confronted this problem, but further investigation of pertinent analytical techniques should be undertaken, perhaps as a research project by an accounting organization.

The potential effects of assessments and payments for social costs on published financial statements should be investigated now rather than after such assessments have become widespread. What are the reporting problems? How should special equipment, such as recycling equipment, be amortized? What are the potential effects on return on investment? on stock prices? on price-earnings ratios? Should contingent liabilities for possible future restoration or removal charges be recognized *now*?

Finally, any changes and problems pertaining to financial reporting will create auditing problems. The public accounting arm of the profession should be giving consideration to the probable nature and resolution of such problems, and to possible effects on the auditor's opinion.

These implications for accounting point to the need for considerable study projects within the accounting profession. Foremost among these would appear to be research projects aimed at developing and field-testing techniques for measuring social costs. Several such projects (in addition to those which have already been completed, primarily by economists) will be needed before we begin to fully understand the problem and to develop practical solutions. Other projects might involve studying the potential effects on business firms of assessments for social costs, demand simulations to determine the effects of higher prices resulting from increased costs, investigation of the probable relative advantage or disadvantage from investing in control equipment versus paying the assessments, and possible changes in investment patterns resulting from changes in return on investment.

All of these studies need not be elaborate and expensive. Practically every geographical area has some industry-caused environmental damage; a project to investigate the cost or "value" of such damage would require little preparation. Several theses and dissertations could easily be based on just such studies.

The research required by the trend toward a system of assessments for social costs can appropriately be undertaken not only by graduate and undergraduate accounting students but also by professional accounting associations, accounting firms, and individual accountants. In fact, such a broad-scale response will be required if the profession is to adequately respond to the new demands of socio-economic accounting.

APPENDIX

Measurement of Social Costs

The most famous calculation of social costs is probably the estimate by investigators for the Mellon Institute of damage done by Pittsburgh's smoke nuisance in 1913. Considering the costs of cleaning and laundering clothes and maintaining and lighting homes, businesses, and public buildings, these investigators arrived at an estimate of $20 per year per person. This figure was adjusted for price-level and population changes in 1959 to arrive at an estimate for total annual air-pollution damage in the United States of $11 billion.[12]

Economists at Carnegie-Mellon University estimated the *health* damages attributable to air pollution at $2 billion in 1963. Their calculations were based on estimates of all costs associated with respiratory diseases (including hospital and doctor bills as well as foregone earnings) and an estimate of 25 percent as the proportion of respiratory diseases associated with air pollution.[13]

Another study was concerned with the effect of air pollution on property values. The researchers argue that such results of air pollution as ailing shrubbery, off-color paint, sooty surfaces, hazy view, and unpleasant odors are taken into account by a home buyer in his offer price. This hypothesis was tested statistically through an analysis of residential property values in three cities—St. Louis, Kansas City, and Washington. Variations in sales prices and rents were correlated with family income, number of rooms, age and condition of property, distance from the center of the city, racial composition of neighborhood, and general educational level of the neighborhood, as well as with two pollution variables—sulphur trioxide and suspended particulates. Although the results, of course, differed among the three cities, a significant inverse correlation was found between air pollution and property values—to the extent that a moderate decrease in air quality (five to fifteen percent) correlated with a significant decrease in property values ($300 to $700 for an average property). Using these results, combined property-value losses from air pollution in eighty-five United States cities were calculated at $621 million for 1965.[14]

"Shadow prices" have been used to estimate the value of outdoor recreational facilities, and hence the social costs associated with damage to such facilities. Such shadow prices might be estimated in several ways, including sample surveys of prospective use rates at alternative fees, calculation of travel costs to and from the recreational site, and determination of prices of comparable services at private facilities.[15] The resulting valuation of outdoor recreational opportunities may turn out to be surprisingly high; fishing rights for one-and-a-quarter miles on the River Lune were sold by auction in 1961 for £20,750.[16]

The cost of "noise pollution" near an airport has been estimated based on the maximum loss that the home-owner in the noisier area is able and willing to bear in order to move out of the area.[17] Mishan argues that a larger estimate would result from the use of the minimum sum such home-owners would accept to put up with the inconvenience.[18]

In the Genossenschaften system of the Ruhr area, total actual water pollution abatement costs are apportioned among enterprises in the system on the basis of relative *dilution* requirements. Each enterprise's effluent discharge is analyzed to determine the amount of water dilution necessary in order that the output not be destructive to fish. The social costs associated with a given enterprise's discharge is thus its pro rata share of total abatement costs for the waterway.[19]

FOOTNOTES

1. "Pollution and the Profit Motive," *Business Week*, April 11, 1970, p. 86.
2. *Ibid.*
3. Allan V. Kneese, "Water Quality Management by Regional Authorities in the Ruhr Area," in Marshall I. Goldman (ed.), *Controlling Pollution: The Economics of a Cleaner America* (Prentice-Hall, Inc., 1967), p. 116.
4. "The Abatement of Pollution," in Goldman, p. 171.
5. *Ibid.*, p. 175.
6. "Paying for Pollution by the Pound," *Business Week*, September 4, 1971, p. 78.
7. "Pollution and the Profit Motive."
8. *Ibid.*, p. 82.

9. "A Pollution Tax is Boomeranging," *Business Week,* April 10, 1971, p. 41.
10. "Paying for Pollution by the Pound."
11. Obviously the same CPA could not both measure and attest to an entity's social costs.
12. Sanford Rose, "The Economics of Environmental Quality," *Fortune,* February, 1970, p. 122.
13. *Ibid.*
14. *Ibid.,* pp. 122–23.
15. James A. Crutchfield, "Valuation of Fishing Resources," *Land Economics* (May 1962), pp. 149–51.
16. *Ibid.,* p. 147.
17. E. J. Mishan, *Technology and Growth: The Price We Pay,* (Praeger Publishers, 1970), p. 38.
18. *Ibid.*
19. Kneese, pp. 121–22.

QUESTIONS

1. What are social costs?

2. How are polluters currently subsidized? How does this lead to a mal-allocation of resources and a diminishment of national well-being?

3. What would happen to the prices of products in disposable packages if producers were assessed for the cost of processing and recycling the resulting trash? What would (or should) happen to local taxes if local government were compensated by producers or through a federal agency for such trash processing costs? As among individuals, how would the burden of trash processing costs shift?

4. By reviewing journals, books, and any other sources find two examples of social cost measurement efforts other than those listed in the appendix to this article.

5. Identify one source of social costs in your community. This might be a plant creating air or water pollution, an airport's noise, congestion surrounding a recreational or commercial facility, litter near a lake or a drive-in restaurant, pollution and noise from vehicular traffic—any of the variety of disamenities which interfere with the enjoyment of life. Suggest ways to measure this social cost—ways to measure the damage done to society. If practical, apply the techniques you have suggested to develop some actual cost estimates.

A proposal that published financial reports disclose information on the firm's responsibility for pollution—and that all such disclosures should meet the tests for attestation by CPAs.

Pollution Control Through Social Cost Conversion

by *Floyd A. Beams &*
Paul E. Fertig

The role of accounting in our current ecological crisis is not passive. Accounting provides information upon which decisions are made—decisions that result in economic and social actions. If the resulting activities disrupt the environment then accounting is, at least in part, accountable for that disruption.

Accounting as an organized profession has the responsibility to transcend the internal viewpoint of a private firm and to develop information which portrays a private firm's role in and contribution to society.[1] Accounting information should lead to decisions that result in the efficient utilization of resources, the conservation of the environment and the equitable allocation of business income. Accounting can assume an active role in controlling pollution by working

SOURCE: Reprinted by permission of the authors and the publisher from The Journal of Accountancy (November 1971), pp. 37–42. Copyright 1971 by the American Institute of Certified Public Accountants, Inc.

256

toward the concept of production costs suggested by President Nixon: "To the extent possible, the price of goods should be made to include the cost of producing and disposing of them without damaging the environment."[2]

This article seeks to show that reluctance of our industrial firms to accept responsibility for damaging the environment is likely to be a major obstacle in our attempts to control pollution. This statement from an executive of "a major U.S. oil and chemical company" may be typical: "Many of us already have the money to spend on cleaning up the dangerous level of pollution, but we are not going to spend it until all of us are forced to do the same."[3] Similarly, accountants have not taken the lead in accepting pollution cost as a private cost for accounting purposes. For example, a recent article entitled "Production Costing in Open Pit Mining" does not mention the possibility that the cost associated with defacing the earth's surface should be considered a production cost.[4] Such omission may not be realistic in view of increasing social pressure on these firms to accept responsibility for the damage caused by their production activities and efforts of some firms to correct it.[5] As we shall see, firms and industries differ greatly with respect to the amount of pollution they create, as well as in the efforts they expend to neutralize it. These differences severely impair the comparability of income reports. Under current reporting practices, those firms which appear to be efficient may be very inefficient. Those firms which have adequate earnings records may be economic failures. Those companies receiving the savings of investors may be the least deserving of additional resources.

HOW ACCOUNTING CONTRIBUTES TO POLLUTION

The dominant motivation for business activities is usually considered to be the profit motive. Profit maximization requires, among other things, the minimization of costs for any given level of activity. This is economic theory. But in accounting for a firm the theory regresses to the proposition that the minimization of private costs is a necessary condition of private profit maximization. Private costs are those measurable pecuniary costs of resources used or destroyed in conducting business activity that are borne by the firm. Not included in the profit maximization formula are those additional costs of resources used or destroyed in conducting business activity that are borne by others or by society. These are the social costs of business enterprise.[6] They are costs in the sense that they represent resource values destroyed by the firm and paid for by others. Typical of such resource destruction is pollution of air, contamination of the streams and deterioration of residential and industrial sites.

Basically a firm which is motivated by a desire to maximize private profits has no incentive to conserve resources which are free goods from its internal point of view. Thus, the expenditures which a firm makes to conserve environmental resources generally conflict with the private profit objective. Not only is there a failure to conserve environmental resources, but the combination of the private profit objective and current accounting practices may lead to excessive use and misuse of air, water and other resources. This occurs when private costs are minimized by wasting environmental resources. Examples of this situation are the dumping of untreated sewage and unfiltered air into the environment.

Such dumping increases social costs while holding private costs to a minimum. The result is a type of income redistribution from citizens and taxpayers to the customers and investors of the polluting firm. The process of minimizing private costs by increasing social costs is also objectionable because the production and distribution activities of a polluter are likely to be inefficient. This will be the case when the total private and social costs of output exceed the private costs which would have to be incurred to produce and distribute the same output without damaging the environment.

These problems which arise from excluding social costs from income measurements are not new. Many accountants have written about the problems and the American Accounting Association has organized committees to conduct research in the areas of Socio-Economic Accounting (1969-1970) and Measures of Effectiveness for Social Programs (1970-1971). The current concern for pollution control and environmental replenishment has created a new urgency for the profession to accept an active role in regard to social costs. On the one hand, accounting is being criticized for contributing to the decay of our environment and, on the other hand, new organizations are being formed to provide information relating to the social responsibility of corporations.

In response to the demand for more information on private enterprise than is provided in typical financial statements, a new organization called the Council on Economic Priorities (CEP) was created. This organization investigates corporations and issues reports on its findings. The purpose of the reports is explained by Alice Tepper, director of the organization: "We would simply like to see social responsibility become, like profits and earnings figures, a standard by which corporate practices are evaluated and exposed to the investing public."[7]

Embedded in this statement are the implications that investors may misdirect their savings by overlooking the social responsibility aspect of corporate operations and that public pressure may be applied for firms to acknowledge social responsibilities. As a stopgap measure, such reports on social responsibility may be tolerable. But in fairness to all parties concerned, the information should be generated according to data accumulation, reporting and attestation principles. Without principles the confidence of the American public cannot be acquired.

There is a tremendous demand for this type of information on social responsibility from widely diverse groups (investors, lawmakers, politicians, economists)—and it is not available. Organizations like the CEP are responding to the demand. Some organizations may try to make impartial, unbiased, complete and accurate reports to the best of their ability—whatever it may be. Other organizations may themselves simply be responding to a profit motivation. These organizations are without standards, without discipline and lacking the professionalism of accountancy with its guardian, the AICPA.

Some perspective as to the nature and extent of current criticism is provided by the following excerpt in which Professor Quigley of the department of history at Georgetown University indicts the accounting profession for its role in the decay of our environment.

> The "firm" was an innovation in bookkeeping techniques, just as the "corporation" was a legal gimmick. Both were man-made and both are imaginary; yet together with the industrial revolution they have made it possible, even likely, that we have already passed the point of no return in environmental pollution.
>
> Establishment of the "firm" was a bookkeeping decision that in calculating profits by subtracting "costs" from "income," "economic costs" would be included but "social costs" would not be counted.[8]

This indictment of accounting was not a passing fancy in Quigley's article; it was his theme. He further explains that Americans

> . . . use falsified accounting techniques and mistaken taxation methods, not only to encourage this process [environmental decay], but to conceal from themselves what is really happening.[9]
>
> The ultimate falsehood of our accounting is to be found in official and semiofficial statistics on the American "standard of living."[10]
>
> Moreover, this whole system of false reporting on the condition of America is solidly sustained by the tax system since the upkeep and maintenance of the most destructive earth-mover is tax deductible.[11]

The remedies for our ecological crisis as listed by Quigley were (1) change the tax system and fiscal policy, (2) revise corporation law and (3) create a system of social accounts.[12]

Although few accountants would be willing to accept Quigley's arguments (to say nothing of his language) or the degree of responsibility he seems to imply that we should accept, the basic message is unmistakable and cannot be ignored. Many segments of our society are at fault and accountants are not beyond criticism.

NONCOMPARABLE FINANCIAL REPORTS

The problem of comparability in financial reporting practices has received considerable attention from the accounting profession over the years. Although many of the problems have never been solved, considerable progress toward more comparable reports has been made. Now the problem of comparability arises again in connection with social costs and environmental pollution. Some companies within an industry are controlling pollution by making current outlays while others are seemingly ignoring the pollution problem. The operations of some industries are more destructive to the environment than the operations of others. Programs of abatement and costs of abatement will also vary by company, by industry and by location. The probable result of these differences is that, other things being equal, the worst polluters will appear to be the most successful and they will likely receive additional resources from the investing public.

An example of these variations comes from a recent government report which estimates that ". . . over half the volume of wastes discharged to water comes from four major groups of industries—paper manufacturing, petroleum refining, organic chemicals manufacturing and blast furnaces and basic steel production."[13] The Council on Economic Priorities mentioned above recently issued a report on the paper industry that notes that "the paper industry has been generally slow to install anti-pollution devices and processes, despite their ready availability. Owens-Illinois and Weyerhaeuser are important exceptions; both companies clean up most of their plants' effluents. Less than half of the 131 mills surveyed have satisfactory air pollution controls; many dump raw wastes into U.S. waterways."[14]

The significance of those social costs which are currently being omitted from the profit calculations of most firms is suggested by the following estimates of Professor Goldman. Goldman estimates that the annual operating costs of pollution control will run 1% to 2% of GNP and 4% to 7% of the value of industrial, agricultural, mining and transportation output. He compares these estimates to the experience of industrial firms which sometimes allocate as much as 10% of their expenditures to pollution control.[15]

Another source estimates that air pollution control will cost $1.94 per $100 of sales for the average iron and steel mills, $2.89 for iron foundries, $3.92 for nonferrous metal plants, $.21 for grain mills and $.95 for cement plants.[16]

Still another source has estimated that industrial spending on pollution control during 1971 will range from 3% to 5% of a total capital investment of about $70 billion—or as much as $3.5 billion.[17]

Comparability of financial reports with respect to pollution cost cannot be achieved merely by insisting on complete disclosure of the voluntary efforts of firms to neutralize pollution and correct the damage. What is needed is a comparison among firms of the damage created by production activities. This comparability can be achieved only through the application of a full-fledged system of accrual accounting.

ACCRUAL ACCOUNTING FOR POLLUTION

The essence of the application of accrual accounting to costs of pollution is based on the proposition that the costs of neutralizing the damage to the environment are costs of production. This means, of course, that costs incurred in connection with current manufacturing activities should be treated as current product costs, and costs incurred to neutralize future pollution should be capitalized and allocated to future manufacturing activities. Costs associated with repairing environmental damage resulting from activities of prior periods should be accounted for as a correction of prior periods' income. Identification of costs of past, current and future activities will often be difficult, but the effort must be made.

The financial position effect of recording these costs may be to change property values as industrial sites are deteriorated and re-established or it may be to recognize liabilities which have neither asset implication nor legal status. These alternate forms are developed below.

Resource Impairment.   The value of an industrial site is dependent upon adequate air and water resources and upon efficient means of waste disposal. When these environmental qualities which give a site its value are impaired, the costs of such impairment must be reflected in the financial reports. If the environment is contaminated by a firm's own production activities, the cost of resources destroyed should be associated with the production activity which gave rise to the site deterioration. Site deterioration due to the actions of other firms or to changes in regulations which reduce the efficiency by which industrial wastes (gaseous, liquid or solid) can be discarded may be considered period costs or losses.

Accounting for site deterioration is similar to depreciation accounting with one important exception. Depreciation cannot be avoided. By contrast it is possible to maintain the environmental quality of an industrial site or even to improve the environmental quality of a site which has been allowed to deteriorate.

Thus the application of accrual accounting suggests that outlays for pollution control that result in a maintenance of existing environmental conditions are current expenses. Outlays to re-establish the environmental quality of a deteriorated site are capital expenditures, provided, of course, that the earlier deterioration was charged to expense or to production. Pollution control outlays to provide for future site maintenance should be capitalized and spread over the period of expected benefit.

Accelerated obsolescence is another area in which accrual accounting applications must be kept modern. Depreciation rates for plants and equipment which do not meet existing pollution control standards may not reflect the obsolescence factor. Consider the following observation of a steel company executive:

> If we put in a unit in 1957 or 1958 to meet the code at that time, we have by no means written it off or gotten our money out of it. Now we're hit with a new standard and we're faced with quite a writeoff, because in most cases it isn't a matter of just adding on; it might mean a whole new facility.[18]

Other examples of actual or potential deterioration of property values resulting from new standards of industrial waste disposal can be found throughout current news. Consider the accounting ramifications of the following regional news items, for example:

> The State Water Control Board of the Commonwealth of Virginia has set July 1972 as the deadline for American Cyanamid Company's Piney River plant to cease polluting the Piney River. The high cost of the new controls which would be necessary to halt the pollution led to the announced closing of the plant and the possibility of throwing 325 people out of work.[19]

> The Saltville, Virginia, soda ash plant of Olin Mathieson Corporation is scheduled for closing by 1972. The history of this plant dates back to 1893 and the reason for closing is simply that the plant cannot meet the prevailing water quality control standards. About 650 people will be out of jobs if the anticipated shutdown occurs.[20]

> Strip mining practices will be banned if the Hechler Bill which proposes to outlaw strip mining becomes a federal law. Strip mining and related operations are estimated to employ about 5% of the labor force in West Virginia.[21]

Liability Recognition.   In addition to the above proposal that resource impairment which results from environmental pollution be recognized and reported on an accrual basis, we propose that expected future outlays for environmental damages which result from past and current production activities be estimated and reported on a current basis. Admittedly, the measurement problems are difficult, perhaps even insurmountable at the present time, but the difficulty makes the problem no less important.

Liability accounting for environmental pollution may take any of several forms. The legal liabilities which result from a firm's violation of existing laws must be reported. Contingent liabilities from probable actions where firms are in violation should also be reported. In addition, firms should accrue liabilities for those expected future outlays which will not create asset values for the firm.

Just as lessees accrue liabilities for restoration of leased property at the termination of their leases, mining companies should accrue liabilities for eventual land restoration during the stripping operations. Similar liabilities should be accrued for the manufacturing companies that are slowly assuming responsibility for cleaning up segments of the public domain. That is, when industrial companies clean up beaches, lakes, rivers and so on, they are not creating property values for the firm. Accrual accounting would seem to require charges to income in the period of contamination rather than in the period of outlay.

There is some evidence that firms would prefer to use cash-basis accounting for pollution control outlays. The following query and answer from an interview between a *U.S. News* reporter and Edwin H. Gott, chairman of U.S. Steel Corporation, illustrates this point.

Q. Is there some way the cost of adding pollution abatement equipment could be passed on to the public other than by price increases?

A. The problem now is that pollution control equipment is classified as a capital improvement. You write the costs off as part of the normal depreciation process. I think the more practical way would be to consider installation of this equipment as an operating expense, part of the current cost of doing business. The installation of the equipment is not done for profit motives, but strictly to comply with regulations.[22]

THE MEASUREMENT PROBLEM

Unfortunately, concerted social action for pollution control has been postponed until the point at which many recognize it as a national emergency and crisis. Time is not available to conduct the research necessary to establish verifiable methods for measuring the costs of pollution at the level of the individual firm. Instead, it appears that pollution costs to the firm in many industries are to be determined by law and regulation. Firms will incur costs, nor necessarily to neutralize the environmental damage they cause, but to maintain the community at some legal standard established by government agency. The enforcement of legal standards could take the form of assessing effluent charges against firms for industrial wastes which they dump into the waterways or the atmosphere. Monitoring devices to detect and measure different types of effluents are available and are being installed in many areas of the country. Effluent rates could be set arbitrarily high to encourage firms to avoid the charges by developing their own programs of abatement. Alternatively, the rates could be set so as to finance regional projects of pollution control.

Perhaps this method of pollution control is unavoidable, but it means that many of the problems of measuring the cost to the firm of controlling pollution will be a matter of law, rather than of technology or economics. This will not be universally true, of course, and the opportunities for voluntary assumption of pollution costs by individual firms will remain in many industries. Therefore, research into the pollution costs to the firm is crucial, and the results can also be used to identify and correct inequities in the laws as they occur. In the mean-time, the accountants' task in the area of measurement is to adapt to changing regulations and costs structures which affect nearly all phases of the reporting system.

RECOMMENDATIONS

In view of the foregoing discussions, we propose that published financial reports disclose information on the responsibility for pollution whether imposed by law or assumed voluntarily by firms. Our proposal is based on the following premises.

First, we have a national commitment toward controlling and reducing environmental pollution. Firms will pay for and pass on to the consumer the cost of environmental resources which are destroyed in the production and distribution processes. Thus, the decisions firms must make are concerned with which pollution control programs to undertake and when to undertake them, within the limits of the law.

Second, in the absence of adequate measurement methods, firms will generally account for pollution outlays as expenses. As indicated above, cash-basis accounting will make the income statements of delinquent firms appear more favorable than statements of firms which are voluntarily assuming responsibility for pollution control. Accounting needs to apply accrual accounting procedures to pollution costs in order to obtain comparability in published reports. The accounting reports should also provide additional disclosures that will give the reader some basis for assessing the responsibility that firms or industries should assume. The demand for information on the social responsibility of firms will be met by others if accounting does not rise to the challenge of supplying it.

Accounting can and should provide disclosures on pollution costs so that financial statement users are informed of company efforts at abating pollution and of the possible lack of comparability in financial statements of different firms. The quantitative data presented in financial reports should meet accounting tests for data accumulation and reporting. All disclosures should meet the tests for attestation.

Our proposal consists of two parts—a verbal description and a quantitative reporting requirement. The verbal description would consist of a dual disclosure in general terms of firm and industry position with respect to pollution control problems. An introductory statement should appear on the financial statements to the effect that a valid comparison of the financial statements of different companies requires consideration of pollution control programs. Keyed to this statement should be: (1) a standard industry footnote which identifies the major pollution control problems within the industry, the goals of the industry in abating pollution, the control standards which have been imposed and the deadlines for compliance with existing standards (this industry note could be prepared by the research staff of the AICPA and supplied to auditors on a quarterly or semiannual basis) and (2) a firm disclosure which relates to the industry disclosure and compares firm and industry pollution problems, regulations, deadlines, goals and programs of abatement.

The second part of the proposal is to require separate disclosure in financial statements of pollution control expenses (income statement), pollution control outlays (funds statement) and pollution control resources (balance sheet). This information will give an investor a basis for determining how one firm's pollution control program compares with the programs of other firms. The current trend toward publicizing dollar expenditures for pollution control is misleading because equal dollar amounts have different implications in different firms and industries. Again the AICPA could serve the profession by providing suggestions for standardized terminology and guidelines for classification of pollution control items.

The recommended disclosures would give investors and the public an opportunity to assess a management's real commitment toward pollution control. They could also provide a stimulus for management to assume an earlier and voluntary responsibility for damages to the environment due to the firm's activities. Such disclosures could lead to an acceleration of the process of transferring social costs into the private cost framework. Procrastination of some firms in undertaking pollution control programs prevents upward adjustments of product prices and puts the socially conscious firm at a competitive disadvantage in terms of earnings per share and stock prices. The recommended disclosures could offset the current earnings per share advantage of the procrastinators by encouraging investors to rely on the additional information to predict long-run earnings per share for all firms.

FOOTNOTES

1. The reader may wish to contrast this viewpoint with Professor Paton's statement that "the notion that the goal of the professional accountant is public or social service is nonsense. His function is to provide the best possible service to his specific clients, the people who pay for his efforts." William A. Paton, "Earmarks of a Profession—and the APB" *(The Journal of Accountancy,* January 1971, p. 41).

2. 1970 State of the Union Message.

3. "Stepped-up War on Pollution," *U.S. News and World Report,* January 11, 1971, p. 20.

4. Robert H. Davis, "Production Costing in Open Pit Mining," *Management Accounting*, January 1971, p. 39.

5. "Hiding the Scars," *Wall Street Journal*, May 24, 1971, p. 1.

6. Observe that the concept of social costs of business enterprise is merely a part of the broader concept, social costs.

7. "Report on Paper," *Time*, December 28, 1970, p. 41.

8. Carroll Quigley, "Our Ecological Crisis," *Current History*, Vol. 59, No. 347, July 1970, p. 9.

9. *Ibid.*, p. 11.

10. *Ibid.*, p. 12.

11. *Idem.*

12. *Idem.*

13. U.S. Department of Interior, Federal Water Quality Administration, *Clean Water for the 1970's: A Status Report*, June 1970, p. 5.

14. "Report on Paper."

15. Marshall I. Goldman, "The Costs of Fighting Pollution," *Current History*, Vol. 59, No. 348, August 1970, p. 81.

16. "Pollution Price Tag: 71 Billion Dollars," *U.S. News and World Report*, August 17, 1970, p. 41.

17. "Stepped-up War on Pollution," *U.S. News and World Report*, January 11, 1971, p. 21.

18. "How Private Industry Combats Pollution," *U.S. News and World Report*, February 15, 1971, p. 46.

19. Summarized from "Holton Joins Fight to Save Nelson Plant." *The Roanoke Times*, December 24, 1970, p. 7.

20. Summarized from "The Price of Ecology: A Small Town Faces Challenge of Industry Loss," *The Roanoke Times*, December 6, 1970, p. B-1. Also see End of a Company Town," *Life*, March 26, 1971, pp. 37–45.

21. Summarized from "Strip Miners Said Racing the Clock," *The Roanoke Times*, April 13, 1971, p. 7.

22. "Foreign Threats to a Basic Industry," *U.S. News & World Report*, October 26, 1970, p. 67.

QUESTIONS

1.   (a) "Accounting information should lead to decisions that result in the efficient utilization of resources, the conservation of the environment

and the equitable allocation of business income." Do you agree? How could accounting information lead to decisions that result in inefficient utilization of resources, destruction of the environment, or inequitable allocation of business income?

(b) Some argue that the accountant's responsibility is to "report the facts" without regard to the effect on decisions and their results. Is this view consistent or inconsistent with the quotation in part (a) above? Discuss.

2. How might accrual accounting for pollution affect the following specific accounts?
   (a) Equipment
   (b) Land
   (c) Accrued liabilities
   (d) Depreciation
   (e) Prepaid expenses

3 Locate annual reports of five corporations which disclose information concerning pollution control costs and efforts. Compare and contrast these disclosures, and evaluate them in terms of usefulness to (a) a potential investor, and (b) you.

4. Summarize in your own words Professor Quigley's criticism of accounting.

5. "The probable result of [different approaches to the pollution problem] is that, other things being equal, the worst polluters will appear to be the most successful . . ." Show through the use of an example how this might work.

*Systems technology and advanced computer
hardware are being applied to problems that
piecemeal approaches can no longer solve.
This article describes how Price Waterhouse
& Company assisted in the application of
such technology to the development of the
first statewide, comprehensive system for
the processing and retrieval of water quality
control information.*

A Statewide Program for Water Quality Control

by Henry S. Sawin

The "environmental crisis" is shaping up as the most important issue of the 1970s. The President of the United States keynoted his program for the coming decade with emphasis on a wide ranging program to clean up the environment and with establishment of the President's Council on Environmental Quality. Governors of practically all of the 50 states have called for action to abate pollution; many have established new state departments to bring together responsibility for environmental control, and more and more states are looking across their borders toward regional cooperation on the problem. Citizen attention is

SOURCE: Reprinted by permission of the publisher from Price Waterhouse Review (Spring 1971), pp. 12–21.

directed to the environmental crisis by daily accounts in the mass media of new pollution crises, and the voters have made known their concern by giving overwhelming approval in the 1970 elections to bond issues that will finance environmental improvement. Student activists, always in the vanguard in advocating social change, have shifted their attention to problems of the environment.

Quantitative estimates of the magnitude of the problem can do little to calm people who do not want to become involved. The country's pollution scorecard reads like this: 7,000,000 automobiles scrapped each year; 30,000,000 tons of wastepaper to be disposed of yearly; 48,000,000 cans and 28,000,000 bottles per year to be processed through waste disposal plants or picked up from the edges of our highways; 1,000,000 tons of garbage to dispose of every day; 200,000,000 tons (90,000,000 tons from cars) of pollutants released into our air every year; national yearly water use of 25 trillion gallons, with practically every user adding one more polluting element.

Traditional piecemeal approaches to pollution control and abatement tend to be a self-limiting solution to the problem. A municipal incinerator, for example, may temporarily solve the problem of disposing of a city's garbage and trash. But it will also quickly create air pollution problems because of its fly ash, smoke, and gaseous output—and even water pollution if residual slag and ashes are dumped into a river, a bay, or the ocean.

For a broad view of the pollution problem and possible solutions, attention is turning to the science of ecology. Since this science is basically a systems approach to the environment, every businessman can grasp its significance. The concept of an ecosystem is that there is a closed loop system of living and nonliving parts that support life cycles within a selected area. The critical subsystems include:

Non-Living Matter—The sunlight, water, oxygen, carbon dioxide, organic compounds, and other nutrients used by plants for their growth.

Plants—From microscopic phytoplankton in water up through grass and shrubs to trees, these organisms convert carbon dioxide and water, through photosynthesis, into carbohydrates required both by themselves and other organisms in the ecosystem.

Consumers—These higher organisms feed on the producers. Herbivores such as cattle and sheep are primary consumers. Carnivorous man and animals such as lions and wolves feed upon the herbivores and are secondary consumers. In marine ecosystems, of course, the rich variety of fish and other animal life forms are the balancing consumers.

Decomposers—Bacteria, fungi, and insects close the loop of the ecosystem when they break down the dead producers and consumers and return their chemical compounds to the ecosystem for reuse by the plants.

Growth and decay are simultaneous and continuous in the ecosystem. In nonhuman environments they tend to balance each other over the long run and equilibrium is maintained in the closed loop system. It is human interference—or pollution—that can drastically disturb the system and its equilibrium.

Looking at the earth as a total ecosystem, it is easy to see the havoc that may occur if the current high level of land-based pollution is extended to the oceans. About 70 percent of the earth's oxygen is produced by ocean phytoplankton. If these floating microscopic plants are killed off by oil spills, chemical and nuclear wastes, the residue from coastal sewage treatment plants, etc., then the life-supporting oxygen supply will be decreased and all animal life threatened.

Lake Erie is a localized example of what can happen to a large body of water. Almost a closed ecosystem, the lake has been classified by some groups as technically "dead"—unable to support life processes because large quantities of organic industrial waste and municipal sewage altered the ecological balance.

Clearly, our environment is threatened—but what can be done about it? It appears that there are four major tasks facing us:

1. In the short run, pollution must be controlled through enforcement of increasingly stringent regulations. Here, current technology for pollution *minimization* and *neutralization* will have to suffice until those things that take longer can be made effective—time does not permit waiting for a NASA-type effort to advance the state of the art.
2. In the short run, systems technology and the power of advanced computing hardware must be applied to the development of new approaches to pollution measurement and control.
3. In the long run, technology must be adopted which will minimize the creation of pollutants in the first place and will economically *recycle* more pollutants into consumable products.
4. In the long run, integrated ecologic models must be developed which will incorporate information from engineering, the natural sciences, and the social sciences to aid man in establishing a non-destructive relationship with the environment.

PENNSYLVANIA'S COMPREHENSIVE SYSTEM

The purpose of this article is to describe one short-run program which is utilizing systems technology and the power of advanced computer hardware to measure and control pollution. The program is being developed by the Commonwealth of Pennsylvania with financial assistance at the federal level from the Office of Water Quality, Environmental Protection Agency, and the professional assistance of our Management Advisory Services Department. It is the first statewide, comprehensive system for the processing and retrieval of water quality control information.

The project's most immediate objective is to establish a workable information system which will assist Pennsylvania's Bureau of Sanitary Engineering in its responsibilities for planning, directing, evaluating, and administering the water quality management program of the state as a whole.

As a demonstration project, a second objective is to develop a system that can be adopted by other state, regional, and federal water pollution control agencies. Meeting this objective will involve providing a demonstration system and a training program in management data systems for personnel of other agencies. To insure transferability to a variety of other situations, the following three underlying criteria were established:

1. Computer programs must be compatible with a second manufacturer's equipment. This will minimize rewriting of programs by another agency.
2. The system must be modular. This will permit others to adopt portions of the system without having to implement it in its entirety.
3. The system must have the ability to interface with the information system of other agencies. This is being accomplished by the adoption of the uniform data elements and coding techniques which have been defined by the Joint Committee of State Sanitary Engineers on Water Quality Management Data.

The commitment by the Bureau of Sanitary Engineering to this program has been significant. Walter Lyon, Director of the Bureau, has created a project team composed of over ten state employees assigned fulltime. The team consists of sanitary engineers, systems analysts, programmers, and forms designers. In addition, a committee of representatives from each functional area and regional office of the Bureau advises on all aspects of the project as it progresses. Our firm provides project supervision and supplements the state's systems analysis and programming effort. The project, which will extend over several years, is currently in its second year. The first subsystems are expected to be available for demonstration and training purposes in the near future.

AN OVERVIEW OF THE SYSTEM

One of the major duties of a field office in Pennsylvania is to take water samples to determine if they meet approved standards; identifying the need for such added facilities as water treatment plants; and then tracking the approval (permitting), construction, and operation of that plant until it is performing in an acceptable manner. Field engineers must not only satisfy the technical requirements for field water samples, but also the legal requirements. It is possible that it might later be necessary to prove in court that the samples were taken correctly and that the water clearly does not meet acceptable water quality standards. The whole process requires much information, a lot of paper work, and effective communication between field offices and the central office as well as with various policy boards and with legislators.

The Water Quality Management Information System being designed minimizes the routine steps performed by Bureau employees and maximizes the available information. It provides this information on a need-to-know basis through the use of such techniques as exception, key item, and stratified reporting. It is expected that these techniques will substantially alter and improve the field of water quality management.

The system includes 11 subsystems. These 11 subsystems and their inter-relationships are shown in Exhibit I. Each is described briefly in the following sections.

PROJECT STATUS SUBSYSTEM

The Water Quality Management Information System maintains data for the Bureau's five water quality programs. These programs encompass, respectively, water supply, sewage, industrial waste, bathing places, and mine drainage. Through the use of the project status subsystem, a Bureau employee (for example, a field engineer or a central office enforcement officer) can get key data on the need for a new facility such as a treatment plant or collection system. He can track the construction status of facilities that have been permitted by the state and funded, and are under construction by municipalities, sewer authorities, private companies, or others. The field engineer regularly receives the project status report and also receives exception reports including lists of all construction projects currently out of compliance with laws and regulations, and an action report which lists schedules which have not been met.

These reports are used by the field engineers to identify the need to initiate action against the owner/operators of facilities to meet scheduled dates. Owner/operators or their consulting engineers receive a computer printed turnaround card on or about the date on which the succeeding construction step was to have been completed. The construction status is entered on the card, which is returned to the department for use in updating the project status file. The monitoring of construction of new facilities and upgrading of existing facilities is a key part of the work of the Bureau.

Another task of the Bureau is to provide to state legislators, the federal government (for information on grants, etc.), and interested citizens information on construction activity throughout the state. Information is required on the locations of projects under construction, expected completion dates, and estimated costs. The compilation of this data has traditionally taken many hours by Bureau personnel. Using the reporting elements of the project status system,

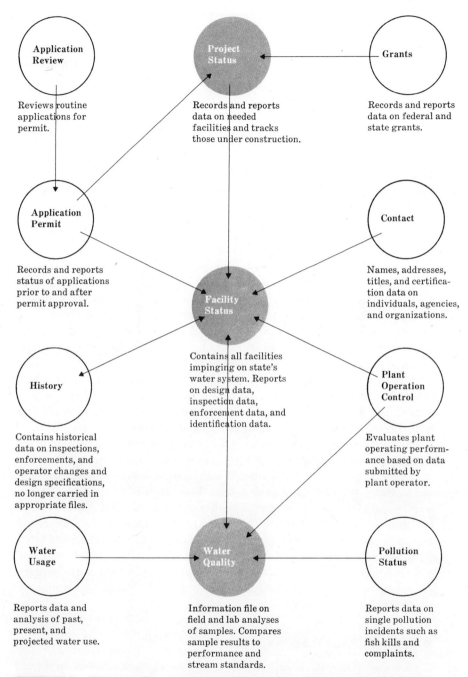

Application Review

Reviews routine applications for permit.

Project Status

Records and reports data on needed facilities and tracks those under construction.

Grants

Records and reports data on federal and state grants.

Application Permit

Records and reports status of applications prior to and after permit approval.

Contact

Names, addresses, titles, and certification data on individuals, agencies, and organizations.

Facility Status

Contains all facilities impinging on state's water system. Reports on design data, inspection data, enforcement data, and identification data.

History

Contains historical data on inspections, enforcements, and operator changes and design specifications, no longer carried in appropriate files.

Plant Operation Control

Evaluates plant operating performance based on data submitted by plant operator.

Water Usage

Reports data and analysis of past, present, and projected water use.

Water Quality

Information file on field and lab analyses of samples. Compares sample results to performance and stream standards.

Pollution Status

Reports data on single pollution incidents such as fish kills and complaints.

EXHIBIT I. Water quality management information system (system modules)

these hours are minimized, the reports are obtained on a timely basis, and the Bureau can more effectively accomplish its mission by assigning its personnel to more critical tasks.

FACILITY STATUS SUBSYSTEM

The data base of the Water Quality Management Information System includes information on all facilities within the state which by law or regulation are included in the water supply, sewage, industrial waste, bathing places, and mine drainage programs. The term "facilities" applies not only to water treatment plants, but also, for example, to sewage collection systems, interceptors, sewers, and sewage discharge points. The facility status subsystem maintains and processes the identification, design, inspection, and violation data for each facility encompassed by the state's five water quality programs.

Identification data including the name and exact location of each facility, design data on which facility permits were based, and construction data is provided to the central and field offices in catalog form for day-to-day reference. Probably the most important aspect of the facility status subsystem, however, is violation and enforcement information and exception reporting. All violation orders and enforcement steps are tracked on the facility status subsystem. The nature of violations, dates on which they occurred, and the steps to be taken and dates to be met by owner/operators are all part of the facility status subsystem data base. This information is reported to the central and field offices in a manner which enables assigned personnel to carry out their tasks of abating pollution and enforcing water quality standards in Pennsylvania.

Exception reports on steps which must be taken to abate water pollution are submitted to the field engineers. The Bureau personnel, upon request, can obtain information on the status of particular enforcement actions whether they fall within the purview of the Bureau or have been assigned to the Legal Department. Preprinted inspection reports are forwarded to the field offices prior to the dates of required scheduled inspections. The issuance of these inspection reports is based on schedules submitted each year by the field offices and based on violations which have occurred. Other items of importance to the Bureau are reports which identify the possible need for new facilities (such as treatment plants) based on populations served which exceed the design populations for which the plants were constructed.

WATER QUALITY SUBSYSTEM

A most important task of the Bureau is, of course, monitoring the quality of waste and waters of the Commonwealth. Samples are taken from both the effluents of particular facilities and throughout the streams and rivers of Pennsylvania. The samples are then laboratory analyzed and the results entered and compared to the water quality file. The system comparisons are to lists of standards for either particular facilities or particular portions of streams to determine if samples meet acceptable water quality standards. Reports are issued to the central and field offices identifying those samples which have not met water quality standards. These reports include background data on past samples and the complete details of current samples. Data on sample results can be obtained upon request for any samples for any facility or stream, and within specified dates.

The water quality subsystem, therefore, is a key element in the Bureau's work, since it supplies sample data for meeting reporting requirements, for stream or facility water quality trend analysis, and for water system modeling and stream profile development. The data availability on a timely basis enables the Bureau to perform functions not previously possible by manual methods.

CONTACT SUBSYSTEM

The state grants operator's certificates to all sewage and water supply treatment plant operators. The Bureau can obtain data on these certified operators through the contact subsystem. Information such as previous experience, test results, educational background, and the type of treatment plant the individual is authorized to operate are all available through the contact subsystem. Certificates and wallet cards (similar to automobile licenses) are issued annually or as required.

Another aspect of the contact subsystem is the availability of a mailing list for all individuals, corporations, agencies, etc., that the Bureau contacts throughout the year. Through the use of an open-ended coding system, the Bureau can retrieve various lists and/or mailing labels for designated levels within a particular type of organization, or for a specific individual. This is useful, for example, when it is necessary to send mailings to chairmen of all watershed associations or citizens committees throughout the state.

The contact system is not as sophisticated an application as, for instance, a modeling application or even the facility status subsystem, but is extremely important in saving many man-hours on the part of technical personnel to enable them to perform other tasks.

GRANTS SUBSYSTEM

Much of the funding for new or upgraded municipal water supply and sewage facilities comes from federal or state grants. In addition, a significant portion of the operating funds of a state environmental agency comes from the federal government. Information concerning grants is maintained in this subsystem and is available to Bureau personnel upon request. Federal and state reports are prepared through the grants subsystem as are those status reports required by the Bureau to better perform its work.

PERMIT APPLICATION SUBSYSTEM

The state issues permits for construction and operation of all types of water treatment facilities. Therefore, a significant task in the central and field offices is review and approval of applications for permits and then assuring that permit conditions are met. Through the application permit subsystem, a field engineer can obtain the permit history of particular facilities or of all facilities within his region. He can refer to his permit application status report to answer many daily questions on the current status of particular applications. Central and field office personnel receive reports on permit conditions which are not being met and which should result in some form of action on the part of field personnel. The permit application, project status, grants, and facility status subsystems interface to assist the Bureau in taking prompt and effective action in this area.

APPLICATION REVIEW SUBSYSTEM

Field offices, as part of the process of approving applications for permits, perform an initial review of submissions from municipalities, industrial plants, and others to determine conformance with rules and regulations and to assure consistency within the application. Applications not meeting overall standards, not including all necessary paper work, or not having internal consistency are returned for completion before a detailed investigation is made of the plans themselves. Many of these tasks are routine and can be performed more efficiently using a computer.

The application review subsystem provides reports for the field office on those applications which should be returned on the basis of this initial review. This subsystem reduces the time required to process an application and the amount of manual, routine work which has previously been necessary in evaluating permit applications, thereby enabling field engineers to spend more time on the more extensive analytical work necessary prior to the issuance of permits.

POLLUTION STATUS SUBSYSTEM

The Bureau's central office and its field offices require information on "single" pollution incidents such as fish kills, accidental spills, or complaints. Information, here, includes the date and location of a particular incident or complaint, the agency or individual reporting it, the type and nature of the condition causing the incident, and the disposition of the complaint. Reports are issued listing open complaints not resolved and listing pollution incidents or complaints within particular geographical areas.

WATER USAGE SUBSYSTEM

The type and rate of water usage has a direct effect on the quality of water. Data concerning the type of use at a particular location and the flow of a stream are collected by field engineers, along with other data, through inspection reports, permits, and laboratory samples. This information, as well as information obtained through agencies primarily concerned with water resources, i.e., quantity of water, is correlated through the water usage subsystem. Reports containing water usage data for problem areas are issued. Information on water quality levels, correlated by type of use and quantity of water, is available upon request through the water usage subsystem.

PLANT OPERATION CONTROL SUBSYSTEM

Water samples taken by operators of water and waste water treatment plants throughout Pennsylvania are forwarded to private, state-approved laboratories for analysis. Sample results, as well as other information on the actual operating characteristics of the treatment plants, are carried by the Water Quality Management Information System. Data is submitted on such items as operating problems, influent and effluent readings of biological oxygen demand, suspended solids or dissolved oxygen, hours operated and bypassed, or chlorination and gallons bypassed. Various validity and consistency checks are made to assure proper submission of samples, and sample results are then compared to acceptable levels for each quality indicator to determine if facilities are meeting required standards.

Thus, the field office obtains current operating data on each treatment plant within the region, without the necessity and expense of inspecting every facility. It can obtain weekly reports of plant operator samples not meeting standards, or of operating characteristics which suggest the need for actual inspections or directives for change in operation of the plants. A major objective of this subsystem is to insure maximum possible efficiency in plant operation.

HISTORY SUBSYSTEM

The need for current data on the quality of water and current enforcement status is critical. Equally important is the need to know past violations, design characteristics, and inspection results. The facility status subsystem carries all open violations as well as those resolved within up to two years previous. However, the evaluation of an owner/operator for permit approval to upgrade a plant might require a complete history of the violations of a facility since its original operation date. The granting of a certificate to an operator for a higher level treatment plant might be influenced by the history of operating efficiency of that operator at a previous facility. The data to answer these types of requests by field engineers are obtained through the interface of the history file with the applicable file carrying the current data.

CONCLUSION

A statewide system to manage the quality of water requires the ability: (1) to process massive volumes of data, (2) to interface with other agencies on water quality problems, and (3) to retrieve data quickly and to act with speed and prevision in making decisions.

Pennsylvania plans to take advantage of advances in the state of the art of computer and information systems technology and to use established uniform data coding systems to develop these abilities. This is a long-range program of which many initial important steps have been completed. It is expected that this system will enable Pennsylvania to better manage the quality of its water, as well as to provide a model system from which other states and agencies can benefit.

HOW THIS SYSTEM APPLIES TO AIR QUALITY CONTROL

The management of air quality and water quality are similar and, in fact, often the responsibility of the same department and field offices in many states. The tasks performed by field engineers in air quality control include performing inspections, enforcing standards, and granting operating permits or emission registrations.

The types of reports described in this article and included as part of Pennsylvania's Water Quality Management Information System could be adapted to an Air Quality Management Information System.

A field engineer pursuing the task of enforcement management for air would request reports, as described for the facility status subsystem, which would identify those violations which have not been abated or do not meet scheduled dates for compliance.

When ambient air samples are taken and analyzed, they would be compared to applicable standards for geographic grid areas and would trigger reports showing areas not within standards. Stack samples not meeting specifications would cause the same type of violation data to be inserted on an emission inventory-enforcement management file that nonstandard effluent samples cause to be put on the facilities file in the Water Quality Management Information System.

Many applications (for example, contact or pollution status subsystems which deal with retrieval of name and address lists or complaint data) would be the same in almost any environmental control system.

In fact, the similarities in day-to-day operating procedures point to future use of combined air and water quality control systems in solving the environmental crisis.

QUESTIONS

1. Summarize Pennsylvania's water quality control system.

2. What were the accountants' contributions to this system?

3. Could this work have been done as well by other professionals such as engineers, mathematicians, computer specialists? Explain.

More than automobiles can be recalled for defective parts.

Annual Report Recall Urged

General Motors Corp. was asked by a private group to recall all its 1969-model annual reports to repair some allegedly defective antipollution claims.

The demand came from the Project on Corporate Responsibility.

In a letter to GM's president, Edward Cole, the group challenged statements on pages 25 and 26 of the annual report. The statements said hydrocarbon emissions have been reduced 80% and carbon monoxide emissions 65%, on 1970 model cars from uncontrolled 1960 model cars. They contended recent Government surveys show that such reductions were made only on prototype cars tested by the Government, and that reductions on most production cars were much smaller.

As a result, "we demand that you recall your 1969 annual report and repair the defects contained in that report," wrote Philip Moore, executive secretary of Campaign GM. GM said it had no comment on the demand.

SOURCE: Reprinted with permission of The Wall Street Journal (April 10, 1970).

QUESTIONS

1. Would you expect claims such as those cited about emissions to be covered by the auditor's opinion? (If possible, examine General Motors' 1969 annual report. Were these claims covered in the opinion?)

2. (a) What standards of truth and accuracy govern unaudited sections of corporate annual reports?

   (b) In your opinion, what standards should apply?

   (c) What standards of truth and accuracy govern advertising in general?

Section VII

National Income Accounting

National income accounting, sometimes called social accounting, socio-economic accounting, or simply economic accounting, is concerned with measuring the economic performance of a nation.

There are several possible indicators of economic performance. The labor force employed, the percentage level of unemployment, the amount of money in circulation, the price index, and the level of federal expenditures are statistics frequently mentioned in news reports. The most commonly cited indicator, how-ever, is the gross national product (GNP). Gross national product is essentially the total current output of goods and services in an economy, valued at selling price.

As a measure of economic activity, there is a great deal of interest in the level of GNP. Business firms base their plans and budgets partially on expectations concerning the level of economic activity. Budgets of governmental units—federal, state, and local—must take into account expected levels of business sales and incomes in order to forecast tax receipts. Investors are interested in the level of economic activity because of its effects on corporate performance and on stock market prices. Even individuals might be interested in the GNP, since its level and rate of growth may provide an indication of the security of their employment.

Despite such interest, the concept of GNP as a measure of total output has come under criticism, especially in recent years. Some argue that a measure which lumps together such outputs as university educational services, pornographic films, life-saving drugs, and dune buggies is not an indicator of the economic well-being of a nation. Others maintain that some output—that which pollutes and damages the environment—should be subtracted, not added, in

measuring national output. Still others feel that an economic measure emphasizes materialism and should be replaced—or at least supplemented—by a measure of the quality of life, national well-being, or similar attributes. (A discussion
of such measures will be found in Section VIII, "Accounting for Social Progress.")

Regardless of the criticisms, national income accounting is a widely accepted
measure of economic activity which influences government policy and business
decisions, and consequently should be understood by anyone who would not be
economically illiterate.

Gross national product can be calculated in three different ways: by market
value of goods and services, by types of purchasers of such goods and services,
and according to the distribution of the revenue from these goods and services
to various income recipients. In terms of market value of goods and services, the
GNP in 1971 was composed of:

Goods output	$ 494.3 billion
Services	443.3
Construction	109.2
GROSS NATIONAL PRODUCT	$1,046.8 billion[1]

Since output is either purchased by someone or is added to inventory, the
GNP can also be classified in terms of expenditures by various classes of final
purchasers:

Individuals—for personal consumption	$662.1	
—residences	40.6	$ 702.7 billion
Business—investment in buildings	38.2	
—investment in equipment	70.5	
—additions to inventories	2.2	110.9
Federal government—national defense	71.4	
—other	26.2	97.6
State and local government purchases		135.5
GROSS NATIONAL PRODUCT		$1,046.8 billion[2]

Essentially, final purchasers are those who actually use the goods or services to
satisfy needs and wants. Most business outlays are costs which go into products

1. Survey of Current Business, February, 1972, p. 10.
2. Ibid. Will not add to total due to rounding.

ultimately consumed by individuals; such costs are consequently reflected in individual expenditures in the above tabulation.

The student of accounting will realize that revenue from services and sale of goods is used to pay wages and salaries and other expenses, with any excess going to the owners of the business as profits. Gross national product can be obtained by adding the incomes of the various participants in the production process, as follows:

Compensation of employees (including military and other govt. employees)	$ 641.9 billion
Corporate profits	80.7
Profits of unincorporated businesses	68.3
Net interest income	35.6
Rental income of persons	24.3
National Income	$ 850.8 billion
Indirect business taxes (e.g., property taxes)	102.1
Depreciation provisions	95.2
Other minor adjustments	– 1.3
GROSS NATIONAL PRODUCT	$1,046.8 billion[3]

The composition of the gross national product is important, but any statistic is useless standing alone; there must be some basis for comparison. GNP statistics are usually compared over time within a country, and also between countries. GNP figures for the United States since 1947 are presented in Table 1, both in current dollars and in constant dollars (i.e., adjusted for the effects of inflation, using 1958 as a base year); the reader may recall the national interest aroused in 1971 when a "trillion-dollar economy" was reached. Table 2 presents a rough comparison of GNP on a per capita basis for all countries with populations of 1 million or more.

Financial statements and other reports are only as good as the raw data on which they are based. Computer technicians often refer to the problem of GIGO, or "garbage in, garbage out." Similarly, if unreliable data is used in compiling GNP estimates, the results may be misleading or even useless. Final GNP estimates are based to a significant extent on financial accounting data, and if such data is unreliable the GNP estimates will suffer accordingly. This relationship between national income accounting and financial accounting is traced in the article by Ralph Lucano.

3. Adapted from Survey of Current Business, February, 1972, p. 11.

TABLE 1.   Gross National Product for the United States in
Current and Constant (1958) Dollars

Year	Current Dollars	Constant (1958) Dollars
1947	231.3	309.9
48	257.6	323.7
49	256.5	324.1
50	284.8	355.3
51	328.4	383.4
52	345.5	395.1
53	364.6	412.8
54	364.8	407.0
55	398.0	438.0
56	419.2	446.1
57	441.1	452.5
58	447.3	447.3
59	483.7	475.9
60	503.7	487.7
61	520.1	497.2
62	560.3	529.8
63	590.5	551.0
64	632.4	581.1
65	684.9	617.8
66	749.9	658.1
67	793.9	675.2
68	864.2	706.6
69	929.1	724.7
70	974.1	720.0
71	1046.8	739.4

Source: U.S. Dept. of Commerce, *1971 Business Statistics* and *Survey of Current Business*, February, 1972.

Since Keynes, governments have attempted to influence the level and nature of aggregate economic activity to achieve various policy objectives such as reduction of inflation, growth in real output, and full employment. Efforts to achieve these objectives are best reflected in the federal budget. This budget, as recently revised, is described in the article by S. C. Yu.

Despite its one-dimensional (economic) nature, national income accounting is a useful way of measuring the progress of a nation. The national income accounts are based to a significant extent on financial accounting data, and thus reflect another important role of accounting in society.

TABLE 2. Gross National Product Per Capita (1969) and Average Annual Growth Rate (1960-69) of Countries with Populations of 1 Million or More.

Country	GNP per CAPITA (US dollars)	GROWTH RATE (percent)
UNITED STATES	4,240	3.2
SWEDEN	2,920	3.4
SWITZERLAND	2,700	2.6
CANADA	2,650	2.8
FRANCE	2,460	4.8
DENMARK	2,310	3.7
AUSTRALIA	2,300	2.9
NEW ZEALAND	2,230	2.0
GERMANY, FED. REP. OF	2,190	3.7
NORWAY	2,160	4.0
BELGIUM	2,010	3.5
FINLAND	1,980	3.9
UNITED KINGDOM	1,890	1.8
NETHERLANDS	1,760	3.1
GERMANY (Eastern)†	1,570	4.1
ISRAEL	1,570	5.3
LIBYA, ARAB REP. OF	1,510	21.7
AUSTRIA	1,470	3.9
JAPAN	1,430	10.0
PUERTO RICO	1,410	6.0
ITALY	1,400	4.7
CZECHOSLOVAKIA†	1,370	3.9
USSR†	1,200	5.6
IRELAND	1,110	3.5
HUNGARY†	1,100	5.5
ARGENTINA	1,060	2.6
VENEZUELA	1,000	2.5
POLAND†	940	5.1
TRINIDAD AND TOBAGO	890	3.8
BULGARIA†	860	6.7
ROMANIA†	860	7.5
HONG KONG	850	8.7
GREECE	840	6.2
SPAIN	820	6.5
SINGAPORE	800	4.5

(Continued)

TABLE 2.   (Continued)

Country	GNP per CAPITA (US dollars)	GROWTH RATE (percent)
SOUTH AFRICA[1]	710	3.8
PANAMA	660	4.8
LEBANON	580	2.1
MEXICO	580	3.4
YUGOSLAVIA	580	4.6
URUGUAY	560	-0.8
JAMAICA	550	3.0
CHILE	510	1.7
COSTA RICA,	510	2.9
PORTUGAL	510	4.9
MONGOLIA†	460	1.0
ALBANIA†	430	4.9
NICARAGUA	380	2.8
SAUDI ARABIA	380	7.1
GUATEMALA	350	1.9
IRAN	350	4.9
TURKEY	350	3.4
MALAYSIA	340	3.8
PERU	330	1.4
IRAQ	310	3.0
CHINA, REP. OF	300	6.3
COLOMBIA	290	1.5
EL SALVADOR	290	1.9
ZAMBIA	290	5.4
CUBA†	280	-3.2
DOMINICAN REPUBLIC	280	0.4
JORDAN*	280	4.7
KOREA (North)†	280	5.9
BRAZIL	270	1.4
ALGERIA	260	
HONDURAS	260	1.1
SYRIA, ARAB REP. OF	260	4.7
ECUADOR	240	1.2
IVORY COAST	240	4.7
PARAGUAY	240	1.0

(Continued)

TABLE 2.   (Continued)

Country	GNP per CAPITA (US dollars)	GROWTH RATE (percent)
RHODESIA	240	0.4
TUNISIA	230	2.1
ANGOLA	210	1.4
KOREA, REP. OF	210	6.4
MOZAMBIQUE	210	3.3
PAPUA NEW GUINEA	210	2.0
PHILIPPINES	210	1.9
LIBERIA	200	1.3
SENEGAL	200	−0.1
CEYLON	190	2.1
GHANA	190	0.0
MOROCCO	190	3.4
SIERRE LEONE	170	1.2
BOLIVIA	160	2.4
EGYPT, ARAB REP. OF	160	1.2
THAILAND	160	4.7
CAMEROON	150	2.0
MAURITANIA*	140	4.6
VIET-NAM, REP. OF	140	1.8
CENTRAL AFRICA REP.	130	0.0
KENYA	130	1.5
KHMER REP.	130	0.5
YEMEN, PEOPLE'S DEM. REP. OF	120	−4.6
INDIA	110	1.1
LAOS*	110	0.2
MALAGASY REP.	110	0.0
PAKISTAN	110	2.9
SUDAN	110	0.6
UGANDA	110	1.7
INDONESIA	100	0.8
TOGO	100	0.0
AFGHANISTAN	—	0.3
BURMA	—	1.8
BURUNDI*	—	0.0
CHAD	—	−1.3

(Continued)

TABLE 2.   (Continued)

Country	GNP per CAPITA (US dollars)	GROWTH RATE (percent)
CHINA (Mainland)†	—	0.8
CONGO, DEM. REP. OF	—	0.2
DAHOMEY	—	0.9
ETHIOPIA	—	2.3
GUINEA	—	2.6
HAITI	—	-1.0
MALAWI	—	1.0
MALI	—	1.2
NEPAL	—	0.4
NIGER	—	-0.9
NIGERIA	—	-0.3
RWANDA	—	-0.8
SOMALIA*	—	1.5
TANZANIA²	—	1.6
UPPER VOLTA	—	0.1
VIET-NAM (North)†	—	3.2
YEMEN, ARAB REP. OF*	—	2.3

Note: In view of the usual errors inherent in this type of data and to avoid a misleading impression of accuracy, the figures for GNP per capita have been rounded to the nearest $10.

[1] Including Namibla.
[2] Mainland Tanzania.
*Estimates of GNP per capita and its growth rate are tentative.
†Estimates of GNP per capita and its growth rate have a wide margin of error mainly because of the problems in deriving the GNP at factor cost from net material product and in converting the GNP estimate into US dollars.
—Estimated at less than 100 dollars.

Source: *Finance and Development,* IX (No. 1, 1972), p. 51. Used with permission.

ADDITIONAL REFERENCES

1.   Gilbert, Milton, and Richard Stone, "Recent Developments in National Income and Social Accounting," Accounting Research, January 1954.

2.   "How We Measure Our Wealth," Nation's Business, August 1967, pp. 78–82.

3. Jaenicke, H. R., "Macroeconomics and Accounting Practice," The Journal of Accountancy, June 1969, pp. 35–39.

4. Littleton, A. C., "Accounting Rediscovered," The Accounting Review, April 1958, pp. 246–253.

5. Lubbert, Jens, "National Accounting—Its Scope and Purpose," The International Journal of Accounting Education and Research, Spring 1966, pp. 44–59.

6. Ruggles, Richard, and Nancy Ruggles, "The Evolution and Present State of National Economic Accounting," The International Journal of Accounting Education and Research, Fall, 1968, pp. 1–16.

7. Sengupta, S., "What is Social Accounting," The Chartered Accountant (India), July 1965, pp. 22–47.

8. Yanovsky, M., Social Accounting Systems (Chicago: Aldine Publishing, 1965).

9. Yu, S. C., "Micro-Accounting and Macro-Accounting," The Accounting Review, January 1966, pp. 8–20.

The Economic Report of the President to the Congress and to the nation contains an analysis of the economy for the given year. Tables in the report present the details for national income, gross national product, savings, earnings, inventories and corporate profits. Financial accounting represents a basic and important source of information in the accumulation of these important aggregate data. The report of savings published in national income presentations compares closely with the statement of the source and application of funds and the statement of retained income. These latter statements which are prepared for financial accounting can readily be recast into the form of statements prepared for social accounting.

Relationship Between Financial and National Income Accounting

by Ralph V. Lucano

SOURCE: Reprinted by permission of the publisher from The Federal Accountant (March 1962), pp. 14–20.

Financial accounting which records the current economic history of one business enterprise is also a contributor to national income accounting, which records the current economic history and progress of the nation and is largely compiled by the Office of Business Economics of the United States Department of Commerce.

National income accounting,[1] or social accounting, deals with the economics of aggregates. It reports the gross national product, national income, personal consumption expenditures, private domestic and foreign investments, and government purchases of goods and services. It also reports gross saving and investment, personal saving, as well as government receipts and expenditures.

NATIONAL INCOME

National income consists of employee compensation, rental income of individuals, net interest, and the income of business enterprises, including an inventory valuation adjustment.

For its estimate of corporate income, the Department of Commerce relies on data tabulated by the Internal Revenue Service. For its estimate of unincorporated business income, the Department uses surveys, censuses, and income tax information. For its estimate of personal saving, the Department of Commerce relies on several residual estimates and on the estimates of changes in assets and liabilities prepared by the Securities and Exchange Commission.

While national income data are partly prepared from sources other than financial accounting reports, and personal saving estimates are prepared without recourse to financial accounting reports, both concepts are closely related to basic financial accounting objectives. As a result, national income data and personal saving data could be developed from the reports customarily prepared by financial accountants for the use of the individual firm.

Even though compensation of employees represents the largest amount in national income, it remains generally a simple concept and the data are obtained without technical difficulty from the reports furnished under the Social Security laws.

The income of business enterprises, incorporated and unincorporated, however, is essentially based on the accounting reports of the single firm, and represents the individual accountant's participation in aggregate economics. At the present time, social accounting is concerned with the income of the entire economy rather than with assets and equities, and the data used are based on the income and expense statements of each firm, rather than on a balance sheet.

ACCOUNTING AND ECONOMIC INCOME

Income is a term with many meanings. It is also determined in various ways. Relying on the accounting assumptions of the stable dollar, continuity of operations, the entity, the fiscal year, and realization of income, the financial accountant computes income and expenses. He has the choice of several accounting methods, such as cash, accrual, installment sales, or percentage of completed contract, for his overall procedure. He has also the choice of methods in valuing specific accounts, such as inventory, depreciation, development expense, organization expense, and bond discount. As each accounting method records income and expenses on a basis different from that of another method, the accounting net income of one individual firm, using its methods, will not be comparable with the income of another firm, using another method, in any one fiscal period.

Financial accounting income also differs from economic income as only one residual is determined, and no attempt is made to allocate the net income to the factors of production, nor is an attempt made to compute imputed income. Therefore, in preparing a report for a board of directors or for management, or in preparing an income tax return, the individual accountant is concerned solely with the accounting and financial needs of his own firm. That he is nevertheless also preparing a portion of the data that will be used ultimately in the determination of the status and the progress of the national economy is usually of little concern to him. And yet, without the use of special procedure and without the preparation of special national income reports, if the accountant is adhering to generally accepted accounting principles, he is preparing some of the basic data that will be merged into the national accounts.[2]

While the variations in methods and valuations may be puzzling to a layman, they appear inevitable in a free enterprise economy. Income tax statutes and regulations, rules of government agencies, and the preference of individual professional accountants accentuate the prevailing disparity of method. The final result, however, should approximate the sought for income data for the aggregate.

CONVERSION OF FINANCIAL ACCOUNTING STATEMENTS INTO SOCIAL ACCOUNTING STATEMENTS

Personal savings is defined by the Department of Commerce as "the excess of personal income over personal consumption expenditures and personal tax and non-tax payments. It consists of the current savings of individuals (including owners of unincorporated businesses) . . ."[3]

Though the report of savings published in national incomes is not prepared in the form and in the wording of financial accounting, it does compare closely with two reports prepared for the individual firm, the statement of the source and application of funds, and the statement of retained income. As the underlying concepts are similar, the statements prepared by financial accounting are easily revised and recast into the form of the statements prepared by social accounting. For example:

Statement of Source and Application of Funds

Funds Available:

Funds obtained from operations	$33,000.00
Charge against net income not requiring cash outlay, depreciation	12,000.00
Increase in current liabilities	40,000.00
Decrease in prepaid expenses	4,000.00
Total funds received	$89,000.00

Funds Used:

Addition to property and equipment	$28,000.00
Increase in inventories	15,000.00
Increase in accounts receivable	6,000.00
Increase in cash	11,000.00
Decrease in long-term liabilities	19,000.00
Dividends paid	10,000.00
Total funds applied	$89,000.00

For the same data, the statement of retained income is:

Profit from operations—1961	$33,000.00
Less dividends paid	10,000.00
Retained income, or savings	$23,000.00

Both of these financial statements can be recast into a simple statement of savings adhering to the Department of Commerce procedure:[4]

Addition to property and equipment		$28,000.00	
Less depreciation charged in the current year		12,000.00	
Net increase in property			$16,000.00
Increase in inventories			15,000.00
Increase in accounts receivable			6,000.00
Increase in currency and securities			11,000.00
			$48,000.00
Less:			
Decrease in prepaid assets (prepaid expenses)		$ 4,000.00	
Increase in indebtedness (net)—			
Increase	$40,000.00		
Decrease	19,000.00	21,000.00	$25,000.00
Net Savings			$23,000.00

Without passing judgment on the accuracy of the amounts reported, it should be interesting to note that while financial accounting does not customarily specify savings in its formal structure, its statement of retained income and its statement of application of funds could be used as a basis for national income savings amounts, if sufficient financial accounting reports were available.

CONTRIBUTION OF FINANCIAL ACCOUNTING

In the national economy, a primary objective is the maintenance of a stable and flourishing free enterprise system, with employment, production and purchasing power at a maximum. Accounting alone, no matter how accurate or comprehensive its reports, is not going to solve the economic problems of inflation, recession, unemployment, overproduction, or misguided investment.

To aid in achieving these objectives, however, the President of the United States, under the requirements of the Employment Act of 1946, presents his annual Economic Report of the President to the Congress and to the nation. The Economic Report contains an analysis of the economy for the given year, including economic developments and outlook, economic policies, and a program for economic growth with stable prices. Many tables are included in the report, and they present the details for national income, gross national product, savings, earnings, inventories, and corporate profits.

It is obvious, therefore, that financial accounting represents a basic and important source of information in the accumulation of these important aggregate data, facilitating our knowledge of current operations and aiding the maintenance of a dynamic economy, and that our aggregate data are related, in part, to the accounting of the individual firm.

NOTE ON CURRENT FORMS OF NATIONAL ECONOMIC ACCOUNTS

In 1957 the Subcommittee on Economic Statistics of the Joint Economic Committee, U.S. Congress, explored national economic income concepts and in its published hearings[5] included the following from *The National Economic Accounts of the United States: Review, Appraisal and Recommendations,* a report to the Office of Statistical Standards, Bureau of the Budget, prepared by the National Accounts Review Committee of the National Bureau of Economic Research:

> The term "national economic accounts" is currently used to refer to a number of bodies of systematically arranged statistical data which have as their focus the economic activities taking place within a nation. There are at present five such bodies of data, treating different aspects of the Nation's

economic activity. These are the national income and product accounts, the input-output table, the flow-of-funds statements, the balance of payments, and the national balance sheets.

(a) National Income and Product Accounts

National income and product accounts are concerned, as the name implies, with income and product transactions. They are designed to show in monetary terms the current productive activity of the economy, distinguishing the current income and outlay associated with specific kinds of economic activities: production, consumption, and investment. They thus consolidate by economic activities the sort of information contained in the profit and loss accounts of enterprises and the budgets of consumers and governments.

(b) Input-output Tables

Input-output tables are also concerned with the current production activity of the economy, but they focus on interindustry relationships, rather than on income and product transactions. Input-output tables, which are usually arranged in the form of a square from-whom-to-whom tabulation, classify industries according to the nature of the processing activities in which they engage. Information is provided on the inputs from other industries and sectors that are utilized by each industry, and on the utilization of the output of each industry in other industries and sectors.

(c) Flow-of-funds Statements

Flow-of-funds statements cover all money and credit transactions in the economy; they thus deal with financial as well as income and product transactions. They provide information on the extension of bank credit, the purchase of securities, and other changes in the assets and liabilities of the different sectors of the economy, as well as on the payments and receipts of income. In contrast with input-output tables, flow-of-funds statements divide the economy into institutional sectors—corporations, unincorporated enterprises, banks, insurance companies, and so forth—rather than into processing industries. Flow-of-funds statements thus are intended to show the financial transactions of various groups in the economy, rather than the physical transformation relationships.

(d) Balance-of-payments Tables

Balance of payments tables embrace on the one hand the international trade statistics, classified by country of origin and destination and by commodity, and on the other hand foreign financial transactions. The classification of commodities tends to be a cross between the industrial breakdown used by input-output tables and the end use breakdown adopted in national income and product accounting. In treating financial transactions, however, the classification system of balance of payments bears a strong resemblance to that of flow-of-funds statements.

(e) National Balance Sheets

National balance sheets show the assets and liabilities of different sectors of the economy. They are closely related to flow-of-funds statements, except that they deal with stocks rather than flows. They are concerned with both the tangible and intangible assets of the economy and the liabilities and equities arising therefrom. National balance sheets ordinarily deal with the same institutional sectors as flow-of-funds statements, since these are the sectors that hold financial assets and liabilities. In addition they must sometimes also deal with the stocks of plant and equipment and with inventories of the various processing industries distinguished in input-output tables.

FOOTNOTES

1. The status of national income accounting is recognized by the American Economic Association, and it is listed under social accounting in the American Economic Review list of dissertations and periodicals. The American Accounting Association, however, does not provide a separate heading for it, but apparently lists national income accounting as income determination, a sub-heading under the theory of accounting, in its list of research projects in accounting published in The Accounting Review.
2. Possibly someday a courageous or intrepid legislator will suggest the filing of annual national income reports in an effort to strengthen our knowledge of national data.
3. National Income, 1954 edition, United States Department of Commerce, Washington, D.C., United States Government Printing Office, 1954; page 60.
4. See National Income, 1954 edition, page 167, for the formal statement.
5. See *The National Economic Accounts of the United States*. Hearings before the Subcommittee on Economic Statistics of the Joint Economic Committee, U.S. Congress, Oct. 29–30, 1957, Washington, D.C.: U.S. Government Printing Office, 1957, pp. 132–133.

QUESTIONS

1. How do financial accounting reports contribute to national income determination?

2. Refer to the most recent Economic Report of the President. What GNP was forecast? Compare this forecast with revised estimates reported in current articles in publications such as The Wall Street Journal, Business Week, and the Survey of Current Business.

3. Although national income is estimated, we do not construct a national balance sheet. Outline the format you would recommend for a national balance sheet. How would you "value" assets? Would you reflect depreciation? Would you have any intangible assets? How would you describe any "surplus?"

4. Business firms may choose among a number of accounting methods for reporting such items as inventories and depreciation. What problems would you expect this degree of flexibility to cause for national income accounting?

5. Obtain the annual report of a company.
   (a) What data from this report would enter into the national income accounts?
   (b) Estimate the value added by the firm.

The federal budget is a major instrument in achievement of national goals. It is widely discussed (especially at election time) and widely misunderstood. The new budget format, introduced in 1968 and designed to be more comprehensible, is described and compared to its predecessor.

Is the New U.S. Budget a More Understandable Document?

by S.C. Yu

Until this year, the federal budget has been prepared under different budget concepts. An innovative budget for fiscal 1969 was presented to the Congress by the President in January 1968. This new budget format is intended to replace the three former budget concepts, all of which have been criticized over the years for their competitive nature and conflicting views.

SOURCE: Reprinted slightly abridged by permission of the author and the publisher from The International Journal of Accounting Education and Research (Spring 1968), pp. 45–66.

The primary purpose of this paper is to examine the new budget in an effort to determine whether or not it is a more understandable and useful document as compared with the old measures. Examination of the underlying concepts as well as the format of the new budget are necessary in making a comparison with the former budget concepts. To begin with then, let us identify briefly the meaning and purposes of the federal budget.

MEANING OF THE BUDGET OF THE UNITED STATES

The budget of the Federal Government represents the President's recommendations for the programs and financial plan of the Federal Government for the coming year.[1] Although this definition of the U.S. budget appears to be quite simple and clear, there are three points which should be clarified and emphasized:

1. It is the President's budget. Although the budget consists of requests of the various Federal Government departments and agencies, these requests must be approved by the President, who in turn submits the budget, together with his "Budget Message," to the Congress. Therefore, it becomes the President's budget, not the budget of the various departments, agencies, or the Budget Bureau.

2. The President, in his budget, does not ask the Congress "to spend," but "to appropriate." In other words, the budget submitted represents the President's requests for congressional action, i.e., "budget authority."[2] The Congress makes the appropriations; the executive branch of the Federal Government does the spending.

3. The actual "programs of spending" of the Federal Government must be in conformity with Congressional action initiated in response to the President's requests. Normally, the submitted budget is dismantled by the Congress during its annual session. After Congress has adjourned, the Bureau of the Budget must reconstruct the budget in accordance with the actual appropriations made by the Congress. This revised or reconstructed budget is known as the "Budget Review," and generally it is not widely publicized.[3] Obviously, the unavoidable delay in releasing the revised budget estimates causes considerable difficulty to forecasters and analysts.

PURPOSE OF THE BUDGET

The Federal budget reflects an overall plan of federal government activities. Because of the significant role played by the federal government in our economy, the budget of the United States must serve many purposes. Officially, the budget represents the President's requests for congressional appropriations to achieve the government's spending program, and serves as a report to the Congress and the public on attempted plans. Economically speaking, the budget is intended:

1. to effect an efficient allocation of resources between the private and public sectors of the economy, and

2. to form a sound fiscal policy—through taxation and spending—for providing high employment, curbing inflation, stimulating growth of the economy, and improving the balance of payments.[4]

THE COMMISSION ON BUDGET CONCEPTS

The concepts and format of the new budget for fiscal 1969 are based almost entirely upon recommendations of the Commission on Budget Concepts. Recognizing the serious shortcomings of the old budget concepts, the President in 1967 appointed a 16-member Commission on Budget Concepts to study the basic concepts underlying the U.S. budget. Although budgetary concepts and procedures have been changed many times since passage of the Budget and Accounting Act of 1921, this is the first time that a commission of this kind was appointed by the President of the United States. The President's Commission was asked to make a critical review of the existing budgets and to recommend "an approach to budgetary presentation which would assist both public and congressional understanding of this vital document."[5] Thus the fundamental objective of the Commission was "to make the budget of the United States Government a more understandable and useful instrument of public policy and financial planning."[6] It was the feeling of the Commission that the conflicting views and competing nature of the old budget measures were the basic causes of confusion and misunderstanding. The most significant contribution made by the Commission was its recommendation for a single, unified budget. In addition, the Commission attempted to remove certain inconsistencies of the old budget measures and to broaden the coverage of the budget. In view of the magnitude and complexity of the Federal budget, this was indeed a formidable task. Its report was submitted to the President on October 10, 1967.

FORMER BUDGET CONCEPTS

There were three basic old budget concepts: (1) the administrative budget, (2) the consolidated cash budget, and (3) the national income accounts budget. In addition, in recent years, a special analysis of flow of government-administered funds has been prepared. The Commission on Budget Concepts pointed out that although each of these old budget measures was designed to serve certain special purposes, their distinctiveness was often lost in the eyes of the public and the Congress.

The Administrative Budget

This budgetary measure covered receipts and expenditures of federal funds owned by the U.S. Government. In other words, it excluded trust funds held in a fiduciary capacity by the government. Accordingly, this budget was incomplete since it covered roughly only about three-fifths of the federal government's total activities. Under the administrative budget the criterion of inclusion and exclusion of government funds was largely a legal concept rather than an economic one. Whether or not the legal basis of excluding trust funds was appropriate, the administrative budget was definitely inadequate for economic analysis purposes. For instance, social security taxes affect personal income just as surely as do income and other taxes. Indeed, the analyst needs a format which includes also the trust funds.

It may be noted that both financial flows (i.e., purely financial transactions) and nonfinancial flows (e.g., purchases of goods and services) were included in the receipts and expenditures of the administrative budget. Distinguishing between these two types of transactions is necessary since purely financial flows generate no real income and product, while nonfinancial flows do. It is extremely desirable, therefore, for analytical purposes, to show financial transactions in a separate category.

The administrative budget generally was on a cash basis, or more precisely, on a checks-issued basis. Of course, an accrual basis is much preferred. With respect to the treatment of all government expenditures as current outlays, the administrative budget should not be criticized unduly here since all the former budget measures followed the same accounting procedure. As a matter of fact, capital expenditures are not recognized in the new budget either. The Commission on Budget Concepts was against a formal capital budget, because of conceptual and practical difficulties. The issue of government capital expenditures is a highly controversial one and certainly is a topic for a separate paper.

The Consolidated Cash Budget

In official government documents, the so-called cash budget is also known as "receipts from and payments to the public." This cash budgetary measure was designed by the Bureau of the Budget and the Federal Reserve Board in the 1940's to compensate for the deficiency resulting from the exclusion of trust funds in the administrative budget, and to meet the needs of the U.S. Treasury. It was consolidated in the sense that both federally-owned funds and trust funds were included on a consolidated basis, i.e., transactions between them were eliminated. It was called a "cash" budget in the sense that it was on a "checks-paid" basis.

The cash budget depicted total cash transactions between the federal government and the public. Consequently, surplus or deficit of the cash budget reflected the needs of the Treasury Department for borrowing from the public or showed its ability to repay public debts. Because of significant increases in the trust funds in recent years, the consolidated cash budget has been regarded as a very important document in the analysis of federal finances.

The National Income Accounts Budget

This budget has been variously called the "Federal Budget, National Income Accounts Basis," the "Income and Product Budget," and the "Federal Sector of the National Income Accounts." Strictly speaking, the national income accounts budget was not a budget but an economic analysis of federal receipts and expenditures. Inasmuch as it is based on the national income accounting framework, this budget depicted only nonfinancial flows.[7] Thus, purely financial transactions, such as loans and repayments of loans, were excluded. With the exceptions of personal income taxes and purchases of goods and services, which were on a payment basis and a delivery basis, respectively, the NIA budget was on an accrual basis. Otherwise, it resembled the cash budget, modified to conform to national income accounting concepts and classification. Because of its significance in economic analysis, the format of the NIA Budget is shown in Table 1.[8]

Flow of Government-Administered Funds

This is a special analysis of government funds. It represented the flow of moneys on a gross basis between the federal government and the public. This special analysis was on a checks-issued basis. As will be discussed later, the coverage of this flow analysis is substantially the same as in the new budget concept. They differ primarily in grossing and netting of certain items. Thus, budget deficit or surplus remains the same under both concepts.

UNDERLYING CONCEPTS OF THE NEW BUDGET

All of the Commission's major recommendations except two (accrual accounting and segregation of loan subsidies) have been implemented in the new budget of the United States. It is hoped that the two recommendations not adopted at present, especially accrual accounting, will be incorporated in the budget in the near future.[9] Following is a summary of the underlying concepts of the new budget.

A Unified Budget

Much of the confusion resulting from the former budget concepts was apparently due to differences in orientation, coverage, and grossing and netting

TABLE 1.   Federal Receipts and Expenditures in the National Income Accounts (In billions of dollars)

Description	1967 actual	1968 estimate	1969 estimate
RECEIPTS, NATIONAL INCOME BASIS			
Personal tax and nontax receipts	64.6	71.0	83.8
Corporate profits tax accruals	31.4	34.3	37.2
Indirect business tax and nontax accruals	15.9	17.1	18.1
Contributions for social insurance	35.7	38.7	43.4
Total receipts, national income basis	147.6	161.1	182.5
EXPENDITURES, NATIONAL INCOME BASIS			
Purchases of goods and services	84.5	92.8	99.4
Defense	(67.6)	(74.4)	(78.8)
Nondefense	(16.9)	(18.4)	(20.6)
Transfer payments	39.8	44.9	49.9
Domestic ("to persons")	(37.7)	(43.0)	(47.9)
Foreign	(2.1)	(1.9)	(2.0)
Grants-in-aid to State and local governments	15.4	18.0	20.0
Net interest paid	10.1	10.7	11.2
Subsidies less current surplus of government enterprises	5.3	4.7	4.5
Total expenditures, national income basis	155.1	171.1	185.0
Surplus (+) or deficit (-), national income basis	-7.5	-10.0	-2.5

Source: *Special Analyses Budget of the United States Fiscal 1969.* U.S. Government Printing Office, p. 22.

procedures. Consequently, there existed discrepancies in receipts and expenditures, and hence in budget surplus or deficit. The most significant feature of the new budget is the unification of the old budgetary concepts. This new unified budget now becomes *the* budget of the United States and supersedes all the old measures. With this new budget, there is no such thing as competing budgets or conflicting views, since there exists now only *one* budget of the United States Government.

Emphasis on Congressional Action

All the former budget measures centered around receipts and spending programs of the federal government. Appropriations, a necessary element of the budget, were given no distinctive treatment. This is undoubtedly a major deficiency of the old budget concepts. While expenditures and net lending reflect the size of the budget, it must be remembered that appropriations are prerequisites to spending and lending. The emphasis placed on "appropriations" (congressional action) is one of the main features of the new budget.[10] Thus, the new budget format presents budget authority in a significant manner and, consequently, provides better information as well as an integration between expenditures and congressional action.[11]

Broad Coverage

In terms of coverage, the new budget is much broader than any of the former measures. In addition to the presentation of "appropriations" as a new category, the new budget comprehensively covers all programs and financial plans of the federal government. Thus it includes both federal funds and trust funds. Furthermore, the budget includes a section labeled "Budget Financing." Finally, it provides information for outstanding debt at the end of the year. Thus, the comprehensiveness of the new budget presents an integrated set of budgetary financial data.

Separation of Loan Activities

In the new budget, lending is classified separately in order to provide a better understanding of the economic impact of the budget on private income and employment. This is accomplished by providing a loan account in the "Receipts, Expenditures, and Net Lending" section of the budget. The net total of this section is called "budget deficit" (or surplus), and replaces the three deficit or surplus figures under the old budgets. Participation certificates,[12] formerly treated as offsets against expenditures, are now classified among borrowing activities as a means of financing.

Netting of Proprietary Receipts

Market-oriented receipts are treated as offsets against related expenditures. This recommendation of the Commission is intended to eliminate inconsistent treatment of business-type or market-oriented nontax receipts. Under the former budget measures, some receipts of this type were so treated; others were not. Consistency calls for equal treatment.

FORMAT OF THE NEW BUDGET

Organization of the new unified budget is based primarily upon the underlying budget concepts discussed above. The "Summary of the Budget and Financial Plan," as shown in Table 2, gives a general view of the format of the new budget. It contains four basic parts: budget authority; receipts, expenditures and net lending; budget financing; and outstanding debt at end of year. Thus the basic structure of the new budget provides an interrelated system of appropriations, spending, and financing. Let us examine briefly the major components of the budget.

Budget Authority

The budget summary starts with budget authority, including both new appropriations and existing appropriations. The former require new congressional action, whereas the latter do not. Placing appropriations at the beginning of the budget reflects not only the significance of congressional action on the requested programs, but also brings out the relationship between appropriations and budgeted spending as well as their logical sequence, i.e., budget authority precedes spending.

Budget Receipts, Expenditures, and Net Lending

This is the second part of the budget. Spending and lending are separately identified through the use of two accounts, the receipt-expenditure account and the loan account. Receipts include all tax and nontax (e.g., fees) revenues, trust funds receipts, and other current receipts. Expenditures cover purchases of goods and services, payments out of trust funds, foreign loans on noncommercial terms, non-recourse domestic loans, and subsidies. The difference between total receipts and expenditures is called "expenditure account surplus or deficit." This surplus or deficit item is an innovative concept of the Commission, which claims that it provides "the executive branch, the Congress, and the public with a useful measure of economic impact for fiscal policy purposes."[13] Lending programs are excluded from calculation of this item because they represent essentially flows of financial assets as contrasted to "income and product" or nonfinancial flows.

The loan account shows loan disbursements and repayments with the exceptions of those included as expenditures. The balance of the loan account is called "net lending." When the balances of these two accounts, i.e., the expenditure account deficit or surplus plus net lending, are combined, the resulting total is called "budget deficit or surplus." It should be emphasized that the term "budget deficit or surplus" is used for the entire budget, whereas the expenditure

TABLE 2. Summary of the Budget and Financial Plan (Fiscal years. In billions)

Description	1967 actual	1968 estimate	1969 estimate
Budget authority (largely appropriations):			
Previously enacted	$135.4	$125.1	. . . .
Proposed for current action by Congress	. . . .	3.3	$141.5
Becoming available without current action by Congress	58.7	69.9	73.1
Deductions for interfund and intragovernmental transactions and applicable receipts	-11.5	-11.8	-12.9
Total, budget authority	182.6	186.5	201.7
Receipts, expenditures, and net lending:			
Expenditure account:			
Receipts	149.6	155.9	178.1
Expenditures (excludes net lending)	153.2	169.9	182.8
Expenditure deficit (–)	-3.6	-14.0	-4.7
Loan account:			
Loan disbursements	17.8	20.9	20.4
Loan repayments	-12.6	-15.1	-17.1
Net lending	5.2	5.8	3.3
Total budget:			
Receipts	149.6	155.8	178.1
Outlays (expenditures and net lending)	158.4	175.6	186.1
Budget deficit (–)	-8.8	-19.8	-8.0
Budget financing:			
Borrowing from the public	3.5	20.8	8.0
Reduction of cash balances, etc.	5.3	-1.0	*
Total, budget financing	8.8	19.8	8.0

	1966 actual			
Outstanding debt, end of year:				
Gross amount outstanding	329.5	341.3	370.0	387.2
Held by the public	265.6	269.2	290.0	298.0

*Less than $50 million.
Source: *The Budget of the United States Government Fiscal 1969,* U.S. Government Printing Office, 10.

account deficit or surplus excludes the loan account (net lending). The Commission strongly recommended that reference to deficit or surplus be properly identified, that the use of the word "deficit" or "surplus" should be avoided, and that the single amount of budget deficit or surplus should not be overly used or emphasized.

Budget Financing

This part of the budget shows how the budget deficit is *financed* (or disposed of in case of a surplus). There are two basic means of financing a deficit, borrowing from the public and reducing cash balances, etc. Budget financing and budget deficit must, of course agree.

Outstanding Debt at End of Year

This last part of the budget gives a summary of the level of federal borrowing (securities) at the end of the year. It shows the gross amount of federal debt outstanding, including the amount of securities held by the public and the amount held by trust funds and other government agencies. In addition, it reveals estimates of the anticipated level of borrowing.

CONCLUSION

The Federal budget is a highly complicated document. Evaluation as to whether or not the Commission on Budget Concepts has made this vital document more understandable and meaningful must be on a relative basis.

From the foregoing discussion, it is seen that the most prominent features of the new budget are the unification of the former budget concepts, and a broader coverage of basic budget elements. Through our comparative analysis, it appears that the new budget format eliminates most of the discrepancies caused by the old competing measures. For instance, instead of three sets of budget totals, there is now only one set of budget figures. The comprehensiveness of the new budget format not only provides a broader budget framework for the federal government, but also allows for presentation of basic budgetary components in a logical sequence. In addition, a number of inconsistent treatments of receipts and expenditures have been removed. It may be noted that the AICPA has fully endorsed the new budget concepts and format. The Institute, in its January 1968 issue of the *Journal of Accountancy* states: "The executive committee of the American Institute of Certified Public Accountants recommends that the federal government adopt, at the earliest practical moment, the modern and progressive budget principles contained in the Report of the President's Commission on Budget Concepts. The executive committee agrees with the

President's Commission that adoption of these recommendations would make the budget of the United States government a more understandable and useful instrument of public policy and financial planning."[14]

A meaningful and penetrating study of the federal budget requires analysis of the components of the budget as well as their relationships. The single deficit or surplus item, as cautioned by the Commission, should not be overly emphasized. Although the new budget replaces the former three deficit or surplus figures with one single "budget deficit or surplus" item, it should be pointed out that the new budget contains another deficit or surplus figure, i.e., the "expenditure-account deficit." Whether or not these two deficit or surplus items will cause any confusion remains to be seen. It may be desirable to give a different name to the "expenditure-account deficit," such as "excess of expenditures over receipts," and to leave the "budget deficit or surplus" item for the total budget.

For economic analysis, data for both financial flows and nonfinancial flows are needed. However, a clear distinction between these two types of transactions is of utmost importance since, for analytical purposes, such a differentiation will bring out the interplay between financial flows and nonfinancial flows.[15] This kind of information is very desirable for decision-making and planning purposes. The new budget, to some extent, does contain this significant feature, e.g., the provision for a separate loan account. However, further identification of these two types of transactions may prove even more desirable.

In general, we may say that a unified, integrated budget system will undoubtedly improve public as well as congressional understanding of the federal budget. However, one must realize that no single budget format is inclusive enough to meet all needs. Discriminatory inclusion and exclusion of budgetary and financial items are often necessary for various analytical purposes. Supplementary analyses, such as the NIA measure and money-flows between the federal government and the public are needed.

FOOTNOTES

1.   Bureau of the Budget, *The Budget in Brief* (Washington, D.C.: Government Printing Office, 1968), p. 5.

2.   *I.e.,* "authority provided by the Congress to obligate the Federal Government to pay out money." *The Budget in Brief, ibid.,* p. 4. Under the new budget, the word "appropriations" is applicable to the present concept of NOA.* See *Report of the President's Commission on Budget Concepts* (Washington, D.C.: U.S. Government Printing Office, October 1967), p. 100.

3.   Professor John P. Lewis and Robert C. Turner present an excellent description of the process of documentation of the Federal budget in their book:

*EDITOR'S NOTE: See footnote 10.

Business Conditions Analysis (2nd Edition, New York: McGraw-Hill Book Company, 1967), pp. 410–16.

4. *Budget in Brief, op. cit.*, p. 5.

5. *The Budget of the United States Government* (Washington, D.C.: U.S. Government Printing Office, 1968), p. 39.

6. *Report of the President's Commission on Budget Concepts* (Washington, D.C.: U.S. Government Printing Office, 1967), p. 1.

7. Non-financial flows refer to generation of income and product. As students of national income accounting well know, income here means factor or cost (a debit) which differs from "income" as recorded by a credit in financial accounting.

8. Those who are not familiar with national income accounting should study closely the classification of receipts and expenditures of this federal sector account and its relation to the national income and product accounts.

9. See *The Budget of the United States Government, op cit.*, p. 40.

10. "Appropriation" may be defined as "an authorization by an Act of Congress to incur obligations and make payments out of the Treasury for specified purposes." Appropriations are the most common form of new obligational authority (NOA). The latter is defined as "authority provided by the Congress to obligate the Federal Government to pay out money." "Authority" is defined as "an Act of Congress which authorizes Federal programs, obligations, or expenditures." This term "sometimes refers to basic substantive legislation, . . . but not actually providing authority to spend." Apparently, there are variations in defining these terms. The Commission recommended "redefining the term appropriations to cover all forms of congressional action which grant authority to obligate the Government to make expenditures." See *Report of the Commission on Budget Concepts, op. cit.*, pp. 7 and 95; also *Budget in Brief, op. cit.*, p. 4.

11. Detailed information about appropriations was customarily shown in the budget appendix in the past.

12. Participation certificates are "interest-bearing instruments representing shares in a pool of Government-held loans. Under present practice, the Government continues to service the individual loans, and takes the loss on any defaults." *Report of Commission on Budget Concepts, op. cit.*, p. 100.

13. *Ibid.*, p. 5.

14. "AICPA Executive Committee Statement on the Report of the President's Commission on Budget Concepts," *The Journal of Accountancy* (January 1968), p. 49.

15. A typical example is the flow-of-funds segment of macroaccounting which portrays the interrelationships of financial flows and nonfinancial flows.

QUESTIONS

1. Define budgeting.

2. Compare federal budgeting with budgeting for a business firm. How are they similar? In what ways are they different?

3. What are appropriations? How are they treated under the new budget?

4. What are the major components of the new budget?

5. Refer to the most recent budget of the United States. (If your library doesn't have a copy of the actual budget, it will be summarized in numerous publications such as Business Week.) How has it grown since 1967? Which components have changed the most percentage wise?

Section VIII
Accounting for Social Progress

The Employment Act of 1946 established the Council of Economic Advisors, provided for the annual economic report of the President, and established a Joint Economic Committee in the Congress. Our system of national income accounts grew out of this legislation; the result is that we now have a reasonably understandable and useful set of data concerning the economic progress of the nation. As indicated in Section VII, the national income accounts are subject to considerable criticism. Our tendency to emphasize a single economic index, the Gross National Product, has been especially criticized as reflecting an overly materialistic value system. In spite of such criticism, however, most would agree that national economic planning and policy-making have been improved with the availability of the information provided by the national income accounts.

As we began to develop reasonably satisfactory economic statistics, interest turned to a broader evaluation of the quality of life encompassing not only economic factors but non-economic factors as well. In response to this growing interest the Department of Health, Education, and Welfare undertook a preliminary study of ways to measure social conditions and progress in the United States. This study, Toward A Social Report, is summarized and discussed in the article by Angus Campbell.

Legislation to establish a social report of the President, analogous to the economic report, was introduced in 1967 by Senator Walter F. Mondale (the "Full Opportunity and Social Accounting Act"). This act, reproduced in its original form in the following pages, was not passed; it was reintroduced in amended form in 1970 but again failed to pass the Congress.

313

Nevertheless, Senator's Mondale's bill drew substantial support and reflects the national interest in developing measures of social progress and conditions.

The objectives of a system of social evaluation such as envisioned in Senator Mondale's bill have been stated as follows:

It would sharpen our quantitative knowledge of social needs.

It would allow us to measure more precisely our progress toward our social objectives.

It would help us to evaluate efforts at all levels of government.

It would help us to determine priorities among competing social programs.

It would encourage the development and assessment of alternative courses without waiting until some one solution had belatedly been proved a failure.[1]

In opposition to a social report, critics argue that we sometimes take security in statistics, feeling that measurement of the problem is tantamount to solving it. In other words, the social report itself might be accepted as sufficient action, and we might never get around to actually trying to improve social conditions. There is also the danger that the relevant factors cannot be adequately measured, and we might fall into the trap of measuring not what should be measured but what can be measured (like the story about the boy looking for a lost quarter under a street lamp "where the light was better" rather than down the street where the quarter was actually lost). Another criticism is that aggregate statistics tend to disguise significant and possibly dangerous details. This point is made by Professor Robert Abelson in the excerpt from his testimony before the Senate Subcommittee on Government Research of the Committee on Government Operations in hearings on Senator Mondale's bill.

The concept of social measurement may have merit—but it could conceivably frustrate the very progress it seeks to encourage.

1. Walter F. Mondale, "Some Thoughts on 'Stumbling Into the Future,' " American Psychologist, XXII (November 1967), page 973.

ADDITIONAL REFERENCES

1. Churchman, C. West, "On the Facility, Felicity, and Morality of Measuring Social Change," The Accounting Review, January 1971, pp. 30–35.

2. Gross, Bertrand, The State of the Nation: Social Systems Accounting (London: Tavistock Publications, 1966).

3. Kreps, Theodore J., "Measurement of the Social Performance of Business," The Annals of the American Academy of Political and Social Science, September 1962, pp. 20–31.

4. Lazarsfield, Paul F., "Accounting and Social Bookkeeping," in Robert R. Sterling and William F. Bentz, editors, Accounting in Perspective: Contributions to Accounting Thought by Other Disciplines (Cincinnati: Southwestern Publishing Co., 1971).

5. U.S. Dept. of Health, Education, and Welfare, Toward a Social Report (Washington: U.S. Dept. of HEW, 1969).

Can we measure the social condition of our society, the quality of life? The recommendations contained in <u>Toward a Social Report</u>, published by the Department of Health, Education, and Welfare, are summarized.

Social Accounting in the 1970's

by Angus Campbell

The theme for my remarks comes from a statement made recently by the President of the United States. In his State of the Union address to the Congress in January of 1970, Mr. Nixon asked the following question:

> In the next 10 years we will increase our wealth by 50 per cent; the profound question is, does this mean that we will be 50 per cent richer in any real sense, 50 per cent better off, 50 per cent happier?

I ask you to examine with me the implications of this statement.

You are aware that there is a growing interest in this country, in both private and public circles, in the concept of national goals. In July of 1969 the President

SOURCE: Reprinted by permission from the January 1971 issue of the <u>Michigan Business Review</u>, published by the Graduate School of Business Administration, The University of Michigan.

created within the White House what he called a National Goals Research Staff. Among the functions of this staff is "the responsibility for developing and monitoring social indicators that can reflect the present and the future quality of American life and the direction and rate of its change." As a nation we have begun to ask ourselves more specifically what is implied by our stated aspirations to "life, liberty and the pursuit of happiness" and how well or poorly these objectives are being secured by the American population.

When we look for ways of assessing the trends in our national life, we find that the most highly developed accounts are those which monitor the nation's economic status. We have learned to depend on the annual report of the Council of Economic Advisers and the increasingly useful and detailed economic accounts which it presents. Indeed, as someone has recently pointed out, these economic indicators have become so much a part of our thinking that we have tended to equate a rising national income with national well-being.

It is apparent, however, from Mr. Nixon's statement that he has begun to question this equation. He is prepared to accept the economist's prediction that the national income will continue to increase over the next 10 years, but he is asking whether the nation will in any real sense be better off or happier. This must be a question that we have all asked ourselves in one way or another in recent years. Since World War II we have seen average family income rise dramatically and the number of families below the poverty line reduced by more than half. We have become a nation of affluence. But during those same years, we have seen a prodigious increase in the crime rate, especially crimes against the person. We are in the middle of a spreading epidemic of the use of drugs. We are experiencing one of the most violent eras in the nation's history. Civil disobedience and civil disorder are an everyday occurrence. It would take a brave man, indeed, to argue that the quality of life in these United States has been improving in the last few years.

Because this discrepancy between a rising national income and a deteriorating national morale has become so apparent and so disturbing, there is now a growing concern for the development of new kinds of accounting which will give more adequate assessment of the national well-being. It is now proposed that along with the economic indicators, which have become a standard feature of national reporting, there should be developed a program of social indicators leading to a social report to the President.

We need these social indicators, not out of simple curiosity as to what the social condition of the country might be at any particular time, but because of their value in helping develop intelligent social policy. The economic data provided by the Council of Economic Advisers are used in countless ways by both public and private agencies. Over time we would expect a well-established set of social indicators to acquire the same kind of value.

We must recognize that while economists have devised various systems of economic accounts by which the nation's economic performance can be assessed, we do not have any such system of social accounts and it will be difficult to develop one. Dollars are fungible and the various components of the economic accounts can, for the most part, be reduced to a common base. The data which would go into a program of social accounting are, in many cases, as readily quantifiable as those in the economic report, but they are not as easily combined and it is not likely that we will be able to devise a single statistic which might be called the gross social product.

It seems apparent that we will have to begin our program of social accounting on a more modest level. Starting from where we are, rather than from where we would like to be, we will begin to assemble and extend those sets of data which have been collected in some systematic way over a period of time and which appear to have value as indicators of the social condition of our society. The Department of Health, Education, and Welfare has recently issued a monograph entitled *Toward a Social Report*, which undertakes to lay out a preliminary outline of what the contents of such a report might be.

The HEW monograph suggests that the social report should begin with a chapter on health and illness. It suggests that the standard data on life expectancy should be extended by an index of expectancy of healthy life, that is, years free of bed disability and institutional confinement. It would undertake to follow trends in mental health and illness and to develop more adequate data on the prevalence of emotional disturbance in the general population. It would examine the very substantial differences in health which exist between the regions and the various groups in our society, and where possible, to compare our health data to those of other countries. As you know, despite our much vaunted system of medical service, numerous other countries have a longer life expectancy at birth than we do and our rates of ulcers, hypertension, and a number of other morbid conditions are relatively high. Our rank with respect to infant mortality rates is low and has been progressively declining in recent decades. The HEW report proposes also to include data regarding the economics of health care, with a monitoring of the cost of medical attention and the adequacy of insurance coverage. An evaluation of our system of health care must take account not only of the quality of care given the individual patient but also of the adequacy of the delivery of health services to the entire population.

The HEW monograph suggests that a second chapter of the social report be devoted to social mobility, to an examination of how much equality of opportunity we have and whether there is more or less than there used to be. Evidence to answer these questions is not voluminous but by comparing the occupational levels of fathers and sons it is possible to demonstrate that considerably less than half of the total variation in occupational achievement among men in this country can be explained by differences in their family background. In other words, there is a considerable degree of movement from one occupational level to a higher one and this mobility does not appear to have declined during recent decades. It is clear, however, that the point at which we fail most dramatically to achieve true equality of opportunity is among our minority groups. Black Americans have much less occupational mobility than whites and this cannot be fully explained by their disadvantages in education or level of skill. We know that black people have made significant gains upward in the occupational ladder during the last 10 years and it is important to continue to monitor this movement, since it provides a particularly revealing indicator of the extent to which our society is coming up to its pretensions of equal opportunity.

A social report must also include information about the quality of the physical environment we live in, since the world around us has a direct effect on the quality of our experience. For many years we Americans have ignored the various forms of pollution which have accumulated around us and now, with that engaging enthusiasm for which we are internationally famous, we seem to have decided to eliminate the problem overnight, certainly not later than 1975. It is apparent that our present pollution crisis results primarily from two factors: (1) our pollution growth and (2) our affluence. The 1970 Census counted over 200 million people in this country and despite the fact that our raw birthrate is very near the low record reached during the Depression, and is at present one of the lowest rates in the world, we are adding 2 million people to our population every year. In other words, we are adding the equivalent of a city the size of Detroit to the population each year. The medium family income is now approaching $9,000 a year and nearly one family in five is receiving over $15,000 a year.

This unprecedented affluence is converted to consumption of all kinds, and one of the byproducts of consumption is pollution.

I do not have the sense that our national goals regarding the protection and reclaiming of our environment are very clear, or that we are very clear about what kinds of costs we are prepared to pay to achieve what we might think of as desirable ends. I feel quite confident, however, that the problem of pollution is going to be with us for a long time and it will obviously be necessary to develop a comprehensive and dependable set of indicators of the quality of the environment on which public policy can be based.

A different type of pollutant which diminishes the quality of life in this country is the array of antisocial acts classified as crime. Any serious program of social accounting surely must attempt to monitor trends in the incidence and character of criminal acts since the presence of crime calls into question the basic values of our society. The unfortunate fact is that the national statistics on crime which we now have available are flawed by serious shortcomings. It is apparent, for example, that despite the fact that our crime rates are higher than those of any other country, they probably grossly underestimate the actual number of crimes committed. National surveys carried out for the President's Crime Commission in 1965 indicate that more than twice as many crimes occur as are reported in the official crime statistics. It is also clear that the FBI Uniform Crime Reports on the incidence of major crimes, being based on the voluntary cooperation of police forces around the country, may contain serious error. Be this as it may, public apprehension regarding crime on the streets is undoubtedly growing and the demand for effective measures to restore law and order is increasingly insistent.

In attempting to cope with our rising rates of crime and violence we are groping for solutions to a problem which seems virtually intractable. I doubt very much if an improved system of crime reporting would provide immediate answers to these problems, but it would at least give us a better definition of our present difficulties and a better basis for estimating the probable consequences of alternative policies proposed to solve them.

Let me mention one further aspect of our social performance which the HEW monograph would like to see more fully accounted. That is the area of learning. The Office of Education has, for a good many years, been keeping rather complete records of the numbers of children of each age cohort who go to school. As you know, young Americans spend far more years in school than did any of our preceding generations and we have now reached the point where four-fifths of our youth complete high school, 40 per cent of them go on to college, and one in five completes a college degree. In comparison to other countries, we are clearly in a class by ourselves. It is a remarkable fact, however, that with all this tremendous investment in our educational system we have no systematic program of national assessment of what this education is achieving. We hear on the one hand that our schools are better than they have ever been, with better-trained teachers, better facilities and modern methods of instruction, and on the other hand that the average high school graduate cannot spell, write a decent English sentence, or do simple arithmetic. It should not be difficult to organize a national program of assessing scholarly achievement, perhaps on a sampling basis, and establishing a set of trend lines that would tell us what in fact our schools are accomplishing. We might find that our complacency regarding such matters is not fully justified. The International Study of Achievement in Mathematics has recently made a comparison of the mathematical performance of American students with that of students from certain European countries; it found that our students had one of the poorest levels of performance of all the nations that were studied.

Up to this point the indicators that I have been discussing do not raise any serious questions of definition or of measurement. I have no doubt that in the course of time these and other indicators will be developed and refined and that, when combined into an annual social report, they will make possible a more rounded assessment of the conditions of life in the nation and of the direction of movement taking place in the way the nation lives. I am not satisfied, however, that these social and economic indicators will tell us all we want to know about what is happening to the quality of life in America. To be sure, we can regard increasing numbers of hospital beds, new housing starts, or college degrees awarded as evidence of gains in the national well-being. But the fact that people are free of physical morbidity does not assure us that they are free of anxiety and depression. The fact that they live in better housing does not tell us that they feel safer on the streets of their neighborhoods. The fact that they have more extended schooling does not guarantee that they feel more self-fulfilled or less alienated. The quality of life must be in the eye of the beholder and it is only through an examination of the experience of life as our people perceive it that we will understand the human meaning of the great social and institutional changes which characterize our time.

I believe that as we move through the 1970's we will need to develop a program of psychological indicators to accompany and amplify the kinds of social indicators that I have been discussing. In my view, we are in great need of a research program devoted to the continuing generation of information regarding the aspirations, expectations, satisfactions, frustrations, attitudes, and values of the American population and of its major subdivisions. I am well aware of the serious problems of measurement which such an effort would involve, but I do not believe that we can arrive at an understanding of what is happening to the quality of life in this country until we find ways of providing ourselves with this kind of information.

Let me suggest two or three kinds of psychological measures to which I would give high priority.

We often hear it said that this country is experiencing a revolution of rising expectations. Circumstances which once seemed normal and sufficient are no longer satisfying. Levels of aspiration have risen rapidly and have produced widespread frustration. These are plausible statements but there is in fact little evidence as to what has been happening to levels of satisfaction and dissatisfaction in the different segments of the population. We know incomes have gone up, that housing is improved and that conditions of work are better, but we cannot assume that these positive changes in the objective conditions of life create corresponding improvement in the subjective experience of life. The current mood of frustration and resentment in the black population of this country demonstrates well enough that a rising standard of living does not necessarily produce a higher level of satisfaction.

Another kind of psychological indicator that I think we badly need is one that would give us a reading on levels of group attachment and group hostility.

One gets the impression these days that our nation is being torn into pieces—young against old, blacks against whites, students against hard hats, hawks against doves, even recently women against men. How much of this is rhetoric and how much is real? Despite the recurrent episodes of racial violence which we are experiencing these days, our surveys at the Institute for Social Research demonstrate that over the last several years peaceful contact between the races has increased in almost all phases of life and that both white and black people are increasingly likely to tell us that they have friends in the other race. We should have far more information on these intergroup attitudes than we have and we should be carefully monitoring them as they change over time.

Finally, I would propose that we make a serious effort to understand the phenomenon of alienation. The daily headlines make it clear that a certain fraction of our population has lost whatever attachment it had to our basic social and political values. The number of hardcore revolutionaries is probably very small, but the number of those who have come to question the validity of our traditional national assumptions may be very much greater.

Alienation undoubtedly has many forms and many causes but, in some degree at least, it reflects a malfunctioning of our society. A healthy society requires a certain degree of consensus, a shared sense of community among its citizens. When there is evidence of sickness, it would appear to be a matter of simple prudence to find a way to measure the severity of the symptoms and to identify the conditions which produce them.

These are examples of variables we should be accounting; you could no doubt suggest others. One reason I am anxious to see systematic measurement of these psychological indicators undertaken is because I believe that without such measurement we can be very easily misled as to what the actual state of public morale is. It is simply not possible to come to a realistic understanding of the complex attitudes and values of a population as diverse as ours by watching television or reading the newspapers. Indeed it could be argued that single-minded concentration on television would virtually guarantee a distorted view of what the public is like. This wouldn't be so important if it weren't for the fact that important decisions regarding social policy are influenced by what decision-makers think the public believes and wants. If they make these decisions on the basis of misconceptions the consequences can be very serious indeed.

May I now conclude my remarks by returning to Mr. Nixon's question "In the next 10 years, will we be 50 per cent richer in any real sense, 50 per cent better off, 50 per cent happier?" I think this is precisely the kind of question the President should be raising with his constituents. It compels us to examine our national purpose and to evaluate the progress we are making toward it. Once we accept Mr. Nixon's implication that the quality of American life cannot be adequately represented by measures of our wealth, we are forced to think about those aspects of human experience which do make life stimulating, rewarding, and fulfilling. I would hope that 10 years from now we will be able to tell the man who is President in 1980 whether the American people are in fact better off or happier than they were in 1970.

QUESTIONS

1. In what way is "social accounting" accounting?

2. Relate national income accounting to current efforts to develop an index of social progress (see readings in Section VII).

3. It is often said that we cannot measure "interpersonal utility," or the relative satisfaction, happiness, and pleasure of individuals. "One man's meat is another man's poison." Since different things make different people happy, is it possible to measure aggregate "happiness" and to determine, as President Nixon asked, whether we are "50 per cent happier?"

4. List the types of information which Toward a Social Report recommends be included in a national social report. Describe the problems you would anticipate in developing such information. What other categories of information do you think would be useful in evaluating the quality of American life?

5. What is social mobility?

6. ". . . these economic indicators have become so much a part of our thinking that we have tended to equate a rising national income with national well-being."
    (a) What, to you, constitutes national well-being?
    (b) Do you think national income and well-being are proportional at all?
    (c) Is "national morale" the same as "national well-being?"

7. Could the method described in "The Modern Management Approach to a Program of Social Improvement" in Section III be used in some modified form to develop an index of social progress or of "quality of life?"

8. You probably have read George Orwell's 1984. Do you think social accounting leads toward or away from the sort of conditions described in his novel? What about Campbell's psychological measures?

*A Bill to promote the public welfare, S.843
in the Senate of the United States, February 6, 1967.*

Full Opportunity
and Social Accounting
Act

DECLARATION OF POLICY

Sec. 2.   In order to promote the general welfare, the Congress declares that it is
the continuing policy and responsibility of the Federal Government, consistent
with the primary responsibilities of state and local governments and the private
sector, to promote and encourage such conditions as will give every American
the opportunity to live in decency and dignity, and to provide a clear and precise
picture of whether such conditions are promoted and encouraged in such areas
as health, education, and training, rehabilitation, housing, vocational opportunities, the arts and humanities, and special assistance for the mentally ill and

SOURCE: Reprinted by permission of the publisher from American Psychologist (November 1967), pp. 974–976. Copyright 1967 by the American Psychological Association.

retarded, the deprived, the abandoned, and the criminal, and by measuring progress in meeting such needs.

SOCIAL REPORT OF THE PRESIDENT

Sec. 3.   (a) The President shall transmit to the Congress not later than March 20 of each year a report to be known as the "social report," setting forth (1) the overall progress and effectiveness of Federal efforts designed to carry out the policy declared in Section 2 with particular emphasis upon the manner in which such efforts serve to meet national social needs in such areas as health, education and training, rehabilitation, housing, vocational opportunities, the arts and humanities, and special assistance for the mentally ill and retarded, the deprived, the abandoned, and the criminal; (2) a review of state, local, and private efforts designed to create the conditions specified in Section 2; (3) current and foreseeable needs in the areas served by such efforts and the progress of development of plans to meet such needs; and (4) programs and policies for carrying out the policy declared in Section 2, together with such recommendations for legislation as he may deem necessary or desirable.

(b) The President may transmit from time to time to the Congress reports and supplementary to the social report, each of which shall include such supplementary or revised recommendations as he may deem necessary or desirable to achieve the policy declared in Section 2.

(c) The social report, and all supplementary reports transmitted under Subsection (b) of this section, shall, when transmitted to Congress, be referred to the joint committee created by Section 5.

COUNCIL OF SOCIAL ADVISERS TO THE PRESIDENT

Sec. 4.   (a) There is created in the Executive Office of the President a Council of Social Advisers (hereinafter called the Council). The Council shall be composed of three members who shall be appointed by the President, by and with the advice and consent of the Senate, and each of whom shall be a person who, as a result of his training, experience, and attainments, is exceptionally qualified to appraise programs and activities of the Government in the light of the policy declared in Section 2, and to formulate and recommend programs to carry out such policy. Each member of the Council, other than the Chairman, shall receive compensation at the rate prescribed for Level IV of the Executive Schedule by Section 5315 of Title 5 of the United States Code. The President shall designate one of the members of the Council as Chairman who shall receive compensation at the rate prescribed for Level II of such Schedule.

(b) The Chairman of the Council is authorized to employ, and fix the compensation of, such specialists and other experts as may be necessary for the carrying out of its functions under this Act, without regard to the provisions of Title 5, United States Code, governing appointments in the competitive service, and without regard to the provisions of Chapter 51 and Subchapter III of chapter 53 of such title relating to classification and General Schedule pay rates, and is authorized, subject to such provisions, to employ such other officers and employees as may be necessary for carrying out its functions under this Act, and fix their compensation in accordance with the provisions of such Chapter 51 and Subchapter III of Chapter 53.

(c) It shall be the duty and function of the Council—

1. to assist and advise the President in the preparation of the social report:

2. to gather timely and authoritative information and statistical data concerning developments and programs designed to carry out the policy declared in Section 2, both current and prospective, to analyze and interpret such information and data in the light of the policy declared in section 2 and to compile and submit to the President studies relating to such developments and programs;

3. to appraise the various programs and activities of the Federal Government in the light of the policy declared in Section 2 of this Act for the purpose of determining the extent to which such programs and activities contribute to the achievement of such policy, and to make recommendations to the President with respect thereto;

4. to develop priorities for programs designed to carry out the policy declared in Section 2 and recommend to the President the most efficient way to allocate Federal resources and the level of government—Federal, state, or local—best suited to carry out such programs; and

5. to make and furnish such studies, reports thereon, and recommendations with respect to programs, activities, and legislation to carry out the policy declared in Section 2 as the President may request.

(d) Whenever the President determines that information or data developed by the Council pursuant to Subsection (c) of this section should be made available to the states and localities he shall provide for the timely dissemination of such information and data to such states and localities.

(e) The Council shall make an annual report to the President in February of each year.

(f) In exercising its powers, functions, and duties under this Act—

1. the Council may constitute such advisory committees and may consult with such representatives of industry, agriculture, labor consumers, state and local governments, and other groups, organizations, and individuals as it deems advisable;

2. the Council shall, to the fullest extent possible, use the services, facilities, and information (including statistical information) of other Government agencies as well as of private research agencies, in order that duplication of effort and expense may be avoided.

(g) To enable the Council to exercise its powers, functions, and duties under this Act, there are authorized to be appropriated (except for the salaries of the members and officers and employees of the Council) such sums as may be necessary. For the salaries of the members and salaries of officers and employees of the Council, there is authorized to be appropriated not exceeding $ in the aggregate for each fiscal year.

JOINT COMMITTEE ON THE SOCIAL REPORT

Sec. 5.   (a) There is established a Joint Committee on the Social Report, to be composed of eight Members of the Senate, to be appointed by the President of the Senate and eight Members of the House of Representatives, to be appointed by the Speaker of the House of Representatives. In each case, the majority party shall be represented by five Members and the minority party shall be represented by three Members.

(b) It shall be the function of the Joint Committee—

1. to make a continuing study of all matters relating to the social report; and
2. as a guide to the several committees of the Congress dealing with legislation relating to the social report, not later than June 1 of each year to file a report with the Senate and the House of Representatives containing its findings and recommendations with respect to each of the main recommendations made by the President in the social report, and from time to time make such other reports and recommendations to the Senate and House of Representatives as it deems advisable.

(c) Vacancies in the membership of the Joint Committee shall not affect the power of remaining members to execute the functions of the Joint Committee, and shall be filled in the same manner as in the case of the original selection. The Joint Committee shall select a chairman and a vice-chairman from among its members.

(d) The Joint Committee, or any duly authorized subcommittee thereof, is authorized to hold such hearings as it deems advisable, and, within the limitations of its appropriations, the Joint Committee is empowered to appoint and fix the compensation of such experts, consultants, technicians, and clerical and stenographic assistants, to procure such printing and binding, and to make such expenditures, as it deems necessary and advisable. The cost of stenographic services to report hearings of the Joint Committee, or any subcommittee thereof, shall not exceed 25 cents per hundred words. The Joint Committee is authorized to utilize the services, information, and facilities of the departments and agencies of the Government, and private research agencies.

(e) There is hereby authorized to be appropriated for each fiscal year the sum of $, or so much thereof as may be necessary, to carry out the provisions of this section to be disbursed by the Secretary of the Senate on vouchers signed by the chairman or vice-chairman.

QUESTIONS

1. Does this bill meet the objectives outlined in <u>Toward a Social Report</u> summarized by Campbell in the preceding selection?

2. To what extent, based on your knowledge of the work of the Council of Economic Advisors and the national income accounts, would this bill result in duplication of national economic accounting and reporting?

3. Assume you are a U.S. Senator participating in the debate on this bill. As assigned by your instructor, prepare a brief argument either for or against the bill.

Testimony given by Robert Abelson, Professor of Psychology, Yale University, before the Senate Subcommittee on Government Research of the Committee on Government Operations, Ninetieth Congress, First Session, S. 843, Full Opportunity and Social Accounting Act.

Testimony on the Full Opportunity and Social Accounting Act

by Robert Abelson

I am certain that a very useful national social accounting system can be established, though one would have to be extravagantly optimistic to suppose that a perfect system is possible. There will certainly be some rather serious gaps at first, particularly in more intangible areas, such as the social morale of minority group members. Although indicators in many areas may be reliable and valid, it is probably not too good an idea to think in terms of a single aggregate index of national social health because such an aggregate would suffer from the conceptual and statistical weaknesses of its weakest components. A profile of indices is probably a more reasonable target.

SOURCE: Reprinted slightly abridged by permission of Professor Abelson and the publisher from <u>American Psychologist</u> (November 1967), pp. 994–995. Copyright 1967 by the American Psychological Association.

329

Pursuing this point further, I would assert that information is likely to be much more useful in aiding appropriate social action when it is examined in differentiated "disaggregated" detail than when it is contemplated in gross, lumped indices. Let me give an example.

As this Subcommittee undoubtedly knows, the Carnegie Corporation has financed a large-scale tryout of a procedure for the assessment of our national educational progress. As presently contemplated, this assessment procedure would yield data on educational achievement in 10 diverse subject matter fields, for 9-, 13-, 17-, and 27-year-olds, males and females, for four regions of the country, and for different gross city size and economic categories. Conceivably, this staggering totality of information could be aggregated into a single index number representing national educational attainment. If the assessment were repeated 5 years later, a second index could be obtained, suggesting in comparison with the first, whether we, as a nation, were progressing or retrogressing in educational attainments.

But of what use would such a simple comparison be? No doubt it could serve as a national rallying symbol, as a cause for cheering or recriminating depending on whether we went up or down. Beyond that it would tell us little unless we looked at relative improvements, in different subsegments of the population, that is, at whether urban slum children, for one example, were catching up or falling behind, and in what subjects, and whether differently for boys and girls, and so on. This example deals only with one area, education, but in other areas the story would be much the same.

QUESTIONS

1. The Gross National Product is a single aggregate index which, despite drawbacks, has proven useful both in national economic planning and also in the private sector. Could a single aggregate national social index be constructed which would be equally useful? Discuss thoroughly.

2. Assume we have a well-developed set of social statistics, which indicate that the quality of American life rose by 13% during the last year. You have just contracted mononucleosis, your best friend has been convicted for marijuana possession and sentenced to 30 years, and your kid brother shows signs of developing into a kleptomaniac in addition to being a compulsive liar. What does the 13% statistic mean to you personally?

Section IX

Accounting and Economic Development

In the introductory section of this book the general contribution of accounting to the well-being of mankind was outlined. It was noted that in economies which have progressed beyond the barter stage, and particularly in complex and highly developed societies, individual happiness and well-being stem to a significant degree from command of economic resources with which to acquire food, clothing, lodging, health services, education, recreation, and other amenities. Typically, individuals pool their efforts in industrial enterprises in order to increase their output and productivity. Assembling such industrial enterprises requires substantial capital. This capital cannot be attracted to an enterprise unless investors are provided with reliable information about the enterprise and its history. Provision of this information is one of the major functions of accounting, and thus accounting contributes in a significant if somewhat indirect manner to economic growth and the well-being of society.

Perhaps the reader is somewhat jaded with economic goods and services and is inclined to decry crass materialism. Well-enough—excessive materialism is an evil and should not be anyone's goal. But in underdeveloped nations materialism is not the issue—at least not to most citizens. Survival, freedom from hunger, reasonably good health—these are goals not yet realized in most nations and these are goals which require some form of economic growth.

331

In any economy based on capitalism and free enterprise, provision of goods and services to members of the society depends on capital formation which requires reliable financial information, which is in turn based on good accounting. In a non-capitalistic economy or one characterized by state ownership efficient management of the national (people's) resources requires effective accounting systems and controls; adequate reporting of state economic activities to permit the people to determine whether their resources are being used for appropriate purposes also requires good accounting. Thus in either form of economoc society accounting contributes in a significant fashion to economic growth and development. This thesis is advanced in each of the three articles which follow.

Enthoven provides a somewhat general and theoretical discussion of the role of accounting in economic development, with particular emphasis on the nature of the information accounting should generate in a developing country. Seiler focuses on enterprise accounting and its importance for efficient management, an essential of economic growth; he also reviews the relatively low status of the accounting profession in underdeveloped countries and the implications of this for economic development. Mahon discusses the need for good accounting for effective capital markets and for efficient tax systems, and suggests how accountants in developed countries can help underdeveloped nations. He argues:

> The evidence strongly supports the premise that [the economic progress of the United Kingdom and other British-linked nations, Canada, the Netherlands, the United States, and several other highly developed countries] and their relatively higher standards of living are at least in part attributable to proper accounting and auditing.

Previous sections of this book have shown how accountants can contribute in specific ways to improvements in their society. This section explores the broader ways in which accounting can aid entire nations to increase the overall well-being of their citizens.

ADDITIONAL REFERENCES

1.   Bevis, Herman W., "The Accounting Function in Economic Progress," The Journal of Accountancy, August 1958, pp. 27–34.
2.   Enthoven, Adolf J. H., "Accounting and Development Programming," The International Journal of Accounting Education and Research, Fall 1967, pp. 107–120.
3.   Enthoven, Adolf J. H., "Economic Development and Accountancy," The Journal of Accountancy, August 1965, pp. 29–35.

4. Linowes, David F., "The Need for Accounting in Developing Social Systems," The Journal of Accountancy, March 1970, pp. 62–65.
5. Linowes, David F., "The Role of Accounting in Emerging Nations," The Journal of Accountancy, January 1969, p. 18.
6. Lowe, Howard D., "Accounting Aid for Developing Countries," The Accounting Review, April 1967, pp. 356–360.
7. Philpott, B. P., "Social Accounting and Economic Planning," The Accountant's Journal (New Zealand), April 1969, pp. 324–332.
8. Ross, J. W., "Accounting in Newly Developed Nations," Cost and Management (Canada), July–August 1967, pp. 43–44.
9. Seidler, Lee J., The Function of Accounting in Economic Development: Turkey as a Case Study (New York: F. A. Praeger, 1967).
10. SyCip, Washington, "Professional Practice in Developing Economies," The Journal of Accountancy, January 1967, pp. 41–45.

*The role of accounting in developing coun-
tries, including its contribution to capital
formation and to government financing
and budgeting, is discussed.*

Accountancy for Economic Development

by Adolf J. H. Enthoven

The dynamic process of developing the less developed countries poses a new demand for an effective and comprehensive methodology and practice of accountancy for both microeconomic and macroeconomic purposes. An improved form of accountancy that will serve the economic development process in the most effective and useful manner must be sought. If, then, we are to create, as I believe we should, an "economic development accountancy" the important questions that we shall have to answer are what type and form of information do we need for this new kind of accountancy and what methodology is required to attain it?

Let me offer some indications of what is involved. In the first place the information to be generated needs to be economically meaningful and useful, reflecting socioeconomic relationships, and geared toward the objectives of development. The standards on which the information is evolved must be part

SOURCE: Reprinted by permission of the author and the publisher from
Finance and Development (No. 3, 1969), pp. 24–29.

of an eco-accountancy "philosophy" or theory. Such a theory, to be economically oriented, would constitute a coherent set of standards and guidelines,
forming a reference framework. The purpose of the framework is to judge the
applicability of the accountancy methodology, and it should accordingly
encompass more than the accepted practices and conventions. Second, the information and evaluations should reflect not only the "hard" information that we
have about past events but also the information (clearly less hard) that estimates
provide about the future. Accountants have historically been obsessed with the
question: is this information accurate and verifiable? In economic development
accountancy they must accept that even information that only approximates to
accuracy may be useful.

Finally, the information should be valued and portrayed in such a form that it
benefits the principal users; it will have to serve both the microeconomic and
macroeconomic sphere. Adherence to a standardized system or plan of accountancy would be of the greatest value in this connection.

Accountancy—in its widest context—may be considered as consisting of four
kinds of activity, pertaining to the eco-financial information to be provided:
(1) identifying, analyzing, processing, classifying, allocating, and reporting;
(2) measurement, evaluation, communication, and the assessment of efficiency;
(3) decision making about human and material resources; (4) accountability and
the facilitating of controls. These activities have applicability to the four branches
of accountancy, i.e., financial accountancy and auditing; cost and management
accountancy; government accountancy and budgeting; and social (national)
accounting.

COLLECTING INFORMATION

In order to shape such a new form of accountancy, certain technical aspects
have to be considered. I have already stressed that the information should be
classified, portrayed, and reported in a more universally standardized manner.
We often find, for example, that similar capital or operating items (or expenses)
are treated differently in different projects or different countries; and different
allocations, amortizations of and valuations (historical vs. current) of capital and
expense items may give a distorted account of income, surplus, and aggregate
result. These distortions in turn may lead to different planning coefficients, such
as shadow prices, input-output relations, and capital output ratios. For purposes
of reporting, measurement, and microeconomic and macroeconomic decision
making, such diversity of presentation and related evaluation is undesirable and
detrimental.

The adoption of a uniform or standardized system of accountancy could
alleviate many basic accountancy problems in developing economies, where
generally we are in any event faced with a lack of information and adequate

accountancy skills. Such a uniform accountancy system or plan would be widely useful; it would serve the business unit, the industry, the social accounts, the development plan and its related economic policies, the government budget, and the fiscal system. The uniformity would above all apply to concepts and terms, the procedures of valuation (inputs and outputs), the method of registration, and the classification of accounts for business, sectoral, and even national purposes. The advantages of such a standardized eco-accountancy system would be easier analysis, evaluation, and comparability; better studies of feasibility and costs; facilitation of fiscal administration, budgeting, control, and auditing; more reliable social accounts; a more unified development of accountancy theory; and improvement in economic planning and policies. International acceptance of such a "uniform accountancy system" would be desirable, as it would facilitate measurement and comparison by countries and expedite capital formation and investment flows.

A great deal of valuable work in standardizing social accounting systems has been carried out by the United Nations, the Organization for Economic Cooperation and Development, and the International Monetary Fund, and the development of a uniform accountancy system will have to be closely coordinated and integrated with these preparations.

For information to be effective for decision making, future cost and benefits have to be measured, incorporating, where possible, economic and technological trends. Comparisons between industries equally require that the information is assessed and allocated on a basis that is economically justifiable. Too often we find that the accountancy rules set forth ways of, for example, allocating expenses, costs, and revenues that are directed exclusively to the requirement of "accounting and stewardship" in a narrow sense.

Long-term development planning and investment requires calculations about future direct and indirect benefits and costs, to determine the most beneficial social or private-financial course of action to follow. Such cost-benefit analysis applies to tactical decisions concerning an enterprise, a project and its components, the comparison between projects, and to development programs. It is an aid for the implementation of a development plan, and its purpose is to quantify—and presumably optimize—the difference between revenues and costs. Such cost-benefit measurements have to be more extensive than an extrapolation of past financial trends, which could lead to the wrong decision-making "model;" it requires a certain economic insight into future behaviors of cost and prices. These factors are influenced by socioeconomic conditions and technological changes and by institutional, organizational, infrastructure, and manpower variations.

Both capital and operating costs and benefits tend to change over time, and this time-value factor is of great importance in the accountancy cost-benefit (and cost-effectiveness) calculations. Time has an economic value, and it is necessary in cost-benefit analysis to compare the benefits and costs, taking into account the interest rate, or discount factor, on future revenues and costs. The costs are generally easier to calculate than the future (discounted) benefits. The interest (discount) rate used—or return obtained—in cost-benefit analysis is a measure of the (marginal) productivity of capital in the economy, and helps to determine whether a project is worthwhile. Such analyses assist in eliminating uneconomic projects and in channeling investments in the most beneficial direction. The projected benefits of a project or program are generally realized over a long period of time, while most of the costs are incurred in the beginning. Relative financial weights have to be placed on revenues and costs, and the weighted sum maximized. Such discounting of benefits and costs, over time, is referred to as the discounted value or discounted cash flow method. The rate of interest—or return required—is a determinant in the feasibility and optimization of a project or program.

It cannot be stressed too strongly that what is really vital to accountancy for economic development is that the accountant, in preparing feasibility studies and other forecasts, has to measure and communicate information about the future. This calls for a greater eco-technical insight and coordination with other disciplines than is found at present. From an auditing point of view it also involves the concept of verification and accountability in a different context; auditing should give an account of the structure in which the entity or project operates. Such operational auditing has to be considered against the economic development environment and trends. Accountancy and auditing have been too much concerned with the registration, allocation, and verification of items considered as monetary entities for the business unit, while too little attention has been paid to the processing, registration, valuation, and evaluation of information from both the microeconomic and macroeconomic point of view. For purposes of administration and control, adherence to traditional historical accountancy/ auditing practices might be required in many countries for some time to come, but it should not constitute the entire scope and aims of accountancy.

Although any processing of information involves certain qualitative judgments, its evaluation for economic development accountancy needs much more in the way of such judgment. Accountancy as it is now practiced essentially conveys quantifiable and verifiable data of a conservative, retrospective nature. Such conventional accounting does not answer to the necessities of calculation and communication in dynamic times. For accountancy to be more effective for microeconomic and macroeconomic purposes, it has to reflect current eco-financial values. The underlying idea is that all goods, services, and value added have an input-output component, which should be assessed according to their current or replacement value.

Accountancy is essentially a processing and registration of values, and such values have to be economically useful. Production is the consumption of existing values to create new values; for example, the current value of a piece of equipment might be stated as the discounted value of its future incorporated working units. Costs are values sacrificed, but they should not be confused with acquisition expenses, which apply to the past, and are of a monetary character.

Such an economic approach to accountancy bridges, in my opinion, the big gap between value and cost and would bring greater unanimity to the concepts of value added, income, capital, and surplus. It will also lead to the needed closer integration between enterprise, government, and social accountancy and will also require a more deeply considered coordination between economics and accountancy.

Accountancy that is concerned with current (i.e., replacement) values does not claim to portray financial certainty, but aims to convey more realistic information about the whole economic, technical, and financial field of interest. This wider information is what is needed for the making of effective decisions in economic development.

In cost-benefit analysis, for example, where we try to compare current and discounted projected costs with discounted forecasted benefits, the need for uniformly *valued* costs and benefits is extremely important. What are benefits and what are costs is largely a question of value determination. Capital-output ratios, which reflect the relationship between the capital investments and the annual resulting income from these investments, equally need information about current value to make them effective for policy making. Again, "current value" accountancy is necessary for input-output analysis; an input-output table, which shows how goods and services interact among industries, is being widely used as an analytical tool and guide to decisions about economic policy.

Current or replacement value does not necessarily mean the actual technical replacement, but rather the economic replacement. The actual replacement price, and the actual decision to replace, might well deviate from the current or replacement value, i.e., the best eco-accountancy value existing at the present moment. In the business economic (micro) sphere such current values pertain particularly to the fixed assets (plant and equipment) and inventories, which were acquired in the past and are "written off" or consumed over a period of years, according to tax laws, the dogma of conventional accountancy, or other arbitrary criteria. Such write-offs (depreciation) of fixed assets generally constitute an allocation of the historical expenditures, which are unrelated to the current valuation of the services being used, or the value of the remaining services still to be incorporated in the asset. Inventories and other assets are generally—under the principles of conventional accountancy—absorbed or amortized on the basis of their historical expense, and reflected in the financial statements at the lower of cost (expense) or market price.

Financial depreciation, amortization, and inventory consumption often form a large part of the cost of production in industry; such cost estimates are being used, among other purposes, for setting selling prices, income determination, the valuation of inventories of goods produced, efficiency and managerial controls, and planning and policy making. Yet such valuation of assets at historical cost has a distorting effect, since it has a tendency to overstate true profitability or surplus.

At the project or business level, current value income determination conveys that only that portion is income—or surplus—which can be consumed without impairing the net capital structure. It is not a mere subtraction between revenues and allocated expenses. Current value accountancy measurements also reflect the setting aside of adequate reserves for the economic replacement of the assets of the business or project, which simultaneously convey the anticipated replacement financing requirements. In many developing economies there is a tendency to distribute the maximum amount of income and where income is historically computed there is a danger that in addition to "true income" part of the actual capital of the enterprise may be distributed as being profit. Especially during periods of inflation and rapid technological change—often encountered in developing countries—adherence to historical cost assessments tends to distort true income, surplus, the decision-making factors, the macro (social) accounts and the planning-policy framework.

The economic implications of current value accountancy are that net income during periods of recession and price decline tends to be higher than when based upon historical accountancy, and the reverse during periods of boom. Current value accountancy would have a beneficial or curbing influence on capital formation and investment decisions when it is required, and would tend to work anti-cyclically. The technique of current value accountancy is then an integral part of "economic development accountancy." The government sector, dominant in many developing countries, could be one of its greatest users and promoters. Underlying the adoption and execution of a current value accountancy approach, which has an impact on the whole economic sphere, are the accountancy postulates, standards, and rules. Each standard or rule will have to be looked at from the point of view of its economic merit, and the methodological frame of reference in accountancy should be more than the sum total of conventional accepted practices. The development of a sound accountancy theory, methodology, and practice requires a clear understanding of the foundation and scope of accountancy.

ACCOUNTANCY IN THE DEVELOPMENT PROCESS

If we want to consider more fully the kind of accountancy needed in planning economic development, we must consider it in three specific fields: development planning, capital formation, and government administration.

Development planning involves the application of rational choices among various patterns of investment. One of the most difficult tasks in development planning is the outlining, screening, selection, and implementation of projects and programs. Import statistics, social accounts data, input-output tables, commodity flows, market studies, and rough cost-benefit calculations might give us an indication of potentialities. However, to prepare, measure, and evaluate projects in accordance with established economic policies and alternatives is a tedious task, and requires the measurement of social and individual benefits and costs. This is an accountancy function.

Cost-benefit analysis, or cost-effectiveness in government, resembles profit maximization for the business firm. It is important that all the benefits and all the cost of a program or project be taken into account. The cost, benefit, and investment return data are also used for the social accounts and other feasibility studies, and these micro data assist in portraying alternative development models. Erroneous or unrealistic cost and benefit information may cause unwise investments and investment fund allocation.

The World Bank has taken considerable initiative in applying sophisticated forms of cost-benefit analysis in its project studies over the past years.

Effective economic planning needs a comprehensive and analytical framework of social (or national) accounts data, and preferably input-output tables derived therefrom. If such social accounts and interindustry data are to be effective, the underlying accountancy information that is available in the private and public sector must be both truthful and economically useful. The techniques of business accountancy are also used in social accounting; they reflect the same equations, they use the double entry debit and credit system, and they both consolidate; however, they diverge in their requirements as regards the classification, valuation, and accumulation of information.

An input-output system gives a more dynamic idea of the economy, and although these tables are hard to prepare—above all in developing countries—they play a vital role in development planning. The accounting information derived from business activities is at the core of such a matrix, and especially with the application of input-output coefficients current or prospective eco-accountancy values have to be reflected. These coefficients help determine the requirements of prospective projects.

Capital-output ratios, reflecting the quantity of output resulting from a unit of capital input, are used as a measuring tool or policy guide in macro and micro planning. In computing the gross, net, or marginal capital-output ratio, the value of the inputs and outputs has to be consistent, incorporating realistic accountancy information and classifications. The basis of depreciation greatly influences the ratio. Comparing historical inputs with current outputs can result in the wrong evaluations and decisions.

Although the techniques involved in input-output tables, capital-output ratios, and cost-benefit analysis are well known, the informational and methodological accountancy requirements have not been adequately evaluated and set forth.

Project evaluation requires a measurement of productivity, and while labor or capital intensity might be desirable from the point of view of those responsible for individual projects it might not be so socially. The degree of labor or capital intensity often depends on the policy objectives of the government, but generally it will be guided by the national income or surplus creation, preferably with the aid of shadow or "accounting" prices. Such shadow or accounting prices are a sort of replacement value under equilibrium conditions relying upon current accountancy information, and they are needed when prices do not reflect real scarcities or surpluses. Such shadow prices may apply to the cost of capital, the cost of labor and foreign exchange and international commodities, and, by their use in economic development, projects could be justified or rejected on a sounder basis of economic reasoning.

The effective implementation and follow-up of a project or program also places a strong demand upon accountancy and auditing as financial and cost statements need to be prepared, cost-benefit assessment and revisions have to be made, and capital and operating financial means and methods to be outlined and secured.

CAPITAL FORMATION AND DEVELOPMENT FINANCE

The existence of sound eco-accountancy will tend to result in the generation of increased individual or social surplus (profit). This in itself can be one of the major sources of capital formation within a country. The availability and execution of sound projects and programs might also stimulate the potential internal and external flow of capital in and to a country. By contrast, the absence of sound projects might cause capital flight. It is an essential aspect of development accountancy, by means of cost-benefit calculations and related measurements, to help identify and implement projects, which should have priority from the point of view of national income, savings, or investment return. Consequently, sound accountancy is able to assist in a more efficient allocation and use of capital and finance funds. The government budget and its fiscal policy can be another major internal source of capital formation, requiring an equally sound accountancy approach.

The accountability, control, and communicating role of accountancy in the enhancement of capital formation is also significant. The availability of comprehensive and reliable financial reporting and appraisals for outsiders, according to certain prescribed standards and rules, will have an effect in building confidence, which in turn tends to stimulate domestic and foreign capital investment.

GOVERNMENT ADMINISTRATION AND BUDGETING

In many developing countries, the public sector is dominant and the increasing range and complexity of governmental activities requires comprehensive governmental accountancy for social accounting, economic policies, planning, management, controls, and accountability.

The government budget—preferably on the accountancy accrual basis—states the government's financial program for one or more years—and this budget can serve as a valuable tool in the formalization of development plans and programs. The budget is to be seen as an essential instrument for defining national aims and plans and goals (benefits) which have to be achieved at the least cost. Tied in to the governmental budgeting system are the account classifications (economic or functional), which are part of the government accounting system.

A fairly recent development in the budgetary field is "performance budgeting," and its further extension, "planning-programming-budgeting" (p.p.b.). While traditional budgeting is aligned to the role of financial stewardship and stresses the financial aspects of expenditures, performance budgeting is oriented to management and cost accounting and tries to measure the benefits and costs of programs, projects, and activities. It tries to build a link between the projects, the plan, and the budget. The adoption and adherence to a "uniform accountancy system" would greatly facilitate integration between planning and budgeting, and could simultaneously serve other microeconomic and macroeconomic needs.

The recording and classification of government receipts and expenditures also covers the area of fiscal administration. Taxation, which can be a potential form of capital formation, is at the core of government operations. Dogmatic accountancy rules and regulations may hamper the growth of an effective tax structure, and meaningful reporting procedures have to be installed based upon sound accountancy standards and rules.

IMPLEMENTING 'ECONOMIC DEVELOPMENT ACCOUNTANCY'

Economic development accountancy, in addition to a revision of existing accountancy thoughts and concepts, a new kind of systematization, and an educational effort to make this widely known and understood, requires institutional effort. Institutes of accountancy, other professional associations, and academic circles should be called in to assist in evaluating and outlining the concepts, standards, and directives. The initiative and/or support for a needed change in accountancy methodology and practices might come also from international organizations such as the World Bank, the International Monetary Fund, and the United Nations and its affiliated agencies, as these organizations are so deeply involved in the direct and indirect generation and application of economic development accountancy information. They might be able to take part in devising and/or making known more effective accountancy norms and practices. Many of the required modifications in the teaching and practice of accountancy—and accreditation of certificates—preferably also could be implemented with the support of international organizations. An attempt should be made to harmonize the accountancy and auditing concepts, standards, rules, and practices gearing these toward demands of economic development. Revisions of the laws and rules covering eco-financial measurements, reporting, and communication will be needed.

Moving accountancy out of its present narrow dogmatic sphere of operation toward a more effective socioeconomic development function will be a slow and perhaps a rather tedious task, but if this objective is not pursued, other disciplines may start filling the eco-accountancy needs, and accountancy may become too important to be left to the accountants. In an earlier article I showed that, in the past, accountancy has adapted itself to the changing requirements of society; now it must respond effectively to the challenge of economic growth and development.

QUESTIONS

1. What are "socioeconomic relationships?"

2. Does the United States have a uniform system of accounting? Would a uniform system be desirable in developing countries? Discuss.

3. Enthoven stresses that, in accountancy for economic development, the accountant must measure and communicate information about the future. In traditional financial and managerial accounting, does the accountant measure and communicate information about the future? Consider this question carefully and discuss fully.

4. ". . . valuation of assets at historical cost has a distorting effect . . ." If this is so, why is historical cost the most widely used valuation method? Discuss fully.

5. According to Enthoven, what problems are caused in developing countries by the use of historical costs?

6. Summarize Enthoven's arguments concerning the use of current or replacement values. Compare this viewpoint with generally accepted accounting principles in the United States.

7. What is an input-output system? (Suggestion: check economics texts.) How would such a system be useful in a developing economy?

8. How can accounting contribute to capital formation in a developing country?

9. Define eco-accountancy.

10. ". . . if this objective [of a more effective socio-economic development function] is not pursued, other disciplines may start filling the eco-accountancy needs, and accountancy may become too important to be left to the accountants." Explain this statement. Do you agree with it?

The status of the accounting profession is considerably lower in most developing countries than in countries like the United States. The possible relationship between this low level of prestige and the low rate of economic growth in such countries is considered in this article.

Accounting, Information Systems, and Undeveloped Nations

by Robert E. Seiler

Large-scale participation by the United States government in programs of assistance for economically depressed countries began in post World War II years with the Marshall plan, developed into the ICA program of the 1950's, and since the early 1960's has been centered in the AID program. This assistance is the result of a growing awareness that the development of depressed nations is economically prudent, although the extent of our participation in the developmental process remains controversial.

The purpose of this discussion is to call attention to the role of accounting in the development of emerging nations, and to consider the relationship between the present low level of prestige enjoyed by the accounting professions of these

SOURCE: Reprinted by permission of the author and the publisher from The Accounting Review (October 1966), pp. 652–656.

nations and the low rate of their economic growth. The term *information system,* which appears with some frequency in this discussion, may be defined as any organized, established methodology for gathering and reporting economic data. Accounting systems, with their dual output of financial reports for external use and control reports for internal management, are an integral and important part of a society's information system. The thesis advanced herein is that the strength and extent of a nation's information system determines in large part the rate at which economic development will progress, and that accounting and accounting systems thus assume an important role in the development of emerging nations.

INADEQUATE FINANCIAL DATA FOR FISCAL PLANNING

One of the most pressing problems facing the underdeveloped nation is the creation of information gathering systems for fiscal planning purposes. Parallel with the construction of such a system is the problem of instilling a reasonable degree of confidence in the system and its output. Until an adequate network of information gathering and reporting systems exists, there cannot be a reasonably sound basis for assessing and gathering taxes, increasing the flow of capital into new or expanded productive facilities, regulating the rate structures of publicly controlled industries, creating a public market for securities, or insuring intelligent negotiations between labor and management.

While poor fiscal planning is not necessarily restricted to underdeveloped nations, it is accentuated in these countries because of the acute shortage of economic resources. One specific instance may be cited in which resources were allocated (budgeted) to the construction and paving of roads by the Minister of Public Works without knowledge of the number of miles of paved or unpaved roads existing at that time, without knowledge of traffic density, and without reasonably accurate construction cost estimates. The data which should have been used were lacking because information-gathering systems were faulty or non-existent. As a result, scarce resources were misallocated, and the bottlenecks existing in that nation's inadequate transportation system were not alleviated.

Economic and fiscal planning is by its very nature a complex matter, and its complexity increases as the effects of more and more variables are measured and included in the analysis. Economic, political, and business leaders in the more industrialized nations, such as ours, depend heavily upon the wealth of existing financial data available to them, and, perhaps to an even greater extent, upon a network of information-gathering systems. Fiscal planning decisions are largely unstructured, necessitating special studies and the gathering of data from many different sources. Thus the information-gathering system in many cases is more valuable than the stock of existing data.

MANAGEMENT DECISIONS WITHOUT FINANCIAL DATA

Since a national economy is no more than the total of a number of individual entities, the aggregate financial condition of a nation's enterprises should determine the over-all health of the economy. Thus, each individual's managerial ability makes a small but definite imprint upon the economic condition of that nation. Each time a production, pricing, or investment decision is made without adequate knowledge of its consequences, the probability of misdirected effort, wasted resources, and economic loss is increased. Thus, economic stability is heavily dependent upon the aggregate managerial ability available within the economic structure.

However, managerial ability cannot be maximized without data-gathering and reporting systems to facilitate the decision-making process. In a number of the less developed countries, information systems which provide reliable financial data are few in number, and the group of managers equipped to utilize even the existing data is small.

In one Latin American country a $26 million plant was constructed for the purpose of manufacturing chemical fertilizer, a commodity badly needed to improve the nation's agricultural productivity. Upon completion, however, it was found that the cost of production was considerably higher than the cost of imported fertilizer; and the plant operated only a few months before being closed. The economic resources invested in the plant and specialized equipment, representing an enormous sum for this small country, were almost completely lost. A more sophisticated entrepreneurial and managerial effort could have prevented this disaster, for sound profit planning and cost projections would have clearly indicated that the project could not succeed.

THE ECONOMICS OF DEVELOPMENT

An area of economic theory frequently called the economics of development has emerged within the last few years. The basic objective of this area of investigation is to isolate and measure the economic forces which shape the developmental process in the less industrialized nations.

A number of significant studies have recently been completed in an effort to gain more understanding of developmental economics. One such study included an economic review of the growth patterns in six of the lesser developed nations. This study provides strong evidence that the availability of natural resources, the one economic factor frequently singled out as the most significant, while important, is not the most crucial factor.[1] If the availability of natural resources were the predominant element, the national income of Indonesia would be higher than that of the Philippines, and Mexico would not have a per capita income and rate of growth over three times that of India. This study concluded that in all six of the nations analyzed there are two elements which, above all else, provide the key to economic development: These are *entrepreneurship* and *trained management*. The supply of capital is a factor which must be considered, to be sure, but there is considerable evidence that even underdeveloped nations have untapped sources of capital *if* the entrepreneurship and managerial elements are available to gather it and put it to work.[2]

It is precisely at this point that the effect of inadequate systems of information processing come into focus, for entrepreneurship and managerial talents cannot be maximized without a foundation of information upon which to base business decisions. Without the availability of a reliable system of gathering financial data the entrepreneurial and managerial efforts are at best halting and inefficient, and scarce capital may flow into those enterprises less likely to succeed.

PRESENT STATUS OF THE ACCOUNTING PROFESSION

Accounting as a recognized discipline is relatively young in even the most advanced countries. At the beginning of this century corporations in the United States reported whatever they pleased, if anything at all, and the government's interest in the financial data of individual enterprises was almost nonexistent. The growth in prestige of the profession paralleled almost perfectly the growth in public awareness of the importance of those data that can be accumulated and interpreted only through the accounting process.

Accounting is hardly known and little appreciated as a process of measuring and increasing the productivity of both the whole and the parts of a complex network of productive elements such as land, equipment, raw materials, people at work, interrelated legal obligations, and invested capital. The level of business education and training in the non-industrialized nations frequently is such that few managers recognize the central purpose of accounting as an information-gathering methodology. It is more frequently viewed as a legally required nuisance, or a means of deceiving the tax authorities. Consequently, the accountant does not enjoy a prestigious position, and his work is considered a low-level, clerical task.

In addition, there is a more subtle factor working against the profession in underdeveloped countries. This is the fact that the productivity of an office worker is more difficult to measure than that of a production-line employee. Success is relative in most office assignments, and distinction between mediocre and outstanding performance is difficult. Production men are frequently heard to complain that they would have been fired long ago if their performance had been as poor as that of the employees behind the office desks. It is precisely this condition in underdeveloped countries that results in the accumulation of the owner's or manager's friends and relatives in the office, where, as one author observed, they make "a last-ditch stand for their right to a quiet, incompetent existence." Consequently, industrial accounting has suffered, and a large number of owners and managers have never realized the benefits of adequate and reliable financial data.

The low level of prestige which the profession enjoys and a corresponding low level of performance by accountants themselves have accentuated the tendency to reduce accounting matters to the status of prescribed rules. The pressure for uniformity has prevented the exercise of sufficient patience to permit accounting and financial reporting practices to grow in a self-regulated fashion. And it seems evident that in those cases where uniform accounting is prescribed, the development of the information gathering system slows perceptively. The case of the Interstate Commerce Commission and the installation of uniform railroad systems within our own country may be cited as an example. Although many accountants felt in 1914 that the prescribed railroad system was a model, within a few decades it was completely outdated and the reporting practices of the industry were far behind those of other industries. Uniform systems are deceptive; for while they seem to represent progress, the short history of experience available at this time indicates that they soon become a liability. Unfortunately, the trend toward standardized systems is so strong in some nations that progress in data gathering and reporting is seriously retarded.

SOCIOLOGICAL FACTORS

There is always a danger of over-simplifying the problems of developing an industrialized economy. Paramount among these is the failure to consider the subtle but powerful sociological forces existing in underdeveloped countries. One of the foremost of these forces is the tendency to believe that success is primarily the result of sheer luck, or an ability to outwit others, rather than the systematic application of effort and creative energy. This philosophy is evidenced by the popularity of lotteries and the intensity of the political struggle in Latin American countries.

Another detrimental force is the inherent distrust of others in a business arrangement. The idea that both parties can benefit through a business transaction is difficult for some societies to accept, and suspicion grows as agreement on a business arrangement is approached. Thus, negotiations over even simple matters may never reach a conclusion, or at best may extend over long periods of time.

Still another powerful force is the inevitable resistance to change. Even though persons most closely affected by a development attest verbally that they are anxious for more industrialization, there is frequently an unspoken desire for industrial failure, thus assuring continuation of the "old ways." This desire for failure may in some cases lead to unconscious sabotage; it is exemplified by the almost deliberate failure to repair equipment brought into many underdeveloped countries.

EDUCATION AS A PARTIAL ANSWER

Education for business is a partial answer to the dilemma, and educational facilities are being created or expanded as rapidly as possible. By early 1963, sixty-six American universities held 118 U.S. government contracts for technical assistance in thirty-nine countries in the fields of education, agriculture, public administration, and business administration.[3] In addition, a large number of private institutions, such as the Ford and Carnegie Foundations, are financing an increasing number of educational endeavors in business administration. Simultaneous developmental efforts must be made in education, agriculture, business, and perhaps most importantly, in the art of government. Without a favorable governmental climate, all other efforts may be wasted.

A number of our present educational efforts in underdeveloped countries include training and instruction in the development of accounting systems and in the use of accounting data. There appears to be growing awareness on the part of developmental economists that the existence of simple but reliable financial data-gathering systems must parallel the educational efforts directed toward the development of managerial ability. Thus, the pressures are strong for rapid development of data-gathering systems; but the existing level of business education is such that the result all too frequently is a legally-required, prescribed, uniform system. While this speeds the data-gathering process in the early stages of development, it is likely to prove a decided handicap in the latter stages. Fortunately, the United States affords an example of the effectiveness of a non-regulated, self governed accounting profession, and accounting developments within this country are closely watched by the budding professional societies of emerging nations.

FOOTNOTES

1. B. Huggins, *Economic Development* (W. W. Norton and Co., 1959), page 81. This study included Libya, Indonesia, The Philippines, India, Italy, and Mexico.
2. For example, see A. O. Hirshman, *The Strategy of Economic Development* (Yale University Press, 1958), page 27.
3. The role of general education in underdeveloped nations is described in detail by R. F. Butts in his *American Education in International Development* (Harper and Row, New York, 1963).

QUESTIONS

1.   What is "entrepreneurship?"

2.   Does the author show a relationship between the low level of prestige enjoyed by the accounting professions in emerging nations and the low rate of their economic growth? Discuss fully.

3.   What does the author cite as the two most important factors in development? What other factors are important? Where does accounting fit in with these factors?

4.   In the United States, did economic and industrial growth cause the growth in accounting, or did the development of accounting encourage and facilitate the industrial development? Would you expect the same relationship to apply in a country now in the developing stage? Explain fully.

5.   "Economic stability is heavily dependent upon the aggregate management ability available within the economic structure." Do you think the United States' economic stability is largely due to the fact that we have a lot of smart managers?

6.   Reread Seiler's last paragraph. How does his advocacy of a "non-regulated, self governed accounting profession" contrast with Enthoven's conclusion that "an attempt should be made to harmonize the accountancy and auditing concepts, standards, rules, and practices gearing these toward demands of economic development?"

Plans for industrializing underdeveloped countries stress technological requisites, slight the necessity for proper accounting skills.

Ledgers
As Much As Lathes

by James J. Mahon

Modern industrialization, like a hothouse plant, is a delicate and complex mechanism. It cannot flourish, or even survive, outside a proper environment. If a nation seeking development is to achieve the fruits of modern technology and industrialization, it cannot plant the industrial seedling in a wasteland of unidentified and unarticulated activities and expect it to thrive; rather, it must first establish an overall environment conducive to its growth and propagation. The essence of that environment is self-discipline, order, and integrity in the planning and sequencing of economic and fiscal activities. A system of recording and measurement must be provided. Commonly accepted accounting practices and related skills to serve as guidelines are typically the means to accomplish this fruitful synchronization of community life. They deserve early attention and the highest priority in any development plan.

Confirmation of this fact may be derived from a recent study made to identify and catalog the technical differences in accounting principles and practices,

SOURCE: Reprinted with permission from the Summer 1966 issue of the COLUMBIA JOURNAL OF WORLD BUSINESS. Copyright © 1966 by the Trustees of Columbia University in the City of New York.

professional auditing standards, and financial reporting customs among various nations.[1] The study, which covered twenty-five countries, demonstrated that a *proximate relationship exists between good accounting and economic progress.* Invariably neither is found without the other. The more developed nations had the more advanced accounting disciplines and the reverse was also true. Of itself, this of course does not prove cause and effect. In fact, from a chronological viewpoint, it is not likely that good accounting *preceded* industrialization in the developed countries. Nor did the two necessarily occur concurrently. Rather, it is probably accounting standards and techniques tended to develop and improve *as a result* of growing industrialization. And as the applications of accounting techniques to recording, measuring, and controlling financial, commercial, and industrial activities evolved and increased, they in turn added to the speed and soundness of economic development. What counts is that in these countries accounting today provides a virtually indispensable basis for economic communication, both within and between the elements of industrial complexes. It is the language of business, public and private.

BASIC TO EFFECTIVE CAPITAL MARKETS

The study corroborates that in the more developed countries proper accounting and related techniques have aided the development of a capital market that enables massive funds to be accumulated from widely dispersed sources and placed at the disposal of industry in general. The investment of this capital in plants and machines and in working funds has contributed substantially to industrial growth, volume, and productivity.

Capital accumulation from diverse sources is dependent to a high degree upon published reports of a business' financial condition and the results of its operations—the credibility of which must not be in doubt. Broad adherence to proper accounting and auditing concepts in the industrialized countries has ensured that accurate information is dispensed to millions of "absentee owners," large and small, who rely on such reports as a basis for their commitments. (Over 20 million Americans are said to own stock in companies listed on U.S. stock exchanges.)

Moreover, the skillful administration of business organizations, and their resultant productivity and profitability, depends in part on effective accounting systems, techniques, and controls. As organizations—publicly or privately owned —become larger and more complex their effective control depends on an orderly collection and presentation of continuous information to those responsible for decision. This flow is in part revealed in the statistics of unit production and sales, in part in the financial expression of costs and returns. Progressively more sophisticated methods of communication, involving electronic collection, storage and retrieval of data as well as fantastically rapid computation, are becoming available, but basically they rest upon and amplify the disciplines that accountants, statisticians and mathematicians have heretofore evolved. The new techniques will simply make knowledge of the underlying disciplines the more indispensable.

EFFICIENT TAX SYSTEMS

Proper accounting has also lent order and integrity to tax remittance and collection. Compliance with tax laws in the more developed nations is generally greater than elsewhere. If the human resources of a nation are to be successfully marshalled in the effort to achieve a satisfactory level of abundance, there must be reasonable political stability, provision for infrastructure facilities, and effective administration of law. This takes money, which, in the absence of inflationary policies, must be obtained by governments through taxes. Without a developed system of accounts the collection of taxes is necessarily reduced to an inadequate base, with many inequities and traditions of evasion.

Adequate accounting systems to support capital markets and fiscal systems are found in the United Kingdom and other British-linked nations, Canada, the Netherlands, the United States, and several other highly developed countries. The evidence strongly supports the premise that their economic progress and their relatively higher standards of living are at least in part attributable to proper accounting and auditing that have facilitated the accumulation and protection of capital, and ensured the effective and productive utilization of funds, manpower, and other resources.

SHOCKING NEGLECT

Granted that effective and efficient industrialization is heavily dependent on sophisticated accounting, it is puzzling that the key role of accounting knowledge has not been accorded a higher priority in plans for boosting the economies of lesser-developed countries. Yet, programs aimed at the ultimate industrialization of developing countries generally tend to emphasize the *technology* of the components of infrastructure—power, communications, transportation, agriculture, natural resources, and basic industries—and to underemphasize the administrative tools for making them work.

Almost all development plans seem to take the position that, given adequate capital for the construction of railroads, power dams, docks, steel and fertilizer plants, together with the necessary technical skills to operate such facilities, economic improvement will follow. This simply is not so, unless proper emphasis is placed on the importance of adequate accounting and related techniques to assure the fulfilment of this vision. The inescapable fact is that the values of accounting are not fully appreciated—or, if appreciated, have not been generally implemented.

As a result, lesser-developed countries are advanced substantial funds from abroad to develop their economic institutions, and proceed to attempt this development without adequate attention to the necessary accounting-oriented controls or systems for the protection and judicious use of the funds themselves, or the efficient utilization of manpower and other resources concurrently employed.

And what happens? Projects spring up all over the place and begin operating in an atmosphere of relative inefficiency and chaos, ungoverned by either internal or external discipline. Efficiency or productivity languishes, inflation sets in, prices soar, political stability wilts, and capital flees abroad. This is followed by frantic pleas to outside sources to replenish capital in an effort to bolster the economy and stave off national bankruptcy—a case very often of sending good money after bad!

Actually, what's needed in most lesser-developed countries is a recognition that a sound accounting base is needed at the *outset* of a nation's development efforts—not as a tardy afterthought.

Recent economic progress in Mexico has demonstrated, among other things, the practical benefits that ensue from a dedication to good accounting. Mexico's development has been relatively orderly and sound—aided, no doubt, by general recognition of the value of a stable government that exercises integrity in the conduct of the nation's economic and fiscal affairs, and relies on sound accounting and related techniques in carrying out its policies. Accounting education and a well-organized accounting profession in Mexico are approaching a high degree of excellence.

Other Western Hemisphere countries are moving in this direction too— although progress has been somewhat slower. A "little SEC" law primarily aimed at disclosure in financial statements exists in Argentina. Brazil recently enacted a stronger corporate disclosure act. The U.S. agency AID and the World Bank are increasingly concentrating on the need for sounder accounting "infrastructures" in countries to which they are advancing assistance and aid. Also, several American universities are "exporting" accounting education to a number of developing South American countries.

TOTAL EFFORT REQUIRED

While these improvements are welcome beginnings, they are still too limited. Comprehensive programs should be initiated at all the *existing* levels of infrastructure—from the lowliest of entrepreneurs to the highest of governmental departments. Good accounting should pervade the entire economy, not only isolated segments. For today's economic institutions are, or should be, inter-related. One depends upon the other. And the absence of proper accounting or accountability in any important segment of the economy increases the possibility of chaos in all.

To be specific, measures of reform are called for most urgently in the following areas:

Governmental Accounting.   Many developing countries have yet to adopt the trustee-stewardship concept of uncompromising integrity, responsibility, and accountability in the organization of governmental departments and divisions; and to introduce budgetary-appropriation and other management-accounting controls and methods for the protection and efficient use of funds, manpower, and other resources.

Taxation.   The enforcement and administration of tax laws require adequate accounts if they are to be based on an appropriate and equitable distribution of the necessary cost of government among the various segments of the population—taking into consideration the potential yield of various revenue sources, the relative costs of collection and enforcement, and the importance of preserving incentive and competitiveness in the economy. Appropriate systems and techniques must also be established for the collection, handling, and proper disposition of the revenues received and for assuring optimum taxpayer acceptance and compliance.

Financial Reporting.   In the area of financial reporting by private financial, industrial, and commercial enterprises, there is a need to adopt a body of generally accepted accounting principles and auditing standards; to establish and support a competent independent accounting profession; to enact and enforce adequate corporate reporting laws and security exchange requirements; and to promote integrity and disclosure in financial reporting. All of these would tend to stimulate the development of capital markets for the attraction of indigenous capital into industry, thus reducing reliance on outside capital. Moreover, they would provide more dependable source data for national statistics upon which intelligent and effective economic planning and policy-making can be based.

Management.   Finally, there is a need for business to have better control data if it is to adopt and use more sophisticated management techniques to achieve maximum productivity, competitiveness, and profits.

To carry out these recommendations, accounting education and training in developing countries should be accorded an urgency at least equal to that of technological education and training. Fortunately, this is now being studied by some of the organizations that can be influential in this area.

HOW THE DEVELOPED CAN HELP

Concrete ways in which the developed world might help young nations to establish, or enlarge and strengthen, a local accounting profession include:

1. The several international banking institutions, or perhaps an agency of the United Nations, could collaborate with an international body of accountants to draft accounting and auditing manuals for use in lesser-developed countries.
2. Pamphlets and other accounting literature from nations with mature professional groups could be supplied and their standard textbooks translated.
3. Societies such as the American Institute of Certified Public Accountants, and corresponding bodies in Canada, Mexico, Britain, the Netherlands, and elsewhere can give counsel on setting up professional organizations.
4. Scholarships could be established for students from developing countries enabling them to study accountancy at accredited schools in the United States and Europe.
5. Major accounting firms in the United States, the United Kingdom, France, Germany, the Scandinavian countries, etc., could institute a policy of accepting more apprentices from developing countries for periods of on-the-job training.
6. Centers could be established in developing areas for educating young people in accountancy and also for assisting businessmen and government officials in accounting matters.

The objectives of these and similar efforts would not be just to permit local businessmen and foreign investors to receive financial statements and have audits performed. Such programs would guarantee the availability of competent, respected professionals to oversee the proper conduct of accounting activities, and, in the long run, this professionalism would generate the prerequisite atmosphere of confidence for the development of an indigenous capital market so sorely needed.

Above all, it must be remembered that to continue attempts at industrialization without providing the means for its measurement and control would be like building a car without an accelerator, a steering wheel, or a brake. No doubt it could be made to operate after a fashion, but its speed, direction, and ultimate fate would be matters of conjecture.

FOOTNOTE

1. *Professional Accounting in 25 Countries,* American Institute of Certified Public Accountants, New York, 1964.

QUESTIONS

1. Proper accounting has "aided the development of a capital market that enables massive funds to be accumulated from widely dispersed sources and placed at the disposal of industry in general." How has accounting aided this process?

2. How does a well-developed accounting profession assist government in the collection of tax revenues? What would be the effect on national programs such as public welfare, health, crime control, and defense if the accounting system should break down? Explain thoroughly.

3. Summarize the accounting reform measures Mahon proposes for developing countries.

4. Based on the articles by Enthoven, Seiler, and Mahon, summarize the potential role of accounting in economic development.

Section X

Other Dimensions

This section presents several additional areas of society in which accountants can be of service. The accountant's role in labor relations is discussed by Harold H. Jack, a labor accountant. The article on political campaign accounting reflects the personal experience of Frank Zaveral, Jr. in two political campaigns. Stuart Walzer discusses the role of the accountant in divorce litigation.

The arts need accountants too, according to the executive director of Associated Councils of the Arts, Ralph Burgard. And the classroom is not the only place accounting should be found on the campus; because of their unique and often rather loose organization, universities are particularly susceptible to defalcations. Max Cooper describes several such defalcations and presents ways to prevent them.

Accounting and financial information of radio and television stations should be made public, according to three public-interest communications groups in their petition to the Federal Communications Commission. This incident raises the question of the extent to which financial information of organizations affected with the public interest should be made available to the public. Should we have a public disclosure law in this country that applies to more than government agencies?

Disclosure of the social effects of corporate activity has been demanded by groups working with Ralph Nader and by others. The possible nature and extent of such "corporate social audits" are explored in the article and editorial from Business Week.

Accounting is an essential part of the government and management of the Navajo Tribe. Contrary to what may be the popular image of a southwest Indian

359

reservation, John L. Keller of Peat, Marwick, Mitchell & Co. describes a complex administrative operation involving a computerized data-processing system accounting for millions of dollars each year.

The areas discussed in this section and throughout this book by no means exhaust the ways in which accountants can serve society and work for its improvement —the possibilities have only been sampled. One objective has been to stimulate the reader's imagination, to encourage him to consider the variety of ways in which he might be able, as an accountant or as one with some knowledge of accounting and its skills, to leave the world a better place in which to live. Hopefully, the opportunities have been shown to be varied and exciting.

ADDITIONAL REFERENCES

1. Corson, John J., "The Great What-Is-It: The 'Social Audit'," Nation's Business, July 1972, pp. 54–56.
2. Demarest, Paul W., "Are Labor Unions Accountable?" Management Accounting, August 1968, pp. 37–43.
3. Fischer, Harry C., The Uses of Accounting in Collective Bargaining (Los Angeles: Inst. of Industrial Relations, UCLA, 1969).
4. Hekimian, J. S. and C. H. Jones, "Put People on Your Balance Sheet," Harvard Business Review, January–February 1967, pp. 105–113.
5. Hess, Robert E., "Labor Unions Look at Accountants," Management Accounting, February 1967, pp. 41–42.
6. Holloway, Frank B., "Cost Accounting for Creative and Non-Profit Activities," The Price Waterhouse Review, Spring 1967, pp. 24–29.
7. "How Much is the Help Worth?" Business Week, December 27, 1969, p. 37.
8. Paine, Frank T., "Human Resource Accounting—The Current State of the Question," The Federal Accountant, June 1970, pp. 57–67.
9. Pratt, Robert R., "Wanted: Management Accountants for U.S. Orchestras," Management Accounting, January 1971, pp. 24–25.
10. Simpson, Paul G., "Church Accounting and the CPA," Pennsylvania CPA Spokesman, June 1970, pp. 6–7.

*AFL-CIO Controller tells how the manage-
ment accountant can assist negotiations.*

The Accountant's
Role in Labor
Relations

by Harold H. Jack

In the book *Horizons for a Profession,* which resulted from a study sponsored
by the Carnegie Corporation of New York and the American Institute of Certified Public Accountants, the conclusion is stated that with respect to accountants' services in labor relations, only arbitration, commercial or labor, appears
to be of any significance at the present time, and this is limited to the larger
public accounting firms. The same is true but to a lesser extent of collective
bargaining and labor negotiation studies. While that study was limited to services
performed by CPA firms, I believe we can say with a reasonable degree of assurance that the results of the study apply equally to licensed public accountants
and to a lesser degree to accountants in industry.

I believe that this lack of participation by accountants in the collective bargaining process is unrealistic.

Certainly, as accountants, more than any other group, we can appreciate that
accounting data constitutes an important segment of the total information which

---

SOURCE: Reprinted by permission of the author and the publisher from
Management Accounting (October 1970), pp. 57, 60, 63.

must be considered by both labor and management in the course of their negotiations. Almost without exception, labor negotiations involve more than hourly wage offers and demands (being a labor accountant, I prefer to think of the latter not as demands but as attempts to secure a fair share of the productive effort). Such matters as working conditions, pensions and profit sharing plans, holidays, vacation—and the list is long and impressive—have long been recognized as proper subjects of the collective bargaining process.

With rare exception, each item which is involved in the bargaining process whether it be offered by management—or demanded by labor—has a cost attached to it. Certainly we can agree that no one is better equipped to measure what the cost is than accountants. The feeling of responsibility to intelligently justify contract proposals probably bears more heavily on the union conscience than on management's. Since we make most of the suggestions we are expected to justify them. The day when the union takes as much or as little as it has the naked power to take has long since passed. In this age of highly integrated social and economic factors, there is a continuing demand that collective bargaining progress be related to community progress. Unions feel this keenly and, therefore, have for many years placed great emphasis on the accumulation and presentation of pertinent economic factors in support of its bargaining performance.

Thus it is not surprising to find a nationally-known corporate industrial accountant, Paul W. Demarest, writing in the August 1968 issue of *Management Accounting:*

> Union accountants have provided sufficient data to their management so that their union is in some cases better prepared than corporate representatives for negotiations.

WAYS TO ASSIST MANAGEMENT

While the type of economic research and analysis required to determine the costs involved in a particular item might be different than anything you have previously dealt with, your background and training would enable you to develop reliable figures. Some of the particular areas in which you could assist management, either by computing projected costs or by furnishing background information which would assist it in the negotiations, include:

- Costs of the proposals advanced by the labor negotiators;
- Special productivity studies;
- Analyses of profit margins to determine ability to pay;
- Calculations of the effect of projected wage increases on profitability if prices cannot be increased;
- Forecasts of profit margins based on sales forecasts and projected wage increases.

Historical summaries and analysis of employee wages and benefits could prove helpful. Such an analysis could take many forms. The amount of information which might be supplied is limited only by your imagination. For example, a historical tabulation of wage rates and benefits stated in total dollars, dollars per hour, and as a percentage of total sales and total costs could provide management with a meaningful guide against which present demands could be measured.

While some of the areas might be beyond those you are used to dealing with, I do not believe that a strong accountant need feel any trepidation about expanding his services to serve management needs.

From the standpoint of possible services which might be rendered to the labor side of the negotiations, consider these possibilities: Special studies of prevailing wage rates in the geographic area; special studies of contract settlements in comparable industries; special studies of cost of living index changes.

Again, these are only illustrations of possible areas of service. There are certainly many additional possibilities.

Those of you who are industrial accountants are probably not too interested in the possible areas of service to labor negotiators, but look again at the items above. Management has a vital interest in knowing how its offer compares with the wage rates in its area of operations, and further that its wage scale is comparable with its competitors, and further that, in relation to the change in price levels since the last contract was negotiated, its offer is fair.

Moreover, if you are dealing with a publicly held company it would be possible to develop important information from labor's standpoint by examination of published reports, SEC filings and other available information.

As you may have deduced, I believe the possibilities for an accountant rendering service in collective bargaining are greater on the management side than on the labor side. This naturally follows. An accountant cannot perform without information, and, without doubt, the amount of information readily available to the accountant makes his role as an advisor to management easier than when he is called upon to act as an advisor to labor. In most instances the information required to perform the various studies and projections which I have previously mentioned is available from the records of the company and need only be assembled and converted to understandable facts and figures. This is generally not true of the types of information required to produce meaningful information for the labor side in the collective bargaining process.

HELPFUL GOVERNMENT SOURCES

Your search for information in this area should begin with the U.S. government. There is available a wealth of information which can be extremely useful. I am sure that you are all aware of the Bureau of Labor Statistics and the regularity with which it publishes the cost of living index, both on a national and local basis.

In addition, a number of publications are available at a nominal cost from the Government Printing Office. Examples of publications which could serve as possible sources of meaningful and helpful information are:

1. *Employment and Earnings and Monthly Report on the Labor Force.* This publication presents the most current information available on trends and levels of employment, hours of work, earnings and labor turnover. It gives not only overall trends, but also shows developments in particular industries in the States, and local metropolitan areas.

2. *Employment and Earning Statistics for States and Areas—based on the 1957 standard industrial classification.* This publication provides historical information on employment and earnings statistics.

3. *Monthly Labor Review.* This publication is the medium through which the Labor Department publishes its regular monthly reports on such subjects as trends of employment and payrolls, hourly and weekly earnings, weekly working hours, collective agreements, industrial accidents, industrial disputes and many others.

4. *Wages and Related Benefits.* This is a series of area wage surveys covering over 60 metropolitan areas.

As I stated earlier, many of you may feel that some of these areas lie outside the accountant's area of competence. While at present this may be, and in large measure is probably true, nevertheless, I don't believe any one of us is precluded from expanding his area of competence. If you will think about it for a moment, I am sure you will agree that each of the areas of possible service which I have suggested deals with facts and figures—and isn't that the meat and potatoes of our chosen field?

To those of you who have not been so involved in labor negotiations, may I suggest you consider getting involved. If you are in public practice, sell your clients—be they management or labor—on the idea that you have something to offer. If you are employed in industrial accounting, and your company is not getting this type of service from its accounting group, let it be known that management is missing a good bet.

The question arises: does the accountant even have to limit himself to merely furnishing facts and figures to the negotiating parties or can he also extend himself into active participation in the collective bargaining process? I personally feel that because of their background, training and broad exposure to people many accountants would make excellent negotiators. However, it would take time for accountants to adjust to the fencing exercises and apparent lack of progress which characterizes many collective bargaining sessions, but again his competence and background should stand the accountant in good stead.

We are determined as labor accountants to help in setting as high a standard as possible for our profession. There will be those who say it is perhaps the heat and the glare of the public spotlight, which seems to be kept well focused on labor unions, that helps to account for this attitude. Perhaps that is so. We also have professional pride.

We think, for example, that this attitude of professionalism and conscientiousness had at least some part to play in the reduction of the premium for fiduciary bonds required of union officers and certain employees under federal labor law. The reduction was made by the insurance companies voluntarily and is the first such voluntary reduction in history.

Mr. Demarest, the corporate accountant to whom I referred to earlier said this in that article,

> The inconsistencies and inadequacies of corporate annual reports have frequently been mentioned in accounting literature. Corporate accountants could take a lesson from the Biennial Report of the AFL-CIO issued to their convention.

We are determined to maintain and improve the record as it stands, and we hope that more and more the scope and effectiveness of the magical collective bargaining process, which has helped make this nation and our system one of the wonders of the world, may be improved by virtue of a more intense interest on the part of the accountant as to the role he can play.   .

QUESTIONS

1. How can public accountants assist unions in labor negotiations? How can they assist corporate managements? Specifically indicate the areas of assistance which could be useful to both sides.

2. Is there any conflict of interest when one accounting firm is engaged to assist a union in negotiations and, elsewhere, is engaged to assist a different corporate management in negotiations with a different union? What if the same union was involved in both negotiations?

3. "If you are dealing with a publicly held company it would be possible to develop important information from labor's standpoint by examination of published reports. . . " Examine the annual report of one large corporation (easily obtained from the corporation itself or from a securities broker, if not in your school's library). Indicate which information in the annual report you would expect labor to be interested in, and why.

4. During the strike by Cesar Chavez' United Farm Workers Organizing Committee in the Rio Grande Valley of Texas, a large corporate-owned farm stated that it could not meet the workers' wage demands without going broke. As an accountant, how would you have gone about investigating this claim to either refute or sustain it?

A partner in the accounting firm of Lester Witte & Company presents some suggestions for accounting for political campaigns, based on his personal experience in two campaigns.

Political Campaign Accounting

by Frank M. Zaveral, Jr.

The typical political campaigner does not concern himself with records dealing with financial matters. Balance sheets and operating statements often have little meaning for the American politician when in the midst of a campaign—a campaign which might be described as a fight for political life. There are at least two prime causes for the absence of politicians' accounting records: (1) clerical workers in a campaign are busy with other matters and the candidate and those close to him have bigger, more pressing problems to contend with than records, including the hurly-burly of the campaign, the problems of organization, constant travel and the abiding worry about the sources of funds; (2) the reports required of candidates by the federal and various state governments are meaningless—reporting requirements, few as they are, are not enforced, records are not audited and, therefore, it is not necessary to spend time keeping detailed records.

SOURCE: Reprinted by permission of the author and the publisher from The Journal of Accountancy (May 1969), pp. 90–91.

However, contrary to the reasoning described above, in order to properly and financially plan the campaign, adequate records should be maintained by candidates' campaign committees. The principles of internal control dictate that some system of records be maintained so that the safety of the assets will be assured. The problem of control over cash, the principal and often the only asset of the campaign committee, is heightened in a campaign because there are many individuals handling cash before it is finally deposited; in some cases it is never deposited, thus increasing the problem.

The basic question in campaign financing is not whether one can afford to spend money, but rather if the campaign can afford *not* to spend money on some vital phase of the campaign strategy. It is as Samuel Johnson described accounting: "Keeping accounts, sir, is of no use when a man is spending . . . money and has nobody to whom he is to account. You won't eat less beef today because you have written down what it cost yesterday." This currently popular philosophy in the campaign circles is false—since money *is* scarce, some expenses might be postponed or eliminated and funds spent for items which may be more promising of providing voter influence if the campaign manager is aware of what funds are available and what expenses have received the most attention so far in the campaign.

There are some items of such importance in campaign accounting, and which my experience indicates are ignored, that I call special attention to them, even though they are elementary.

Subsidiary List of Contributors.   A knowledge of who contributes could be vital when conducting a subsequent campaign; also, a subsidiary list of contributors could be helpful in establishing the desired internal control over cash receipts.

Deposit Detail.   All deposits should have some detail to indicate the source of the cash deposited; i.e., contributions, sale of dinner tickets, etc.

Prenumbered Receipts and Checks.   Standard control items to be sure, but often overlooked by campaign committees.

Invoice Approval.   The organized lines of purchase responsibility I have observed were so weak that the campaign could foreseeably pay for items it never received. The campaign should have one or two individuals responsible for all purchases or contract commitments. Often, nearly everyone connected with the campaign orders materials, office supplies, etc., and no central control is maintained.

Record of Pledges.   It is not uncommon for a political committee to accept pledges for contributions and then bill the pledger at a later date. It is obviously important to keep some kind of memorandum record to be sure that action is taken to collect the pledge. If an individual volunteers labor to a campaign, proper facilities should record his offer of help and he should be contacted when his help is needed.

Use of Books of Account. Check stubs alone are not sufficient financial records. Even a spread sheet analyzing expenses could be sufficient.

Petty Cash. The imprest system should always be used. Related to this area is the absolute necessity that all receipts be deposited; no cash should be kept out of the deposit for use as petty cash, for paying bills, etc. If all cash transactions are conducted through the bank, the bank records provide a ready available record of all cash received and disbursed.

Income and expense classifications are not currently established on a national basis for the use of campaigns. Hopefully, the states will eventually require adequate reporting by candidates and committees so that researchers and political scientists can correlate success with the level of expenditures and the public can determine where the funds are coming from and where they are going.

Indeed, standard published reports, based on a uniform system of accounts, could well be the catalyst needed to suggest new methods of campaign financing so that funds might be available to those candidates not supplied with overly abundant fortunes. Herbert E. Alexander in *Money, Politics, and Public Reporting* (Citizens Research Foundation, Princeton, N.J., 1960) has suggested certain accounts which would provide the information necessary for adequate reporting. Using his recommendations as a base and utilizing my experiences with campaigns, I suggest that the accounts described below become a uniform system of accounts for campaign committees.

The recommendations I propose, as to general matters and the chart of accounts, should be an adequate starting point for helping a campaign control its financial affairs. I hope that my comments will inspire new action toward uniformity in accounting and full reporting of political committees in the United States—reporting which the lieutenant governor of Colorado has described as "the best ethical measure for candidates for public office."

Income (Receipts):

Account Number	Account Name and Explanation
401	Contributions—cash donations
402	Sale of Dinner Tickets—fund-raising dinner
403	Sale of Movie Tickets—fund-raising movie
404	Sale of Reception Tickets—fund-raising reception
405	Loans—receipts from loans
406	Miscellaneous

Expense (Disbursements):

Account Number	Account Name and Explanation
501	Salaries
502	Travel Expense—should include all expenses for travel, including employees
503	Broadcasting
–01	Radio—all costs incurred in producing radio programs and "spots"
–02	Television—all costs in producing a television advertisement
504	Publicity and Literature
–01	Newspapers and periodicals
–02	Printing, distribution of literature
–03	Billboards
–04	Trade, party publications, program advertisements
–05	Bumper stickers
–06	Buttons, badges and decals
–07	Photo supplies
–08	Other
505	Office Expenses
–01	Telephone and telegraph
–02	Postage and freight
–03	Rent
–04	Utilities
–05	Equipment (rental)
–06	Stationery
–07	Supplies
–08	Renovation of headquarters (if applicable)
–09	Other
506	Fund-Raising Costs—could be detailed to match with the appropriate income classification
507	Miscellaneous
–01	Payment of loans
–02	Professional services
–03	Other (including filing fees)

QUESTIONS

1. Summarize the potential role of accounting in a political campaign.

2. What is "internal control?"

3. Why does the author emphasize the control of <u>cash</u> in a political campaign?

4. ". . . the campaign could foreseeably pay for items it never received." Using an example, show in detail how this might happen.

5. What is an "imprest system?" (Check an accounting dictionary or textbook.)

6. Obtain the financial report of a candidate for public office. (These are often published or summarized in newspapers during a campaign, or may be obtained directly from a candidate; in many states they are required by law.) Evaluate it for completeness and usefulness to voters, and compare it with others obtained in your class.

Accountants can be of service to both parties in divorce litigation, and through objective advice and testimony may help reduce the acrimony which often accompanies these intensely personal and emotional proceedings.

The Role of the Accountant in Divorce Litigation

by Stuart B. Walzer

The accountant has an important role to play in divorce situations. His services are required both in cases which are settled through negotiation and in cases which are litigated. Unfortunately, the accountant's active participation is often overlooked, to the detriment of his client's cause.

THE ORDER TO SHOW CAUSE HEARING

A crucial phase in any litigated divorce case comes at the Order to Show Cause hearing. The hearing takes place shortly after the divorce is filed. The husband is

---

SOURCE: Reprinted by permission of the author and the publisher from the California CPA Quarterly (December 1965), pp. 18–20.

required to "show cause, if any" why alimony pendente lite (pending litigation), child support, and interim attorneys fees should not be awarded to the wife. The order made at this hearing will often remain in effect for a year or more until the full scale trial can be held.

The key issues at this hearing are economic. These issues can be framed simply: (1) What can the husband afford to pay to the wife for her support and the support of the minor children? (2) What does the wife reasonably need to support herself and the minor children? The court takes into account the past standard of living of the parties in determining what the wife and children will need.

It is at this hearing that the accountant can often play a decisive role in the future course of the litigation. Through an objective presentation of facts and figures his testimony can clear the air of much of the emotionalism surrounding the case. Unfortunately, this is a time of so much stress that the participation by an accountant is overlooked by one or both of the parties.

THE ACCOUNTANT'S ROLE AT THE ORDER TO SHOW CAUSE

What happens when the accountant gets to the hearing? It should be stressed that the accountant must generally be present in person. There is no form of written account prepared by an accountant, whether in affidavit form or otherwise, which will be admissible into evidence unless both parties agree to admit the document. The opposing side will seldom agree to the admission of a written account unless the accountant is present and appears prepared to testify. When the accountant is present, the judge or commissioner can be counted on to pressure both sides to accept the written account as substantially "what the accountant would testify to if called as a witness." The original document is then handed up to the judge for his perusal, while a copy is handed to opposing counsel. The submission of the written account is subject to the accountant being available for cross examination. The accountant must be prepared to undergo stringent cross examination as to the items set forth in his account. He can, however, refer to his notes and to any supporting documents which he may have brought with him.

CONTENT OF THE WRITTEN ACCOUNT

The written accounts which are submitted to the court and opposing counsel are of extreme importance. They should by all means be kept simple. The trial calendar at Order to Show Cause hearings is crowded beyond belief. The judges and commissioners who hear these matters are under great pressure to expedite the hearings. Therefore, anything which cannot be readily digested in a few minutes is less than worthless.

When the accountant appears on behalf of the husband the written account should show the husband's true income and the demands against this income. It should show the outstanding community* obligations and the monthly payments on these obligations. As the manager of the community the husband is going to be required to meet these payments. The court should have a realistic picture of the amount of outgo, and the amounts which will be left to meet the needs of the wife and children and of the husband. The accounts should be as illustrative as imagination can make them. For example, rather than to set forth "food" as an item of the husband's expense, the item might better be titled "Cost of dining out in restaurants."

It may be helpful to the court to submit a separate sheet with a breakdown of proposed alimony and support figures which the husband feels he can live with. The sheet should contain projected figures, showing how the proposed payments will work out for the wife and children and also for the husband.

TAX SAVINGS

Tax savings can be made at the Order to Show Cause hearing if someone is alert enough to recognize them. Alimony is deductible by the husband and taxable to the wife. If the husband is inclined to be generous in his tender of support, the court will not take it amiss if he suggests that the bulk of his monthly payment be denominated alimony. Frequently the court will grant such a request. Also, one of the children may require extraordinary medical or dental care, such as psychiatric treatment or orthodontia. Unless the payment is made directly by the husband to the physician, neither party may be in a position to take a medical deduction. The wife cannot take the deduction, even though she makes the payment, unless she pays more than half the support of the child and is entitled to claim the exemption on the child. The husband, while he pays more than half of the support and claims the exemption, may nevertheless be barred from deducting the medical expense unless he himself makes the medical payment. A request to the court that these payments be made directly by the husband to the physician will generally be granted, with a pro rata reduction in the child support.

IMPORTANCE OF EARLY ACCOUNTING TESTIMONY

It is probably unwise to defer accounting testimony until the full scale trial of a divorce action. The interim order for alimony and child support which is made

*EDITOR'S NOTE: "Community" is used here to mean common or joint, as between husband and wife.

at the first hearing strongly influences the trial judge at the time of the full scale trial. The trial judge will often take the position that the parties have had a year or more to adjust to the standard of living established by the Order to Show Cause. In many instances he may adopt the so-called interim order outright. This fact is well known to attorneys and has a strong influence on their negotiations towards a settlement. Negotiations tend to hover in the neighborhood of the amounts set for alimony and child support at the time of the Order to Show Cause.

THE WIFE'S NEED FOR ACCOUNTING TESTIMONY

Up until now I have emphasized the husband's need for an accountant's testimony at the Order to Show Cause hearing. If the affairs of the community are at all complex the wife may be in even greater need of accounting testimony. It is a fact that in many marriages the wife knows little or nothing of the nature or extent of the community assets. She often knows little or nothing of her husband's earning picture. Witness the recent case of the woman who had lived in extreme poverty during her entire married life while married to a man worth $18 million. In order for the wife to establish that her husband has the ability to meet an adequate support order the wife may require an audit of the husband's business records. But where can the wife get accounting services if the husband keeps her penniless? The answer is that at the very commencement of the proceedings the wife should move for the appointment of an accountant of her choice and request that the accountant's fee be paid by the husband either out of the community or out of his current earnings. Such a request is generally viewed with sympathy by the court. The wife should not be put in the position of walking into the all-important Order to Show Cause hearing with no information as to her husband's true financial picture. She need not do so if she will take the appropriate steps to get an accountant appointed by the court.

THE FINAL TRIAL

In a case which is contested all the way the parties will ultimately come to a full-scale trial. Once again accounting testimony may be critically important. This later trial offers what may be the last opportunity to correct the earlier order. For example, the judge at the Order to Show Cause may have deliberately set the support payments on the high side, counting on the husband to supplement his earning with invasions of the community property. By the time the full-scale trial rolls around any liquid assets in the community are likely to be dissipated in meeting the court order. What is left will be divided in some proportion between the husband and the wife. The important fact is that the wife will get her share of the community and it will no longer be available to supplement the husband's earnings. His source for meeting the support order will be gone. This must be shown to the court in graphic form. Only well-developed accounting testimony can be counted on to show the court that the husband cannot possibly meet the existing support order in the future and that it must be reduced.

In conclusion I should point out that in 1963, 93,000 domestic relations cases were filed in California. These cases made up the largest single category of filings. It is apparent from these figures that there exists a large body of litigation in which accounting services are sorely needed. It may be up to the accountants to educate their clients to this need.

QUESTIONS

1. Summarize the potential role of an accountant in divorce litigation.

2. An attorney in a divorce litigation is an advocate whose proper role is to present his client's position most favorably. Is the accountant's role similarly one of advocacy, or should his attitude be one of complete independence and neutrality, just "presenting the facts?" If the accountant should be independent, why does the author propose that both sides should engage accountants?

3. Do you agree with the author that "accounting services are sorely needed" in divorce litigation, or does this proposal appear to be aimed primarily at developing more business for accountants? Explain.

The executive director of Associated Councils
of the Arts makes a plea for help from
accountants.

Accountants:
The Arts Need You

by Ralph Burgard

The Megalopolis Philharmonic Orchestra is celebrating its 50th anniversary season in one of America's larger cities. Its Viennese-born conductor is happily awash in a Mahler cycle, while the orchestra manager finds himself inundated by a sea of nonmusical problems including a faltering maintenance fund campaign, an inefficient box office accounting system inherited from a previous manager, and a new union contract which will increase the orchestra's budget from $1,700,000 to $2,500,000 in three years.

In the Megalopolis suburb of Rosedale, the Rosedale Little Theatre is about to open its sixth season with *Bus Stop*. Samuel Powers, the director and only paid member of the company, is frantically whipping his volunteer actors into a thespian frenzy while trying to write a Sunday newspaper ad and to rationalize a financial report to his board, due the following day, which will reveal that the books are three months behind. What is more, he has no idea how much money has been received in season ticket sales.

Jerry Wintergreen, a prominent Megalopolis painter, is ruefully contemplating his morning mail which contains a letter from his New York dealer ecstatically

SOURCE: Reprinted by permission of the publisher from H&S REPORTS (Autumn 1968), pp. 26–29. Copyright 1968, Haskins & Sells.

reporting some favorable reviews of his latest show, and a notice from the Internal Revenue Service that he owes the federal government $1,800 because of inaccurate returns filed in 1966 and 1967.

Successful corporate leaders have long proclaimed that business is an art as well as science; but only recently has management of the arts been recognized as business.

Scenes like the hypothetical ones above are being reenacted daily in American cities. They offer accountants an unparalleled opportunity to use their skills and judgment to improve the quality of American life by assisting artists and art institutions. In turn, the accountant and his wife can add a new dimension to their lives by participating in the world of painters, musicians, actors, dancers, and such art institutions as museums, theatres, and symphonies.

Since World War II, America has seen an unprecedented growth in the numbers of arts institutions and interest in them. For example, Associated Councils of the Arts, the national organization for state and city arts councils, estimates that in the United States there are now 30 professional and 1,450 avocational symphonies; 28 professional and 5,000 avocational theatres; 620 art museums; 740 opera companies and 230 dance companies. In Canada there are about 40 arts councils under professional direction, some 40 symphonies and 102 art museums.

THE ARTS DO NOT PAY THEIR WAY

Income from memberships and ticket sales cannot fully pay the costs of running a professional symphony, theatre, or museum. Major orchestras must raise between 20 and 70 per cent of their annual income from contributions in order to make ends meet. With museums the percentages run higher.

A recent study financed by the Twentieth Century Fund[1] showed that the gap between expenditures and earned income (ticket sales, memberships, class fees, etc.) is increasing steadily each year. In 1964 this report indicated an income gap of $23,000,000 in the professional performing arts alone. By 1975 this gap between income and expense may rise to $60,000,000.

The creative and performing artists are among the most underpaid workers in the American economy. A professional dancer in our finest companies still earns less than a stenographer. Only a handful of painters and sculptors can earn a subsistence solely from the sales of their works. The average symphony musician is still paid less than a schoolteacher. In this sense, the artists have been the principal subsidizers of the arts in our country. The Baumol-Bowen report, cited above, indicates that in the period 1929-64 the average professional performer's wages increased 2.5 times over their original level, while manufacturing workers' wages increased 4.2 times, and schoolteachers' pay rose 4.4 times.

There is a severe shortage of trained administrators. In the halcyon pre-income-tax days, Colonel Henry Higginson, President of the Boston Symphony Orchestra, would simply write a check at the end of the season covering the orchestra's deficit and send the orchestra manager blithely on vacation until the first fall rehearsal. Today, fund raising comes much harder and must be organized as a yearly campaign. Furthermore, the changing character of American society, and of urban life in particular, has directly affected the role of arts institutions. The administrators of symphonies, museums, and theatres are not only faced with the continued necessity of improving artistic standards and the perennial problems of adequate financing, but also with such diverse projects as serving suburban audiences, improving the quality of arts education in local schools, providing programs for low income areas, and securing adequate parking at the concert hall or theatre.

Every theatre, museum, or symphony that advertises for an artistic director is likely to receive 100 applications. On the other hand, inquiries for a business administrator or manager are fortunate to inspire four to five replies from people ill-trained to direct the fortunes of a community enterprise involving, in many cases, hundreds of thousands of dollars. As a result, every arts institution, large or small, is in need of expert advice on financial and statistical matters. They can use all the help they can get from volunteers who know money and figures and books.

WHAT CAN ACCOUNTANTS DO?

Many accountants may at first treat any suggestion of helping the arts with dismay, quickly followed by disclaimers of competence, including an inability to understand modern art and tone deafness inherited from one's grandmother. They should take courage from Samuel R. Rosenbaum, a prominent lawyer and long-time officer of the Philadelphia Orchestra, who has stated: "The most dangerous board member of an orchestra is one who feels he knows a little bit about music."

Moreover, most of the problems will sound remarkably familiar to those encountered in a normal business day. Solutions to these problems may be grouped in the following general categories: fiscal planning, tax advice, and managerial counsel.

The accounting practices of such institutions as symphonies, theatres, and museums are likely to be a jumble of leftover systems inherited from past administrators or board members with a background in banking. When one considers that the average term of a performing arts administrator is about three years, it is easy to understand why uniform accounting procedures are as yet unknown to arts organizations. The leadership of most of them would be delighted to find a volunteer, or a board member, trained in accounting, who can set up the books, draft a budget form that is intelligible to the board, or establish an efficient system of accounting for contributions to the annual fund campaign.

Rapidly expanding arts institutions are finding it necessary to plan far ahead of the current fiscal year. However, translating five-year artistic goals into budgetary terms is an unfamiliar process to most arts administrators and a skilled accountant can be of the greatest help in this area, even if he is tone deaf.

Today there are more than 500 community arts councils in this country that sponsor cooperative programs involving a number of arts organizations. These projects include developing new audiences for the arts through central promotions, building an arts center, planning a school program in all the arts, or sponsoring an annual united arts fund campaign. Eighteen cities, including St. Louis, New Orleans, Cincinnati, and St. Paul, are undertaking such campaigns and the number is steadily growing. The central budget committees for these campaigns function in much the same way as their counterparts in health and welfare. They require people with a thorough fiscal background who can interpret audits and budgets. All budget committees need at least one accountant volunteering his time in this capacity.

TAX ADVICE

Most arts institutions qualify as tax exempt under section 501c(3) of the Internal Revenue Code. They must cope with an increasing stream of government report forms, including the annual 990-A return, the state fund campaign registration form, withholding, social security, and entertainment tax exemption forms. Very few arts organizations have a director who can handle these tax matters efficiently, and to the best advantage of the institution. An accountant skilled in tax work who volunteers to advise him would be welcomed with open arms.

Equally with organizations, the individual artists, because of the complexity of their affairs, need tax help from skilled professionals. Artists have been placed on this earth to enrich our lives by creating music, paintings, sculpture, plays, dances, and films. We should not expect them to include among their talents a detailed knowledge of IRS forms. Rubin Gorewitz, a New York CPA, is well known in the artistic community as a financial advisor to artists. Mr. Gorewitz recently recalled a time when he had tried to persuade John Cage, the noted composer, to learn more about fiscal administration for the benefit of an organization on whose board they both served. Mr. Cage gently replied that he had 40 years of uncompleted artistic projects in his head and only 20 years left to live. Mr. Gorewitz did not try to refute this disarming logic.

There are few creative artists who do not need advice on virtually every aspect of their financial affairs. In this respect the accountant can act as the liaison between the artist and his fiscal world. Advice can include preparation of annual returns, establishing a simplified record system for tax purposes, or drafting a foundation presentation, a process somewhat analogous to the preparation of an SEC prospectus.

Mr. Gorewitz warns that the accountant should not try to teach the artists accounting. This will only confuse and disturb both artist and accountant. In effect, the accountant assumes the role of fiscal advisor so the artist can devote more time to that which he knows best—his art.

MANAGEMENT COUNSEL

In the administrative affairs of organizations and individuals good judgment is essential. Accountants, trained in the analytical approach to problem solving, can use this to great advantage in arts administration. They may help the administrator to cope with costing problems or prepare a foundation proposal. They may also exert valuable leadership as members of boards of directors.

A prime example in this respect is Homer Sayad, partner in charge of the Haskins & Sells St. Louis Office, who has made outstanding contributions to the cultural life of that city. Persian by birth, Mr. Sayad came to St. Louis 14 years ago via London and Chicago after the merger with Deloittes.* Since then he has served as president of the St. Louis Opera Theatre and chairman of the budget committee of the Arts and Education Council of Greater St. Louis. He has been president of the latter organization since 1965. His wife Elizabeth has been equally active in cultural affairs, serving on the board of the Missouri State Council on the Arts and as founder and first president of the New Music Circle, an organization sponsoring concerts of contemporary music. Michael Newton, director of the Arts and Education Council in St. Louis, has high praise for Mr. Sayad's contributions. Mr. Newton says that accountants can render great service to arts organizations because they "think in an orderly fashion and may also act as a bridge between the arts organizations and potential sources of funds."

A few years ago, one of Broadway's leading angels took an informal survey of his fellow businessmen-angels to determine why they invested in theatre productions. The results quickly revealed that profit was not the principal motive. Veteran play investors know that the chances of finding a hit are slender indeed. Instead, it was the desire to be associated with the exciting world of the theatre. One businessman summed it up by noting that although every angel was

*EDITOR'S NOTE: This refers to the merger of Haskins & Sells with another accounting firm.

naturally concerned with his investment, most would prefer, instead of a box office report, a personal note from the producer enclosing some reviews from out-of-town tryouts and a progress report on the star's sprained ankle.

This personal involvement and participation in the arts can provide new experiences and insights into the quality of life itself. Rubin Gorewitz says it succinctly: "Artists provide all my entertainment; they make me happy, so I feel I owe them something in return."

Businessmen throughout the country are beginning to acknowledge the essential role the arts play in our lives. Recently, 80 of the nation's top corporate leaders formed the Business Committee for the Arts, under the chairmanship of C. Douglas Dillon, former Secretary of the Treasury, to stimulate support of the arts by the business community. Their example is being followed by countless others who clearly foresee how the arts may contribute to the quality of urban life.

A recent statement by George M. Irwin, an Illinois businessman and chairman of the Associated Councils of the Arts, reflects a growing recognition by business firms that other factors besides a year-end profit are essential to corporate success:

> Corporations are beginning to realize the importance of supporting activities in the arts on both a local and national basis, as a forward-looking policy of enlightened self-interest. They could well become tomorrow's most important arts patrons, supplying not only money, but also talented manpower and service.

The same might be said of men and women who possess the accounting skill which our cultural organizations badly need today. By lending their talents they can derive benefits in personal satisfaction that cannot be measured in dollars.

FOOTNOTE

1. Baumol, William J. and Bowen, William G. *Performing Arts—Who Pays the Piper?* Twentieth Century Fund: New York, 1966.

QUESTIONS

1. Identify and list the arts programs in your community (use newspapers, yellow pages, inquiry, etc.).

2. Outline a basic accounting system which would be adequate for an artistic program or institution. List the records, documents, and controls required.

3. "In turn, the accountant and his wife can add a new dimension to their lives. . ." Could the author have as well said "the accountant and her husband?" Explain.

4. Why do the performing arts cost so much more than they earn in revenue?

5. Describe the problems encountered in the arts with which accountants can help.

6. The article suggests that the most dangerous board member of an arts institution is one who feels he knows a little bit about the arts. Is the converse true—that the artist is dangerous who thinks he knows a little accounting—or should artists be encouraged to learn the rudiments of accounting?

The loose organization in most universities presents unusual temptations to petty embezzlers. This article describes several such defalcations and offers ways by which they can be prevented.

Overcoming the Defalcation Problem in Colleges and Universities

by Max E. Cooper

Case studies of defalcations in colleges and universities point up workable control actions that may be taken to reduce the problem greatly. Educational institutions generally have more security problems with funds for a number of reasons; among them are the following:

1. The widespread employment of temporary help, primarily students, leads to rapid turnover. Temporary personnel generally are not as well trained as permanent employees in commercial organizations and frequently may not have great interest in the work or loyalty to the organization.

SOURCE: Reprinted by permission of the publisher from Lybrand Journal (No. 3, 1967), pp. 13–17.

2. Salary scales are frequently lower than in industry, so that supervisory personnel sometimes may be in short supply or less competent than in commercial organizations.

3. The mental attitudes of executive and clerical personnel frequently tend toward the one "big family" concept, and a feeling of complete trust in all members of the organization results. Internal control then tends to be weaker, as control procedures may be neglected.

4. For reasons of economy, the nonacademic sections are often understaffed at the executive and supervisory levels, resulting in weak control over operations.

5. Internal auditing may be either lacking or not extensive enough.

In addition to the foregoing problems, most colleges and universities have a wide diversity of operations which result in the receipt of income in a number of physical locations. For example, many schools operate cafeterias, student centers, bookstores, real estate rental operations, university presses, hospitals or dispensaries, barber shops, ticket sales, counselling centers, etc. All these operations are responsible for the collection of income. Many are too small to justify staffing or procedures which would provide effective internal control. The only logical answer to the control problems is a well-trained internal audit staff providing an aggressive program of internal audits. Unfortunately, few small colleges have internal audit staffs and many large schools do not have adequately trained staffs or properly comprehensive internal audit programs.

The result of these conditions is that defalcations sometimes occur. Case studies of a number of incidents and corrective action to prevent recurrences follow.

MAIL ROOM: PETTY CASH PROBLEM

A defalcation of approximately $25,000 was made from a $100 petty cash fund over a 10-year period. The mail room manager put in fictitious petty cash purchases of postage, charging the postage inventory. To prevent an inventory shortage from showing up at the end of the year, the manager periodically increased billings to certain departments which either neglected to—or could not—check their bills. The inventory control account was therefore kept in balance with the actual physical inventory of postage.

The peculation started with small and occasional fictitious purchases. Over the years, the amount and frequency of the fictitious petty cash vouchers were increased. During the final year, about $2,000 was taken without raising suspicions of the personnel processing the petty cash vouchers or of the departments which received the fictitious charges. Ultimately, however, the unusual activity in this petty cash fund was discovered by a supervisor.

Internal Audit.   Regular periodic inspection of the activity in all petty cash funds within the university was instituted. Periodic internal audits were also initiated to verify that amounts billed for services rendered agree with job records of cost of services performed.

BOOKSTORE: CASH RECEIPTS

A bookstore cashier obtained money from the cash register by using discarded register receipts as the basis for payouts of fictitious returns of sale items and fictitious purchases of used books. The procedures in force required the student to return new book purchases or to sell used books to a supervisor who would, in turn, give a credit memo to be turned in to the cashier for money.

However, the procedure was neglected by the supervisor, and the cashier was permitted to obtain the necessary forms and approvals on his own. The defalcation was reported to the college by a third person.

Supervisory Approval Required.   The opportunity for this peculation was avoided by the strict reactivation of the normal procedures requiring a student to obtain, personally, supervisory approval for all refunds. Refunds of any sort in excess of $5 were paid by check mailed to the student.

Used books were subsequently purchased by the store from a segregated room where a clerk appraiser authorized payment on a special controlled form. Total payments made by the cashier were then balanced with the total value of the physical inventory of the books purchased for the day.

FICTITIOUS VOUCHERS

A department secretary, turning in fictitious vouchers for part-time student help, requested that the checks be mailed to her for delivery to the students. She then endorsed the checks and retained the proceeds. In the course of bank reconciliations and reviews of canceled checks, the frequent endorsement of checks to this particular secretary was noted. Investigation disclosed the fraud.

Checks Mailed to Payee.   All checks are now mailed directly to the payees by the bursar, and periodic internal audits are made of payments to part-time student help, including test confirmations of amounts of payments received.

INVOICES: DUPLICATE PAYMENTS

An assistant supervisor in the controller's office prepared a check on a real estate operating account using an invoice from a previously paid voucher. The check was made payable to a building and loan association. The assistant supervisor requested that the check be returned to him for delivery to an attorney who was, in turn, to deliver the check to the building and loan association for certain title papers. After the check was properly signed, it was returned as requested. The assistant supervisor then used the same typewriter on which the check had originally been prepared to insert below the name of the payee building and loan association "for deposit to the account of John Jones" (his name). He deposited the check to his account in the building and loan association and later withdrew the funds.

After the check had cleared and the bank account had been reconciled, he extracted the check and voucher from the files and destroyed both.

A supervisor in the controller's office noted inflated expenses charged to the particular building and investigated the apparent duplicate payments. The check and voucher were missing, of course, but a microfilm copy of the check was obtained from the bank through which it had cleared. The assistant's name and endorsement appeared on this check.

Invoices Regularly Canceled.   To avoid similar manipulations of accounts, all checks are now mailed to the payees by the bursar and invoices are canceled as the checks are issued.

TRAVEL ADVANCES: FORGED

A departmental accountant requested fictitious travel advances for research personnel in his department. He obtained the checks, ostensibly for delivery to the payees, forged endorsements and cashed the checks. This defalcation was disclosed through the normal periodic follow-up on unaccounted-for travel advances. Disclosure was delayed, however, because initial follow-up was by form letters which were transmitted through the accountant and, of course, he did not deliver them.

Controls Instituted.   Procedures were changed to provide for faster follow-up (including telephone contacts after thirty days) of unaccounted-for travel advances, and a study was undertaken to determine the feasibility of direct delivery of advances to requesters.

PAYROLL: CONTINUING WAGES

A research worker who resigned was continued on the payroll by her sister-in-law who was the contract administrator. A department head finally noticed that the terminated employee's name was still appearing on current operating statements.

Signed Approvals of Payroll Reports.   Rules against relatives working in the same department are now strictly inforced, and a quarterly payroll report is circulated to all department heads for signed approvals.

DONATIONS: CASH RECEIPTS

The development office collected gifts from donors and issued personalized receipts. The checks were forwarded to the cashier for deposit without the cashier's issuing a receipt to the development office. A cashier extracted cash from the register in the amount of one such check. The credit to the gift account for that day's deposits was short by the amount of this check.

The development office noted the missing check from the operating statement of the gift account. A follow-up with the donor disclosed that the check had been cleared with proper endorsement. Actually, three cashiers were working out of the same change fund, and since no receipt was issued, it was not possible to determine which cashier handled the transaction. This left the college in the extremely uncomfortable position of knowing that one of its three cashiers had pocketed money.

Cashiers' Receipts.   Each cashier has been given her own change fund and cashiers' receipts must be issued for all deposits received from every source.

SPECIAL CONFERENCE: FEES

An assistant from the bursar's office collected fees for a special conference directly at the site, giving hand receipts from a special receipt book which had been withdrawn from the bursar's office. The assistant retained all cash that was collected, stuck the checks in a desk drawer and made no deposit. The controller's office and the manager of the conference failed to note the lack of any revenue from this conference. The defalcation was not discovered until a member inquired by mail why her check had not cleared. The investigation following this request disclosed the lack of a deposit and the defalcation.

This case provides an example of the extreme breakdown of control and supervisory functions that can happen in a college or university. It went unnoticed for almost two months because of the following breakdown in supervision and internal control.

1. The bursar's office clerk in charge of the receipt books failed to charge out and account for the receipt book used in this case because the person obtaining the book was her supervisor.
2. The bursar exercised no control over a member of his staff who was making collections outside the normal control routine of his office.

3. The supervisor in charge of the conference failed to review her accounting reports as to completeness and accuracy.

4. The controller's office failed properly to review the operating statements and account for all normal revenue.

While the controls and policies instituted in each of these situations were uncomplicated and quite direct, the fact that they were required demonstrates the need for improved, formalized control and supervision of funds within an institution.

ADMINISTRATION POLICY

The elementary safeguards that were introduced have wide applicability and should not be limited to the particular situations given. Consideration should be given to the introduction, in all departments of the university, of the following policies:

1. mailing of all checks to the payee;
2. cancellation of invoices as checks are issued;
3. auditing of expense reports for all cash advances within two weeks of stated termination of travel or other activity for which the advance was made;
4. requiring approvals signed by department heads for monthly or quarterly payroll reports;
5. auditing of income and expenses of all special conferences, projects, etc., within a two-week period following their termination;
6. approval of department heads of the record and closing of account for all special conferences, projects, etc.; and
7. regular internal audits to determine that control procedures are effective.

The financial administration should assess the particular situations within the institution that would require special supervision and attention. These variances of costs and income, when encountered, can then be dealt with by applying the required internal controls. Thus unusual conferences, travel or petty cash funds will be handled with the controls and supervision established for the particular activity, and the procedures will be known and become more routine. It again should be emphasized that, frequently, proper internal audit follow-up will represent the only practical control technique.

QUESTIONS

1. Does your school have an internal auditor? How large is his staff? What does he do?

2. What is a petty cash fund?

3. Critics of university administrations often argue that "a university should be run like a business." In what ways is this assertion valid? How is it not valid?

FCC Asked to Require That Stations Disclose Financial Data to Public

Three public-interest communications groups asked the Federal Communications Commission to require the nation's radio and television stations to make their annual financial statements available for public inspection.

The groups also asked the Commission to require stations for the first time to disclose how much money they spend on specific types of programming, such as news, public affairs and locally-produced programs.

Broadcasters currently are required to file annual financial statements with the Commission, but the individual reports generally are kept confidential.

Stations are required to disclose "program expenses" in those reports, but they don't have to categorize those expenses by program type. The petition challenging the current requirements was filed by The Stern Community Law Firm, The National Citizens Committee for Broadcasting and The Citizens Communications Center, all Washington-based organizations.

SOURCE: Reprinted with permission of The Wall Street Journal (July 22, 1971), p. 6.

The groups argue that both the FCC and the courts have held that a station's performance at license-renewal time is measured substantially by the amount of time and money it "reinvests" in community-oriented programming. However, the groups contend that anyone considering challenging a station's license is handicapped because the station's financial information is "hidden from public view."

QUESTIONS

1. To what extent are the financial statements of large U.S. corporations available to the public?

2. Should the financial statements of radio and television stations be more public than those of other businesses? Why?

3. (a) What information of public interest might be disclosed in the detailed financial statements of:
    (1) a television station
    (2) an electric company
    (3) an automobile insurance company
    (4) a large military contractor
    (5) a paper manufacturer
    (6) an automobile manufacturer
    (7) a CPA firm
    (b) Obtain the financial statements of at least two firms from the preceding list. Is the information you listed as being of public interest disclosed?

*The "corporate social audit" is advocated
as a way of reporting on corporate social
responsibility, although warnings about
potential pitfalls are also offered.*

The First Attempts
at a Corporate
'Social Audit'

The hottest—and possibly the fuzziest—new area of controversy in accounting centers on something called "the corporate social audit." Hounded by critics from Ralph Nader to their own disgruntled stockholders, some of the biggest U.S. companies, including BankAmerica Corp. and American Telephone & Telegraph Co., are looking into ways of measuring their performance in activities that affect the society around them or at least assess the true costs of such programs. If normal financial accounting causes debate, as it does today, the corporate social audit is sure to cause even more.

No one even agrees on what a social audit is and on who should do it, let alone on how to set about doing it. To shed some light on what is happening in the field, two professors at the Harvard Business School have just completed a year-long research project, concentrating on a handful of companies that have tried to devise some measures of how well they are meeting their social responsibilities. Their findings and recommendations appear in a new book, *The*

SOURCE: Reprinted by permission of the publisher from Business Week (September 23, 1972), pp. 88–89, 91–92.

Corporate Social Audit, to be published by the Manhattan-based Russell Sage Foundation early next month.

Co-author Raymond A. Bauer says most companies do not know the scope of their present social programs. "When one stops to think about it, this lack of information is not so surprising," write Bauer and his colleague, Dan H. Fenn, Jr.

"There has been little reason or incentive for corporate officials to report such activities or even catalogue them, much less to pass information on their failures up the line," they say. "Since these activities have not been relevant data for evaluation and promotion, they have not shown up in the offices of top management except on a very hit-or-miss basis."

LOW RISK VALUE

Bauer and Fenn recommend a four-step social audit which they say is "reasonably demanding, but should prove valuable at low risk to the firm." First, the company would make an inventory of its activities that have a social impact; then it would explain the circumstances that led up to these activities; next there would be an informal evaluation of those programs that are most relevant, perhaps by an outside expert; and finally, the company would assess the ways in which these social programs mesh with the objects both of the firm itself and of society.

Bauer and Fenn say that when they began the study a year ago only a handful of companies had tackled anything faintly resembling a social audit. Now, they say, they hear almost every day of another company thinking of assessing its social contribution. Fenn, who also is director of the separately endowed John F. Kennedy Library, singles out two characteristics common to most companies doing social audits: First, they are large companies. Second, "They have pretty lively, imaginative, somewhat courageous leadership."

"It seems to me there's this feeling of being under a certain amount of public scrutiny," Fenn continues. And Bauer muses: "I think that lurking in the back of any one of these guys' minds is this notion: If somebody started clobbering me in that area, how could I answer him?"

Bauer says he first got interested because the whole social accountability area was in such a mess. Talking about the book, he says: "Social audit was a phrase being thrown about, but there was no defined content." In Fenn's view, the social audit is "a cutting edge" and something that has to be worked out if the social responsibility of business is to have any real meaning or bite to it. "I came to feel that in this whole murky, messy area, the social audit was the best handle to grab on to," he told *Business Week*.

Much confusion arises simply from the use of the word "audit," which suggests a set of dollar figures certified by some outside authority. That may come some day in the social area, in much the same way that financial accounting and auditing gradually evolved. But as Bauer and Fenn write: "The notion that somehow social performance will be integrated with financial performance envisions that a baby which has not yet started to crawl will some day run."

CHURCHES AND STUDENTS

The idea of a corporate social audit has captured the imaginations of social critics, businessmen, consultants, and professional accountants alike. Such groups as the Council on Economic Priorities, the National Council of Churches' Corporate Information Center, and the student-led Committee for Corporate Responsibility all have tried their hands at auditing individual companies' social performance in the areas of minority hiring, defense contracting, or pollution. A number of mutual funds, including the Dreyfus Third Century Fund, have been launched with the policy of investing only in what are deemed to be "socially responsible companies," based on the fund managers' assessment of social performance.

On the business front, management consultants such as Arthur D. Little, Inc., and Abt Associates, Inc., have been helping clients work on social audits, as well as undertaking the same kind of audit on their own companies (see next page). And just last month, the American Institute of Certified Public Accountants appointed an eight-man committee to help develop "standards and techniques for measuring, recording, reporting, and auditing social performance."

Many a top executive is intrigued, whether he sees it as a way of appeasing outside critics, of satisfying his own conscience and curiosity, or of guiding his company's decision-making. But the few guidelines previously written have been visionary and theoretical, and of little help to a company trying to "measure the immeasurable"—the impact of its social programs in terms of costs, benefits, performance, or even profits.

The biggest problem of all may well be internal. Bauer and Fenn note that the audit team at one company could not get safety records from one of its divisions, even though regular reports had to be filed with the U.S. government. And Bauer tells of a manager in charge of his company's social audit who is keeping his plans secret from his fellow executives. "I don't dare let them know what we're up to until we get the president to sit all the vice-presidents down and tell them this is the law," he explained.

WHERE RESISTANCE LIES

In their book, Bauer and Fenn explain the resistance from the lower echelons: "The process and outcome of the audit might take up their time and disturb

Abt Associates Inc. Social Balance Sheet

Year ended December 31, 1971 with comparative figures for 1970

Social Assets Available	1971	1970
Staff		
Available within one year	$ 2,594,390	$ 2,312,000
Available after one year	6,368,511	5,821,608
Training Investment	507,405	305,889
	9,470,306	8,439,497
Less Accumulated Training		
Obsolescence	136,995	60,523
Total Staff Assets	9,333,311	8,378,974
Organization		
Social Capital Investment	1,398,230	1,272,201
Retained Earnings	219,136	–
Land	285,376	293,358
Buildings at cost	334,321	350,188
Equipment at cost	43,018	17,102
Total Organization Assets	2,280,081	1,932,849
Research		
Proposals	26,878	15,090
Child Care Research	6,629	–
Social Audit	12,979	–
Total Research	46,486	15,090
Public Services Consumed Net of Tax		
Payments	152,847	243,399
Total Social Assets Available	$11,812,725	$10,570,312
Social Commitments, Obligations, and Equity		
Staff		
Committed to Contracts within		
one year	$ 43,263	$ 81,296
Committed to Contracts after		
one year	114,660	215,459
Committed to Administration within one		
year	62,598	56,915
Committed to Administration after		
one year	165,903	150,842
Total Staff Commitments	386,424	504,512
Organization		
Working Capital Requirements	60,000	58,500
Financial Deficit	–	26,814

(Continued)

Abt Associates Inc. Social Balance Sheet (Continued)

Facilities and Equipment Committed to Contracts and Administration.	$ 37,734	$ 36,729
Total Organization Commitments	97,734	122,043
Environmental		
Government Outlays for Public Services Consumed, Net of Tax Payment	152,847	243,399
Pollution from Paper Production	1,770	770
Pollution from Electric Power Production	2,200	1,080
Pollution from Automobile Commuting	10,493	4,333
Total Environmental Obligations	167,310	249,582
Total Commitments and Obligations	651,468	876,137
Society's Equity		
Contributed by Staff	8,946,887	7,874,462
Contributed by Stockholders	2,182,347	1,810,806
Generated by Operations	32,023	8,907
Total Equity	11,161,257	9,694,175
Total Commitments, Obligations and Equity	$11,812,725	$10,570,312

regular operations; expose deep political and philosophic differences within the firm; usurp prerogatives (who has the right to see personnel files?); create anxiety that new standards of evaluation are suddenly being applied; stimulate debate over tough issues like who should see the data; and reveal findings that may prove embarrassing if exposed to the public either deliberately or unintentionally. . . . In some decentralized companies it seems to smack of 'headquarters' meddling and kibitzing."

Fenn says that he knows of one company evaluating its executives on social performance as well as on financial results. Executives do not get bonuses unless they are performing up to standard on such things as minority hiring. But he concedes that this kind of company policy is rare. The book points out that moving into the social audit area entails a certain amount of risk. "And it's not the firm that takes the risk, but some poor bastard down the line," Bauer says.

One key problem lies in reaching an agreement between those who make the audit and those who use it as to what is feasible and useful. "This is a matter of social communication and the establishment of social trust," Bauer and Fenn write. "Considering the state of trust between the business community and the general public, this may be where the problem lies."

In their book, Bauer and Fenn devote much space to the elaborate "cost-benefit" social audit model developed by management consultant Clark C. Abt, whose company published its own detailed, complex "social income statement" and "social balance sheet" in its 1971 annual report to shareholders.

NUMERICAL CAMOUFLAGE

Such a quantitative exercise may be helpful for internal decision making and planning. In Bauer's view, however, putting in the numbers at this point may camouflage what the public is most interested in knowing. "Frankly, we're just skeptical about being able to convert social benefits exclusively into dollar terms," Bauer says.

Many companies are concentrating on the cost side of the cost-benefit equation and are trying to measure what they call the "true costs" of their social programs, as opposed to the merely out-of-pocket costs. For example, a telephone company that recently hired large numbers of unskilled employees from minority groups is trying to determine what its true costs were when its complaint rate soared.

While such measures may be important for internal control, cost-based social audits, such as have been proposed by accountant David F. Linowes of Laventhol, Krekstein, Horwath & Horwath, could be misinterpreted if released to the public. Bauer cautions that such public reports might make an inefficient management appear to be more socially responsible than an efficient management.

"At this stage of the game, we ought to get away from an exclusive concentration on dollar measurements," Fenn insists, "and explore other ways in which some of these measures can be made." The ultimate form of the social audit may look quite different from the form that has evolved for a financial audit, he says, "and we should be willing to accept that fact, rather than try to push (the social audit) into the acceptable financial auditing box."

TWO KINDS OF BALANCE

Some economists have suggested that equal weight should be given to two kinds of balance sheets, the financial and the social. Bauer is skeptical. "The social critics aren't going to give a damn about the financial," he says. "As a matter of fact, if the financial balance sheet looks good and the social looks bad, they're not going to add them. They're going to subtract them."

Other companies are trying their hands at "performance audits," which attempt to measure the progress of corporate programs against well-defined standards. This can work well in the area of hiring and pollution, where local or national guidelines have been spelled out. Bauer and Fenn suggest three other "reasonable candidates" where performance measures might be applied, even in dollar terms: improved recruiting as a result of the company's socially responsible image; improved consumer acceptability; and improved investor acceptability.

But in many areas of social concern, there are no accepted standards against which to measure performance. Even where standards exist, social critics are constantly pressuring companies to do more. As Bauer and Fenn put it: "Social responsibility is a moving target."

Fenn contends that the community at large is not so much interested in the results of various social programs as in the answer to one key question: Is this company really trying? He and Bauer believe that the most effective kind of social audit—one that would get information to the public so it can answer that question—lies in what they call "process audits." Simply put, a process audit is a rather sophisticated, insightful description of what is being *done* through a particular social program, as contrasted with trying to measure what is being *accomplished* and how effective it is, which is the focus of a performance audit.

THE GAO JOINS IN

Bauer points to a study that the General Accounting Office made of one particular series of training programs as an example of a "sensible" process audit. "What they did was sit down and say why the hell was this program set up?" Bauer says. And as he describes it, these were the questions that the GAO explored: "What was the supply problem? You know, what sort of people did you have looking for jobs? What was the demand problem? What sort of jobs were available? What sort of programs were set up? How well did they match the demand? Who went in? Did the people go into the various programs in proportions that were reasonably close to what the demand for jobs was? What proportion got through the program? What proportion got placed?"

Fenn says, "We think that the process audit will reveal the nature of a company's effort better than either the dollar figures or performance figures. If you look at what a company is doing," he adds, "and make it possible for people to judge the seriousness with which management takes this, then it's a valid piece of information. They can judge for themselves whether this is a company that is responsible."

Bauer says that he thinks a social audit can be most useful these days when executives sit down and say, "Let's look at what we're doing and how we're doing it." Most companies, he contends, do not even know that.

He and Fenn acknowledge that companies are going to be reluctant to make such reports public if the results are not favorable, but they argue that if nothing but laudatory reports come out, there is likely to be even more of a credibility gap. "I don't think there's going to be any real credibility until companies start reporting things on which they're not doing so well," Bauer says. "People will just look at the report and say, 'Well, what didn't they tell us?' "

He urges companies to "get on the learning curve," because he feels that the social audit will be in increasing demand. "Keep it simple enough that you can do it," he advises. "Be reasonably sure that you're going to have a product that's going to be useful when you get through. And above all, be sure that you've started learning.

"I think a number of companies are ready to buy that," Bauer says.

A Business Week editorial

What is a Social Audit?

Sometimes the best way to understand a thing is to try to measure it. For this reason if no other, the increasing interest in the corporate "social audit" is a healthy development. Corporations that have accepted the idea of social responsibility can answer their critics by reporting just exactly what they have done and what results they have achieved in such areas as minority employment and pollution control. At the same time, they can sharpen their own judgment by the reporting process and make better decisions as to which programs work and which do not.

It would be a great mistake, however, for companies to try to put exact figures on values that are still immeasurable by any known technique. There is a deceptive precision about figures that can imply certainty where only the crudest approximations are possible. Thus, any dollar figures on a program to employ marginal workers will be misleading because the out-of-pocket costs can be measured fairly accurately but the benefits can only be guessed.

The day may come when it is possible to present a social income statement and a social balance sheet stating costs and benefits in dollars. But for the present, such a report would conceal more than it revealed.

SOURCE: Reprinted by permission of the publisher from Business Week (September 23, 1972), p. 104.

Businessmen embarking on a social audit should remember that the important thing is to learn rather than to prove a point. As Harvard professor Raymond A. Bauer advises: "Keep it simple enough that you can do it. Be reasonably sure that you are going to have a product that's going to be useful when you get through."

It has taken financial accounting over 500 years since the invention of double-entry bookkeeping to reach its present, still-imperfect shape. Social accounting may move faster, but it still has a long way to go.

QUESTIONS

1. What is a "corporate social audit?" How is a "process audit" different?

2. What is to prevent a company from presenting a social report which shows only its good side?

3. Contrast the idea of a corporate social audit with proposals for a national social report described in Section VIII of this book.

4. (a) Compare the Abt Associates "Social Balance Sheet" with a standard balance sheet. How is it different? How is it similar?

   (b) Is the Abt statement more informative to you than a regular balance sheet? If so, in what specific ways?

   (c) Interpret the changes shown (1970 to 1971) in Abt's equity accounts.

5. (a) Criticize the Business Week editorial.

   (b) Now defend it.

*With the help of accounting, the tribal com-
munity begins to move at a quickening pace.*

The Long Walk
of the Navajo

by John L. Keller

*Back in 1951 when the Albuquerque office of Peat, Marwick, Mitchell & Co.
began work for the Navajos, almost as much time was spent on the road as on
the books. In those days the two accountants on the assignment brought sleeping
bags and drove across dirt roads to reach their client, headquartered 160 miles
west of Albuquerque just inside of the Arizona state line. The Navajos' lean
budget in those days drew most of its income from a trickle of fees for hunting,
fishing, and trading post licenses.*

*But times have changed on the reservation. Today the unique Navajo engage-
ment requires the combined efforts of a half-dozen members of the Albuquerque
office management group and twice that many staff accountants. The author of
this article, an honors graduate of The University of Notre Dame, was the Peat,
Marwick, Mitchell & Co. partner in charge of the Navajo engagement.*

The Navajos plugged in to the world of big business late in the 1950s when
immense oil and gas reserves—which supply more than half of the tribe's annual
income of $25 million—were discovered on their reservation in the four corners
country where New Mexico, Arizona, Utah and Colorado join.

SOURCE: Reprinted by permission of the author and the publisher from the
Winter 1969 issue of <u>World</u>, published by Peat, Marwick, Mitchell & Co.

Since that time tribal enterprises have been established to bring jobs, income and improved living conditions to the reservation's citizenry. Industry has begun to appear, a community college is scheduled to open this month, and a shopping center on the reservation is ready for business. New paved roads, leading to some of the most starkly beautiful scenery in the world, have opened hitherto inaccessible areas to dollar-bearing tourists. Campsites have been developed, fishing and hunting promoted, and new lodges put up.

Surplus tribal funds are being invested in high-yield securities, jobs previously held by outsiders are increasingly going to Navajos, new housing and construction have emerged and electrification has spread across the distant land. The Navajos, who in 1968 completed the centennial celebration of their peace treaty with the United States Government, are moving ahead from a neglected past into a future of hope. At the same time, however, they are beginning their second hundred years as a part of the U.S. with the clear intention of preserving their own culture and unique identity.

The contemporary scene of blossoming commerce and industry is far removed from the nomadic life of hunter and raider that the Navajo enjoyed when Spanish conquistadors entered his world early in the 17th century. The Spanish introduced the Navajos to horses, sheep and livestock, as well as weaving and the working of silver into jewelry. They also introduced colonization in communities along the Rio Grande River, which eventually led to warfare between the Navajos and the Spanish settlers. The Navajos were still resisting the white man when Americans replaced Mexicans after the Mexican War in 1848.

It was not until 1864, when Colonel Kit Carson—using scorched earth and starvation tactics—finally subdued them. Some 7,000 Navajos, most of the existing tribe at the time, were marched to Fort Summer in the eastern part of the New Mexico Territory. During the forced march and subsequent four-year confinement, infamously referred to as "The Long Walk" by Navajos, at least 1,500 of them died from sickness, starvation or injury. In 1868, representatives of the U.S. Government signed a treaty with Navajo leaders allowing tribal members to return to the area now comprising the Navajo reservation.

Under the provision of the treaty, each Navajo family started its "new" life with a small supply of corn and a few head of sheep. Despite the hardships encountered on their return to the reservation, the Navajos survived and proliferated until today their population is estimated at 125,000. Succeeding generations continued to live off the sparsely grassed plateau land, raising sheep and livestock.

The Navajos, who speak a sing-song Athabascan dialect, remained loyal to many of their historic beliefs. They seek to live harmoniously with nature. The Navajo word for "beautiful" also means "joy"; it appears often throughout Navajo chants. The medicine man remains an important figure on the reservation. In a society without a written language, he is the one who passes on the tribe's heritage and culture as well as preserving honored beliefs from the past.

In the medicine men's account of the tribe's origin, there was an underworld of darkness where the people (referred to by themselves as *Dineh*) lived in peace. But the *Dineh* quarreled and were forced to leave the dark world, emerging through a series of upper worlds by a hole in the sky into the white, or present, world. With the aid of the gods, they brought with them material from the underworlds for the four sacred mountains which today are the approximate boundaries of the 25,000 square mile reservation.

In 1937 a Constitutional Assembly convened from which evolved the tribe's present form of government. The Navajo reservation is divided into 100 districts, called chapters, that elect representatives to four-year terms on the Tribal Council. The Chairman of the Council, who is the chief executive and administrative officer of the tribe, is also elected to a four-year term together with a Vice Chairman. The current Chairman is Raymond Nakai, a resourceful leader, who is in his second term of office.

The Vice Chairman is Nelson Damon, who in addition to his other executive duties, chairs the 18-man Advisory Committee that establishes the agenda for the Tribal Council.

Chairman Nakai directs and coordinates the day-to-day affairs of the tribe through its three divisions, Administration, Resources, and Public Services.

The Administration Division is headed by Edward McCabe, Jr. Included in it are the departments of the controller and the treasurer, as well as purchasing, data processing, vital statistics and personnel. One of the division's innovations is a successful self-insurance program for workmen's compensation.

Investment of surplus funds in high-yield securities has been high on the Administration Division's list of priorities. Tribal deposits in excess of $50 million had been allowed to remain in 4% interest-bearing accounts in the U.S. Treasury.

In 1966, the tribe received permission to withdraw funds from the U.S. Treasury. Later an independent investment counseling firm was retained to recommend investments, including all forms of debt and equity securities. These achievements represented the culmination of more than five years of effort on the part of tribal officials and PMM&Co. to utilize surplus tribal funds for the development of a sound and diversified investment program. Addressing the Tribal Council during the presentation of audit reports in October 1967, Donald E. Brunton, controller of the tribe, pointed out that in the year ended June 30, 1967, total tribal income had increased by more than $700,000 because of the new investment program. Prompt depositing of tribal receipts and the use of cash forecasts to minimize unproductive checking account balances further increased tribal income in recent years.

Much to the surprise of the uninitiated, the tribe has its own data processing department. In 1958, the controller's department leased a key punch, sorter, collator and IBM 401 tabulating machine. Today, the former data processing section has achieved full departmental status and processes information for the controller, the Navajo Tribal Utility Authority, the police department, and other tribal activities. The department is currently utilizing an IBM 360/20, with a 360/30 installation under way, for over 125 computer applications, including such diverse programs as utility billings, costs of construction projects, livestock statistical information, traffic and crime statistics, as well as tribal payroll and general accounting records.

The Administration Division's purchasing department functions through a centralized system that aims at solving the logistical headaches of dealing with more than 100 tribal departments scattered across the reservation. An encumbrance system records purchase orders as they are sent to vendors, and receiving warehouses have been placed in key areas.

The development of natural resources on the reservation is supervised by the Resources Division, headed by Norman L. Bowman. During the last 10 years the tribe has derived revenues in excess of $176 million from its natural resources. Besides oil and gas reserves, which account for more than one-half of all tribal revenues, there are substantial deposits of soft coal, uranium and other strategic minerals that are largely undeveloped.

The Resources Division also promotes the improvement of livestock. Ram and bull breeding stock are available at nominal cost to encourage Navajos to improve their herds. Lack of water has always been an obstacle to the animal production industry and farming. In the last 10 years, the Resources Division through its ground water development has drilled more than 1,000 wells that have partially alleviated the scarcity of water.

The division established a public works program to provide temporary jobs for unemployed Navajos. Conducted at the chapter level, construction crews earned $3.7 million during 1968 building roads, water storage facilities and other community facilities.

A major project for Resources Division personnel is the development of tourism on the reservation. With the completion of paved highways and airstrips, spectacular scenic attractions are now within reach of the average tourist. Hollywood, long aware of the reservation's beauty, has used Monument Valley, with its imposing rock formations standing on the desert floor like isolated skyscrapers, as the locale for many westerns.

Lake Powell, with its thousands of miles of spectacular shoreline, is rapidly being developed, as are campsites in the mountain areas which are noted for their fishing and hunting.

The tribe has plans on the drawing boards to build a marina and recreational complex at Padre Point on Lake Powell and a recreational complex at Black Creek Canyon. New motels were constructed near the entrance to Monument Valley and Canyon de Chelly (pronounced *da shay*), one of the least known and most beautiful canyons in the nation. Additional facilities were established at the eastern boundary of the Grand Canyon National Park. In an attempt to build up its tourist trade, tribal leaders may institute conducted tours.

The Public Services Division, directed by Wilbur W. Dixon, carries the bulk of responsibility for construction on the reservation, and for other programs of public services provided by the Navajo Tribe. During the past 10 years, more than $50 million in tribal funds were spent on buildings and other improvements, with the largest slice of that funneling through the division's design and construction department and its heavy equipment pool. Homes, tribal buildings, roads and earthen dams were completed. One hundred tribally owned residential units and 650 low-rent houses were constructed by the design and construction department in the last three years. In addition, nearly 1,000 residential units were built under the auspices of various governmental agencies to replace the traditional six-sided Navajo hogan.

The basic objective of the design and construction department and the heavy equipment pool has been to provide job opportunities for Navajos. The intentional use of frequently unskilled Navajos by these departments resulted in substantial overall operating losses that might appear untenable in the ordinary world of commerce. However, these jobs provided a living wage for a considerable number of Navajo families, with nearly $2 million in wages being paid during the past year, and produced Navajos sufficiently skilled to successfully compete for employment off the reservation.

One of the largest departments in the division is the Navajo police department. More than 200 men operate from five district substations on the reservation. The tribe retains jurisdictional authority over crimes committed on the reservation, except those designated as Federal crimes or those of non-Indians, through its police department and its judicial branch, which is comprised of trial courts presided over by judges appointed by the Tribal Chairman with the approval of the Tribal Council.

Another aspect of the Public Services Division operations is the quest for industrial development. In 1968, $4 million in tribal funds was appropriated to attract industry to the reservation. When asked what the tribe had to offer industry, Chairman Nakai wryly replied: "We have an abundant labor pool at wage rates below those of other parts of the country; air, rail and highway accessibility; substantial resources in the form of coal, gas, and electricity; land to build on and a spectacular country with clean air, free from smog and freeways. What do New York, Chicago, and Los Angeles have to offer?"

Tribal efforts to lure new industries are beginning to pay off. In 1967, an electronics plant was constructed at a cost of $600,000 and leased to the General Dynamics Corporation. At peak operational capacity, more than 200 Navajos will be employed with an annual payroll of $1 million.

In November 1968, formal dedication ceremonies opened the first Indian-owned shopping center on the reservation. The center, constructed by the tribe at a cost of $650,000 with 30,000 square feet under roof, is leased to FedMart Corporation.

Industrial parks have been established at several points on the reservation. Among the occupants are the Semiconductor Division of Fairchild Camera and Instrument Corporation, EPI-Vostron, Cardinal Plastics, Navajo Concrete Projects and Babyline Furniture Company. Payrolls from these employers raised living standards for hundreds of Navajo families.

Undoubtedly the single most significant achievement in improving environmental conditions on the reservation has been accomplished through the establishment of the Navajo Tribal Utility Authority (NTUA), a tribal enterprise. Tribal enterprises are given a permanent capital contribution and are then free to operate commercially as a business entity without budgetary or day-to-day supervisory control from the tribal government.

NTUA was created in 1959 to furnish the reservation community of Shiprock, New Mexico, with electrical power. The Authority has since expanded into natural gas, water, and sewer utility operations, and substantially expanded its electric service. The growth of the utility can best be illustrated by comparison of the investment in utility plant and service which in 1961 was slightly less than $2 million with that of $18.9 million in 1968.

Total revenues from the sale of utility services amounted to $2,680,000 for the year ended June 30, 1968, with payroll expenditures on the reservation of approximately $985,000. The Authority provides permanent jobs for 154 employees, all but 10 of them Navajos. The Authority, headed by C. MacEddy, performs countless minor tasks not normally associated with a utility. They range from answering frantic calls to unclog drains to servicing television sets before Saturday's ball game.

The tribe's most spectacular and by far most economically successful enterprise is Navajo Forest Products Industries (NFPI). The reservation contains 500,000 acres of ponderosa pine timberland. A small sawmill started in the 1930s has given way to a vastly expanded lumber business. Since the formation of NFPI in 1958 the town of Navajo, New Mexico, 30 miles north of tribal headquarters at Window Rock, has been created. It now has 175 new houses, paved streets, a post office, fire station, and an elementary school nationally recognized for its design and curriculum.

A $12 million sawmill and cut stock plant, having eight acres under foot, turn out 40-45 million board feet of Navajo pine each year. Controlled logging practices assure that cut-over areas will be reseeded by nature. An added benefit of the lumber entreprise is the 400 miles of roads logging crews have cleared. Inside the sawmill, two giant double cut band mills capable of producing 100,000 board feet of lumber per shift are operated by skilled Navajo sawyers.

During 1968, a finger-joining and millwork plant began operations to more effectively utilize what had previously been waste. Byproducts include chips for paper mills in the area, and decorative bark and soil conditioners.

The mill employs 450 Navajos who annually earn $1.6 million. Most of them learn their skills on the job or are sent to vocational schools. The enterprise also joins in considerable in-service training together with the Bureau of Indian Affairs.

Since its inception 10 years ago NFPI has racked up a hefty $2.5 million profit, and has paid stumpage charges to the tribal coffers totaling $2.8 million.

Another enterprise, the Arts and Crafts Guild, enabled Navajos to bolster personal income while helping preserve an important aspect of their heritage. The enterprise provides raw materials on consignment to craftsmen. The finished products, which include world famous Navajo rings and turquoise jewelry, are purchased by the Guild for wholesale distribution in the Southwest and for retail sale through the Guild's six shops on the reservation.

The tribe's revolving credit fund, established in 1948, assists both enterprises and individuals. Loans are made to cover costs of construction, business and farming ventures, and for educational purposes. The fund has 350 outstanding loans with balances totaling $1.1 million. It is administered by the Bureau of Indian Affairs and a committee of the Tribal Council.

The Office of Economic Opportunity also is represented on the reservation. Begun during the tenure of Chairman Nakai, it is locally known as the Office of Navajo Economic Opportunity (ONEO) and is headed by Peter McDonald. The agency conducts 11 programs and employs 3,000 persons. All but 30 of them, including McDonald, are Navajos.

One of ONEO's most successful programs is its Operation Headstart for pre-school age children. Approximately 25% of all children in that age bracket attend Headstart classes. Other phases of the ONEO include community development construction projects and a neighborhood youth corps. Both draw heavily on the ranks of the unemployed, who are taught basic skills on the job. All of the ONEO projects are determined by the Navajos themselves at chapter meetings.

As the diversity of tribal operations increased throughout the years, so did the role of Peat, Marwick, Mitchell & Co. The original engagement with the Navajos in 1951 was in connection with a 100-year audit to be used in the preparation of claims brought by the tribe against the Indian Claims Commission. The special audit was to extend from 1848—the year in which the Treaty of Guadalupe Hidalgo was signed by Mexico, ceding what is now Arizona and New Mexico to the United States—to 1948, the termination date set by the Indian Claims Commission.

The results of the examination were ultimately given to the tribal legal counsel for use in the still-pending claims cases. As an outgrowth of this assignment, the first audit of the tribal treasurer was made as of May 31, 1951. Over the years, PMM&Co. has worked closely with tribal officials providing a variety of services, varying from the tabulation of votes for the tribal faii beauty pageant, to assisting in the evaluation of economic development proposals. The firm also has provided temporary administrative assistance, and has helped locate qualified personnel for jobs when skilled Navajos were unavailable. Some of the most difficult assignments included the development of accounting systems to adequately reflect the tremendous growth and diversity of the various tribal operations. The Albuquerque office regards the Navajo engagement as its most challenging, and at the same time most rewarding client. The rewards come from the fact that PMM&Co. has the opportunity to take part in the emergence of a people into a modern economic society. The challenge of the Navajo Tribe is not the difficulties caused by their many operating problems, but rather to foresee and keep pace with the rapidly changing needs of their economy.

Although the problems of the Navajo often appear insurmountable and the solutions agonizingly slow, progress is and has been the story of the Navajos.

Perhaps the tribal outlook is best summarized in excerpts from the inaugural address of Chairman Nakai:

It has been said that the Navajo Tribe is the largest and richest Indian tribe in the world. That we are the largest tribe in the world, we are convinced. That we are the richest is very questionable. One does not have to travel very far on the reservation to be exposed to dire poverty, the grinding poverty to which the Navajo Indian resigned himself to endure over a great and sorrowful period of years. But . . . let us not live in the past. Let us look to the future with enthusiasm and hope.

Speaking at a central celebration some time later the Chairman further stated:

We are, indeed, on the threshold of great achievements for our people in the fields of education, industrial development and economic well-being. The next decades will witness giant steps forward in these areas. Yes, we are on a 'long walk' again—a walk toward achievement for all that is good for our people.

QUESTIONS

1. Contrast the Navajo Tribe with a developing nation.

2. How is the Navajo Tribe like a state? How is it like a business?

3. Is the Navajo Tribal Utility Authority a private business or a public enterprise? Explain.

4. What is the Navajo annual income? List the various sources of income.

5. Is vote tabulation in a beauty contest accounting? Why was a public accounting firm used for this tabulation?

6. Thoroughly describe how you would expect to find accounting used on the Navajo reservation. What services has Peat, Marwick, Mitchell & Co. provided over the years?

Questions

DATE DUE